AMERICAN
THEOCRACY

ALSO BY KEVIN PHILLIPS

American Dynasty

William McKinley

Wealth and Democracy

The Cousins' Wars

Arrogant Capital

Boiling Point

The Politics of Rich and Poor

Staying on Top

Post-Conservative America

Electoral Reform and Voter Participation

Mediacracy

The Emerging Republican Majority

KEVIN PHILLIPS

AMERICAN
THEOCRACY

The Peril and Politics of Radical Religion, Oil,

and Borrowed Money in the 21st Century

VIKING

VIKING
Published by the Penguin Group

Penguin Group (USA) Inc., 375 Hudson Street, New York, New York 10014, U.S.A. • Penguin Group (Canada), 90 Eglinton Avenue East, Suite 700, Toronto, Ontario, Canada M4P 2Y3 (a division of Pearson Penguin Canada Inc.) • Penguin Books Ltd, 80 Strand, London WC2R 0RL, England • Penguin Ireland, 25 St. Stephen's Green, Dublin 2, Ireland (a division of Penguin Books Ltd) • Penguin Books Australia Ltd, 250 Camberwell Road, Camberwell, Victoria 3124, Australia (a division of Pearson Australia Group Pty Ltd) • Penguin Books India Pvt Ltd, 11 Community Centre, Panchsheel Park, New Delhi– 110 017, India • Penguin Group (NZ), Cnr Airborne and Rosedale Roads, Albany, Auckland 1310, New Zealand (a division of Pearson New Zealand Ltd) • Penguin Books (South Africa) (Pty) Ltd, 24 Sturdee Avenue, Rosebank, Johannesburg 2196, South Africa

Penguin Books Ltd, Registered Offices: 80 Strand, London WC2R 0RL, England

First published in 2006 by Viking Penguin, a member of Penguin Group (USA) Inc.

10   9   8   7   6   5   4   3   2   1

ISBN 0-670-03486-X

Printed in the United States of America
Maps by Jeffrey Ward
Designed by Carla Bolte

This book is dedicated to the millions of Republicans, present and lapsed, who have opposed the Bush dynasty and the disenlightenment in the 2000 and 2004 elections.

PREFACE

THE AMERICAN PEOPLE ARE NOT FOOLS. THAT IS WHY POLLSTERS, INQUIRING during the last forty years whether the United States was on the right track or the wrong one, have so often gotten the second answer: *wrong track.* That was certainly the case again as the year 2005 closed out.

Because survey takers do not always pursue explanations, this book will venture some. Reckless dependency on shrinking oil supplies, a milieu of radicalized (and much too influential) religion, and a reliance on borrowed money—debt, in its ballooning size and multiple domestic and international deficits—now constitute the three major perils to the United States of the twenty-first century.

Shouldn't war and terror be on the list? Yes—and they are, one step removed. Both derive much of their current impetus from the incendiary backdrop of oil politics and religious fundamentalism, in Islam as well as the West. Despite pretensions to motivations such as liberty and freedom, petroleum and its geopolitics have dominated Anglo-American activity in the Middle East for a full century. On this, history could not be more clear.

The excesses of fundamentalism, in turn, are American and Israeli, as well as the all-too-obvious depredations of radical Islam. The rapture, end-times, and Armageddon hucksters in the United States rank with any Shiite ayatollahs, and the last two presidential elections mark the transformation of the GOP into the first religious party in U.S. history.

The financialization of the United States economy over the last three decades—in the 1990s the finance, real-estate, and insurance sector overtook and then strongly passed manufacturing as a share of the U.S. gross domestic product—is an ill omen in its own right. However, its rise has been closely tied to record levels of debt and to the powerful emergence of a debt-and-credit industrial complex. Excessive debt in the twenty-first-century United States is on its way to becoming the global Fifth Horseman, riding close behind war, pestilence, famine, and fire.

This book's title, *American Theocracy,* sums up a potent change in this country's domestic and foreign policy making—religion's new political prowess and its role in the projection of military power in the Middle Eastern Bible lands—that most people are just beginning to understand. We have had theocracies in North America before—in Puritan New England and later in Mormon Utah—but except in their earliest beginnings, they lacked the intensity of those in Europe, such as John Calvin's Geneva or the Catholic Spain of the Inquisition.

Indeed, most of the Christian theocracies touched on by historians shared two unusual and virtually defining characteristics. First, they were very small in geographic terms. Second, and more important, they were the demographic results of migrations by true believers. The population of John Calvin's sixteenth-century Geneva was swollen by French Protestant refugees, and the Dutch Reformed Calvinists of the Netherlands got a kindred infusion from Flemish refugees fleeing Spanish-controlled Antwerp. The Massachusetts Bay Colony, in turn, was built by English Puritan emigrants, and the nineteenth-century Mormons in Utah represented still another Zion-bound migration. As for Spain, despite militant Catholicism and the infamous Inquisition, it was too large and varied a nation to fit the small-scale theocratic pattern. Seventeenth-century attempts to shut down Spanish theaters, gambling houses, and brothels failed, and the golden age of Spanish literature and art—from Cervantes to El Greco—flourished in Toledo and Madrid under court, church, and noble patronage despite periodic homosexual reports and scandals that the Inquisition did not greatly pursue.[1]

Theocracy in America is of this lesser breed. The United States is too big and too diverse to resemble the Massachusetts Bay Colony of John Winthrop or sixteenth-century Geneva or even nineteenth-century Utah. A leading world power such as the United States, with almost three hundred million people and huge international responsibilities, goes about as far in a theocratic direction as it can when it satisfies the unfortunate criteria on display in Washington circa 2005: an elected leader who believes himself in some way to speak for God, a ruling political party that represents religious true believers and seeks to mobilize the churches, the conviction of many voters in that Republican party that government should be guided by religion, and on top of it all, White House implementation of domestic and international political agendas that seem to be driven by religious motivations and biblical worldviews. All of these factors and many more are discussed at length in part 2 of this book.

The three threats emphasized in these pages could stand on their own as menaces to the Republic. History, however, provides a further level of confirmation. Natural resources, religious excess, wars, and burgeoning debt levels have been prominent causes of the downfall of the previous leading world economic powers. The United States is hardly the first, and we can profit from the examples of what went wrong before.

Oil, as everyone knows, became the all-important fuel of American global ascendancy in the twentieth century. But before that, nineteenth-century Britain was the coal hegemon and seventeenth-century Dutch fortune harnessed the winds and the waters. Neither nation could maintain its global economic leadership when the world moved toward a new energy regime. Today's United States, despite denials, has obviously organized much of its overseas military posture around petroleum, protecting oil fields, pipelines, and sea lanes.

But U.S. preoccupation with the Middle East has two dimensions. In addition to its concerns with oil and terrorism, the White House is courting end-times theologians and electorates for whom the holy lands are already a battleground of Christian destiny. Both pursuits, oil and biblical expectations, require a dissimulation in Washington that undercuts the U.S. tradition of commitment to the role of an informed electorate.

The political corollary—fascinating but appalling—is the recent transformation of the Republican presidential coalition. Since the elections of 2000 and especially of 2004, three pillars have become increasingly central: (1) the oil–national security complex, with its pervasive interests; (2) the religious right, with its doctrinal imperatives and massive electorate; and (3) the debt-dealing financial sector, which extends far beyond the old symbolism of Wall Street. In December 2004 *The New York Times* took up the term "borrower-industrial complex" to identify one profitable engine of exploding consumer debt.

That name does not quite work, but we can hardly use a term like the credit-card / mortgage / auto-loan / corporate-debt / federal-borrowing industrial complex. This is a problem still searching for its Election Day Halloween mask. In any event, the rapid ballooning of government, corporate, financial, and personal debt over the last four decades goes a long way to explain why the finance sector, debt's toll collector, has swollen to outweigh the manufacture of real goods. We are in the midst of one of America's most perverse transformations.

George W. Bush has promoted these alignments, interest groups, and their underpinning values. His family, over multiple generations, has been tied to a politics that conjoined finance, national security, and oil. In recent decades, operating from the federal executive branch, the Bushes have added close ties to evangelical and fundamentalist power brokers of many persuasions. These origins, biases, and practices were detailed in my last book, *American Dynasty: Aristocracy, Fortune, and the Politics of Deceit in the House of Bush* (2004). The present volume, therefore, revisits mostly the family's influence in helping these trends and guiding these constituencies.

Over three decades of Bush presidencies, vice presidencies, and CIA directorships, the Republican party has slowly become the vehicle of all three interests—a fusion of petroleum-defined national security; a crusading, simplistic Christianity; and a reckless credit-feeding financial complex. The three are increasingly allied in commitment to Republican politics, if not in full agreement with one another. On the most important front, I am beginning to think that the southern-dominated, biblically driven Washington GOP represents a rogue coalition, like the southern, proslavery politics that controlled Washington until Lincoln's election in 1860.

But the national Democrats have their own complicity. Their lack of understanding and moxie has contributed to the mutation of the GOP. Without that weak and muddled opposition, both before and after September 11, the Republican transformation would have been impolitic and perhaps impossible.

Clearly the pitfalls of petro-politics, radical religion, and debt finance have to be addressed in their own right. However, I have a personal concern over what has become of the Republican coalition. Forty years ago, I began a book, finished in 1967 and taken to the 1968 Republican presidential campaign, for which I became the chief political and voting-patterns analyst. Published in 1969, while I was still in the fledgling Nixon administration, *The Emerging Republican Majority* became highly controversial. *Newsweek* identified it as "The political bible of the Nixon Era."

In that book I coined the term "Sun Belt" to describe the oil, military, aerospace, and retirement country that stretched from Florida to California, but debate concentrated on the argument—since fulfilled and then some—that the South was on its way into the national Republican party. Four decades later, this framework has produced the triple mutation that *this* book will discuss.

Some of that evolution was always implicit. If any region of the United States had the potential to produce a high-powered, crusading fundamentalism, it was Dixie. If any new alignment had the potential to nurture a fusion of oil interests and the military-industrial complex, it was the Sun Belt that helped to draw them into commercial and political proximity and collaboration. Wall Street, of course, has long been part of the GOP coalition. On the other hand, members of the Downtown Association and the Links Club were never enthusiastic about "Joe Sixpack" and middle America, to say nothing of preachers such as Oral Roberts or the Tupelo, Mississippi, Assemblies of God. The new cohabitation is an unnatural one.

Little was said about oil in *The Emerging Republican Majority*, partly because I knew I would be in the government when the book appeared. Still, oilmen liked its political thesis, and I fleshed out an analysis still relevant today—that the nation's oil, coal, and natural-gas sections, despite their intramural differences, would be regional mainstays of the new "heartland"-centered GOP national coalition. Hitherto, these interests had been divided by the political Mason-Dixon Line. That division would and did end.

While studying economic geography and history in Britain some years earlier, I had been intrigued by the Eurasian "heartland" theory of Sir Halford Mackinder, a prominent early-twentieth-century geographer. Control of the heartland, Mackinder argued, would determine control of the world. In North America, I thought the coming together of a heartland—across fading Civil War lines—would determine control of Washington.

Wordsmith William Safire, in his *The New Language of Politics* entry on the heartland, cited Mackinder. He then noted that "political analyst Kevin Phillips applied the old geopolitical word to U.S. politics in his 1969 book *The Emerging Republican Majority*: 'Twenty-one of the twenty-five Heartland states supported Richard Nixon in 1968. . . . Over the remainder of the century, the Heartland should dominate American politics in tandem with suburbia, the South and Sun Belt–swayed California.'"[2]

This was the prelude to today's "red states." Mackinder's worldview has its own second wind because his Eurasian cockpit has reemerged as the pivot of the international struggle for oil. In a similar context, the American heartland, from Wyoming, Colorado, and New Mexico to Ohio and the Appalachian coal states, has become (along with the rest of the onetime Confederacy) the seat of a fossil-fuels political alliance—an electoral hydrocarbon coalition. It cherishes SUVs and easy carbon dioxide emissions policy, and applauds preemptive U.S. air strikes on uncooperative, terrorist-coddling Persian Gulf countries fortuitously blessed with huge reserves of oil.

Because the United States is beginning to run out of its own oil sources, a military solution to an energy crisis is hardly lunacy. Neither Caesar nor Napoléon would have flinched, and the temptation, at least, is understandable. What Caesar and Napoléon did not face, but less able American presidents do, is that bungled overseas military embroilment, unfortunate in its own right, could also boomerang economically. The United States, some $4 trillion in hock internationally, has become the world's leading debtor, increasingly nagged by worry that some nations will sell dollars in their reserves and switch their holdings to rival currencies. Washington prints bonds and dollar-green IOUs, which European and Asian bankers accumulate until for some reason they lose patience. This is the debt Achilles' heel, which stands alongside the oil Achilles' heel.

Unfortunately, as much or more dynamite hides in the responsiveness of the new GOP coalition to Christian evangelicals, fundamentalists, and Pentecostals, who muster some 40 percent of the party electorate. Many, many millions believe that the Armageddon described in the Bible is coming soon. Chaos in the explosive Middle East, far from being a threat, actually heralds the awaited second coming of Jesus Christ. Oil-price spikes, murderous hurricanes, deadly tsunamis, and melting polar ice caps lend further credence.

The potential interaction between the end-times electorate, inept pursuit of Persian Gulf oil, Washington's multiple deceptions, and the credit and financial crisis that could follow a substantial liquidation by foreign holders of U.S. bonds is the stuff of nightmares. To watch U.S. voting patterns enable such policies—the GOP coalition is unlikely to turn back—

is depressing to someone who spent many years researching, watching, and cheering those grass roots.

Four decades ago, although *The Emerging Republican Majority* said little about southern fundamentalists and evangelicals, the new GOP coalition seemed certain to enjoy a major infusion of conservative northern Catholics and southern Protestants. This troubled me not at all. During the 1970s and part of the 1980s, I agreed with the predominating Republican argument that "secular" liberals, by badly misjudging the depth and importance of religion in the United States, had given conservatives a powerful and legitimate electoral opportunity.

Since then, my appreciation of the intensity of religion in the United States has deepened. Its huge carryover from the eighteenth and nineteenth centuries turns out to have seeded a similar evangelical wave in the twentieth and early twenty-first centuries. In 1998, after years of research, I published *The Cousins' Wars,* a lengthy study of the three great English-speaking internal convulsions—the English Civil War of the 1640s, the American Revolution, and the American War Between the States. Amid each fratricide, religious divisions figured so strongly in people's choosing sides that persisting threads became clear—pietists and puritans versus high-church adherents, and a recurrent conviction by militant evangelicals, from the 1640s to the 1860s, culminating in the American Civil War, that theirs was the cause of liberty and the Protestant Reformation. The overall analysis and its documentation were taken seriously enough that the book became a finalist for that year's Pulitzer Prize in history. Indeed, my wife and I were sufficiently impressed by the historical roles of the scores of eighteenth-century churches we visited—from the pastel Caribbean stuccos of Anglican South Carolina to the stone fortresses of Presbyterian Pennsylvania and the white Congregational meetinghouses of New England—to think of writing a book on them sometime (we still do).

Such was religion's enduring importance in the United States when it was trod upon in the 1960s and thereafter by secular advocates determined to push Christianity out of the public square, a mistake that unleashed an evangelical, fundamentalist, and Pentecostal counterreformation that in some ways is still building. As part 2 will explore, strong theocratic pressures are already visible in the Republican national coalition and its leadership, while the substantial portion of Christian America committed to theories of Armageddon and the inerrancy of the Bible has already made the GOP into America's first religious party.

Its religiosity reaches across the board—from domestic policy to foreign affairs. Besides providing critical support for invading Iraq, widely anathematized by preachers as a second Babylon, the Republican coalition's clash with science has seeded half a dozen controversies. These include Bible-based disbelief in Darwinian theories of evolution, dismissal of global warming, disagreement with geological explanations of fossil-fuel depletion, religious rejection of global population planning, derogation of women's rights, opposition to stem-cell research, and so on. This suggests that U.S. society and politics may again be heading for a defining controversy such as the Scopes trial of 1925. That embarrassment chastened fundamentalism for a generation, but the outcome of the eventual twenty-first-century test is hardly assured.

Book buyers will understand that in these United States volumes able to sell two or three hundred thousand hardcover copies are uncommon. Not rare, just uncommon. Consider, then, the publishing success of end-times preacher Tim LaHaye, earlier the politically shrewd founder (in 1981) of the Washington-based Council for National Policy. Beginning in 1994 LaHaye successfully coauthored a series of books on the rapture, the tribulation, and the road to Armageddon that has since sold some *sixty million* copies in print, video, and cassette forms. Evangelist Jerry Falwell hailed it as probably the most influential religious publishing event since the Bible.[3] Several novels of the *Left Behind* series rose to number one on the *New York Times* fiction bestseller list, and the series as a whole almost certainly reached fifteen to twenty million American voters. Political aides in the Bush White House must have read several volumes, if only for pointers on constituency sentiment.

In that respect, the books were highly informative. LaHaye's novels furnished hints rarely discussed by serious publications as to why George W. Bush's 2002–2003 call for war in Iraq included jeering at the United Nations, harped on the evil regime in Baghdad, and pretended that democracy, not oil, was the motive. LaHaye had authored essentially that plot almost a decade earlier. His evil antichrist, who had a French financial adviser and rose to power through the United Nations, was headquartered in New Babylon, Iraq, not far from the Baghdad of Bush's arch-devil, Saddam Hussein. The fictional Tribulation Force, which fought in God's name, represented goodness and had nothing to do with oil, which was one of the antichrist's evil chessboards.

Twenty years ago, *The New York Times* would not have considered LaHaye for the bestseller list, and my scenario of his writings influencing the White House could only have been spoof. Not so today. In a late-2004 speech, the retiring television journalist Bill Moyers, himself an ordained Baptist minister, broke with polite convention. He told an audience at the Harvard medical school that "one of the biggest changes in politics in my lifetime is that the delusional is no longer marginal. It has come in from the fringe, to sit in the seat of power in the Oval Office and in Congress. For the first time in our history, ideology and theology hold a monopoly of power in Washington."[4]

I would put it somewhat differently. These developments have warped the Republican party and its electoral coalition, muted Democratic voices, and become a gathering threat to America's future. No leading world power in modern memory has become a captive, even a partial captive, of the sort of biblical inerrancy—backwater, not mainstream—that dismisses modern knowledge and science. The last parallel was in the early seventeenth century, when the papacy, with the agreement of inquisitional Spain, disciplined the astronomer Galileo for saying that the sun, not the earth, was the center of our solar system.

Conservative true believers will scoff: the United States is sui generis, they say, a unique and chosen nation. What did or did not happen to Rome, imperial Spain, the Dutch Republic, and Britain is irrelevant. The catch here, alas, is that these nations also thought they were unique and that God was on their side. The revelation that He was apparently not added a further debilitating note to the later stages of each national decline. Perhaps the warfare, earthquakes, plagues, and turmoil of the early twenty-first century are unprecedented, but the religious believers of yesteryear also saw millennial signs in flood, plagues, famines, comets, and Mongol and Turkish invasions.

Over the course of the last twenty-five years, I have made frequent reference to these political, economic, and historical (but not religious) precedents in several books, most recently in *Wealth and Democracy* (2002). The concentration of wealth that developed in the United States in the long bull market of 1982–2000 was also a characteristic of the zeniths of the previous leading world economic powers as their elites pursued surfeit in Mediterranean villas or in the country-house splendor of Edwardian England.

This volume, to be sure, is mostly about something other than wealth. Its concluding chapters in part 3 concentrate on the perils of debt, albeit that is also a financial excess. As we will see, wealth and debt have often overextended together in the modern trajectories of leading world economic powers. In a nation's early years, debt is a vital and creative collaborator in economic expansion; in late stages, it becomes what Mr. Hyde was to Dr. Jekyll: an increasingly dominant mood and facial distortion. The United States of the early twenty-first century is well into this debt-driven climactic, with some critics arguing—all too plausibly—that an unsustainable credit bubble has replaced the stock bubble that burst in 2000.

Unfortunately, as my subtitle argues, three of the preeminent weaknesses displayed in these past declines have been religious excess, an outdated or declining energy and industrial base, and financialization and debt (from foreign and military overstretch). The examples have been clear, and they thread my analysis in this book. The extent to which politics in the United States—and especially the governing Republican coalition—deserves much of the blame for this fatal convergence is not only the book's subject matter but its raison d'être.

CONTENTS

Part I

OIL AND AMERICAN SUPREMACY

1

Fuel and National Power

Control energy and you control the nations.
—Henry Kissinger

You and your predecessors in the oil and gas industry played a large part in making the twentieth century the "American Century."
—Secretary of Energy Spencer Abraham, speech to the
American Petroleum Institute, 2002

Not a day goes by without some new disclosure, some new bit of headline evidence that our brilliant energy success comes at great cost—air pollution and toxic waste sites, blackouts and price spikes, fraud and corruption, and even war. The industrial-strength confidence that was a by-product of our global energy economy for most of the twentieth century has slowly been replaced by anxiety.
—Paul Roberts, *The End of Oil,* 2004

THE STAKES COULD HARDLY BE HIGHER. SINCE THE EARLY TWENTIETH century, the world's age of oil has also been its era of American supremacy. Few doubt the interrelationship. Not merely a symbol of U.S. global power, petroleum has been its fuel for military might, twentieth-century manufacturing supremacy, and the latter-day SUV gas-hog culture. Oil abundance has always been part of what America fights *for,* as well as *with.*

Until recently, Americans have managed their oil age well. Like previous watershed energy regimes, ours has been an idiosyncratic mastery, a timely conjunction of a resource base, technical proficiency, and popular awareness. Put differently, over the last several hundred years each leading global economic power has ridden an emergent fuel resource into the pages of history. From the late eighteenth century to the early twentieth century, Britain did so through its pioneering skill with abundant coal. America's years at the helm, in turn, were driven by national engagement with the next major fossil fuel, oil.

The twenty-first century's oil-supply uncertainties have rekindled U.S. scholarly interest in the historical phenomenon of resource wars, which are now obviously looming more ominously than ever. Equally important, then, must be the strategic grasp of resource bases by modern world powers. This chapter's thesis is that unusual abilities to exploit a single energy resource for profit and for power—literal and political— have been vital to the rise of the leading world economic powers.

These supremacies have overlapped with, though they have not fully paralleled, inventive relationships with decisive fuels. The downside, so far, has been that the country able to seize a unique energy opportunity has lacked the wherewithal to manage the next one. Thus, the inevitable twenty-first-century global transition from oil to a postoil regime—be it natural gas, hydrogen, more nuclear reliance, renewable energies, or various hybrids of cleaned-up fossil fuels—could see the United States displaced by a new leading economic power, probably an Asian one. China's early history of innovations in hydraulics, natural-gas use, and deep drilling may be relevant.

This is not to embrace some vaguely Marxian mineral determinism— linking nations' power to natural resources in a way that downplays factors such as religion, nationalism, or charismatic leadership. What seems clear is that fuel has been one of several pivots. Thereafter, over generations, the world's energy leaderships—seventeenth-century Dutch ingenuity with water, wind, and wood, British aptitude with coal, and the U.S. cleverness with oil—have invariably developed related infrastructures of corporate, governmental, and cultural commitment. One generation's innovations become a later era's entrenchments.

Britain, on the cusp of decline, naïvely faced the military and economic future shock of 1914–1945 with a sooty transportation and energy structure still rooted in the mid-Victorian commercial geography of coal fields, canals, railroads, and ironmongers. The United States, for its part, is entering the twenty-first century with a resource base of declining oil and gas production and a grid of aging power plants, pipelines, and refineries.

Serious ledgers must also include the maintenance cost of a population blithely dispersed to suburbs and exurbs under the psychologies of cheap gas and oil that dominated in the forties, fifties, and sixties, recently reinforced by the current migration to "micropolitan" areas along outer suburban interstate-highway corridors. When U.S. gasoline prices reached three dollars a gallon in 2005, media reports began to capture the trauma among rural, small-town, and exurban Americans who drove to distant jobs. Other legacies range from the assets inertia of oil behemoths such as ExxonMobil to the potential insolvency of the onetime Detroit automobile giants, as SUV manufacturing becomes less magically profitable than it once seemed.

With U.S. oil production slumping inexorably from its 1970 peak and replacement options unclear, Americans have already embraced one historically familiar recourse: military seizure of portions of the Middle East, expected by 2020 to have two-thirds of the world's remaining oil resources. Global demand among other nations will press even harder than it does now. As supplies tighten, the countries of Latin America and Asia, especially China, India, and Japan, all with ballooning fuel needs, will also scheme and compete for them. Energy analysts have begun incorporating military reminders—the high past incidence of wars fought over natural resources—into some of the books published recently in North America, volumes with stark messages such as *The End of Oil: On the Edge of a Perilous New World; Blood and Oil: The Dangers and Consequences of America's Growing Dependency on Imported Petroleum; The Party's Over: Oil, War, and the Fate of Industrial Societies;* and *Crossing the Rubicon: The Decline of the American Empire at the End of the Age of Oil.* These, along with other, more technical, works, marshal expert geological analyses behind the proposition that, at the very least, world oil supplies will be tightening in the 2010s and 2020s even as commercial demand mushrooms.

Discussion of the American politics of this global conundrum will follow in chapter 2, leading into analysis of the mainsprings of U.S. petroleum imperialism in chapter 3. However, this first chapter aims to set a basic scene: the United States is a longtime oil power—at best an oil and gas power—and the aging of its energy infrastructure, guarded by a globally aggressive, entrenched-interest political coalition, is a harbinger of costly confrontations and military embroilment likely to lead to national decline.

Human nature has hardly been remolded. Prehistoric societies were often at blows over natural resources: food, water, and wood for fire and shelter. Modern history has been only slightly more subtle. Natural resources caused or aggravated sixteenth-, seventeenth-, and eighteenth-century wars to secure Baltic timber and naval stores, North Atlantic fisheries, East Indies spices, Caribbean sugar and salt, as well as New World gold and silver. After the industrial revolution, fossil fuels such as coal and oil moved into great-power gun sights.

Many resource grabs have succeeded. The broader dilemma for the twenty-first-century United States, unfortunately, has a financial twist. Past leading powers have eventually suffered from imperial hubris—a misplaced cocksureness that leads them into a strategic overreach they can no longer afford. The result has often been a humbled hegemon, left with crippling debt burdens, lost trade advantages, a stricken currency, and increasing vulnerability as rivals increase their stature as creditor nations, financial centers, and technological innovators.

To be sure, not all trends follow early-stage extrapolations. History may take decades to adjudicate whether the United States will be saluted for regaining its earlier global oil supremacy or disrespected for pursuing its ambitions into the footprints of earlier powers that miscalculated and stumbled.

What can safely be said is this: the longtime proven fuel of American power is running low—and at an extraordinarily inopportune time. The consequences of this will necessarily affect the global strength of the dollar, which gives U.S. strategists a double challenge.

A Brief History of Western Fuelishness

Foolishness about fuel history deserves its own noun. Candid discussions by senior U.S. officials about the peaking of American oil production back in 1970 and the not-too-distant peaking of global output have been rare, to say the least. This cavalier behavior has ignored geologists' calculations regarding the aging and depletion of world oil resources, which have generally been proved out since the seventies. Another mistake has been to date the petroleum era—its history, politics, and economics—back no further than 1859, when America's first oil well was drilled in northwest Pennsylvania. The implication, at least, is that there is little older precedent that matters.

Politically and historically, this is myopic. Oil is no modern energy discovery. The word itself goes back to the Greek *elaia,* which became *oleum* in Latin, then *oile* in Old French and medieval Anglo-French.[1] The Bible, especially Genesis, has references to asphalt, tar, and naphtha. Medieval Mesopotamia and Persia had local oil bureaucrats. In Renaissance Europe, some oil came from olives, some from fish, lard, seeds, nuts, and rocks. According to some, the word "petroleum" (Latin for "rock oil") first appeared in *De re metallica,* the 1556 treatise by German-born George Bauer (writing as Georgius Agricola), widely regarded as the father of mineralogy; other scholars date its usage to the fourteenth century. So-called rock oil was produced in several parts of Germany and eastern Europe. All of this matters.

By the Middle Ages, Basques and Scandinavians were killing whales for oil in the Bay of Biscay and the North Atlantic. After Spain's great armada was scattered and sunk in 1588, a desperate Spanish navy pressed into service whale-wise Basque seamen. Many chose instead to sail with the Dutch, who by the 1620s wound up in control of a much-expanded European whaling trade. This centered in waters around Spitsbergen, the barren 15,000-square-mile island just north of the Arctic Circle, then Dutch-held and known as Amsterdam Island. There, oil production for the lamps of Europe bred a roistering milieu not unlike that in later industrial boomtowns in the United States.

By 1637 the Dutch apparently had more than three hundred whaling ships and eighteen thousand men at Spitsbergen. The new flensing and boiling techniques developed by the Hollanders to produce whale oil created a sprawling industrial landscape resembling a seaside Hades: endless carcasses, huge saws and knives, deep vats, row after row of storage tanks, with fires and smoke clouds lurid in the Arctic half-light.[2] The biggest of these mammalian giants, sperm whales sixty to seventy feet long, produced a whopping five hundred to eight hundred gallons of oil.

Procuring whale oil was a serious European enterprise. The Dutch, without peer in seagoing commerce, used it for soap; lighting for streets, households, and industry; lubricants for machinery; cosmetics (lipsticks and perfumes); and even sophisticated paints. Art historians credit local oil-refining techniques for the mastery exhibited by the Dutch and Flemish painters of the sixteenth and seventeenth centuries. Linseed oil made from seeds crushed in nearby windmills improved paints enough that Rembrandt, Vermeer, and others could make major advances in precise lines, light, shade, and perspective.[3] Indeed, municipal illumination took a great leap forward because of a painter, Jan van der Heyden: he invented the street lantern, which burned through a night on a mixture of processed oils. Amsterdam adopted it in the 1670s for what some historians call the first proper system of city street lighting.[4]

Only some of these uses were displaced by John D. Rockefeller's later mass production of petroleum, since that was not always the preferred ingredient or lubricant for a given purpose. Wildlife conservationists, for example, later lamented that "the First World War provided a large market for explosives using glycerin from baleen whale oil provided by British and Norwegian whaling in the Antarctic."[5] French perfumers, Swiss watchmakers, and many others continue to demand special oils.

After a century Dutch whaling (and broader Dutch maritime enterprise) lost its edge, and in the 1720s leadership passed to British colonial New England, most notably Massachusetts. That state, not Pennsylvania, saw the first American energy boom. More broadly, the preeminence of Dutch, British, and American companies in the international petroleum business goes back to the whaling and maritime eras. This adds centuries to the larger U.S. and Western trajectory of economic and energy-resource maturation. Our oil culture is getting old.

Nantucket was the first major center, and before long sixty American whaling ships were in the Davis Strait near Greenland. By 1768 Nantucket alone had 125 whaling ships and exported its oil directly to Britain.[6] English and Scottish ports briefly moved ahead after the British navy captured many American whalers during the American Revolution and the War of 1812. However, Massachusetts always bounced back in peacetime, and by 1820 New Bedford, the greatest port of all, took over, captaining the pursuit of the fierce but especially oil-rich sperm whales later immortalized by Herman Melville in *Moby-Dick*. Absorbing the fleets of other nearby whaling centers, New Bedford in 1845 sent ten thousand seamen in more than three hundred ships to bring home its greatest receipts: 158,000 barrels of sperm oil, 272,000 barrels of other whale oil, and 300,000 pounds of whalebone (much in demand for corsets and suchlike).[7]

Like twentieth-century oilmen, the Dutch, British, and New England whalers generally opened up new territories as they depleted familiar ones. The sequence of whaling grounds led from the Bay of Biscay, Greenland, and Labrador to Spitsbergen and the European Arctic, the Gulf of St. Lawrence, Brazil, Chile, the South Pacific, Japan, and by the mid-nineteenth century, Kodiak, Kamchatka, the Bering Sea, and the nearby Alaskan Arctic.[8] Petroleum exploration produced a similar migration of geologists—from Pennsylvania, eastern Europe, the Russian Caucasus, and Persia to the Dutch East Indies, Oklahoma, Texas, California, Mexico, Venezuela, the Persian Gulf, Saudi Arabia, west Africa, Alaska, the North Sea, and the South China Sea. Each time, resource depletion demanded increasingly far-flung searches.

The petroleum that attracted thirty thousand fortune seekers to Civil War–era Pennsylvania found much the same market as whale oil. Illumination was foremost, then lubrication, soap production, medicinal remedies, and paints. The Seneca Indians who lived along Oil Creek, a tributary of the Allegheny, had long used the local oil seepage in their especially fearful war paint, a distant cousin of the medium of the Dutch masters. After "Colonel" Edwin Drake drilled the first local oil well in 1859, Pennsylvania businessmen acknowledged whale oil as a forerunner. The author of *Petrolia: The Landscape of America's First Oil Boom* wrote that "more than any other product, whale oil whetted the human appetite for clean, efficient, and affordable illumination. . . . The American whaling fleet defined the process of the hunt and refining technology, thereby establishing dominance over the fishery. Most importantly, this dominance established trade markets to disperse whale oil illumination internationally. Illumination proved to be so integral and basic a technology that Americans readily purchased the expensive oil. This success, however, aroused a grassroots desire for a less expensive alternative."[9]

Mid-nineteenth-century Americans were a literate and reading people. Demand for nighttime illumination far exceeded the four million barrels of whale oil produced each year by refineries in New England and New York. It was for this reason that Drake's Connecticut backers sent him to the Oil Creek valley. Journalists and entrepreneurs recognized the continuity. The first oil gushers in Venango County prompted hurrahs akin to seamen's "thar she blows" for the spout of a large sperm whale. In 1861 *Vanity Fair* published a cartoon showing formally attired whales attending a ball honoring Drake's well, pausing to toast the new technology that had spared them.[10]

Cheap and plentiful, the new fuel soon carried energy use to revolutionary levels. But these few paragraphs should make one thing clear: oil was no physical or commercial bolt from the blue. Three centuries of development cannot, in the words of one technology-proud U.S. oil museum, be dismissed as a few thousand barrels of kerosene produced from rock oil hand-dug by peasants in eastern Europe.* The dioramas and paintings of whale-crazed Spitsbergen in Amsterdam's Rijksmuseum portray one of the earliest serious industrial landscapes. From Romania to Norway, from bamboo-drilling China to the flowing springs along the Caspian Sea that so impressed Marco Polo, the medieval period had known oil in many varieties. Greek fire (similar to napalm) was a famous war weapon. And even two prominent early versions of the internal-combustion engine, portal to the peak-oil era, used lesser fuels: Henry Ford's original Model T burned ethanol made from corn, and Rudolf Diesel's 1892 invention was designed to run on peanut or vegetable oil, both easily made.

In the modern age of oil geopolitics after World War I, it was not coincidental that Britain and the Netherlands, along with the well-endowed United States, owned the preeminent oil giants, the famous "seven sisters": Esso, Texaco, Socony, Socal, Gulf Oil, British Petroleum (then the Anglo-Persian Oil Company), and Royal Dutch/Shell. For Britain and Holland the explanation lay in maritime and imperial history—the legacy of far-flung empires and spheres of interest. During the 1890s the oil fields that grew into Royal Dutch were found in the Dutch East Indies archipelago that traders from Holland had originally seized for spices in the 1620s. The Caribbean islands of the Dutch Antilles, colonized in the 1630s in pursuit of trade and salt deposits, also paid off three hundred years later. Some oil was found locally, and Royal Dutch obtained concessions for the rich new oil fields in next-door Venezuela. Huge and profitable refineries went up on the Dutch island of Aruba.

Imperial reach also gave Britain access to Persia, in particular, as well as to Borneo, Burma, and Trinidad, along with several protected Persian Gulf sultanates. The nineteenth-century handicap of the coal-rich British was a dearth of curiosity about petroleum. Despite some early exploration in central Burma, serious attention did not develop until the Anglo-German naval and strategic rivalry that gripped both nations after 1900. Until then, Persia and Mesopotamia were principally way stations to India,

---

*Indeed, most scholars now credit F. M. Semenov, a Russian engineer, for drilling the first oil well near Baku in the late 1840s.

the distant jewel in Britain's imperial crown. When the British struck oil in Persia in 1908, it was at the site of the ancient fire temple at Masjid-I-Sulaiman. The explorer responsible, mining engineer William D'Arcy, was also an avid Bible reader, his interest piqued by scriptural reference to the naphtha pools that burned endlessly in ancient fire temples.

D'Arcy's find soon led to the Anglo-Persian Oil Company, which later became Anglo Iranian, and ultimately British Petroleum. But considering that a French archaeologist had found local oil seepages in 1892 and that reports to England of large quantities of oil in Persia dated back to the sixteenth century, the British were slow to act.[11] Britain had all the coal it needed for industry and commerce, so oil initially became important because of naval needs. Awareness in the United States had much deeper economic antecedents.

As we will see, the oil finds of the 1920s were too little and too late to resurrect Dutch and British global economic hegemonies, each of which had a trajectory of 125–140 years. Britons simply did not have the feel for oil that they had for coal. The fact that the Americans, British, and Dutch all have oil assets and are close allies in the twenty-first century may not matter much in resolving the next pivotal issue: whether the all-important U.S. oil infrastructure and culture can transform itself. The clock is clearly ticking.

The political establishment's reluctance to acquaint the American electorate with this dilemma involves three particularly glaring problems: (1) unwillingness to speak of the present oil crisis in the full context of geological, economic, and military history; (2) failure to understand the past vulnerability of great but idiosyncratic national energy cultures losing their familiar footing; and (3) refusal to discuss the evidence of oil-field depletions and insufficient new discoveries that shows petroleum production moving toward an inflammatory worldwide shortage in a matter of decades. Candor is rare and its lack costly in such watersheds, having also been scarce in the Dutch United Provinces circa 1720 and in Britain just a century ago.

The Dead Hand of Yesteryear's Success

The evidence is that leading world economic powers, after an energy golden era, lose their magic—and not by accident. The infrastructures created by these unusual, even quirky, successes eventually became economic obstacle courses and inertia-bound burdens.

This chapter's emphasis will be on the United States as the vulnerable oil hegemon, an essential perspective for evaluating developments both in domestic politics and about the American military protectorate in Iraq. However, this is best prefaced by a brief look at what made and then undid the United Provinces of the Netherlands as the wind and water hegemon from 1590 to the 1720s and what made and then, more important, unmade Britain as the coal hegemon from roughly 1760 to 1914. More was involved than merely fuel, but the rise of coal-based industry left the Dutch further behind and elevated Britain. Oil, in turn, played a major role in the U.S. displacement of Britain.

Simon Schama, the historian, interpreted Holland's seventeenth-century golden age as a triumph of "moral geography." The small seaside United Provinces of the Netherlands, with so much of its surface area in islands and reclaimed land, represented a victory of people over water: "infirmity into strength, water into dry land, mud into gold."[12] He argued further that hydrology and reformed religion went together. Even as the Protestant Hollanders redeemed their country in the 1580s and 1590s by expelling Spanish Catholic rulers, they were reclaiming hundreds of thousands of acres from the sea. Both redemptions fed a sense of being special. "The making of new land belongs to God alone," proclaimed sixteenth-century hydraulic engineer Andries Vierlingh, "for he gives to some people the wit and strength to do it."[13]

Actually the Dutch achievement went even further. From the 1580s until the disruptive European wars of 1688–1713, the Dutch built the foremost global trading empire of that time. Tamers of the seas, they were also the best designers of ships—from small, handy trading vessels (*fluyts*) to whaling ships and herring "buses." The Dutch led in navigation; they ran the lucrative herring fisheries and North Atlantic whale trade; their navy dominated the sea lanes to Asia; and their engineers penned up the waters of the Zuider Zee with dikes, hydraulics, and windmill-driven pumps. At their peak, the Dutch boasted the world's biggest shipyards, the global center of commerce and finance (Amsterdam), the largest share of world trade, and overseas outposts from Brazil to New Amsterdam and from Japan, China, and India to the Cape of Good Hope.

More than just a communications network and global highway, water for the Dutch was also a sea of riches (herring, cod, whales, polder that became farmland, and salt, the vital preservative). Flooding itself became a weapon, used to trap or keep out Spanish troops when Dutch generals retreated behind their inner "Water Line." Leiden University, in 1600, established a school for fortification engineers that taught water warfare.[14] Not surprisingly, a Hollander invented a powerful type of fire engine — pipes as thick as a person's thigh, powered by pumps able to throw water three hundred paces.[15]

But water was not the only source of Dutch power. By filling the sails of the world's largest merchant marine—estimates ranged from six thousand ships to an unlikely ten thousand—wind also drove the single most important element of the Dutch economy. Flat and breezy Holland also harnessed air currents to drive the machinery of several thousand windmills. Following the seventeenth-century updating of the camshaft and crankshaft, these workhorses attained a surprising sophistication. The first Dutch oilseed-grinding mill was established in 1582, the first paper mill in 1586, and the first timber-sawing mill in 1592. By the early eighteenth century, the best mills were equipped with automatic regulators that controlled the speed of rotation, adjusted the pitch of the fan blades for maximum power at a given wind speed, and oriented the fan so that it faced directly into the wind.[16] Fifty-one Alkmaar mills used for drainage could pump out water at a combined rate of one thousand cubic meters per minute, the volume equivalent of a swimming pool one hundred feet long and wide and five feet deep.[17] In the Zaan, Europe's principal industrial district, nearly one thousand windmills powered large-scale shipbuilding, as well as the precursors of the food, paper, and timber works still located there.

By the mid-eighteenth century, as commercial and military power passed to industrializing Britain and populous France, Holland's importance in trade and production was waning. Dutch seamanship, fisheries, and shipbuilding all had lost their earlier reputations by 1750. Specialists in Dutch history offer many explanations. Some have emphasized war and rivals' mercantilist economic policies: the cumulative damage done to Dutch trade routes and maritime capacity by the late-seventeenth-century and eighteenth-century wars with France, together with the tariffs or outright prohibitions imposed by many countries on certain foreign goods, all of which hurt Dutch industries and shipping. The diffusion of Dutch technical expertise across Europe was also a problem. So was the reorientation of many Hollanders toward investments rather than hands-on commerce, seamanship, or engineering. Most historians agree that Dutch maritime and technical endeavors became less likely to innovate, and the British, in particular, moved ahead. Moreover, the republic had negligible coal and iron deposits, whereas well-supplied Britain was about to knit the two together in the industrial revolution. Coal, iron, and the steam engine overwhelmed the windmills that had been so advanced two centuries earlier.

The British era dated from 1763 and the defeat of France after seven years of war. Coal was already putting its dusty fingerprints on Britain's economic future. Indeed, one scholar calls that prowess notable enough that an early coal-fired "first industrial revolution" took place in the England of the seventeenth century. No other eighteenth-century nation remotely matched Britain in coal resources and knowing what to do with them.[18]

Mines in northern England had begun shipping substantial cargos to London by sea during the reign of Queen Elizabeth. Despite its acrid smoke, coal was used for heat and to assist in glass making, brick making, dyeing, iron working, and metallurgy. In mining regions it frequently replaced wood, which was becoming scarce and cost two to three times more. By 1700 England burned 2.5 million tons of coal each year, the great bulk of Europe's consumption. To one French visitor in the 1720s, coal was "the soul of English manufactures" for serving so many trades and domestic purposes elsewhere still fueled by wood.[19]

The major innovations that made coal the grand enabler of industry were all British. Blacksmith Thomas Newcomen developed the first steam engine, installed in 1712 to pump water from a coal mine. In 1769 James Watt built a pump that was much more powerful and thus usable in all kinds of factories (not just mines with nearly free coal at hand). In the 1780s, the development of the puddling and rolling processes consummated the ability to smelt pig iron with coke (coal baked to burn off impurities), which made possible the shift of furnaces and foundries from remote forests to what would become large industrial districts near coal fields.

Transportation as well as iron making came to be concentrated in the coal fields. A pathbreaking English canal, completed by the duke of Bridgewater in 1761, linked his coal mines at Worsley to the fledgling industrial center of Manchester. The cost of coal there dropped by half. Other coal-carrying waterways followed. Tracks of iron-reinforced wood, laid in the late eighteenth century to carry coal-bearing wagons from the mines to the rivers and seaports, inspired the idea of replacing horses with coal-burning steam engines. In the 1810s George Stephenson, a colliery engine-wright, perfected what became the first locomotive. By 1830 the island kingdom mined four-fifths of the world's coal, and in 1848 produced more iron than the rest of the world put together.[20] Taken together, coal, iron, steam engines, and railways *were* the industrial revolution.

By the end of the nineteenth century, more than half of the British towns of more than fifty thousand people were situated on or near coal fields.[21] The regional redistribution of English population in the eighteenth and nineteenth centuries to the north and Midlands was likewise coal driven, historians agree. This was also the zenith of British invention, much of it by skilled craftsmen and engineers, not men of scientific learning. Because of this idiosyncratic imprint, British metallurgy—to take one example—was mostly a collection of small family firms, the sort that cherished and maintained old machinery.

Large-scale U.S. and German iron and steel enterprises, backstopped by research laboratories and technically attuned university systems, cut a new swath in the early 1900s and left British competition behind. Cambridge historian Correlli Barnett, in *The Collapse of British Power,* wryly described Britain circa 1914 as "in many ways a working museum of industrial archaeology. Here clanked on tirelessly not only the actual machines but, not so tirelessly, the techniques and outlook of 1815–50— marvels of inventiveness and progress in their epoch but transformed by the passage of time into quaint memorials of the original Industrial Revolution."[22] Some still survive in popular British museums, a fate also overtaking the machinery of U.S. oil and automobile culture.

By Queen Victoria's death, coal mining itself was more efficient in Germany and America. Despite large-scale British production, many mines were old, with the cheaper-to-reach coal already taken. The most revealing dimension involved coal derivatives, which until the 1850s had been a British-dominated field. A geologist in coal-rich Scotland had extracted sal ammoniac from soot in 1756, and two decades later another Scot began the exploitation of coal as a source of coal tar and chemicals. Coal gas for illumination, developed in the 1790s, was first used to light British factories at night during the Napoleonic wars. As late as 1856 William H. Perkin, a trained chemist, discovered the first aniline dye based on coal distillation.

Thereafter, innovation shifted to Germany, abetted by British willingness to export large quantities of coal tar. By 1914 drugs and dyestuffs had become a German near monopoly and prime export; much the same materials were critical for making high explosives. According to the postwar *History of the [British] Ministry of Munitions,* "In August, 1914, therefore, the Germans were in the fortunate position of being able to turn with ease the vast resources of a flourishing coal-tar industry to the production of high explosives."[23] Britain, in short, had been left at the gate. The spirit of Newcomen, Darby, and Perkin had been missing for at least a generation.

Just as the Dutch had been left behind by the eighteenth-century industrial revolution, some economic historians suggest that coal-shaped Britain was left behind by a "second industrial revolution" circa 1900 that elevated chemicals, petroleum, and electrical engineering, all industries requiring large firms, scientific laboratories, educated workforces, and economies of scale. Whatever one calls the transformation, the Britain of 1900–1914 lagged, with a handful of explanations prevailing. As the inevitable consequence of "having gone first," late-nineteenth-century Britain had a huge investment in plants, equipment, and early techniques that were outdated a generation or two later. Trouble also lay with the prominence of family firms run by engineers, tinkerers, and craftsmen ill equipped to make the transition to economies of scale and mass marketing. The unplanned structure of railroads, in turn, was so widely acknowledged a drag by 1872 that both the British inspector of railways and *The Economist* called for state ownership as a remedy.[24]

Critics also dwelt on how the estate-owning elite of the time looked askance at industry, science, and technology, favoring instead the sort of education that trained the next generation to read Greek and Latin and prepare for Parliament or the Indian Civil Service. Planning and efficiency, alien in this infrastructure, became a much-criticized deficit of early-twentieth-century Britain. A group of leading academic and public figures who called themselves "the Coefficients" organized to discuss possible solutions, including the formation of a national "efficiency party" under former prime minister Lord Rosebery.[25]

To sum up, by 1914 Britain's energy infrastructure had gone from dominance to incipient crisis in a single century. After World War II, when the coal industry was finally nationalized, one commentator described the nation's prime resource base this way: "Psychologically and physically, it was in a dreadful state. The legacy of the pre-war period was not only an old-fashioned, ill-equipped and inefficient industry, but a store of bitterness and suspicion in the heart of the miner against the treatment he had received at the hands of the colliery owner."[26]

History repeats only in outline, so the United States must find its own pathway. But the general parallel is the basis for worry. The United States began the twenty-first century as the leading world economic power, but one already eighty to one hundred years into an oil- and gas-related dominion. Some symptoms of aging, like the displacement of manufacturing by finance, were already writ large in gross-domestic-product data. The conventional energy infrastructure—from pipelines to refineries—was already being described by private and government experts as partly outdated, difficult to overhaul, and vulnerable to attack and sabotage. But there was also an aging problem right at the heart of America's once globally preeminent oil and gas resources.

The Aging American Energy Infrastructure

Like the British of 1900, Americans a century later were slow to grasp the possibility that a steep price might have to be paid for the graying temples of what had once been a pioneering fuel culture and infrastructure.

Twenty-first-century oil rests on more than corporations, plants, and pipelines. Any realistic catalog must also include government subsidies and preferences, entrenched bureaucracies and interest groups, foreign relationships, political party coalitions, and recurring Middle East war patterns. These will be discussed in the next two chapters. This one, however, will look at the physical and economic causes and symptoms of sclerosis: the sheer age of the U.S. oil industry, the zenith and depletion of U.S. oil and gas reserves (the so-called Hubbert peak), the structural weakness of the huge U.S.-based international oil corporations (superannuated goliaths desperate for Middle East oil), and the weakness of U.S. automotive giants, which have lost most markets save those for trucks, large cars, and sports-utility vehicles.

In the long history of oil in the United States, coal was a short-lived rival. Despite resources larger than Britain's, the United States never became a true coal culture. That was because settlers, for some 250 years after the settlements at Jamestown and Plymouth, kept moving west, clearing land, and cutting down trees. Sheer availability made the new nation a wood-burning culture. Even in the centennial year of 1876, the United States took twice as much energy from firewood as from coal.[27] Coal pulled ahead in the mid-1880s, cresting as a source of three-quarters of U.S. energy in 1910, when oil was already beginning its rapid military and industrial ascent. Unfashionable and dangerous to mine, coal put its industrial-era stamp on only a few regions, principally Appalachia and kindred southern portions of Ohio, Indiana, and Illinois.

Oil, with its romance and overnight opportunity, caught the American fancy from the start. So avidly did New Englanders pursue whales for their prized oil that in 1775 the British statesman Edmund Burke saluted their pluck on the floor of Parliament: "And pray, sir, what in the world is equal to it? . . . No sea but what is vexed by their fisheries. No climate that is not witness to their toils."[28] The 1859 find in Pennsylvania, in turn, promoted the biggest oil boom since Spitsbergen, but few local residents were too surprised. Cartographers had been recording petroleum in Pennsylvania since Lewis Evans's 1755 map of the middle British colonies.[29] Sixteenth-century Spaniards had found puddles in Louisiana and oil slicks off the coast of California.

A folk culture was gestating. Native Americans recommended oil to soldiers during the American Revolution as a cure for frostbite. George Washington himself bought an oil spring in 1771. Many other early-nineteenth-century venturers put it in lamps and medicine bottles, probably including John D. Rockefeller's father, a quack who peddled patent medicines. In what became the oil regions, small springs and seeps were commonplace. In addition to Pennsylvania's Oil Creek and West Virginia's Kanawha River ("Old Greasy"), oil had turned up in Kentucky, Ohio, and other parts of western Pennsylvania, frequently as a by-product of searching or drilling for salt.[30]

Rockefeller himself was caught up in more than simple greed in the post–Civil War years when his Standard Oil Company, formed in 1870 in Cleveland, ruthlessly suppressed the chaos of competition among oil refiners. Order of some kind was necessary. Unlike coal, petroleum was subject to disastrous overproduction, which periodically collapsed prices. The Pennsylvania oil fields initially became a mecca for gamblers and speculators, bringing Titusville and Oil City local oil exchanges by 1871. Ida Tarbell, a daughter of the Pennsylvania oil fields who went on to write *The History of the Standard Oil Company,* said of the fortune hunters, "Life ran swift and ruddy and joyous in these men."[31] People danced to such tunes as the "American Petroleum Polka" and the "Oil Fever Gallop."

More than silver, more than gold, oil was the enterprise through which Americans of the industrial era could strike pay dirt, and, as exploration moved westward, many did. Western Pennsylvania led to Ohio and then to Kansas. As early as 1851, Kit Carson and Jim Bridger discovered an oil spring at Poison Spider Creek, just west of present-day Casper, Wyoming.[32] In 1861, lured by news of oil seepage in California, Demetrius Scofield packed up and left the Pennsylvania fields. In 1876 he bought the California Star Oil Works north of the little town of Los Angeles, and he went on to become the first president of Standard Oil of California.

Coal built few large fortunes. But by the turn of the twentieth century, the oilmen—and in a decade more, automobile makers such as Henry Ford and Horace Dodge—topped the lists of great American wealth, a superiority that peaked in the early 1980s following a decade of steep hikes in the price of petroleum. At the century's end, oil money was half Texas crude and half eastern refined—mellow, leather-bound fortunes steeped in the fourth- and fifth-generation respectability of Rockefeller foundations, Mellon art collections, and Harkness pavilions.

In the 1920s, British visitors were already struck by oil's pervasiveness in American culture. Two of them, E. H. Davenport and S. R. Cooke, set down this 1923 comparison:

> Travel but a little in the country and you will gain the impression that the modernism of the United States flowed from its oil wells. Outwardly, oil occupies there the place which coal occupies in Great Britain. The oilfield derrick is as familiar a landmark to the American as the pit-head wheels to the worker in our "black country." The oil-tank car is as ubiquitous on his railroads as the coal-truck is on ours. . . . His wayside is dotted with the petrol-pump, and at night illuminated oil "filling stations" make his streets beautiful. A network of oil pipe-lines underlies his country, more extensive than the network of railways overlying ours. . . . Does not the American partly live in oil?[33]

Certainly many Americans spent long hours in oil-powered vehicles. As automobiles took over from horses and buggies after World War I, they outstripped equine muscle with 40-, 75-, and 120-horsepower engines. In 1929, the United States was estimated to have more than two-thirds of the world's cars. The Germans, incurably mechanical, described the American economic and cultural giddiness of the 1920s in auto-motive terms: "Fordismus."[34] By 1950 Americans were consuming more than one-third of the world's energy output and nearly half of its oil, with gasoline as the single leading product. (Nearly two-thirds of U.S. oil consumption was in this form.) No oil expert could ignore the great American automobile craze. In 2004, after the United States had ruled global automobile ownership for a century, it was still a truism that "hav-ing a car is a way of assimilating in America and, more often than not, it's also the only way of getting around. Public transit systems are rarely found outside of the cities, and they carry with them the stigma of cater-ing to those people who can't afford a car. With the automobile being such a necessity and also a symbol of status, is it any wonder that America views life through a car windshield?"[35]

Along with highways, service stations, motels, and such, the American oil infrastructure also enabled and supported major demographic and residential change, as seen in the extraordinary twentieth-century re-molding of U.S. population distribution. To make the obvious analogy, it paralleled in magnitude, if not flow, the redistribution that coal had wrought in Britain. Following the huge 1901 Spindletop oil discovery in Gulf Coast Texas, when wells able to produce one hundred thousand barrels per day dwarfed previous five-thousand-barrel capabilities, Ameri-cans concluded that supply was enormous, verging on endless. Two more decades ushered in the petro-landscape described by Davenport and Cooke. Coal continued to lead for a while in percentage terms, but America's prevailing twentieth-century corporate, transportation, energy, and resi-dential infrastructure was being shaped around petroleum.

A century later, Spindletop's glories were only a recollection, like the boom times of Oil City, Pennsylvania. It lived on as a museum—fifteen old buildings from the boom years. As for the huge east Texas fields dis-covered in the late 1920s and early 1930s—Daisy Bradford no. 3, Lathrop no. 1, and the rest—by 2004 production there had fallen from 160 million barrels a year in 1936 to just 10 million. In Midland, the oil capital of the West Texas Permian Basin, the major companies began leaving the area in 2000, and some studies suggest that the local oil industry will be gone by the 2020s. "The U.S. oil industry is very old," Paul Holtberg, a senior re-searcher with the RAND Corporation, cautioned in 2002. "There's no question that the resource here has been drilled more heavily than any-where else in the world."[36]

Back in 1956, Marion King Hubbert, an American geologist working for Shell, had brought out a set of calculations interrelating the dates of the major U.S. oil-field discoveries, their rates of production, and the peaks that he saw inevitably following. Fossil fuels such as oil, natural gas, and coal, squeezed into being by millions of years of massive pressure on concentrations of animal and plant matter, are not renewable. Using geological computations, Hubbert predicted that extraction of oil in the lower forty-eight states—Alaska had not yet been tapped—would maximize between 1965 and 1970.[37] To the surprise of laymen, the peak did come in 1970, after which overall production in the lower forty-eight dropped steadily, despite all sorts of new tax breaks and breakthroughs in drilling technology.

By the time Hubbert died in 1989, he had attracted numerous disciples—many grouped in a professional organization called the Association for the Study of Peak Oil and Gas (ASPO)—who applied his basic methodology to other regions and nations.[38] In Alaska production peaked in 1988; in Canada and Mexico, during this decade. Output in the former Soviet Union, which first peaked in 1985–1987, was the subject of considerable disagreement two decades later.[39] Both major North Sea producers are said to have maximized output—Norway in 2004 and Britain in 2000—even though local drilling began only in the 1970s.

A short explanation of the "peak" concept is in order. Geologists define it as the point at which at least half of a field's reachable oil has been extracted. After this stage, getting each barrel out requires more pressure, more expense, or both. Output shrinks accordingly. After a while, despite nominal reserves that may be considerable, more energy is required to find and extract a barrel of oil than the barrel itself contains. By then, production becomes uneconomic—at least until the price of oil rises or the cost of extraction drops.

Although the experts do not agree how close world oil production is to its peak, pessimists believe that it is close, and even relative optimists see it only two or three decades away. Matthew Simmons, a Texas consultant who has advised George W. Bush's White House, pinpointed the aging problem in a 2002 report, "The World's Giant Oilfields," for the Colorado School of Mines. The "120 largest oilfields produce close to 33 million barrels a day, almost 50 percent of the world's crude oil supply. The fourteen largest account for over 20 percent. The average age of these 14 largest fields is 43.5 years."[40] By 2004 Simmons and others were expressing concern that Saudi output might already have peaked—unconfirmable, of course, until seen later in the all-knowing rearview mirror.

Two thousand four was also the year that Royal Dutch/Shell acknowledged overstating its oil and gas reserves by 20 percent, bringing a major plunge in its share price. British Petroleum had downgraded its production goals several times during 2002, said analysts, because it couldn't find enough oil in its existing fields.[41] To all the major oil companies, finding new production resources was a never-ending challenge. Jon Thompson, the president of ExxonMobil Exploration, wrote in a 2003 company publication, "We estimate that world oil and gas production from existing fields is declining at an average rate of about 4 to 6 percent a year. To meet projected demand in 2015, the industry will have to add about 100 million oil-equivalent barrels a day of new production. That's equal to about 80 percent of today's production level. In other words, by 2015, we will need to find, develop and produce a volume of new oil and gas that is equal to eight out of every 10 barrels being produced today."[42]

The year 2005, with its high oil prices, brought more candor about future supplies from the major oil companies and the press, if not from the Bush administration. "Big Oil Warns of Coming Energy Crunch," reported the headline in the *Financial Times*.[43] In a new advertisement ExxonMobil acknowledged that "the world faces enormous energy challenges. There are no easy answers." Meanwhile, a company publication, "The Outlook for Energy: A 2030 View," predicted that oil production ouside OPEC would peak in just five years.[44] Chevron chief executive officer David J. O'Reilly told a Houston audience that in the new international energy equation, "relative to demand, oil is no longer in plentiful supply. The time when we could count on cheap oil and even cheaper natural gas is clearly ending."[45] Major financial institutions with oil exposure, like Deutsche Bank and the Bank of Montreal, began to take sides in the peak oil debate or endorse the case that Saudi oil production had probably peaked, with all that implied for the future.[46]

In a similar vein, prominent figures in the industry began to acknowledge that new oil discoveries were languishing. Arthur Smith, chairman of John S. Herold, Inc., consultants, noted that recent data "show the number of major oil discoveries continues to decline each year. We are living off inventory. That's confirmed by all the data we've collected on the industry."[47] Several months earlier, *Petroleum Review* editor Chris Skrebowski had reported similar study findings: that among eighteen nations providing 30 percent of the world's daily crude oil output, production was declining at a rate of 5 percent a year, "and those procedures still with expansion potential are having to work harder and harder to make up for the accelerating losses of the large number that have clearly peaked and now are in continuous decline."[48] When the informational dam broke, candor came in a flood.

Some models predicted that the production of non-OPEC countries, including the United States, Britain, Canada, Russia, Norway, Mexico, and Angola, would collectively peak around 2010.[49] This implied a future concentration of pricing leverage in the OPEC states, led by Saudi Arabia and the other Gulf countries, where the collective peak is thought to be further off. By 2025 OPEC might control a large portion of the remaining reserves. Not surprisingly, speculation about Saudi production itself peaking brought quick rejoinders from Riyadh. Yet important doubts had been planted, and they were kept alive in 2005 when the Saudis could not increase production enough to keep prices from soaring.

Critic of Hubbert's methodology raised valid caveats: that major reserves were larger than realized (and still increasing through new discoveries) and that a combination of high prices and increasingly sophisticated extraction techniques should make it economic to pursue higher rates of recovery from existing deposits. New drills, they pointed out, could reach depths of ten miles, move in any direction, and even detect oil and gas electronically.[50] Deepwater drilling has excited particular expectations, and some have cast their eyes toward the Arctic preserves.

Peak theorists countered that politicians, government agencies, and OPEC leaders all have major vested interests in soothing worries about the need for crash programs to find oil substitutes. Note was made that back in 1985, many OPEC nations had inflated their estimated oil reserves because doing so allowed them to increase their production quotas. The optimism of official agencies such as the U.S. Geological Survey (USGS) and the Energy Information Agency, in turn, was suspect because of their responsiveness to White House pressure. As far back as 1919, the USGS released gloomy estimates of upcoming U.S. production, by some accounts to justify the American case for sharing in the post–World War I division of Ottoman

Empire oil. In 1973 Congress called for an investigation of the USGS for not anticipating or drawing attention to the U.S. oil-production peak of 1970.[51]

However, even in these government circles, optimists put the peak of global oil production only a bit closer to the middle of the century—say, 2025 to 2035—than to its beginning. That still left the United States of 2025 in the difficult position of needing to import roughly three-quarters of an expected thirty million barrels per day of consumption. At the same time, environmental experts emphasized yet another aging process: the global climate change caused by twentieth-century manufacturing and energy consumption, which overloaded the atmosphere with carbon dioxide. An abrupt climate-change scenario, released by the Pentagon in 2003 but quickly disavowed by the White House, discussed the potential peril to U.S. national security from rising world energy consumption and the likelihood of resource wars.[52]

In the 1980s, as natural gas assumed a greater role in the United States alongside oil, geologists identified a Hubbert peak for U.S. gas production around 1989. By 2000, the cautions from Texas had escalated. *Oil & Gas Journal* reported in 1999 that the Texas gas industry, with one-third of the nation's production, had to drill 6,400 new wells just to maintain output, in contrast to 4,000 new ones the year before, and the Associated Press reported similar ratios nationally.[53] Two decades earlier, offshore drillers in the Gulf of Mexico had frequently found large gas reservoirs of one hundred billion cubic feet or more, but by 2002 discoveries averaged only 5 percent of that size.[54]

Within the United States, the infrastructure for transporting natural gas made hardly anyone happy. Short pipelines are one thing, but carriage over long distances is a challenge—considerably more expensive than moving oil because the gas must be liquefied and carried under pressure. Some Washington policy makers looked for rescue to Canada, Mexico, and the North American Free Trade Agreement. Although rising oil prices made large-scale but high-cost extraction from Alberta's oil sands increasingly economic, getting more natural gas to the United States from Canada's Mackenzie Delta faced other obstacles. The pipeline needed cost $20 billion and was opposed by the Canadian provinces and aboriginal tribes whose lands would be crossed.[55] The larger dilemma is that North America doesn't have much of the world's natural-gas reserves—Asia, the

Middle East, and North Africa dominate—although the United States alone has been consuming 25 percent of the world's annual output.

*Embattled American Oil and Automobile Goliaths
and the Premise of Middle Eastern Rescue*

Age and longevity can be rewarded in America, but they do not favor the oil giants. Despite the huge profits record oil prices bestowed on the two remaining U.S. oil giants, their weaker international circumstances can be glimpsed in lost rankings. In the 1930s and 1940s five of the seven sisters that dominated international oil were American. Now only ExxonMobil (2) and Chevron (7), both of which gained needed scope through 1999 mergers, fly the Stars and Stripes. The other eight leading firms are Saudi Aramco (1), the National Iranian Oil Corporation (3), Petróleos de Venezuela (4), British Petroleum and Royal Dutch/Shell (tied for 5), Total (8), Pemex (9), and PetroChina (10).[56]

Four of the ten are government-owned oil companies empowered by various reorganizations and nationalizations: Pemex, formally Petróleos Mexicanos (1938), the National Iranian Oil Corporation (1979), Petróleos de Venezuela (1976), and Saudi Aramco (1980). PetroChina, principally state owned, is the largest oil company in the People's Republic. That gives Asia and Latin America five out of the top ten, a major comedown for the former seven sisters. From the 1930s to the 1960s, the seven counted much of this oil production their own, but after nationalization spread across the Middle East and Latin America the share of global oil reserves held by the four American and British giants fell to just 4 percent in 2001.[57] Not surprisingly, the companies deeply resent this turnabout and would like to see it reversed by privatization, especially in the Middle East.

In the 1960s commentators described the big American and British firms as "integrated" oil companies because they controlled the whole sequence of production from oil field to pump. But the rise of the rival state-owned companies over the last four decades prompted some U.S. analysts to coin a new term for the Western behemoths: obsolescent "supermajors." Forced into seeking more strength through mergers during the 1990s, the resulting megafirms, also including French Total, soon found themselves consumed with the challenge of replacing every million barrels sold with a freshly discovered million. Finding small fish was not enough; the behemoths needed the latter-day equivalent of giant sperm whales, and the hunting grounds were shrinking.

Experts saw only a few options. The majors could tilt more toward natural gas, made easier because overseas gas producers had no OPEC-type quotas to constrain output. Alternatively, they could hope to gain oil resources by relying on Washington pressure to break up the state-owned firms guarding the spigots in the Persian Gulf. In the years before the 2003 U.S. invasion left Iraq's oil production in disarray from disrepair and insurgent attacks, ExxonMobil and Chevron had both smacked their lips over sharing access. ExxonMobil, foreign observers reported, hoped to get the Majnoon field, with its twenty to twenty-five billion barrels.[58] As early as 1995, *The Wall Street Journal* reported a consensus that Iraq, with its huge resources and very low production costs, was "the biggie" in terms of future production and oil-firm global pecking order.[59]

Those stakes took dollar form in early 2004 when the New York–based Global Policy Forum published calculations of how much the U.S. and U.K. oil giants stood to make from control over Iraqi oil reserves estimated at close to four hundred billion barrels: "In order to understand the magnitude of these profits, it is useful to know that the worldwide profits of the world's five largest [private] oil companies in 2002 were $35 billion. Our estimate of the 'most probable' annual profits in Iraq are $95 billion, three times this sum!"[60]

Even if these estimates were too high, Iraq had become shorthand for oil-company salvation. With the giants caught up by a kind of assets inertia similar to that of British coal and railroading in their own heydays, transformations appeared daunting. In his book *The End of Oil,* Paul Roberts opined that "from the standpoint of an oil company's long-term profitability, this inability to hit targets or replace reserves is akin to a diagnosis of cancer—and the industry knows it. . . . The market now watches company production numbers and so-called reserves-to-production ratios—or how many years a company's reserves will last—as closely as it used to watch profits."[61] Clearly, the potential multiplier of the stock prices (market capitalization) of ExxonMobil, Chevron, Royal Dutch/ Shell, and BP from dividing up Iraq's resources stood to be a cork popper.

Before leaving this discussion of the oil companies, it is relevant to touch on the industry's aging-workforce problem. "Gray hair is in this year," Larry Nation of the American Association of Petroleum Geologists told the *Houston Chronicle* in 2004. "There simply aren't younger geologists to take on the job. It's like a slow-moving train wreck, and here it is."[62] The reasons given included distrust of oil and gas as a boom-bust business, belief that it is an "old guys'" business and environmentally unsound, and unwillingness by families to relocate to obscure and sometimes dangerous places in the third world. However, Stephen Holditch, a former president of the Society of Petroleum Engineers, said these American views did not apply in Africa, Latin America, and Russia. In Cairo, he said, "they're jumping at the chance."[63]

On the positive side, at least the oil firms did not confront the "legacy" problems—the crippling hangover of pension and health costs—that had begun to dog the competitiveness of yesteryear's automobile and airline industry stalwarts. At General Motors, for example, each current worker supports 2.4 retirees, an ultimately unsustainable equation. For now, the oil industry is too rich to have that particular problem.

The aging of the U.S. electricity supply and power grid, serious as it is, can be put to one side as we concentrate on the aging of the American oil culture; electricity is small stuff next to transportation. Cars and trucks burn an overwhelming two out of every three barrels of oil used in the United States. Airplanes use another 10 percent. Power plants, by contrast, are only minor oil burners, as of 1998 being 56 percent coal fired, 21 percent nuclear driven, 10 percent gas burning, and 10 percent hydroelectric.[64] The critical yardstick of an adequate U.S. oil supply—or any turn toward efficiency and conservation—must be automotive.

ExxonMobil's grandparent, Standard Oil, would have been 130 years old as the century turned in 2000; Ford was ninety-seven and General Motors ninety-two. Their old age, much less secure, was succinctly summarized by *The New York Times* in 2005: "Ford and G.M., the last two predominantly American-owned automakers, have been struggling to compete against Asian and European rivals. Both have been losing market share despite heavy spending on rebates, and both are weighed down by soaring health care and pension costs. Standard & Poor's has the debt of Ford and G.M. rated one notch above junk bonds, a precarious position for two of the largest corporate borrowers."[65] By the end of 2005, their bonds had fallen into junk status.

Union labor contracts are part of the vise. Wall Street analysts use "enormous legacy cost burden" language to explain why the two firms would rather produce extra vehicles than idle plants temporarily. "If you can generate some contribution to cover those legacy costs," said analyst Maryann Keller, "you will spend money on incentives in order to keep the production lines running. It is more expensive to close the production lines and have people idle. Remember, if the production line is closed, not only do those legacy [pension and health] costs continue, but also the workforce that is temporarily unemployed receives 95 percent of their normal wages."[66]

According to one study by the Federal Deposit Insurance Corporation, "the U.S. automobile industry shows the effects of pension costs on the bottom line. The results of a Prudential Financial study state that pension and retiree benefits represent $631 of the cost of every Chrysler vehicle, $734 of the cost of every Ford vehicle, and $1,360 of the cost of every GM car or truck. In contrast, an article in the *Detroit Free Press* reported that pension and retiree benefit costs per vehicle at the U.S. plants of Honda and Toyota are estimated to be $107 and $180, respectively."[67] Longevity and diminished competitiveness went hand in hand. Predictions mounted that Toyota would soon replace GM as the world's leading carmaker.

Inside Ford and GM, meanwhile, the biggest profits are made not by the manufacturing segment but by the two financial arms: Ford Credit and General Motors Acceptance Corporation (GMAC). Both are giants in the accounts-receivable world. At Ford the nuts-and-bolts automotive sector made $850 million before taxes in 2004, while Ford Credit racked up a record pretax profit of nearly $5 billion.[68] Both companies' credit subsidiaries, it must be added, go beyond auto loans to services ranging from leases to mortgages and money-market instruments. The new bottom line, one could argue, is that manufacturing results have given way. Actual production of goods has become the showroom for a loan-origination business. In 1986 Salomon Brothers forecast exactly this kind of era in which credit operations would be the lucrative side of the business.[69]

Without that financial backstop, the two firms might have become historical artifacts by the end of the twentieth century. The irony is that during the 1930s, 1940s, and 1950s the auto-making big three worked to push the U.S. transportation system into car dependence. Led by GM, the automakers acquired bus manufacturers and lines, then promoted diesel buses to displace both intercity rail transportation and electric transit systems. GM also acquired railroad-engine manufacturers, converting their production from electric trains (the norm in 1935) to trains that by 1970 were almost wholly diesel run.[70] According to foes, while GM made some money from diesel buses and railroad engines, the larger purpose was to channel the public toward car purchases, where the firm's huge profits lay.[71] Critics often exaggerate, but this case seems broadly supportable.

In recent years, ironically, the sales of small and cheaper cars in the United States, once the preoccupation of Henry Ford's Model T culture and GM's early Chevrolet marketing, has slipped into foreign hands. Late in 2003 Toyota passed Chrysler in overall monthly sales, and the GM-Ford-Chrysler market share of all U.S. vehicle sales dropped to under 60 percent. The overall U.S. market share of GM alone dropped to under 30 percent from more than twice that in 1970. Of the compact and mid-size cars sold in 2003, 45 percent and 39 percent, respectively, were imports, principally Japanese.[72] Limited intercity rail and urban mass transit facilities mean that little of the automobile demand can be diverted that way.

Vulnerable automakers have spent much of the last three decades dodging potentially fatal bullets. In the late 1970s and 1980s, Chrysler was bailed out by a federal loan, while Ford was kept afloat by the deep pockets of its founding family. In the 1990s SUVs mounted the rescue, and in the 2000s the job was achieved by lucrative financial units, despite costly rebates and interest-free loans to keep the public buying.[73] Whether the automakers will exist a decade or two hence may matter less than the nature of the forces that will chop them down or repackage their surviving parts. The financial side certainly has hazards, in that both GM and Ford borrowed huge sums in the low-interest bond market in recent years to plug holes in their pension funds and fund the costs of their vital incentive plans. Skeptics pictured a pyramid of credit risk, vulnerable to an interest-rate crunch that could leave the car companies shut out of unsecured borrowing.

On the manufacturing front, both companies might have gone under had they not found the "SUV loophole" in the mid-1980s. As Japanese manufacturers figuratively ate Detroit's lunch, Ford and GM survived by shifting ever more of their production into SUVs and other light trucks that were (1) exempt from the U.S. fuel-efficiency standards applied to automobiles, and (2) profitable to a critical degree, even though such vehicles were so heavy in carbon-dioxide emissions as to have a limited market in other countries.

Through these choices, the automobile companies have painted themselves into a strategic corner. In 2003, the Washington-based World Resources Institute published a survey in which chart after chart showed the manufacturers that are rooted in the U.S. market—Ford, GM, and DaimlerChrysler—turning out most of their sales volume in SUVs and heavy cars and scoring worst in carbon-dioxide emissions. The institute's ultimate measurement, the "carbon intensity" of each automaker's profits, found that "Ford and GM derive more than three quarters of their profits from high carbon-emitting vehicles, because their profits are disproportionately attributable to light truck sales."[74]

To a considerable extent, the U.S. automobile companies' tight corner is also America's. More than most other industries, the surviving U.S.-owned manufacturers are vulnerable to negative economic and energy changes. Should oil and gasoline prices further implode the U.S. domestic SUV and large-car market, imperiling domestic manufacturers, ever more of the smaller cars Americans drive will be foreign made, worsening a U.S. global trade imbalance already inflamed by the surging cost of oil imports. The nations once-proud auto culture could turn into yet another framework for escalating U.S. global indebtedness.

The 2006–2008 politics looks to be confrontational. Unless the Bush administration can submerge the problems facing U.S. automobile manufacturers, motorists, and daily commuters in some new and successful foreign diversion—U.S. mismanagement in Iraq having only aggravated the oil supply and terrorist threats—the political dependence of the Republican national coalition on automobiles, gasoline, and drivers stands to be a battleground. During the first George W. Bush administration, that reliance dictated an attempt to turn the Persian Gulf into an American filling station so as to maintain high energy consumption; during the second, disillusioned constituencies became visibly at risk.

2

The Politics of
American Oil Dependence

Oil provides a unique springboard for analyzing the American society and the problems of power that it poses.
—Robert Engler, *The Politics of Oil*, 1961

Oil is a kind of original sin in American politics. It's a big, messy (sometimes dirty) business, and it has touched everyone and everything in our political system, from the days of the Rockefellers to Bush and Gore.
—David Ignatius, *The Washington Post*, 2000

What makes the new Bush administration different from previous wealthy cabinets is that so many of the officials have links to the same industry—oil.
—BBC News, January 2001

THE GLORY OF THE TWENTIETH CENTURY IS NOW THE BURDEN. OIL HAS soaked deeply—in all likelihood indelibly—into the politics and power structure of the United States, partly because over two bountiful centuries it has also seeped, spouted, and oozed up from so many sections of so many states. More than a fuel, oil became a heritage and also the basis of a lifestyle. In the 1920s Bruce Barton, an advertising man who became a Republican congressman from New York, described gasoline as "the juice of the fountain of youth," a national revivifier through the excursions and explorations it made possible. Eighty years later oil still stands for American independence and fulfillment.

31

Politics has reflected this association. For all the intermittent popular arousal against "the creeping, crawling black monster" of Standard Oil and later against "Big Oil," there is also a sense of bounty. Hundreds of local petro-cultures, blending entrepreneurialism and folk history, have underpinned the towering concentrations of wealth and influence built during America's global oil hegemony.

And tower that wealth has. Fully half of the sixteen richest U.S. companies in 1948 were oil firms. A generation later, the initial *Forbes* survey of the four hundred richest Americans (1982) set out the largest personal and family fortunes. Of the top thirty, more than half had origins in petroleum, America's black gold. As for the millions of small stakeholders— the oil-stained yeomanry of the Allegheny, Pecos, or Williston basins, and the mere part-timers making fifty or one hundred dollars per month from the output of a derrick or two—their contribution was to lobby hard in Cheyenne, Topeka, or Baton Rouge and pose for group photographs published in the inside pages of the Mid-Continent Gas and Oil Association monthly as evidence of grassroots commitment.

At the grass roots oil rarely gushed, but it frequently trickled with modest to middling reward. Twentieth-century Oklahomans saw more than 750,000 wells drilled, with oil struck in seventy-two of seventy-seven counties. A half dozen Los Angeles neighborhoods played host to more derricks than palm trees (and on most days, nearby Huntington Beach counted more drillers than bathers). When Senator Paul Douglas from prairie Illinois, where winter blew cold, led a 1954 fight against the oil-depletion allowance, the industry's cherished federal income tax break, advisers cautioned that even in that corncribbed state, more than one-third of the counties had gas or oil production.[1] Politicians found ratios just as high in Montana, Kansas, and Kentucky.

In ten or fifteen states, many Atlantic, oil and gas deposits were virtually nonexistent. From Maine to Florida, hints of offshore drilling were shouted down as a threat to fisheries, lobsters, and tourism. New England officeholders, in particular, have been ready to blame the Sun Belt for fuel-oil costs, which has prompted Texans to respond with caustic bumper stickers: "Drive Fast, Freeze a Yankee." Nationally, support for the industry outweighed opposition, inasmuch as twenty to thirty states counted oil and gas as a middling to big business, a proud part of local history, or both. Moreover, when the pride and self-interest of the American automobile culture are added to the commerce of energy—as politically they must be—the balance of power has been as unmistakable as the torque of a 1970s Cadillac or the blessing of air-conditioning in summer traffic jams. Environmentalists raise a credible voice but usually a less influential one. Voters have come to expect cheap gasoline, electricity, and gas and oil heating—as well as the comfort, mobility, and personal independence that hydrocarbons facilitate.

Americans constitute the world's most intensive motoring culture. For reasons of history and past abundance, no other national population has clumped so complacently around so fuelish a lifestyle. For many citizens the century of oil has brought surfeit: gas-guzzling mobile fortresses, family excursions on twenty-thousand-gallons-per-hour jet aircraft, and lavishly lit McMansions in glittering, mall-packed exurbs along outer beltways. Against a backdrop of declining national oil and gas output, Americans consume 25 percent of world energy while holding just 5 percent of its energy resources. As the new century began, Americans enjoyed a lifestyle roughly twice as energy intensive as those in Europe and Japan, some ten times the global average.[2] Of the world's 520 million automobiles, unsurprisingly, more than 200 million were driven in the United States, and the U.S. car population was increasing at five times the rate of the human population.[3] How long that could continue was not clear.

John and Jane Q. Citizen mostly ignore these trends and details, and know nothing of geologist Hubbert's bell-shaped charts of peak oil. Senior oil executives sometimes discuss them in industry conferences, but elected officials—many with decades of energy platitudes under their belts—typically shrink from opening what would be a Pandora's box of political consequences. Oil was there for our grandfathers, they insist, and it will be there for our grandchildren; it is part of the American way.

The politics of oil dependence in the United States, in sum, is ingrained and possessive—a culture of red, white, and blue assumptions of entitlement, a foreign policy steeped in covert petroleum emphasis, and a machismo philosophy of invade-and-take-it. But before pursuing these cultural aspects, we must examine the political infrastructure: oil's growing influence on party politics and the presidency, together with the uniquely powerful role it has played in U.S. foreign policy over the years.

The Emergence of Oil and U.S. Party Politics

Almost from its birth, the industry put conspicuous political muscle on display in its home region: Pennsylvania, Ohio, and West Virginia. Oliver Hazard Payne, a wealthy Cleveland refiner and early ally of John D. Rockefeller, rose during the 1870s to become treasurer of Standard Oil, supervising the Ohio-based company's financial liaisons with federal and state politicians. This was an era infamous for the easy equation of money and power. In 1884 Payne is said to have handed out enough to convince the Democratic Ohio legislature to send his father, Congressman Harry Payne, rather than some other party stalwart, to the U.S. Senate. Four years earlier, Standard had helped elect to the U.S. Senate a friendly West Virginia oilman, Johnson N. Camden, whose company, renamed Consolidated Oil, had already been secretly bought out by Rockefeller. Camden, too, was a Democrat.[4] Like most other magnates, Rockefeller sought friends in both parties. As for Republican Pennsylvania, reformer Henry Demarest Lloyd sardonically (and famously) observed that Standard had managed to do everything with the state legislature but refine it.

Access and power flourished, although by the 1890s the Rockefeller fortune, relentlessly attacked by muckraking journalists, had become the nation's most controversial. In party terms, the Pennsylvania and Ohio oil lands sat in Republican regions, but beginning in 1901 geology favored existing or soon-to-be-admitted Democratic states with the gushers at Spindletop and major finds in Oklahoma and Louisiana. By the time Franklin D. Roosevelt ran for the White House in 1932, even grander fields had opened up in eastern Texas, ensuring that state's future as America's top oil and gas producer. This geography may have influenced Roosevelt to select crusty Speaker of the House John Nance Garner of Texas as his running mate. Ironically, the New Deal coalition came undone thirty-six years later under the first Texas-bred *president*, Lyndon Johnson. For the liberalizing national Democratic party, Johnson's oil ties turned out to be a lagging, not leading, indicator.

Oil's bipartisan geography ensured the industry power regardless of party control in Washington. The east Texas discoveries of 1930–1931, followed by a 1932–1933 glut and price collapse, led to petroleum becoming a major preoccupation-cum-beneficiary of the New Deal. In 1926, Washington Republicans had jumped the oil-depletion allowance from a piddling 5 percent to a lucrative 27.5 percent, but they also dropped top federal income-tax rates low enough to mute the rewards of the allowance. The Democratic Congresses of the 1930s, herded along by tough Texan trail bosses, kept the high allowance and liberalized it. Meanwhile, the maximum federal income-tax rate rose to 91 percent, a cross-hatching of liability, shelter, and relief that revalidated oil's nickname of "black gold."[5]

Many oilmen, especially Texans and southerners but even some in the Rockefeller apparatus, backed Roosevelt in his first race when oil needed help.[6] Coal interests generally stuck with the GOP, which increased Democratic openness to oil. In addition to the depletion allowance, New Deal collaboration included price supports for oil and import restrictions. Roosevelt also signed so-called hot-oil legislation. Pushed by the big companies, this 1935 statute prohibited interstate oil transfers, typically by small shippers, at prices below those set by state regulators.[7]

Between them, state and federal regulation created something of a maze. Eventually, oil imports from abroad would be managed through a two-tier system in which U.S. producers received considerably more than the per-barrel price set in global markets.[8] Because a boom-or-bust commodity like oil required some regulation to minimize gluts and price collapses, a degree of government involvement was critical. Further, World War I had already illustrated oil's national-security importance.

Liberals and reformers howled at favoritism, usually castigating the federal tax breaks, so lucrative that they often put wealthy oilmen on the defensive. Oklahoma senator Robert Kerr, the multimillionaire head of Kerr-McGee oil and for a brief time in the 1950s a presidential hopeful, wryly pitched an audience of skeptical border-state farmers by stating his respect for "the right of any American to be against any racket he isn't in on."[9]

Oil-state members of Congress kept the machinery in good repair. The historian Robert Caro noted that even before Roosevelt became president, "Texans were elected on December 7, 1931, not only to the Speakership of the House but to the chairmanships of five of its most influential committees. Lyndon Johnson's first day in the Capitol was the day Texas came to power in it—a power the state was to hold, with only the briefest interruptions, for more than thirty years."[10] Beyond Capitol Hill, other federal pressure was usually suspect.

By World War II, Texas oilmen were lamenting "incipient socialism" in the regulatory approach of Roosevelt and the executive branch. The Democratic share of the presidential vote in upper-income Houston precincts, tabulated by analyst Samuel Lubell in 1956, mirrored the souring Petroleum Club mind-set: a grateful 57 percent in 1936, then a slump to 29 percent in 1940, 18 percent in 1944, 7 percent in 1948, and 6 percent in 1952.[11] Texas oilmen were learning to whisper Republican nationally even if they still spoke Democratic in Tyler, Temple, or Fort Worth.

The state remained the top U.S. oil and gas producer through the entire 1932–1968 New Deal political cycle and most years thereafter, riding one socioeconomic updraft after another, although not in California's league. Between 1930 and 1970, per capita income in Texas gained on the national average, while remaining slightly below it.[12] Meanwhile, population climbed. From fifth place nationally in 1930, the Lone Star State nearly doubled its head count and had climbed to fourth by 1970 while northern states slipped. Notwithstanding local free-enterprise breast-beating, the federal spending that came Texas's way was an especially vital gravy train.

So was oil's increasing centrality to the national economy. Between 1930 and 1946, the annual U.S. consumption of petroleum products roughly tripled to 1.8 billion barrels and then rose threefold again to 5.4 billion barrels by 1971.[13] During this developmental spurt, petroleum became the feedstock for the production of paints, plastics, pharmaceuticals, and textile fibers, and it furnished the gasoline for the automobile age and the suburbanization of America, with all of its housing developments, malls, and office buildings. The aerospace and aviation industries, closely tied to military spending and tourism, also ran on petroleum. Because of this oil-based ascendancy over the rest of the world, mirroring innovation as well as profligacy, the United States by 1955 was using more than one-third of the annual global energy output. Indeed, at this peak of America's postwar global advantage, U.S. per-capita energy consumption was fully six times that of the next-ranking nation.[14]

The quarter century after 1945 marked the apogee of the American car culture. Most males of an age still remember Kaisers, Nashes, DeSotos, and Packards and recall the various big oil companies by their free road maps and snappy promotional images: Socony Mobil's red-winged Pegasus, Amoco's flaming torch, Shell's orange scallop shell, Sinclair's emerald brontosaurus, and so on. And behind the symbols purred giant profit centers. In 1919, only four oil companies had made the U.S. top sixteen ranked by assets: Standard Oil of New Jersey (Esso), Socony, Gulf, and Sinclair. By 1935 the number had doubled to eight: Esso (1), Socony (4), Standard Oil of Indiana (5), Socal (10), Texaco (11), Gulf (12), Shell (15), and Sinclair (16), and the roll call for 1948 was quite similar.[15] Pump-side appeal humanized the remote corporate behemoths—and a half century later, the service-station clutter and auto-showroom sparklers of the forties and the fifties, evoking nostalgia, had become the objects of an upscale collectors' market.

Behind oil stood the rest of the corporate auto culture. Of the other eight top U.S. corporations at midcentury, five manufactured vehicles (autos, trucks, tractors) or their steel frames. Gasoline, oil, and the internal-combustion engine were kings of the road, and the world's best highway system was their palace parade grounds. If the oil industry in America had two seemingly placid golden decades, domestically and globally, they were the 1950s (especially) and the 1960s, despite gathering storm clouds. After 1970, oil nationalizations in the Middle East and the rise of OPEC wrote a new script: oil was to gain a degree of influence on the White House unimaginable in 1959 or 1965.

Oil's Strengthening Grip on the American Presidency

The man in the White House from 1953 to 1961, former general and World War II Allied supreme commander Dwight D. Eisenhower, provided an early hint of the accession to come. He had been born in oil country—Denison, in north-central Texas—although he grew up in eastern Kansas. The thirty-fourth president was also a lifelong advocate of the internal-combustion engine. As a young army officer who had earlier commanded a tank-training unit, Eisenhower helped to lead a mid-1919 Washington-to-California motorcade of some eighty-one cars, trucks, mobile repair shops, and motorcycles. Partly funded by Willys, Packard, Mack, and General Motors, some of whose test vehicles came along, the expedition's purpose was to display the growing prowess of motor transport and publicize the need for two-lane highways. Indeed, records showed that poor roads limited the convoy to an average of fifty-eight miles per day and an average speed of six miles per hour, but millions of voters and politicians were impressed.[16]

Thirty-three years later, as the 1952 Republican presidential nominee, Eisenhower swept all the southern oil centers from west Texas to the Mississippi River delta, the first GOP candidate to do so. Once in office, he followed through on his campaign promise to support the jurisdictional claims of California and the Gulf Coast states to offshore or "tidelands" oil. Most fitting of all, he presided over the massive expansion of America's postwar interstate-highway program (now officially the Dwight D. Eisenhower Interstate Highway System). Among his cabinet appointees were a Texas oil executive (Robert B. Anderson) as secretary of the treasury, and a Detroit automobile-company president ("Engine Charlie" Wilson of General Motors) as secretary of defense.

The new national party politics of oil was beginning to cohere. Even so, the regional split—a typical Texas executive, for example, cast Republican ballots at the national level but supported local Democrats for Congress—would stick until the 1960s, when Richard Nixon, Eisenhower's vice president, sought to complete the transformation. He had narrowly lost Texas in his first presidential race in 1960 because of the home-state muscle of Lyndon Johnson as the vice-presidential nominee. Then he finished slightly short again in 1968, although winning nationally. Like much of the press, Nixon credited the influence of the retiring Texas Democratic president, as well as the state-level exertions of Johnson's longtime chief lieutenant, John B. Connally, then Texas's popular Democratic governor. Between them, Johnson and Connally had close ties to most of the state's oil-connected power brokers: Clint Murchison, the Richardson-Bass family, George Brown, and many others. To co-opt this element, realignment was needed, and Nixon reached the White House with a prairie-sized complex about Texas.

Nixon had an oil-state childhood himself, the makings of a classic love-hate relationship. Biographers have emphasized his campaign contributions dating back to the 1940s from oil forces such as the reclusive Howard Hughes, Standard Oil of California (Socal), and Los Angeles–based Union Oil. However, the thirty-seventh president was also personally molded by an oil boom—in the rich eastern fields of the Los Angeles basin of the 1920s—much like the roaring milieu that had bred the Texas Democrats. Few other Republican politicians could say the same.

Some background is in order. In 1903 California overtook Texas as the nation's leading oil producer, and it was to do so again several times during the 1910s and the 1920s. In 1919 Nixon's father, Frank, left his unsuccessful lemon grove and for several years worked as a roustabout for Union Oil. In 1921 Union struck the huge Santa Fe Springs find near the Nixon family homes in Yorba Linda and later Whittier. Before long, Santa Fe Springs and two other fields in the Los Angeles basin—Signal Hill and Huntington Beach—had again pushed California ahead of Texas. Booming Los Angeles became the world's biggest oil port, while related traffic through the Panama Canal boomed.[17]

In his everyday travels, the young Nixon would have whiffed occasional oil and gas fumes, and locally that smell connoted "Oildorado." In 1924, when Nixon was eleven, oil surpassed agriculture as the state's leading industry. By itself, the Los Angeles basin that year produced 230 million barrels of crude oil and 300 billion cubic feet of natural gas. Not far from Nixon's home, an overenthusiastic developer named a subdivision Petroleum Gardens.[18] "The nearest gushers and pumps," wrote one chronicler, "could sometimes be heard from Yorba Linda, an audible drum of prosperity and sometimes sudden riches thumping over the quiet tract with its struggling or aborted lemon groves. Like the citrus gold coast, oil seemed a miracle within ordinary reach. . . . Though oil was never discovered on the hill, both [Nixon's mother] Hannah and Richard would tell writers that a strike had come after they left, and that the family might have been wealthy."[19] Instead, the 1920s in crowd at Whittier High School—teenagers whose Hacienda Country Club parents represented minor Santa Fe Springs oil money—paid little attention to the awkward outsider, who carried away the memory.

Nixon recalled absorbing, as a boy, some of his populist father's anger at Standard Oil and enthusiasm for 1924 Progressive presidential nominee Robert LaFollette.[20] Nevertheless, as a young lawyer in the late 1930s and later as a successful GOP candidate for Congress and the U.S. Senate, Nixon took the supportive positions expected of the typical Republican nominee in an oil-rich section of oil-rich southern California. As president, though, he sometimes acted contrary to industry views.

For example, he cut the oil-depletion allowance, considered scrapping the oil-import restrictions backed by the big companies, and approved both price controls on oil in 1971 and their renewal in 1973.[21] Nixon likewise signed a wide variety of environmental legislation. Also, his belated proposal to meet the growing national energy crisis, set out in a November 1973 energy-independence message, included far-reaching conservation measures like Sunday gas-station closings and a federal speed limit of 55 mph.

Nixon's preoccupation was not with the history or details of energy policy but with party politics: the realigning of Texas's oil-lubricated moderate-to-conservative Democrats. His goal was a trifecta joining Texas, Florida, and California—oil, retirement centers, and aerospace—in a Sun Belt presidential and congressional alliance under a Republican banner. Their differences notwithstanding, Eisenhower, Johnson, and Nixon all illustrated the increasing salience of oil for post–World War II presidents.

The depth of Nixon's commitment to this coalition became clear in his two sequential Texas strategies. Through 1969 and 1970 he sought the election of a moderate conservative, internationalist, pro-oil Republican to the Senate: Texas congressman George H. W. Bush. Victory, it was thought, would immediately make the new senator a vice-presidential possibility. Some of Nixon's early White House memos and discussions cited getting Bush elected as a reason for several of the administration's pro-oil positions.[22] But in 1970 Bush's second defeat in the Texas U.S. Senate race—he had also lost in 1964—scotched that scenario.

Nixon's follow-up, from 1971 to 1974, directly aimed at luring part of Texas's Johnson-Connally Democratic faction into "New Majority" Republicanism. Johnson was initially hostile. Connally, though, took up the cudgels, signing on as treasury secretary in 1971, captaining Democrats for Nixon in the 1972 landslide, getting Nixon's backing to succeed Vice President Spiro T. Agnew in 1973, and winding up as the damaged president's preferred political heir for 1976. Watergate and Nixon's forced resignation destroyed any Connally prospects, but the continuity is the message: even in the face of Watergate and OPEC, Texas was always on Nixon's mind.

But what neither Democrats nor Republicans expected until too late was so traumatic a watershed in the global oil business. The energy revolution of the 1970s, marked by the price of oil climbing from under $3 per barrel in 1970 to $31 in 1980, quickly forced strategic reappraisals. The new battle was defined in 1973, when Secretary of State Henry Kissinger and others in the cabinet promoted, just short of openly, a plan for using U.S. airborne forces to seize the oil fields of Saudi Arabia, Kuwait, and Abu Dhabi. Years later, in 2003, after the second U.S. invasion of Iraq, old hands with good memories harked back to 1973 and began to talk of a "Thirty Years War" over Middle Eastern oil.[23]

It is just possible, as chapter 3 will pursue, that the United States crossed a mid-1970s Rubicon in fateful response to a crush of related events: the topping out of U.S. oil production in its 1970–1971 Hubbert peak, multiple Middle Eastern nationalizations of Western oil interests (Iraq 1972, Libya 1975, Iran 1979), and the last surge of new OPEC members (the United Arab Emirates 1967, Algeria 1969, Nigeria 1971, and Ecuador 1973). Those years also saw the first OPEC price hikes (winter 1973–1974) and the Washington response of thinly veiled invasion threats in 1973–1975. When we look back on the three subsequent decades, it is now possible to describe a much grander convergence of forces: (1) oil's evertightening grip on Washington politics and psychologies; (2) the cumulative destabilization of the Middle East; (3) the rise of varying degrees of radical Christianity, Judaism, and Islam around the world; (4) the biblical and geopolitical focus on Israel; and (5) the reemergence during the 1990s of eastern Europe, the Middle East, and the Caspian republics as the unstable but pivotal thirty-nation borderlands of the vague Eurasian "heartland" strategically pinpointed by Sir Halford Mackinder, the British political geographer, at the beginning of the twentieth century.

For our immediate purposes, however, it suffices to list the obvious new challenges and imperatives that pushed their way into 1970s political debate. One was the need to regularize world oil prices and get normal markets working again. Then there was America's pressing need to block Soviet ambitions in the Middle East and ensure its own access to the Persian Gulf, which became a staple of bipartisan assurance. A third concerned the various options for U.S. energy "independence": far-reaching conservation measures, stepped-up domestic oil production, emphasis on solar and other renewable energy sources, and the development of new non–Middle Eastern petroleum sources. The fourth, a quiet imperative, was that OPEC uphold the dollar as the currency in which oil purchases had to be made and then recycle the petro-dollars thus earned through purchases of U.S. bonds and weapons systems. And, of course, Washington made it a priority to keep the Arabian Peninsula safe for the House of Saud, a close ally since World War II. Politically, all were spokes that led back to the same hub: *petroleum.*

The 1980 race for the White House touched on these and two more immediate crises: 1979 had witnessed the seizure by radical Iranians of fifty-three American hostages, as well as the Soviet invasion of Afghanistan, a potential move toward the Persian Gulf. In the Republican primaries, Texans Connally and Bush squared off with ex–California governor Ronald Reagan. The latter's easy victory over them—Texas oilmen were prominent in his cheering section—quickly led to a new Lone Star State stratagem. Reagan picked Bush as his running mate, annoying conservative stalwarts but reaching out to Texas and eastern Establishment interests alike.

This was America's first national election focused on the Middle East and oil, and the Republican victory resonated. By the time Reagan and Bush sought reelection four years later, Texas—God-fearing, nationalist, and oil rich—was the gleaming clip on three of the GOP's principal ideological suspenders: the Sun Belt, the Petroleum Belt, and the Bible Belt. As the Grand Old Party became Houstonized, Fort Worthified, and Wacoed, the state stopped voting for Democratic presidents.

California, by contrast, started backing them in 1992. The old Pacific command post of the Nixon and Reagan GOP, increasingly environmental and conservation minded, had largely forgotten Oildorado and was becoming the mainstay of what conservatives called "the Left Coast." And as the Cold War wound down in the 1990s, even California's mid-century aerospace plants, navy yards, and military bases—pointed west to face imperial Japan, divided Korea, or demanding Vietnam—became ghosts of an electoral Christmas past. Economic and political heft slid toward the state's increasingly ascendant sectors: high technology and entertainment, industries in which chief executives frequently had ponytails, hosted liberal Democrats, and tagged companies with un-Republican names such as Yahoo!, Google, Pixar, and DreamWorks SKG. Petrodiplomacy was peripheral to this worldview. Hubbert's peak might as well have been a second-echelon ski resort near Lake Tahoe.

Nevertheless, by 2004, as George W. Bush claimed a second term in the White House, Wall Street, the religious right, and the military-petroleum industrial complex were all eating at the same political table, although wise GOP strategists insisted on separate seatings. The father-and-son Bush presidencies had put a new interest-group imprint on the Republican party. Indeed, six of its seven presidential tickets between 1980 and 2004 had included a Bush, and five of those six had won. Even so, one family's prominence told only part of the tale.

The Texification of America was the key ingredient. Yesteryear's Bush family bases in Ohio and Connecticut could not have sustained an oil-era dynasty. Texas now had the proper accent. During those same seven elections between 1980 and 2004, four different Lone Star State residents had gotten themselves on Republican or Democratic national tickets or become major independent nominees: both Bushes, Lloyd Bentsen, and Ross Perot. In 2000 GOP vice-presidential nominee Dick Cheney, a Texas resident, would have been number five until he switched his domicile to Wyoming to sidestep the legal problem of a ticket having two Texans.* No other state had anything like this access to power; Ronald Reagan had been the last of the Californians. National GOP politics had a new regional ladder, and government policy-making a new bias.

By the turn of the century, in addition to becoming the second-most populous state, Texas had also transformed itself into the most Republican of the top ten—a bulwark of party and ideological strength in Congress, as well as a major launching pad for capturing the White House. Texas Republicans and their compatriots in Alabama or Indiana increasingly spoke the same language. Quite literally, the lexicon of national politics had acquired an essential new prefix: *petro.*

Let's plot the path that took winners to the White House. Until mid-century, petroleum-related entries were rare on a presidential résumé. One exception, James Garfield, had been an early northeastern Ohio oil investor before his election in 1880. The president chosen in 1928, Herbert Hoover of Iowa, was an industry intimate—a mining engineer who, in his earlier days, had undertaken oil surveys and even brokered a few South American properties to Standard Oil.[24] A scholar to boot, he had translated into English the 1556 German-language masterwork in which the term "petroleum" first appeared in print. However little he understood the Great Depression, Hoover knew oil.

*As specified in the U.S. Constitution, the presidential electors from Texas could not have cast their votes for a Texan for president and a second Texan for vice president. Two different states had to be represented.

But as we have seen, it took the deepening of the oil connection under Eisenhower, Johnson, Nixon, and Reagan to set the scene for petro-prefixes and Texification. In naming George H. W. Bush as his running mate in 1980, Reagan loosely followed Nixon's outline, enlisting not just a Texan but the first full-fledged oilman to make a national ticket. Eight years later, when Bush became the first former oil executive to reach the White House, *both* major-party tickets included an oil-savvy Texan. The Democratic vice-presidential nominee, Senator Lloyd Bentsen, was an insurance-company president with past petroleum corporate directorships. The press routinely characterized him as "close to the oil industry."

Through these years, oil's potent influence in U.S. politics was inadequately expressed by raw dollar tabulations—the $159 million the oil and gas industry gave to American politicians between 1990 and 2002 or the $256 million contributed by the transportation sector.[25] What counted at least as much was the dearth of countervailing money or power. Thus, in one Washington showdown after another, oil could keep its tax breaks, coal-fired power plants could be exempted from clean-air legislation, the auto industry could stave off tougher fuel-efficiency standards, and oil and gas could beat back target dates for putting renewables like solar, wind, and water power into the U.S. energy mix. The influence built up over many decades can fairly be described as normally unbeatable: a first-class political, lobbying, and regulatory infrastructure.

In fairness to U.S. industry, though, the political clout and periodic scandals of oil and gas are hardly limited to the United States. British Petroleum, for example, was linked to bribery in Azerbaijan and Kazakhstan in 2001 and 2002, and the *Financial Times* commented that "while the days of [government] ownership have long passed, BP's ties with the British government are still so close that rivals call it 'Blair Petroleum.' . . . One Whitehall insider says there is a 'meeting of the minds' between Tony Blair and Browne [Lord Browne, the BP chairman], who is a regular visitor to Downing Street. . . . This rapport is reinforced by the presence on Browne's staff of former New Labour officials still close to Number 10."[26] Sarcastic references to "Blair Petroleum," by no means a onetime barb, also appeared in *The Guardian* and *The Scotsman*, as well as in Germany's *Der Spiegel* and Russia's *Pravda*.

Across the channel, thirty out of thirty-seven senior executives of Total, the French oil giant, on trial in 2003–2004 were convicted of taking kickbacks and embezzlement. The evidence also made clear that Total, despite privatization, remained a principal arm of French intelligence for information and skulduggery in former French-colonial Africa. The outraged judge who presided over the trial, Eva Joly, wrote a book entitled *Is This the World We Want?* about institutional corruption in the French Republic.[27] Indeed, throughout Asia, Africa, and Latin America the oil industry is so routinely associated with political corruption that the International Monetary Fund actually titled research on one emerging African oil supplier "Escaping the Curse of Oil?"[28]

Not surprisingly, political and global forces also kept escalating the oil industry's ties to the U.S. presidency. In 1992, two of the three White House contenders were Texans. For all the billions that Ross Perot made in computers, after his 1988 sale of Electronic Data Systems to General Motors he diversified into real estate and oil and gas.[29] The 1996 election, for its part, seemed to offer nary an oilman, but 2000's Republican ticket, Texas governor George W. Bush and Halliburton chief executive Dick Cheney, was *all* oil—two ex–oil company presidents on the same slate, absolutely unprecedented, even if it had sidestepped being all Texan. Enterprising journalists found another petroleum connection to the Democratic nominee, two-term vice president Albert Gore. *Washington Post* columnist David Ignatius frowned at "the bizarre prospect of a presidential campaign in which three of the four candidates have intimate personal links to the oil business." Drawing on accounts of the Gore family, he told how Albert Gore Sr., as a Tennessee congressman in the 1950s, had taken a "substantial profit" from a cattle-breeding partnership arranged by Occidental Petroleum chairman Armand Hammer. After Gore Senior left the Senate, Hammer made him chairman of Island Creek Coal, an Occidental subsidiary. The Gore connection, some believed, helped to constrain the FBI from investigating Hammer's controversial relationship with the Soviet Union. On taking up the Tennessee Senate seat, the younger Gore also took up the Occidental relationship. He received "more than $300,000 through the early 1990s—his largest source of income outside his congressional salary—from a land deal his father had made with Hammer in 1973."[30]

While hardly a scandal, this background seems to have imposed a major inhibition. No Democratic nominee so entangled could easily confront the connections of the two oil-sector Republicans—and despite some unusual openings, Gore held back. Those openings included a Bush political genealogy that on one side reached back to the controversial practices of Standard Oil in the Ohio of the 1900s and, on the other side, to Wall Street attempts to refurbish the post–World War I Soviet oil industry. Since Samuel S. Bush and George Herbert Walker a century ago, four generations of Bushes have worked in the oil business, the investment business, or both. I discussed this vocational embroilment and its presidential ramifications at length in my 2004 book, *American Dynasty: Aristocracy, Fortune, and the Politics of Deceit in the House of Bush,* so I will only make brief mention here.[31]

More than any other U.S. political family, the Bushes exemplify the interaction of oil interests, the financial sector, the military-industrial complex, and the intelligence community. They have represented—arguably, they have also helped bring together—the constituencies that the Republican national coalition of the early 2000s has come to serve. First, however, we must lay an additional short track along which to follow the emergence of oil and its extraordinary relationship with both American foreign policy and the nation's intelligence community.

Oil's Unique Role in U.S. Foreign Policy

By the time of the Civil War, oil had achieved a special relationship with Washington and its conduct of international relations. President Ulysses S. Grant, visiting in 1871, recalled for Pennsylvanians that "the discovery and production of petroleum aided materially in supplying the sinews of war, [and] as a medium of [foreign] exchange, taking the place of cotton."[32] With southern commodities such as cotton unavailable for export markets, Abraham Lincoln's embattled government had counted on oil to procure foreign exchange and goods from European markets. Pennsylvania barrels—converted forty-two-gallon whiskey containers— filled in for Georgia bales.

The War Between the States was America's first war in which oil supplies became a target. In May 1863, three thousand Confederate cavalry under General W. E. Jones raided the Burning Springs wells just outside of Parkersburg, West Virginia, and torched 150,000 gallons of the expensive, high-quality oil produced there.[33] Such was the first flare of oil's strategic importance.

John D. Rockefeller, in his 1909 *Random Reminiscences of Men and Events,* recalled, "One of our greatest helpers has been the State Department. Our ambassadors and ministers and consuls have aided to push our way into new markets in the utmost corners of the world."[34] But he left out a key explanation for the government's interest. Standard Oil was the biggest U.S. company, putting a hundred ships to sea, buying and selling oil in Latin America, Germany, and the Far East. It also operated a global intelligence system. "By 1885," according to one historian, "seventy percent of the Standard's business was overseas, and it had its own network of agents through the world, and its own espionage service, to forestall the initiatives of rival companies or governments."[35]

Moreover, by 1909 oil was transcending its market as kerosene, the large but humdrum U.S. export of the fuel-lamp era. Instead, as Germany built a Berlin-to-Baghdad railway and British admirals verged on a massive upgrading of their battle fleets by conversion from coal-fired to petroleum-burning engines, oil was truly marching as to war. From Pennsylvania and Texas to Romania and the Russian Caucasus, petroleum resources were shaping up as the new fulcrums of great-power rivalry.

While the admirals and generals plotted, the importance of Standard, Royal Dutch, and the smaller-scale Anglo-Persian multiplied. The course of empire could be altered if added speed and maneuverability from new oil-fired engines could someday allow Britain's fifteen-inch-gunned *Queen Elizabeth*–class superdreadnoughts to trap the Kaiser's coal-burning squadrons—or by some reverse scenario. Far in the background was another possibility still barely considered: were American dominance of international oil production to continue and harden, power itself could migrate across the Atlantic.

The years prior to 1914 saw sixpenny thrillers become current-affairs manuals. Parliaments barely knew where secret services ended and oil-company activities and munitions marketing began. The war itself raised control of petroleum to high strategy. In 1916 a British raid under Colonel "Empire Jack" Norton-Griffiths crippled the Romanian oil fields before Germans took them, in 1917 Berlin's oil-powered submarine warfare threatened vital Allied fuel deliveries, and 1918's last-minute Turkish drive to refuel the Central Powers was too late in capturing Russia's Baku oil fields. Combat did indeed become petroleum-centric in 1917–1918 once Allied trucks, tanks, airplanes, and gasoline—80 percent of the fuel shipments in this period came from America—replaced wagons, cavalry, and horses.

The Armistice uncorked both celebrations and further schemes. Allied leaders boasted, in the words of French premier Georges Clemenceau, that "oil is as necessary as blood" or that "the Allies floated to victory on a wave of oil," as phrased by a British War Cabinet member, Lord Curzon.[36] However, for foreign offices, chancelleries, and state departments with eyes to read and ears to hear, the revelation of secret Franco-British plans to divide the resources of the Turkish empire, along with U.S. political schemes in Mexico, another major producer, had their own urgency. The great postwar oil hunt had already begun.

The governments of Britain and France, both wed to substantial state ownership and control of strategic oil resources, had colluded in the clandestine Sykes-Picot Agreement of 1916 to carve up the postwar Middle East. France was to get primacy in Syria and Lebanon, while Britain took control of Mesopotamia and Jordan, with Palestine to be under international control. No change was made to London's existing sphere of influence in Persia and the Persian Gulf. Modified in private talks and at a postwar conference in San Remo, the reshuffling also proposed a more or less three-parts British, one-part French split of the oil resources in what became Iraq. To fulfill this arrangement, France got the German quarter-share of the old Turkish Petroleum Company, while Britain kept most of the rest. Initially, the United States was to be excluded.

The British moved to take charge in the Middle East. In 1918–1919, more than one million of His Majesty's forces had arrived to make up what became a de facto regional occupation force. Britain and France each dreamed of a Texas on the Tigris, pumping cheap fuel for automobiles, army motorized brigades, and the great battle fleets berthed in Toulon, Portsmouth, and Scapa Flow.[37] As chapter 7 will detail, there was also a sense on Britain's part—expressed with some candor by Prime Minister David Lloyd George—of returning to the holy lands in a modern-day Crusader role.

Postwar ambitions in London for a global oil coup—projects were also afoot in Latin America, Russia, and the Far East—also encompassed corollary hopes of countering the nascent U.S. challenge to British dominance in international finance. These machinations have been described with great élan and geopolitical detail in the many books dedicated to oil's grand (or not-so-grand) twentieth-century saga.[38] Books explaining the competition and rivalries of the 1920s went so far as to describe "oil wars" between the erstwhile allies.[39]

No one can mistake the nationalism and neomercantilism of the U.S. State and Commerce Departments during the postwar decade and into the 1930s. In 1921 the British ambassador to the United States, Sir Auckland Geddes, wrote to the Foreign Office about Washington's intentions "to treat us as a vassal state so long as our [£4.7 billion war] debt remains unpaid."[40] On the other hand, in 1919 Sir Edward Edgar, a figure in Royal Dutch/Shell's Venezuela operations, had written in a British journal that two-thirds of the improved oil fields of Central and South America were passing into British hands, while the Shell Group was prevailing elsewhere. "America before long," contended Edgar, "will have to purchase from British companies, and to pay for, in dollar currency in progressively increasing proportion, the oil she cannot do without, and is no longer able to furnish from her own store."[41]

Besides being naïve, Edgar was impolitic. Still, Britain now took oil seriously. Also in 1921, Lord Curzon, Britain's foreign secretary, dismissed U.S. demands on behalf of Standard Oil. No concessions, he said, would be allowed to American companies in Mesopotamia or elsewhere in the British Middle East.[42] The United States, Curzon suggested, already had all the oil it needed.

By this point Washington, too, acted as if it half owned Standard Oil, and national honor was at stake. The State Department pressed the British and Dutch with counterthreats: Congress, already launching investigations, could decide to prohibit oil investments by foreigners or to designate British- and Dutch-owned U.S. oil fields as naval reserves, so as to bar any resale.[43] The Bank of England also depended on U.S. central bankers' supporting the wobbly British pound, as the New York Federal Reserve Bank did several times during the 1920s.[44]

By 1925 both explicit and veiled pressures from Washington had obliged Britain to open up Iraq to Standard of New Jersey and Socony. (The two received a 20 percent share in the new Iraq Petroleum Company.) Standard of New Jersey also took over the former German oil concessions in the Dutch East Indies. One American chronicler has pithily summarized: "To some these successive intercessions in behalf of oil were viewed as fulfilling the moral purposes and political needs of the natural overseas extension of nineteenth century manifest destiny. To the less reverent they earned Charles E. Hughes, Secretary of State from 1921 to 1925, the title of Secretary for Oil. And more significantly, these moves announced that the United States and its corporate citizens were now in truth world powers, with continuing economic interests on every continent."[45] Looking back from the twenty-first century, we can call oil supremacy a game the United States always played to win.

Herbert Hoover, the oil-wise U.S. commerce secretary, would have welcomed sharing Hughes's putative title. By one brisk interpretation, he "privately asked Standard Oil of New Jersey to ingratiate itself with Arab culture and turn the oil sheiks away from the Brits and Germans toward the red, white, and blue."[46] Or as one Gulf Oil executive recalled, "representatives of the industry were called to Washington and told to go out and get it."[47] Within a decade or so, American deal makers had taken their cue.

In 1927 Pittsburgh-headquartered Gulf—owned by the family of Treasury Secretary Andrew Mellon—bought the oil concession in Kuwait, soon taking the Anglo-Persian Oil Company into partnership there to satisfy the British. The next year Socal won the franchise in Bahrain, and by 1933 it had also arranged a concession from Saudi ruler Abdul Aziz ibn Saud, whose territory had unwisely been ignored by the British. Then in 1936 Socal and Texaco negotiated a deal to split the combined Saudi Arabian and Bahraini concession evenly between them, for which Socal in return picked up a share of Texaco's fields in the Dutch East Indies.[48]

Two years later the left-leaning Mexican government of President Lázaro Cárdenas nationalized foreign oil holdings, squeezing the British out of another nation where they had made strong inroads before 1914. Though still 90 percent coal-burning at home, Britain did significantly enlarge its overseas oil resources between the world wars. Nevertheless, as important Middle East producers took on American relationships, the United Kingdom lost any real hope of perpetuating its economic hegemony into the new oil era—indeed, it fell short well before the deeper dislocations that accompanied World War II.

By the thirties U.S. oil companies overseas found themselves in quasi-official positions roughly comparable to those of Royal Dutch/Shell and Anglo-Persian in the British orbit: senior American oilmen were a kind of auxiliary diplomatic and foreign service, while the firms themselves could count on Washington's help. In *The Seven Sisters,* Anthony Sampson concluded that "to radical critics, it looked as if the State Department had simply abdicated the whole process of oil diplomacy to the oilmen. The government, however much they might distrust the oilmen, were not prepared to set up their own organization. They preferred to use the oil companies, at a discreet distance, as the instruments of national security and foreign policy."[49] No other U.S. industry had a comparable position.

The Second World War, which was also rife with petroleum objectives and rivalries, fully established the United States as both global oil hegemon and economic commander in chief of the West. This eased, although it did not end, the old oil squabbles with the British and French. However, strategists in the State Department, the Pentagon, and headquarters of the U.S. oil giants well knew that another wrenching adjustment loomed. While at war from 1941 to 1945, the United States had been drawing down its own oil, while one geological survey after another identified the Middle East, with the world's biggest reserves, as the next great regional supplier. The fifties and sixties were to provide a relative lull; then the unique relationship between oil and government in the United States would once again take center stage.

Not that Americans of 1952 or even 1966 worried about this much. The Cold War was the obvious threat, the Soviet Union the great enemy. The Middle East, at least in the minds of Long Island or Peoria, was still the Hollywood movie set of casbahs and camel drivers. Equal complacency guided the U.S. automobile culture of oversized cars with oversized tail fins, as well as the oil-burning proliferation of airlines, suburbs, and regional shopping centers. However, before we turn to the 1970s and the subsequent three-decade rise of petroleum-driven U.S. foreign policy (and two presidential generations of the oil-backed Bush family), it is necessary to consider another dimension: the buoyant but ultimately parochial political culture that developed around oil, its local production, and its vast consumption in the twentieth-century United States.

Oil and Automobile Culture and Twenty-First-Century American Politics

After 150 years of national exuberance, most Americans cannot be expected to easily separate oil's uncertain future from its prolific past—the romance of gushers and boomtowns, the march of the population across the continent, the fuel supply that never lost its abundance, a citizenry far more residentially and vocationally mobile than their European ancestors, and the endless celebration of the open road, to say nothing of nearly a century of national success. Memories are becoming dangerously nostalgic. Whatever their great-grandparents thought of John D. Rockefeller, whatever their parents thought (or still think) of big oil, twenty-first-century Americans display a growing fondness for the old gusher sites, gas stations, and Gulf, Esso, and Mobil signs.

Museums are proliferating, especially in the leading energy states, gathering what Europeans might call the detritus of empire: the last of the old Kern County (California) oil derricks, a shell-shaped Shell service station from the 1920s, replicas of World War II oil tankers, ancient gas pumps (with ancient prices), and yellowed newspaper headlines touting the flag-bedecked opening of the Pennsylvania Turnpike in 1940 or the crowd that raced out from Beaumont in 1901 to see Spindletop spout. The California Oil Museum outside Los Angeles, capital of America's highway mentality, takes pride in its collection of gas-station artifacts.

Particular nostalgia seems to attach to architecture of America's post–World War II automotive heyday: drive-in movies and hamburger joints, roadhouses and ancient motels, as well as gas stations meticulously restored to their 1947 or 1954 appearance. Ohio, for example, is home to a thriving Society for Commercial Archaeology. The spring 2004 issue of its journal featured an article on early neon signs: "The Landscape of Spinning Sombreros and Electrified Tepees: Restoring New Mexico's Route 66 Signs." Washington State, in turn, has a Lost Highway Museum, while a St. Louis firm called Primarily Petroliana handles "oil and gas swap meets and auctions, featuring gas station antiques, oil industry collectibles and auto industry memorabilia."[50] Clearly, the reminiscence is fond.

The United States has fifteen to twenty widely listed oil and gas museums and thirty or so less-noted county and regional facilities. Of the total, more than half are in Texas, Oklahoma, California, Pennsylvania, Louisiana, and Kansas. Unusual exhibits range from the offshore oil rig "Mr. Charlie," open to the public at the International Petroleum Museum and Exposition in Morgan City, Louisiana, to the collection of fifteen Spindletop-related buildings at Texas's Spindletop–Gladys City Boomtown Museum.

The pride of each local oil culture is palpable. Ohioans date their state's oldest drilled well to 1814, but it was sunk in pursuit of salt. The Oil and Gas Museum in West Virginia, in turn, says that its oldest well—at Burning Springs near Parkersburg—dates to 1860, while nearby oil operations may antedate Pennsylvania's 1859 strike. The Norman No. 1 Museum in Neodesha, Kansas, boasts a replica of what was supposedly the oldest drilled well west of the Mississippi.[51]

Little-known bits of petroliana appear everywhere. The California Oil Museum, headquartered in Union Oil's 1890 office building, has an exhibit showing how Native Americans used oil seeps. Curators in Louisiana insist that oil was first discovered locally by the 1543 expedition of Hernando de Soto. The Oil and Gas Museum—Appalachian and contentious—describes George Washington as the "first petroleum industry speculator" by dint of his 1771 purchase of 250 acres in what was then Virginia that had an oil and gas spring.[52] Enthralled readers can subscribe to *Oil-Industry History*, published in Meadville, Pennsylvania, or *"Check the Oil!"* a journal of American petroliana.

I emphasize this petro-culture not for its own sake but for several larger reasons. First, the obvious politics of local pride and affectionate memory, which reaffirms the intensity of the decisive energy culture. Second, the striking resemblance to the latter-day memory lanes of two other great energy cultures that changed too little or too late. Britain has dozens of major coal and railway museums, thickest in the north of England, where coal midwived the first railway steam engine and where the industrial revolution unfolded during the first half of the nineteenth century. In those years Britain produced and consumed more than half of the world's coal.

The Dutch take the same pride in their sturdy dikes and well-preserved seventeenth- and eighteenth-century windmills, some one thousand of which still stand. These, too, are prime attractions for visitors, the best being grouped into six open-air museum parks. Two hundred and fifty years ago, the Zaan district just outside Amsterdam was Europe's first industrial complex, with nine hundred or so windmills. Some survivors were famous enough in their day to have nicknames like "De Kat," a grinder of coloring materials, and "De Schoolmeester," reputed source of the parchment used for the American Declaration of Independence.[53]

The larger point, of course, is that because the twenty-first-century

United States has a pervasive oil and gas culture from its own earlier zenith—with an intact cultural and psychological infrastructure—it's no surprise that Americans cling to and defend an ingrained fuel habit. Many of the museums and exhibits date from the 1980s. The hardening of old attitudes and reaffirmation of the consumption ethic since those years may signal an inability to turn back.

The chance to do so came a quarter century ago. From the late seventies to the early eighties, oil consumption in the United States underwent a powerful reversal. Energy-using Americans had been scared. In 1976 the political combination of the Watergate scandal, the energy crisis, inflation, economic recession, and military collapse in South Vietnam (1975) dominated that year's election and cost Republicans the White House, albeit only by a thin margin. The new Democratic chief executive, former Georgia governor Jimmy Carter—by vocation a peanut grower and by religious belief a Sunday school–teaching Baptist—had campaigned on a reformist vision. Even Texas gave him a narrow victory, casting its final twentieth-century vote for a Democratic president.

Forswearing the trappings of the imperial presidency, Carter left his limousine to walk down Pennsylvania Avenue on Inauguration Day in January 1977. Weeks later he made an energy speech on television wearing a cardigan sweater. In mid-1979 the embattled president underscored the second OPEC oil crisis by asking for "the most massive peacetime commitment of funds and resources in our nation's history to develop America's own alternative sources of fuel from coal, from oil shale, from plant products for gasohol, from unconventional gas, from the sun." Nixon, before being completely overwhelmed by Watergate, had taken a similar but less ambitious tack on energy independence. Soon thereafter Congress passed the Energy Policy and Conservation Act of 1975, which among other things mandated a doubling of passenger-car fuel economy by 1985. Carter went further in 1977, declaring "the moral equivalent of war."

The ideology and culture of the four Carter years were broadly anti-imperial, as they stressed energy conservation; peace (rather than arms sales) in the Middle East; skepticism of CIA clandestine operations and the overthrow of foreign governments; reduced conspicuous consumption; federal missionary work on behalf of solar power and renewable energy sources; smaller automobiles; and the enactment of a 55 mph federal speed limit. Carter also promoted government restraint in budgetary matters and a vague attempt to crystallize "less is more" and "smaller is better" viewpoints, both of these in opposition to earlier mandates to spend, build, produce, and consume.

Militarily the Carter White House spoke softly and also managed to carry a pretty small stick. After the revolutionary government of Iran in 1979 seized fifty-three Americans from the U.S. embassy, the air rescue mission Carter ordered in the spring of 1980 failed. With the helicopters downed in the Iranian desert a symbol of his greater ineptitude, Carter lost the 1980 election and is remembered as a weak president.

The 1975–1985 revolution in energy efficiency, however, was a relative success. Together with spiking oil prices, a conservationist ethic tightened America's energy belt. Between 1977 and 1985—and in the face of an expanding economy—oil demand *fell* by more than one-sixth.[54] The percentage of oil consumed in the United States annually that had to be imported shrank from 46 percent to 30 percent. Inasmuch as two-thirds of the petroleum used in the United States went to keep automobiles on the road, the CAFE standards enacted in 1975 were a linchpin in this reduction. Where the average car in the United States got just fifteen miles per gallon that year, the figure by 1985 was twenty-five. California was in the forefront, having followed Governor Jerry Brown's call to move away from dependence on nonrenewable fossil fuels.

Nationally, new homes were often twice as energy efficient as similar-sized predecessors. Appliances made even bigger gains. New refrigerators, for example, used only one-quarter the power of pre-1970s models.[55] As for the U.S. manufacturing sector as a whole, its energy efficiency improved by 30 percent between 1977 and 1986.[56] The conservation "weapon," once fired, was probably at least as efficient as the military option would have been.

With roots in different economic and energy cultures, conservatives and liberals were inclined to ignore the other side's partial successes, preferring to resort to caricature. Republicans quipped that Carter's call for energy conservation as the "moral equivalent of war" could be summed up by its acronym, "meow." Absent a policy synthesis and compromise, the complex of economic, lifestyle, and foreign-policy issues that propelled U.S. oil politics swung in the conservative direction again.

By the mid-1980s, support for energy conservation was ebbing. For one thing, the Reagan-Bush administration had been lukewarm to it, reducing spending on solar energy by two-thirds, deemphasizing efficiency, and moving the spotlight back to petroleum.[57] Nevertheless, as things turned out, the Republicans' 1981 emphasis on increasing oil supply as a means of lowering prices was justifiable, just like Carter's 1977 focus on efficiency and alternative fuels. Market forces rewarded the GOP emphasis.

As the OPEC nations responded to U.S. urgings or simply produced oil in quantities far beyond their quotas, prices fell. Over five years, they declined by roughly two-thirds, from $31–$35 per barrel in 1981 to $27–$30 in late 1985 and to just $10–$11 at the low point in 1986.[58] Steep enough to devastate many Texas producers, this collapse quickly made irrelevant the 1980–1981 cost comparisons between oil and alternative-energy sources. Hundreds of Texas oilmen filed for bankruptcy, Houston real estate plummeted, and the bottom fell out of the market for cowboy art, but in the nation as a whole oil made a comeback with consumers by regaining price acceptability.

Plummeting oil and gasoline prices soon put the ignition key back into the great American automobile culture. Further federal tightening of fuel-economy standards was rejected in 1985, and Detroit also took advantage of the statute's permissive standards for light trucks by developing its soon-to-be bestsellers: sport-utility vehicles. For ten years, technological improvement had concentrated on fuel economy. Now automobile manufacturers returned to their pre-1973 priorities: power, acceleration, and speed.

American foreign policy also hit the accelerator, as the Reagan and Bush administrations mounted a series of punitive expeditions against provocative foreign regimes from Grenada (1983) and Libya (1986) to Panama (1989) and Iraq (1990–1991). The embrace of high-powered automobiles, air strikes, and invasions, all departures from the Carter mind-set, drew on distinctly Republican values. The war to expel Iraq from Kuwait was oil-related, undertaken in part to protect the American lifestyle, as President George H. W. Bush acknowledged. Once military power had secured Middle Eastern oil supplies again, television news clips showed the forty-first president roaring along the Maine coast at the wheel of his rakish, high-speed Cigarette boat, *Fidelity*. The broader symbolism leaped out: guilt complexes and hair shirts were gone, and with a Texas Republican at the helm the United States was back to practicing gunboat diplomacy and taking what it wanted.

The election of Bill Clinton in 1992 made surprisingly little difference. The sort of Bubba Democrat who had a wink in his eye and often an AstroTurf cushion in the back of his bachelor pickup truck, Clinton kept the U.S. air patrols flying over Iraq, launched occasional missile strikes, and domestically sought to make the good times roll. The auto manufacturers did their part: SUVs rolled off the production lines in steadily increasing numbers. By 1999 48.3 percent of the new sales in the U.S. automobile market came from minivans, light trucks, and SUVs.[59]

Hair shirts made no comeback in 2000, either. On the contrary, Americans were driving more miles in bigger cars, living in even more remote suburbs, and (when they could afford them) buying larger, showier, gadget-stuffed houses at least twice as energy intensive as those in Europe and Japan. In the late nineties, as the stock-market bubble swelled toward its 2000 puncture, investors were especially drawn to new varieties of conspicuous consumption, backstopped by the belief that technology had initiated a new era of prosperity and U.S. supremacy.

In destroying the World Trade Center on September 11, 2001, al-Qaeda struck at a nation already concerned about the economic implications of the 2000 stock-market slide and the bounce-back of oil prices to the thirty-dollar-per-barrel range after touching lows near ten dollars in 1998. Under George W. Bush, petroleum and security issues become intertwined to a degree that favored the Republicans in the same way as the 1980s fatigue with Carter-type energy politics had. To a majority of the public, conservation was overshadowed by support for more two-fisted responses to the energy problem, and even activists had become reluctant to use the term because of its image as a 1970s relic.[60] Most of all, an oil, automobile, and national-security coalition had taken the driver's seat in Washington. The president and vice president came from the oil industry, and the White House chief of staff, Andrew Card, was the former president of the American Automobile Manufacturers Association.

The Hydrocarbon Coalition and the 2004 Election

By any serious historical standard, George W. Bush won a tight race in 2004. Yet its closeness was revealing, following an intense, if rarely candid, election-year discussion of American security, including the supposed benefit of preemptive Middle Eastern invasions in preventing terror attacks and diminished lifestyles at home. Narrow margins tend to highlight polarizations. George W. Bush did not carry the states where most of the September 11 victims had lived. New York's and New Jersey's experiences with damage and death were not decisive election factors. Religious divisions, striking indeed, were more influential and will be analyzed in part 2. Yet among the factors that had spurred the GOP electorate—a vital backdrop for the next chapter's discussion of petro-imperialism—one can discern several surprisingly influential oil, gasoline, and automobile relationships.

A large number of voters work in or depend on the energy and automobile industries, and still more are invested in them, not just financially but emotionally and culturally. These secondary cadres included racing fans, hobbyists, collectors, and dedicated readers of automotive magazines, as well as the tens of millions of automobile commuters from suburbs and distant exurbs, plus the high number of drivers whose strong self-identifications with vehicle types and models serve as thinly disguised political statements.

In analyzing the Bush coalition, we can start with energy's influence as an enterprise. For the most part, the oil, gas, and coal regions were in red states. Of the top ten oil and gas producers, California alone—atypical in its parallel sensitivity to conservation themes and electricity overcharges—supported Democrat John Kerry in 2004. The Bush energy coalition also included coal, an industry and workforce particularly vulnerable to environmentalists' hostility and proposed agendas on carbon-dioxide emissions. Just two of the top ten coal states backed Kerry: Pennsylvania (4) and Illinois (7). Three coal producers—Kentucky, West Virginia, and Tennessee—were among the states giving Bush his biggest gains between 2000 and 2004, although evangelical and fundamentalist religion may be the larger explanation. States with little or no oil, gas, or coal output, by contrast, ranked high in the Kerry bloc. On the 2004 electoral map, the "heartland" hydrocarbon or fossil-fuels coalition displayed a bolder profile than it had four years earlier.

The U.S. car culture has strong regionalisms. The thirteen states with 75 mph speed limits—eight in the mountain West, North Dakota, South Dakota, Nebraska, Oklahoma, and Texas—all lopsidedly backed George W. Bush for reelection. Fast-shooting country is also fast-driving country. None of these states backed Jimmy Carter in 1980, either.

As for automobile-manufacturing employment, the leading states— Ohio, Michigan, and Illinois—divided their electoral votes between the parties in 2004. However, because they are closely balanced electoral pivots, analysts assume that they—Ohio and Michigan in particular—can swing on an issue that puts the industry at risk. Fuel-economy standards tough enough to threaten America's SUV production and culture might serve.

Car preference turned out to be a revealing guide to presidential preference, according to a 2004 survey of 2,500 drivers sponsored by Kelley Blue Book, the automobile valuation guide. Merely driving with any frequency (as opposed to bicycling, subway riding, or whatever) correlated among adults with a pro-GOP bias; drivers polled seven points more favorably for Bush than did the overall electorate. Predictably the president led by a country mile among drivers of Fords, Chevrolets, large SUVs, and full-sized pickup trucks such as the Chevy Suburban or Ford F-Series.[61] Smaller, ad hoc samplings also put the Republican incumbent out front among upscale owners of Porsches, Jaguars, and large GM models. Readership samples of magazines such as *Car and Driver, Motor Trend,* and *Road & Track,* mostly male, would presumably have produced two- or three-to-one pro-Bush margins.

Kerry, besides winning nondrivers, prevailed narrowly among aficionados of convertibles, presumably youthful. He also led handily among those selecting fuel-efficient imports such as Toyotas and Subarus. Volvos, with their Swedish safety emphasis, have been the stereotyped liberal choice, but five out of six owners of fuel-saving hybrids picked the Massachusetts senator, his biggest edge.[62] In the United States more than elsewhere, a preference for conspicuous consumption over energy efficiency and conservation is a signal of a much deeper, central divide.

Spectators at NASCAR events and other stock-car races were wooed so ardently by the Bush campaign that their decision making became the basis of an election-year metaphor. In addition to attending races, George W. Bush sought NASCAR driver endorsements, enlisting top names to stump for him in Pennsylvania, West Virginia, Ohio, and Michigan.[63] One survey showed Bush with the support of 54 percent of "NASCAR dads"—defined as blue-collar males who watched at least one televised NASCAR race during the year. However, fans in the speedway stands, the ultimate enthusiasts, were more lopsidedly supportive.[64]

Another White House effort pinpointed exurbanites—voters who live in remote suburbs and towns, many of them interstate-corridor "boomburbs" full of new houses and recent arrivals. The newest residential classification, fully deployed by the Census Bureau in 2003, is "micropolitan"—coined to describe areas that lack the city of fifty thousand people required for metropolitan status but that are "too urban to be rural."[65] Like the other terms, "micropolitan" is too sweeping, but it steers our conceptions of these places in a useful direction.

In states such as Ohio and Florida, such areas—increasingly identified with particular interstate highways (Florida's much-heralded I-4 corridor and Ohio's still unsung I-76, I-80, and I-71)—are starting to have more voters than the often Democratic urban and inner-suburban metropolitan areas. In Florida, Bush flew into sites along the I-4 and I-75 corridors for effective late-campaign rallies. After the dust settled, Democratic and Republican consultants alike credited the NASCAR dads and "security moms" along I-4 for much of the GOP victory margin.[66] Ohio saw Bush weaken in the big metropolitan counties compared to his showing in 2000, but his gains in the twenty-nine micropolitan areas more than made up for it. Bush and Cheney both made final-week stops in Wilmington, Ohio—population just 12,187 in 2004 but a fast-growing node along the I-71 corridor between Cincinnati and Columbus.[67]

Some 573 micropolitan areas housed fully one out of ten Americans at the time of the 2000 census, and according to Robert Lang, director of the Metropolitan Institute at Virginia Tech, they backed Bush in 2004, 61–39.[68] Twenty-seven of Ohio's micropolitan areas went for Bush, and ten of Florida's eleven. Many micropolitan areas overlap with the nation's hundred fastest-growing counties, which are likewise pro-Bush.[69]

Instead of being affluent, most of these regions are middling in income and education, "filled with young families, most of them white, many of modest means, willing to trade time for space—accepting longer commutes into urban areas so they can afford homes."[70] According to a post-election examination of Ohio's Clinton County, where Wilmington is, some local newcomers "drive to jobs in Dayton and Cincinnati and even an hour north to Columbus."[71]

If the Census Bureau ever profiles counties by per-capita gasoline usage, these places will rank high, altogether appropriate for demographic products of the interstate-highway system. Besides the innate thirst of

SUVs, some of the last quarter century's surge in U.S. oil consumption has come from Americans driving more—some twelve thousand miles per motorist per year, up almost one-third from 1980—because they as a whole live farther from work.[72] In consumption terms, exurbia is the physical result of the latest population redistribution enabled by car culture and the electorate that upholds it.

In assessing their political motivations, coming years will see thousands of exurbanites—now a full 10 percent of the national electorate—stretched out, figuratively at least, on psychiatrists' couches and sociologists' survey sheets. Still, a few conclusions already seem obvious. Family values are central—if by this we mean having families and accepting lengthy commutes to install them in reasonably safe and well-churched places. In the 1970s such households might have been fleeing school busing or central-city crime; in the post–September 11 era, many sought distance from "godless" school systems or the random violence and terrorist attacks expected to occur in metropolitan areas. Although many of the migrants likely had conservative leanings to begin with—thereby taking a GOP vote out of Cleveland or Cincinnati even as they added one in a micropolitan area—religious and political socialization processes in the exurbs could be expected to intensify their views. In moving to small-town America, many shed earlier urban Democratic registrations.

While SUVs became a particular phenomenon after the events of September 11, increased personal safety-consciousness, other heavy vehicles also gained cachet. By 2003 the machismo emphasized by Detroit spread to large cars with names such as Dodge Viper and Mercury Marauder. Press accounts quoted buyers half joking that they would have bought an Abrams tank had one been available. The Marauder VT version, indeed, boasted a 444-horsepower engine, about one-third the size of one of the engines propelling the World War II Martin B-26 Marauders flown on long-distance bombing raids against Japan. That's a lot of engine just to hit a sale at a suburban shopping mall.

Nevertheless, the bigger psychological change after September 11 came among women, not men. Democratic pollster Celinda Lake reported in 2004 that "women have almost twice the sense of risk as men do. They think a member of their family might be a victim of terrorism."[73] Marketing executives generally concurred that married women saw big cars as protection for themselves and their children, not vehicles with which to work off road rage. By late 2003, according to *Road & Track,* 40 percent of the vehicles classified as trucks were being bought by women, and the election-year survey for the Kelley Blue Book found Kerry trailing Bush by a three-to-one ratio among such security moms.[74]

The significance here is difficult to overstate. Election Day and post-election polls for 2004 come in many flavors—the network exit polls, for example, put Kerry ahead—but sticking with Lake's survey is useful for focusing on women. Whereas men produced a small 2000–2004 Democratic gain—Kerry got 44 percent as opposed to Gore's 42 percent—security-consciousness among women favored Bush. Here Gore's 54 percent became Kerry's 51 percent, with the decline concentrated among married women, where Gore's two-point lead in 2000 reversed into an eleven-point Bush margin.[75] Granted there was a post–9/11 mood shift in the national climate, the emotional crystallization came from the Bush campaign's skill in stimulating apprehension among married mothers in middle-class urban/suburban or exurban areas—multidimensional fears of what might happen in their homes, in their cars, at their schools, or in any public place that terrorists might choose to attack. Single, childless women, by contrast, did not follow this pattern.

For many national Democratic strategists, whose screens ping at a one-point rise in central-city poverty or a scowl from Hollywood contributors, the angst of middle America—Hummer purchases by fearful housewives, micropolitan buildups along interstate-highway corridors, NASCAR excitement, and a Pentecostal drift in the Hispanic lower middle class—apparently failed to register. By contrast, even such obscure but relevant data as county-level breakouts on the distribution of Florida's 350,000 concealed-weapon permits was entered into shrewd Republican calculations of voter psychologies along the I-4.[76] Fear was there to be tapped, and the Bush-Cheney team collected by the bucket.

But tapping fear raises the hope that it can be ameliorated by the tappers; failure, to be sure, would carry a high penalty. Should U.S. policies collapse in some oil-supply cutoff, large-scale terrorist success, economic crash of the dollar, or deep disenchantment with White House misrepresentations, public anger could shift from Middle Eastern terrorists and oil dangers to deceit and incompetence in Washington and thus to the ballot box. Like a bicycle, the innately unsteady GOP coalition with such disparate elements is enormously dependent on forward motion.

By the end of 2005, Interstate Corridor residents had a particular new discontent: soaring fuel prices.

The Republican national coalition's unusual outlook must be underscored by an additional energy-related point. Some 30 to 40 percent of the Bush electorate, many of whom might otherwise resent their employment conditions, credit-card debt, heating bills, or escalating costs of automobile upkeep (from insurance to gas prices), often subordinate these economic concerns to a broader religious preoccupation with biblical prophecy and the second coming of Jesus Christ. The explanation is mostly theological and will be pursued accordingly. But there is a strong connection to oil, gas, and energy—a tie that inhibits American policymaking deliberations.

In 1983 James Watt, Ronald Reagan's secretary of the interior, was forced to resign because of pressure from environmentalists who regarded him as hostile to their cause. Part of the suspicion lay in Watt's conservative religion—he was the first cabinet secretary to belong to the Pentecostal Assemblies of God—and in suppositions that he was preoccupied with waiting for Christ's second coming rather than with environmental stewardship. This was an early instance of a connection that has since become more controversial, and interest in Watt rekindled in 2001 when his protégée, Coloradan Gale Norton, was named secretary of the interior by George W. Bush. Norton had worked for Watt at the Mountain States Legal Foundation in 1979–1981 and again at the Interior Department. Like Watt, she was seen by the environmental movement as a foe.

Come 2004, Watt participated in a series of interviews conducted in Denver with former interior secretaries. His introduction, by Patricia Limerick of the Center of the American West at the University of Colorado, harked back two decades to his resignation. She noted that "this person [Watt] did not say that because the Second Coming was imminent, we must squander and trash our resources. He said, 'Since the Second Coming may be upon us, we must behave as good stewards in anticipation of that reckoning.'"[77]

The distinction is important given how critics have misquoted Watt, for which Bill Moyers and several major print media apologized in 2005. In practical terms, however, the new centrality of "stewardship"—the theology underpinning the religious-right environmental and energy policy—likewise demands attention. Scholars of religious politics such as University of Akron professor John Green describe those elements ignoring the environment as they wait for the rapture, or second coming, as a "fringe" movement.[78] By sophisticated standards, that may be.

However, like the widely held belief in Armageddon, fringe ideas touching the environment or natural resources may influence fifteen, twenty, or even thirty million adults, and not a few are well-placed officeholders. Somewhat ironically, the Book of Genesis theology that true believers bring to bear on matters relative to the environment, global warming, carbon-based fuels, petroleum geology, and the age of the earth has a particular influence on congressmen, senators, cabinet officers, and presidents from states such as Oklahoma, Texas, New Mexico, Colorado, and Wyoming, much as left-liberal ideology commands its best access to politicians from Massachusetts, New York, and the Pacific Coast.

Liberal Democrats, in mishandling the Watt debate, generally went for the easy mockery—biblical worldview politicians waiting for the Second Coming, yuk-yuk—while ignoring the existence of a powerful Republican, conservative, and theological infrastructure related to energy and environmental subject matter. Watt, in short, is only the tip of a politico-religious iceberg that is far larger now than it was when he left office in 1983.

We will return more broadly to the new theology underpinning much of the Republican party and its coalition in part 2. What deserves attention in these chapters is the significance for U.S. energy and resource policies of the biblical worldview held by key conservative power brokers in Washington. In Congress, the two most notable are Texan Tom DeLay and Oklahoman James Inhofe, chairman of the Senate Environment and Public Works Committee. Both men call the federal Environmental Protection Agency a "gestapo" and have favored its abolition. In the Oval Office itself, Texan George W. Bush doubts evolution and global warming and believes in the Bible; the question is only one of degree.

Evangelical religion is clearly beginning to inhibit science and geology. In recent years, as evangelicals have gained importance, corporations have begun to take note, hiring more Washington lobbyists with biblical worldviews or Christian right connections. In Texas and Oklahoma, and across the South and some Rocky Mountain states, the connections among the boardrooms, petroleum clubs, and conservative preachers are well established. Colorado is a particularly important example, given the relationships centered on the beer-rich Coors family. For three decades, and with considerable national significance, it has been at the junction of the religious right and laissez-faire natural-resource, energy, and environmental policy.

Brewer Joseph Coors—the founding father, at least in political terms— was closely involved during the 1970s and early 1980s in helping to fund and build four organizations that became linchpins of the GOP's business-religious axis: the Washington-based Heritage Foundation, the Mountain States Legal Foundation, the Council for National Policy (co-founded by preacher and author Tim LaHaye), and, more marginally, the Coalition on Revival (bridging the theological gap between the rapture believers and the Christian Reconstructionists who believe a theocratic type of government must be built before Jesus will return).[79]

Since the 1980s the impact of this axis during Republican administrations has been particularly notable within the sections of the federal government that regulate the environment, mining, oil and petrochemicals, ranching, and logging—in short, the principal units charged with resources stewardship (the Environmental Protection Agency and the departments of the Interior and Energy). Three interior secretaries—James Watt, Donald Hodel (later also energy secretary), and Gale Norton—at some point held positions in the Mountain States Legal Foundation or the Council for National Policy, as had Anne Gorsuch, a Reagan-era EPA administrator. All four have been associated with permissiveness toward regulated industries. Watt and Hodel, in turn, have been closely associated with the religious right (Hodel, after leaving government, held top positions in three related organizations: the Christian Coalition, the Council for National Policy, and the Colorado-based Focus on the Family).[80]

During the 1980s and much of the 1990s, little attention was paid— save for the Watt episode—to whether the procorporate or antienvironmentalist views of the four were ideological or theological. But that changed in the late nineties as religious-right leaders and their allies were aroused by the criticisms put forward by liberal environmental groups and church organizations led by the National Council of Churches. These included charges that conservative fundamentalists and evangelicals cared little about the environment, preferring to rely on the biblical instruction in Genesis 1:28 to subdue the earth and have dominion over it. Such was the argument, for example, of Norman Geisler, president of the Southern Evangelical Seminary. Genesis, he says, "gives us the divine mandate to use the resources that are there."[81] Others thought that the old argument needed a little more polish.

In 2000 a number of religious conservatives—including stalwarts Richard Land of the Southern Baptist Convention, James Dobson of Focus on the Family, and D. James Kennedy of Florida's Coral Ridge Ministries—launched a new organization called the Interfaith Council for Environmental Stewardship. Human beings, its declaration read, were given stewardship by God "to be fruitful, to bring forth good things from the earth." Moreover, "sound theology" was needed to help guide the environmental decision-making process.[82] Other council tenets and pronouncements emphasized private property rights and economic development.

The moderate-to-liberal National Council of Churches, in turn, linked its 2004 pro-environmental drive to the organization of the National Religious Partnership for the Environment, urging a brand of stewardship that paid more attention to global warming and less to *Left Behind* literature.[83] But even prominent centrist theologians took umbrage at conservative attitudes toward the environment. Martin Marty, of the Institute for the Advanced Study of Religion at the University of Chicago, did so in defending a Lutheran colleague, Barbara Rossing, who had written a book calling the rapture a "racket." Theologian Rossing, Marty wrote, was going back to a first love: "Biblical understanding of the environment and ecology. She had better hurry—if the Rapture people get their explosive, Jesus-the-Terminator way, there may not be much environment left to be cared for."[84]

The evidence that natural-resource issues are taking on theological as well as political overtones is mounting. As we will see, theology is creeping into ever more nooks and crannies of the national debate. Although the exact portion of the GOP electorate taking an end-times view is unknowable, polls suggest that close to a majority of those who voted for Bush believe the Bible to be literally true.

The most intense believers split into two principal camps. The first, so-called dispensationalists, who interpret current events such as tsunamis, oil spikes, and wars as confirming that end times are at hand, usually don't worry about energy policy. Indeed, they cite a biblical verse mentioning costly wheat, barley, and oil as predictions of shortages of food and fuel.[85] In dispensationalist Tim LaHaye's bestselling *Left Behind* series, some of his heroes obtain SUVs to go off-road during the earthquakes of the tribulation. Reconstructionists, by contrast, believe that the world must be made over theocratically, along biblical lines, before Christ will return. Neither faction has fossil fuels, climate deterioration, or the energy efficiency of the U.S. manufacturing sector on its agenda.

Both camps deplore the efforts of geologists and climatologists to sway voters and policy makers through Hubbert-peak analyses and scientific interpretations of global-warming data. Their biblically viewed world is at most ten thousand years old, not the millions of years established by scientists, whose insistence on this longer time frame is said to usurp God's prerogative. In considering stem-cell research or Iraq-as-Babylon, depleting oil or melting polar ice caps, the thought processes of such true believers have at best limited openness to any national secular dialogue. The Republican party entertains no such public debate. Economic conservatives in the oil and gas, coal, and automobile industries may not believe in end times, but their opposition to regulatory environmental prescriptions and tougher fuel-efficiency standards makes them ally with the economically undemanding religious right.

This facet of current U.S. energy politics may yet turn out to be one of the most pernicious. No leading world economic power has ever maintained itself on the cutting edge of innovation and development with a political coalition that panders to biblical inerrancy. But we are getting ahead of our narrative. George W. Bush has been in the White House only for weeks, and he is looking for a chance to attack Iraq. It is time to turn to the new fusion of oil, foreign policy, and overseas military intervention that has come together in what can be called petro-imperialism.

3

Trumpets of Democracy,
Drums of Gasoline

Oil has literally made foreign and security policy for decades. Just since the turn of this century, it has provoked the division of the Middle East after World War I; aroused Germany and Japan to extend their tentacles beyond their borders; the Arab oil embargo; Iran versus Iraq; the Gulf War. This is all clear.

—Bill Richardson, U.S. Secretary of Energy, 1999

A quick look at the map is all it takes. It's no coincidence that the map of terror in the Middle East and Central Asia is practically interchangeable with the map of oil. There's Infinite Justice, Enduring Freedom—and Everlasting Profits to be made.

—*Asia Times*, 2002

The need to dominate oil from Iraq is also deeply intertwined with the defense of the dollar. Its current strength is supported by OPEC's requirement (secured by a secret agreement between the U.S. and Saudi Arabia) that all OPEC sales be denominated in dollars.

—Peter Dale Scott, 2003

He [Karl Rove] turned out millions of the foot soldiers on November 2, including many who have made the apocalypse a powerful driving force in modern American politics. . . . It's why the invasion of Iraq was for them a warm-up act, predicted in the Book of Revelation. . . . A war with Islam in the Middle East is not something to be feared but welcomed—an essential conflagration on the road to redemption.

—Bill Moyers, 2004

EACH EPIGRAPH ON THE PRECEDING PAGE DISTILLS A DIFFERENT ASPECT OF the 2003 invasion of Iraq. They are all compatible, though, because the attack, while at bottom about access to oil and U.S. global supremacy, had other intentions. One was to fold oil objectives into the global war against terror. A second was to cement the U.S. dollar's hegemonic role in global oil sales—and thus in the world economy. A third was to keep the invasion's purpose broad enough to allow the biblically minded Christian right to see it, at least partially, as a destruction of the new Babylon, on the road to Armageddon and redemption.

None of these motivations excuse the fundamental deceits of Anglo-American policy makers. Speaking on behalf of George W. Bush, White House press secretary Ari Fleischer insisted on February 6, 2003, that "if this had anything to do with oil, the position of the United States would be to lift the sanctions so the oil could flow. This is not about that. This is about saving lives by protecting the American people." Defense Secretary Donald Rumsfeld had in November 2002 likewise declared that "it has nothing to do with oil, literally nothing to do with oil." British prime minister Tony Blair, for his part, told members of Parliament in early 2003: "Let me deal with the conspiracy theory idea that this is somehow to do with oil. There is no way whatever if oil were the issue that it would not be infinitely simpler to cut a deal with Saddam."[1]

All three statements, each of which came back to haunt its maker, are all but lies. Oil *was* a critical factor. The thin, partial truth of these denials— very thin, very partial—lay in the fact that broader concerns were also at work. For one thing, as we will see, the Bush administration knew that the oil-peak crisis probably posed strategic dangers far beyond those publicly acknowledged. The dollar's role as the world's reserve currency was also tied to oil. Besides which, seizing Iraq as a military base–cum–oil reservoir would allow U.S. troops to be pulled out of vulnerable Saudi Arabia, where their presence was breeding discontent and terrorism.

At the same time, biblically attuned prowar constituencies would have been alienated by any emphasis on oil or any oil-related peril to the U.S. dollar. In the *Left Behind* series, which religious-right leader Jerry Falwell called the most influential books since the Bible, the godly heroes did not deal in oil; only the malevolent antichrist, based in New Babylon, did that. This aligns with the insistence that the United States and Britain were fighting not for oil, heaven forfend, or to stop OPEC or Islamic leaders from pricing petroleum in euros, but to bring freedom, liberty, and democracy to the Middle East. This hoary claim, the pedigree of which dates to the post–World War I period and the phraseology of President Woodrow Wilson and the British foreign secretary, Lord Curzon, bears little relation to the last century of actual Anglo-American regional involvement.

As the drumbeat for war in Iraq sounded in 2002 and early 2003, part of the ensuing confusion arose because practically none of the true stakes or political motivations were acknowledged: oil, the oil-linked value of the dollar, and religious expectations alike. But one hundred years of petro-imperialism in the Persian Gulf were about to come to a head.

The Hundred Years Oil War

The idea of a latter-day Hundred Years War does not sit easily in the contemporary mind. We think of our technology-fed world as too fast, too intense, to permit such a long engagement. The only hundred-years war generally recognized in Western history was the one fought in western France between 1337 and 1453. Over that long century, the French generally squeezed out the English, whose rulers also claimed to be kings of France. The English general defeated in 1453, John Talbot, earl of Shrewsbury, was a famous knight whose name lives on in that of an estimable Bordeaux wine. Medieval warfare centers such as chateaux Castelnaud and Beynac on the Dordogne add to the lure of vineyards and Michelin stars. Enjoyable travel routes and tours help bring pleasure and history together.

Perhaps one day visitors will drive up the Tigris River to tour sites and battlefields of the Hundred Years Oil War that has devastated Iraq and Iran. More pretentious, freedom-related explanations will seem irrelevant. For now, though, it is hard to imagine travel posters for Fallujah, Nasiriya, Mosul, or the steamy Shatt el-Arab, the estuary of the combined Tigris and Euphrates near Kuwait. But the hundred-year duration is clear enough, the subject matter was indeed oil, and English speakers—British, Americans, Australians, New Zealanders—were invariably among the arms bearers.

Americans wound up as the leaders, but the epic began in 1897, when a nervous local sheikh asked the British to assume a protectorate over Kuwait, then a minor outpost of Turkish Mesopotamia. With oil widely reported in the Tigris-Euphrates Valley, Germany had begun the Berlin–Baghdad Railway, hoping to negotiate for Kuwait as its Persian Gulf terminus. The British took it first. By 1914, the Germans had negotiated oil rights as far as Mosul, as Britain had for Kuwait, which at that time had less promise.[2] When war broke out, Turkish Mesopotamia quickly became a battleground, and British units slowly moved upriver from Basra. They fought through Nasiriya and Kut, losing badly at first but eventually overcoming German-led Turkish troops. Luckily for the British War Office, the first local German commander, Field Marshal Colmar von der Goltz, a crack strategist who beat them at Ctesiphon and Kut, died of typhus in 1916.

Realizing the future stakes, British and French diplomats made a secret arrangement in 1916, the Sykes-Picot Agreement mentioned earlier, for a postwar split of oil-rich Mesopotamia: the Mosul region to be under France, the rest under Britain. However, deciding that they needed Mosul, too, British troops kept fighting after the November 1918 armistice, captured the city in December, and installed themselves. Other satisfactions were provided for the French, notably accepting that they might occupy portions of defeated Germany.

In 1922 Turkey sought to take back Mosul from Britain but failed. Lord Curzon, foreign secretary, famously insisted that the influence of oil on British policy was "nil." "Oil," he said, "had not the remotest connection with my attitude, nor with that of his majesty's Government, over Mosul."[3] Mocked in Parliament and the press, Curzon ultimately took to the pages of *The Times* in 1924 to plead his case, but most historians have scoffed at his claim.[4] There is something about oil that makes high officials lie.

Despite several promises of self-determination to the Arabs, a 1920 rebellion in Iraq caused the British to tighten control through a surprising and unprecedented instrument: the fledgling Royal Air Force. According to Stephen Pelletière, professor at the U.S. Army War College, "this was the first known use of airpower as a constabulary. . . . In time, the British expanded the use of the RAF, sending it on all sorts of assignments. For example, it would bomb the tribes to soften them up for visits from the tax collector."[5] Controversy persisted, but so did the RAF. Iraqis, in turn, repeatedly rose up. One Iraqi historian recorded thirty significant violent outbreaks of some sort between 1919 and 1958, when the British finally left Iraq.[6]

Nineteen forty-one brought a new menace into the oil wars. In pursuit of both petroleum supplies and Middle East hegemony, German troops moved into Egypt and threatened Cairo. Berlin simultaneously pressured the collaborationist Vichy French regime in Syria to help seize control of next-door Iraq. For a month or so in May 1941, German and Italian aircraft—Heinkel bombers, Messerschmitts, and Savoia-Marchettis—pounded the British airfield at Habbaniya, sixty miles from the capital, in support of a pro-German Iraqi faction that had prosecuted a successful coup in Baghdad.[7] Fierce fighting also raged around Fallujah, a scene revisited sixty-two years later. However, the pro-German Rashid Ali clique soon fled to Persia as British relief columns advanced from Palestine and, once more, upriver from Basra.

The Iraqi campaigns of two world wars are reasonably well documented in Britain (and have been the backdrop for some fascinating novels).[8] So is the long history of British regional pursuit of oil. Likewise well understood is the British government's usual preoccupation with oil and geopolitics, not democracy, although few Americans recall either set of precedents. This may help to explain why Prime Minister Blair's pretenses that oil was not involved in 2003 were dismissed by the British press while the U.S. media generally spared George W. Bush's assurances.

The first half century set the patterns: first, oil has always been a central motive of Western attempts—German, British, Russian, American—to invade Iraq or Iran or overthrow a local government; second, oil geography has made the Persian Gulf and Tigris-Euphrates Valley into one of the region's great military corridors. Arguments for an oil-premised Hundred Years Oil War have been made by James A. Paul of the UN-based Global Policy Forum, by Swiss journalist William Engdahl in *A Century of War,* and less categorically by Stephen Pelletière in his political chronicle *Iraq and the International Oil System.*[9] The span seems compelling, but it inconveniently undercuts most of the Anglo-American pretenses raised in 2002 and 2003.

Washington practitioners of realpolitik posit a shorter, America-centered Thirty Years War, starting in 1973, when James Schlesinger, secretary of defense in the Nixon administration, contacted senior British officials about joining the United States in a joint airborne attack to seize the oil fields in Saudi Arabia, Kuwait, and Abu Dhabi.[10] The immediate source of American frustration was the 1973–1974 Israel-Arab war and the related Arab and OPEC embargo on oil shipments to the United States and the Netherlands. The British were cool to the possible 1973 attack, but then secretary of state Henry Kissinger returned to the same theme two years later in an article written under a nom de plume for *Harper's Magazine*.[11] In 2002, as the United States prepared for war, James Akins, the U.S. ambassador to Saudi Arabia from 1973 to 1975, recalled how the *Harper's* article laid out a case for the United States' solving its oil problem by seizing Saudi oil fields and installations. He alleged that Kissinger had also promoted the idea to journalists in a deep-background briefing. Of the war about to start in 2003, Akins said, "It's the Kissinger plan. I thought it had been killed, but it's back."[12]

In either British or American chronology, it is impossible to fully separate Iraq from Kuwait (which was carved out of Iraq) or Iran, which shares an eight-hundred-mile border with Iraq. After World War II, when Washington gained precedence within the Western alliance, the American CIA, not British intelligence, stage-managed the 1953 overthrow of elected Iranian prime minister Mohamed Mossadegh. His principal transgression had been to nationalize the British-owned Anglo-Iranian Oil Company, although Washington also feared Soviet influence. Under the restored Shah, Reza Pahlevi, Iran then became a client state principally of the United States. Anglo-Iranian Oil, although readmitted at the head of a new consortium, was obliged to yield a 40 percent share to U.S. oil firms.[13]

Recently it has come to light that U.S. intelligence also planned a coup in 1959 against Iraqi prime minister Abdul Qarim Qasim, like Mossadegh a nationalist. The effort, which came to nought, allegedly included hiring a twenty-two-year-old named Saddam Hussein.[14] By the 1960s the strategic importance of the entire Persian Gulf to the United States had been defined and upheld by a series of presidents beginning with Franklin D. Roosevelt. The underpinning for each expression of White House concern was just what had motivated Whitehall: oil.

The events since 1973 are reasonably well known. In 1979 Iranian radicals overthrew the Shah, taking fifty-three American embassy employees hostage. President Carter's helicopter rescue mission to get them back failed, but they were released on the day in 1981 when Ronald Reagan was inaugurated. Between 1980 and 1988, as Iraq and Iran fought a war over boundary issues with a subtext of oil geography, the United States, Britain, and several other nations were selling arms to both sides. At the same time, Washington and London cooperated in clandestine arrangements to provide Iraqi leader Saddam Hussein with dual-use materials that facilitated Iraq's pursuit of chemical, biological, and nuclear weapons.[15] William Safire, the *New York Times* columnist and former Republican White House aide, labeled the behavior of the United States, Britain, and Italy as "Iraqgate" and refused to support George H. W. Bush for reelection in 1992 because of his backstairs involvement in it.

In retrospect, the two Iraq wars of 1991 and 2003 displayed striking parallels. Both Iraqgate and the 2002–2003 imbroglio over alleged weapons of mass destruction produced lackluster investigations in Washington (by congressional bodies) and London (by law lords).[16] Both invasions were lubricated by deceits—in the first instance regarding the Iraqi armored threat to Saudi Arabia and the fabrication that Iraqi invaders had ripped three hundred premature Kuwaiti babies from hospital incubators; in the second involving the unsustainable charges that Saddam Hussein had weapons of mass destruction. Former CIA desk officer Pelletière minces few words on this, saying that the behavior of the Americans and British in the run-ups to both wars bore a disturbing similarity to "the Big Lie" used by the Germans in launching World War II. At the very least both governments have been deceitful toward "their respective publics—they are manipulative towards them, to an extreme degree."[17]

Unfortunately, as we can see, this behavior goes back nearly a century. While both governments have talked of Arab freedom and self-determination, the reality has more often involved a chorus of "Onward, Christian Soldiers"—or "Onward, Oil Producers"—with a persistent allegro of punitive aerial bombing.[18] Perhaps the last word should go to the late scholar Edward Said: "Every single empire, in its official discourse, has said that it is not like all the others, that its circumstances are special, that it has a mission to enlighten, civilize, bring order and democracy, and that it uses force only as a last resort."[19]

The Real Map of Iraq

In Baghdad's Iraqi National Museum, left wide open to looters in 2003 by careless U.S. military planners, dozens of wall maps explained Iraq's achievements as the cradle of world civilization: its invention of writing and the wheel, the birth of mathematics, and the establishment of the first code of laws (Hammurabi's). By most archaeologists' accounts, the museum and the National Library were world-class institutions with unique collections.

Even so, the first major building to be surrounded and occupied by American soldiers was the one housing truly vital maps and artifacts: the Iraqi Oil Ministry. Here were thousands of seismic portraits of the nation's oil fields, the subterranean keys to Majnoon, northern Rumaila, West Qurna, and many more. World opinion had little difficulty in mistaking U.S. priorities.

Primitive oil-related cartography may go back to ancient times, since the area in and around Iraq held the world's oldest oil culture. To the north was Azerbaijan, Persian for "garden of fire." In Iraq and Iran, governments as early as the 800s appointed a *wali-al-naft* or oil minister in each region to control, regulate, and tax production. The Persian province of Faris, according to tenth-century records, paid an annual tribute of ninety metric tons of oil to light the palace of the caliph.[20]

Nevertheless, the oldest relevant map of Iraqi oil fields seems to be the one that ran in the London-based *Petroleum Review* of May 23, 1914, under the attention-getting caption "The Petroleum Deposits of Mesopotamia: A Second Baku in the Making." Both oil and asphalt fields were included, as was the Berlin–Baghdad Railway, which Britons feared might give Germany the edge in future regional development.[21] Presumably even more detailed maps were used by French and British negotiators to plot their wartime division of postwar Mesopotamia.

From the 1930s to the 1960s, in the words of oil historian Anthony Sampson, the reorganized Middle East had "two kinds of maps: some showing the names and outlines of the nations, most of them comparatively new; and others showing the region cut up into squares along the coast, marked with the initials—IPC, KOC, ARAMCO, AOC—representing the consortia of oil companies, nearly always including some of the Seven Sisters. To the companies it was these squares which were the real geography: Saudi Arabia was Aramco-land; Iran meant all the seven; Kuwait was Gulf and BP."[22]

The oil maps, in short, had long been the ones that mattered. For the U.S. and British oil companies, losing these concessions to the nationalizations of the 1970s was infuriating. The irony with respect to Iraq was that for one reason or another, the 1970s were the only decade of heavy pumping and large oil revenues. Production had been kept low during the glutted thirties, and it then stagnated during World War II. By 1948 Iraq's commercial production was just one-seventh that of Iran and one-sixth that of Saudi Arabia.[23] Then between 1980 and 1988, the drawn-out Iran-Iraq War curbed output in both countries. Next came the Gulf War in 1991, followed by the effects of United Nations sanctions from 1990 until the subsequent invasion of Iraq in 2003. Over the last decade or so this chronology of Iraq's surprisingly limited oil production has become relevant again for a simple reason: given that relatively little of Iraq's oil has been pumped, *most of it is still in the ground.*

As the dust of the first Gulf War settled, oil companies from Texas to China began wondering which among them would gain access when the United Nations sanctions were lifted. By 1995 *The Wall Street Journal* and other publications were reporting the American fear: that if Saddam Hussein could escape UN sanctions and give Iraq's lush concessions to non–Anglo-American companies, he could realign the global oil business.[24]

In the meantime, UN sanctions were essential in preventing Iraq from exporting oil beyond the middling amount allowed and also in preventing competitive foreign investments. So long as the United States and Britain could keep these sanctions in place, using allegations concerning weapons of mass destruction, Saddam could not implement his own plan to extend large-scale oil concessions (estimated to be worth $1.1 trillion) to French, Russian, Chinese, and other oil companies.[25] Most analysts concluded that he hoped to enlist those three nations, which had seats on the UN Security Council, to get the sanctions lifted.

As the buzzards circled, Iraq became the prize piece needed to complete three interrelated Washington jigsaw puzzles: the rebuilding of Anglo-American oil-company reserves, transformation of Iraq into an oil protectorate–cum–military base, and reinforcement of the global hegemony of the U.S. dollar. This brings us to the next critical set of maps, the ones used in 2001 by Vice President Dick Cheney's National Energy Policy Development Group to mesh America's energy needs with a twenty-first-century national-security blueprint. This group pursued a mandate, in collaboration with the National Security Council, to deal with rogue states and "actions regarding the capture of new and existing oil and gas fields."[26]

Never intended for public scrutiny, the three Middle East maps and their supporting documents came to light in the summer of 2003 under a federal court order. The most pertinent displayed Iraq's oil fields, pipelines, and refineries, with a supporting list of "Foreign Suitors for Iraqi Oilfield Contracts." As of 2001, more than sixty firms from thirty countries—most prominently France, Russia, and China, but also India, Japan, Indonesia, Canada, and Germany—had projects either agreed upon or under discussion with Baghdad. Nothing could have been less popular in Washington or London.

Canadian writer Linda McQuaig of the *Toronto Star* offered this juicy description: "The southwest is neatly divided, for instance, into nine 'Exploration Blocks.' Stripped of political trappings, this map shows a naked Iraq, with only its ample natural assets in view. It's like a supermarket meat chart, which identifies various parts of a slab of beef so customers can see the most desirable cuts. . . . Block 1 might be the striploin, Block 2 and Block 3 are perhaps some juicy tenderloin, but Block 8—ahh, that could be the filet mignon."[27] The French oil giant Total was to get the twenty-five-billion-barrel Majnoon oil field: "there goes the filet mignon into the mouths of the French."

What these maps left unsaid was how relatively untouched—or at least untapped—the Iraqi fields were. But Cheney's team would presumably have studied the history of Iraqi oil output. Since the turn of the twentieth century, later explained Leonardo Maugeri, a senior vice president at the Italian oil and gas company ENI, "only 2,300 wells have been drilled in Iraq, compared with about 1 million in Texas. A large part of the country—the western desert area—is still mainly unexplored. Iraq has never implemented advanced technologies—like 3-D seismic exploration techniques or deep and horizontal drilling—to find or tap new wells. Of more than 80 oilfields discovered in Iraq, only about 21 have been at least partially developed. . . . [I]t is realistic to assume that Iraq has far more oil reserves than documented so far—probably about 200 billion barrels more."[28] Not a few geologists suspected that the former Mesopotamia might have more left than Saudi Arabia.

Fadel Gheit, a prominent New York–based oil analyst, used words more appropriate to a movie publicist: "Think of Iraq as virgin territory. . . . This is bigger than anything Exxon is involved in currently. . . . It is the superstar of the future. That's why Iraq becomes the most sought-after real estate on the face of the earth. . . . Think of Iraq as a military base with a very large oil reserve underneath. . . . You can't ask for better than that."[29]

Defining American Petro-Imperialism

Old-fashioned colonialists, regal and unembarrassed, took physical control of territories, sent in ostrich-plumed governors, minted coins, and printed local postage stamps on which kings or queens gazed proudly over scenes of natives cutting cocoa pods or harvesting tea. By contrast, petro-imperialism—the key aspect of which is the U.S. military's transformation into a global oil-protection force—puts up a democratic facade, emphasizes freedom of the seas (or pipeline routes), and seeks to secure, protect, drill, and ship oil, not administer everyday affairs. Still, the way in which the United States has begun to organize its national security and military posture around oil is hardly new in spirit, albeit unprecedented in scope.

Nations have always been concerned about resources vital for fuel or war-making capacity. In the seventeenth and eighteenth centuries that meant timber and naval stores (tar, turpentine, and the like), which explained both the Dutch and the British preoccupation with access to the Baltic. In the mid-seventeenth century the Dutch ambassador to Denmark bragged of his nation's fleet that "the oaken keys of the Sound [between Denmark and Sweden] lie in the docks of Amsterdam."[30] Similarly, between 1658 and 1814 British squadrons were sent some twenty times to maintain the "freedom" of that sound.[31]

The future United States was also a naval supply yard. By the middle of the eighteenth century, Britain obtained many of the towering masts so vital to the Royal Navy's line of battle from giant pine trees in colonial Maine, then still a part of Massachusetts. Bureaucracy as well as profit was generated by marking, protecting, cutting, and transporting the "king's trees," to which the Crown paid real attention. Towns had to be laid out with oddly angled roads and central greens to permit passage of the huge trees. One such angle is still visible in the colonial-era center of Freeport, Maine, on the tidal and accessible Harraseeket River.

In switching to coal and steam in the nineteenth century, navies also pursued a minor-league "carbon imperialism"—the establishment by Britain and other powers of global networks of coaling stations. The United States set up a half dozen in the Pacific, and the British had scores in both hemispheres. British historian Niall Ferguson, in his book *Empire*, contended that "a map showing the principal US military bases around the world looks remarkably like a map of Royal Navy coaling stations a hundred years ago."[32] Compared with the developments of latter-day petro-imperialism, however, the coaling stations were one-dimensional. Regions were not seized for coal deposits; small bits of territory were merely leased as facilities for use in providing warships with coal, usually brought in from elsewhere.

A better analogy to today's American practice can be found in the client oil states set up by the British after World War I. To Lord Curzon, the optimum was an "Arab facade ruled and administered under British guidance and controlled by a native Mohammedan and, as far as possible, by an Arab staff. . . . There should be no actual incorporation of the conquered territory in the dominions of the conqueror, but the absorption may be veiled by such constitutional fictions as a protectorate, a sphere of influence, a buffer state and so on."[33] He might have been speaking of post-2003 occupied Iraq.

What's different about current U.S. petro-imperialism is that the leading world economic power, whose idiosyncratic fuel base is petroleum, is also the nation worried—for good reason—about running out of oil. By contrast, when the declining Britain of 1919–1953 was belatedly chasing oil, with only partial success, its home economy was still more than 90 percent dependent on coal, almost all of it locally mined. Besides which, Britain's principal ally, the United States, was the world's leading oil and military power. As of the 2000s, by contrast, the United States has no cousinly power dominant in hydrogen or natural-gas production. As a consequence, the whole Western world-power continuum that has more or less controlled global trade and finance since the 1600s could yield to the rise of Asian countries.

With this changing picture, it's not surprising that the linkage of oil and national security took on new dimensions. In 1992, after the Gulf War, then secretary of defense Cheney gave Halliburton, the energy-services company, a contract to study the privatization of some Pentagon functions. The company duly reported back and obtained more funding to, in essence, design its own broader opportunity. In 1993, after George H. W. Bush had been defeated for reelection, Cheney briefly pondered a 1996 presidential race of his own but withdrew, and in 1995 he took the post of chief executive officer at Halliburton. Thereafter, he led a steadily expanding enterprise—Brown and Root had been acquired decades earlier, but the purchase of Dresser Industries in 1998 doubled Halliburton's size—into a pathbreaking role. The company became a major federal "energy war" contractor and, partly because of Cheney's connections, a private-sector bridge between the oil industry and the military-industrial complex.

Another transformational company of the nineties, likewise manned by prominent figures from the departing Bush administration—George H. W. Bush himself and Secretary of State James A. Baker III—was the Carlyle Group, partly funded by rich Saudi investors. Military and Pentagon contractors were conspicuous on the list of Carlyle subsidiaries. One was the Vinnell Corporation, close to the CIA, which held contracts to train the security and internal police forces of countries including Turkey and Saudi Arabia. Other contractors unrelated to Carlyle went even further, providing thinly disguised mercenaries and paramilitary forces for unofficial operations overseas.

Despite the threats of 1973–1975, it took oil nearly two more decades to become a reason for direct U.S. military intervention overseas (as opposed to CIA-led overthrows or large arms sales). The occasion was Iraq's 1990 invasion of Kuwait and the 1991 U.S.-led war for its expulsion from there. Saddam Hussein had told U.S. officials beforehand that his invasion was based on oil-related provocations—first, Kuwait's alleged slant-drilling of Iraqi oil fields just over the border, and second, the Kuwaiti efforts through OPEC to drive down oil prices to deny Iraq the revenues supposedly needed to rebuild after eight draining years of war with Iran.[34]

Once the United States decided to eject Iraq from Kuwait, however, Saddam's rationales became irrelevant. When President Bush mobilized American forces, he commented matter-of-factly that "our jobs, our way of life, our own freedom and the freedom of friendly countries around the world would all suffer if control of the world's great oil reserves fell into the hands of Saddam Hussein." Secretary of Defense Cheney was even more vociferous: "Once he [Saddam] acquired Kuwait and deployed an army as large as the one he possesses," Cheney argued, the Iraqi leader was "in a position to be able to dictate the future of worldwide energy policy, and that gave him a stranglehold on our economy."[35] Compared with the pretenses of 2002–2003, these statements were relatively candid.

It was not only in and around the Persian Gulf that oil dominated American foreign policy. Bush's decision to intervene in Somalia in late 1992, supposedly for humanitarian reasons, was later proved by the investigative journalism of the *Los Angeles Times* to have been substantially oil driven. Four large U.S. oil firms—Chevron, Amoco, Conoco, and Phillips—had exclusive concessions covering two-thirds of Somalia that were put at risk when the nation's pro-Western government was overthrown. Although the U.S. government spoke of "peacekeeping" and company spokesmen denied motivations of oil rather than of humanitarian relief as "absurd" and "nonsense," the newspaper noted that Bush himself in 1986 had dedicated a Texas-run oil facility in nearby Yemen, an occasion when he emphasized regional oil development. Equally to the point, Conoco had allowed its corporate compound in Mogadishu to be made into a de facto U.S. embassy a few days before the marines landed in the capital. These circumstances, the *Times* concluded, led "many to liken the Somalia operation to a miniature version of Operation Desert Storm."[36]

Oil-based foreign policy persisted under Bush's Democratic successor, Bill Clinton. Captivated by mid-nineties assessments of the energy potential of the Caspian Sea region, Clinton in 1995 announced "strategic partnerships" with Uzbekistan and several other newly independent republics in former Soviet central Asia. Several U.S. companies had already negotiated oil or gas deals with Kazakhstan and Azerbaijan. In a 1998 book, *The Grand Chessboard*, Zbigniew Brzezinski, a former Democratic White House national-security adviser, touted the Caspian and central Asia as a strategic pivot in much the same way Britain's Mackinder had before World War I.[37] Brzezinski's strategic recommendations, to be sure, had a more specific oil and gas focus.

Because the landlocked Caspian was inaccessible to oil and gas tankers, pipelines became an early petro-imperial focus. Along with Britain's

Blair, Clinton became a patron of the Baku–Tibilisi–Ceyhan pipeline. He also promoted a route from the Black Sea across the Balkans to Albania. Meanwhile, General Anthony Zinni, the U.S. Centcom (Middle Eastern) commander, opened military conversations with the new republics. By the time Clinton left office in January 2001, he could point to other minor Kipling-esque innovations: the Silk Road Strategy Act of 1999 and the April 2000 launching of the Central Asian Border Security Initiative. But by 2002, oil companies drilling in the Caspian and finding little began to conclude that its energy potential had been overblown.[38]

In 1997–1998 observers had generally dismissed petroleum-related interpretations of Clinton's commitment of U.S. military forces to the Balkans. The principal allegation was that European and U.S. intervention was really about making southern portions of the former Yugoslavia safe for pipelines bringing Caspian oil from Bulgaria on the Black Sea to Albania on the Adriatic. In 2002 the *Asia Times* offered an even broader indictment: "All countries or regions which happen to be an impediment to Pipelineistan routes towards the West have been subjected either to a direct interference or to all-out war: Chechnya, Georgia, Kurdistan, Yugoslavia and Macedonia."[39] Few in the West listened.

In fact, oil-transportation considerations must always have lurked in the background. Late 2004 saw Albania, Macedonia, and Bulgaria sign a pact to begin the trans-Balkans pipeline's construction. Much of the financing came from the U.S. government's Overseas Private Investment Corporation and private American firms, as originally proposed in 1996, when the corridor involved had been laid out as part of the Clinton administration's South Balkan Development Initiative.[40]

Whatever Clinton's expectations for the Caspian, he more than maintained the oil-related status quo in Iraq. He launched major attacks with aircraft and cruise missiles in January 1996, June 1996, and December 1998; he deployed troops near Iraq's borders in 1997 and 1998 (Operations Phoenix Scorpion and Desert Thunder) after Baghdad had proposed oil concessions to Russia, China, and France; and on October 31, he signed the Iraq Liberation Act of 1998, calling for regime change in Baghdad. Two months earlier Clinton had signed another finding (PL 105-235) that accused Iraq of building weapons of mass destruction, failing to cooperate with the United Nations, and being "in material and unacceptable breach of its international obligations."[41] This insistence, as we have seen, was essential to keeping

Saddam Hussein hogtied by UN sanctions and thus unable to implement the French, Russian, and Chinese concessions.

For boldness, though, none of the Clinton-era actions could compare with the far-reaching Great Game propositions of the onetime strategists for the first Bush administration gathered around Cheney and the Project for a New American Century. "Regime change" in Iraq became code for a second invasion. The Bush-Cheney administration, on taking office, embraced an oil "forward strategy" with instant intensity. Plans were discussed in the spring and summer of 2001—well before the events of September—for hamstringing Iraq and convincing the Taliban in Afghanistan to accept construction of an American (Unocal) pipeline from Turkmenistan through Kabul to Karachi, Pakistan. Talks with the Taliban continued in the summer of 2001 but apparently soon collapsed. Duplicity seems to have been in the catbird's seat. Multiple press reports from sources in Pakistan and elsewhere, all officially denied in Washington, had the American government planning to attack Afghanistan sometime in the autumn.[42]

Then the world changed. Besides intensifying existing oil and Middle Eastern pressures, on September 11, the attack on the World Trade Center gave Washington policies a convenient new all-inclusive justification: fighting terror was about everything, and everything was about fighting terror. Oil motivations, rarely a popular or easy foreign-policy justification, could now be submerged within a primal response to a deep-seated national combination of fear, loathing, and outrage. Petroleum strategy could now become only a minor facet of an antiterrorist mobilization. In the wake of September 11, hardly anyone made the argument, which would be widespread by 2004, that America's oil quest and tactics had been provocative in the Middle East. This was especially true of the placement since 1990 of (nonbeliever) U.S. troops on the holy Saudi Arabian soil to which devout Muslims have made centuries of pilgrimages.[43]

Occasionally, the blurring of distinctions between energy, antiterror, and military considerations in U.S. policy making was obliquely acknowledged. In 2003 former White House speechwriter David Frum wrote in his Bush political biography, *The Right Man,* that "the war on terror" was designed to "bring new stability to the most vicious and violent quadrant of the Earth—and new prosperity to us all, by securing the world's largest pool of oil."[44]

Centcom, Eurcom—and Oilcom?

In 2004 Michael Klare, a theorist of the global resumption of resource wars, summed up the increasingly obvious: oil, no longer a mere commodity, had become a national-security matter, thereby falling under the purview of the Department of Defense and warranting protection "at any cost, including the use of military force."[45] Oil-premised military commitments, he argued, were being conflated with the war on terror: "anti-terrorism and the protection of oil supplies are closely related in administration thinking. When requesting funds in 2004 to establish a 'rapid-reaction brigade' in Kazakhstan, for example, the State Department told Congress that such a force is needed to 'enhance Kazakhstan's capability to respond to major terrorist threats to oil platforms' in the Caspian Sea."[46] Notably, Condoleezza Rice, who as Bush's national-security adviser dwelt on terrorism, had made her commercial bones during the 1990s as a director of Chevron with a specialty in Kazakhstan negotiations.

Others pointed to the changing dispositions of the U.S. military, notwithstanding their minimal amplification in the Pentagon's 2003 Global Posture Review. To sticklers, the 2003 report understated the new oil and gas preoccupation by omitting de facto bases in Afghanistan, central Asia, the Balkans, and the Persian Gulf. From west Africa to the Strait of Malacca, evidence aplenty suggested that future U.S. base locations would be tied to oil resources and oil-transport considerations.[47] Several commentators used the term "base mania" to describe the string of installations guarding the pipeline corridors and oil-production centers of the new imperial frontier.[48]

Misleadingly cataloged by the Pentagon or not, the transformations were legion. Southcom, the U.S. forces' Southern Command, had units in Colombia protecting Occidental Petroleum's interest in the Caño Limón pipeline; Colombian national forces scheduled for similar pipeline duty, subsidized by U.S. military aid, were training under U.S. Army Special Forces personnel at Fort Bragg, North Carolina.[49] Eurcom, the European Command, supervised U.S. forces instructing the military of the Caucasian republic of Georgia on how to protect the soon-to-be-completed pipeline from Baku through Georgia en route to the Turkish coast.

By 2003 Pentagon officials, also under the rubric of "fighting terror," had begun to talk about permanent bases in Senegal, Ghana, and Mali in west Africa, the latter being another rising oil region under Eurcom jurisdiction.[50] According to *The Wall Street Journal*, "a key mission for U.S. forces [in Africa] would be to insure that Nigeria's oilfields, which in the future could account for as much as 25 percent of all U.S. oil imports, are secure."[51] That summer, General Charles Wald, the deputy Eurcom commander, visited oil-producing Gabon and the potential oil center of São Tomé, where the United States was contemplating constructing a naval base and paying for feasibility studies on the construction of a deepwater port. General James Jones, the Eurcom commander, announced that navy carrier battle groups would shorten future visits to the Mediterranean and "spend half the time going down the west coast of Africa."[52]

Like so much about oil, Jones's preoccupation can best be understood by looking at a map, where Nigeria, Chad, Cameroon, Gabon, Equatorial Guinea, São Tomé and Principe, Congo, and Angola cluster along or near west Africa's Atlantic coast. São Tomé's importance—the islands have become a U.S. focal point—lies in the output expected as international oil companies explore and develop promising offshore fields in the waters between these islands and Nigeria.[53] Controllable by U.S. naval power, west Africa and its waters could be a middling rival to OPEC—or at least it could help stave off a supply crisis for another four to six years.

Pacific Command headquarters, in turn, announced plans to deploy a small-boat squadron to protect oil shipping in the Strait of Malacca, the strategic waterway between Malaysia and Sumatra that opens into the South China Sea near Singapore. Sometimes the troops deployed were hirelings. In Indonesia, Exxon paid the expenses of local forces guarding the company's large gas field in Aceh, northern Sumatra; local residents called them "Exxon's army."[54]

Centcom, the Florida-based controller for most of the Middle East, had its AOR (area of responsibility) broadened in 1997 to include the oil-rich Caspian basin: Kazakhstan, Kyrgyzstan, Tajikistan, Turkmenistan, and Uzbekistan. Several became home to U.S. facilities set up after September 11: Khanabad in Uzbekistan and the Manas air-force base in Kyrgyzstan.

Such redeployments, Michael Klare wrote, lead to an inescapable conclusion: that the American military "is being used more and more for the protection of overseas oil fields and the supply routes that connect them

to the United States and its allies. Such endeavors, once largely confined
to the Gulf area, are now being extended to unstable oil regions in other
parts of the world. Slowly but surely, the U.S. military is being converted
into a global oil-protection service."[55] Under these circumstances, somewhere near the office of the Joint Chiefs of Staff in the Pentagon's E-Ring,
one can hypothesize a top-secret overall command center boasting the
shorthand for ultimate petro-responsibility: *Oilcom*.

Hardly anyone expects these priorities to be temporary. Over the coming decades the United States, if it remains unchastened, seems sure to
require ever greater quantities of imported oil, the bulk from countries
that are hostile or at least potentially unstable. The latter description fits
many presumed exporters: Iraq, Saudi Arabia, Kuwait, the United Arab
Emirates, Venezuela, Colombia, Nigeria, Equatorial Guinea, Angola, Indonesia, and conceivably Russia. Just as in two world wars, oil supplies and
transports will need to be guarded—this time as they flow *toward* the
United States.

In a series of reports, the Washington-based Center for Strategic and
International Studies has acknowledged this political hazard. Outside the
Gulf region, which has its own medieval characteristics, many vital oil
suppliers "share the characteristics of 'petro-states,' whereby their extreme dependence on income from energy exports distorts their political
and economic institutions, centralizes wealth in the hands of the state,
and makes each country's leaders less resilient in dealing with change but
provides them with sufficient resources to hope to stave off necessary reforms indefinitely."[56]

Unfortunately, oil has been corrosive across much of Asia, Africa, and
Latin America. Besides fueling deeply rooted antagonisms among ethnic
and religious groups clumped together within artificial ex-colonial boundaries, as in Nigeria and Indonesia, sudden infusions of petroleum wealth
into poor countries matter-of-factly promote corruption, cronyism, civil
war, or the emergence of strongmen. And from west Africa to the Red
Sea and the Caspian, companies have proved quite willing to employ
bribery and corruption, promote civil violence, or even encourage war.
Outside of North American or European countries, where some form of
democracy previously existed, it has never spouted from an oil derrick or
developed under the tutelage of ExxonMobil, BP, or Halliburton. To characterize the 2002 political milieu of Gabon, an International Monetary

Fund working paper used the title "Escaping the Curse of Oil?"[57] In the petro-imperial age, this prospect seems daunting.

Iraq: Multiple Constituencies and Special-Interest Countdowns

The deceit-cloaked invasion of Iraq in 2003 may never command a full or satisfactory explanation. Nevertheless, a near-final decision to invade seems to have been made in early 2001, for reasons that had mounted steadily since 1997. Vice President Cheney, with his successive positions at the junction of the business and government pipelines connecting oil, national politics, and the Pentagon, must have played a pivotal role. Indeed, this triple expertise may explain the July 2000 decision to slate him as George W. Bush's running mate.

During the election year and 2001, five political and policy endgames—all felt by important constituencies to be pressing or even desperate—appeared to be under way in the United States, in what was historically an extraordinary convergence. The first was a rising preoccupation on the part of oil geologists and among some thinkers in Washington that not only had American oil production peaked but global oil production outside of OPEC might be within five to ten years of doing so. To believers, this demanded action.

The American oil giants and their lesser compatriots also had corporate time sensitivities. Concerned over slackening new oil discoveries, the big companies feared that their futures depended on whether U.S. or foreign firms obtained access to the huge, barely tapped, and pivotal reserves of Iraq. Huge profits were at stake.

A third set of jitters involved finance. A handful of Americans, aware of the interplay of oil and currency flows, worried about OPEC's potential threat to the dollar. Their fear was that should the cartel decide to end the American currency's virtual monopoly on oil pricing, the dollar would plummet, sending shudders through the U.S. economy and its overextended debt structure.[58] Indeed, Iraqi, Iranian, and Venezuelan currency maneuvers were already visible as the dollar sagged in late 2002.

Climatologists pondered a fourth countdown. Many contended that soaring twentieth-century use of hydrocarbon fuels had poured carbon dioxide into the atmosphere at a rate that was responsible for major global climate change. In 2002 the U.S. Defense Department's internal think tank, the Office of Net Assessment, commissioned a dire-case evaluation, published a year later under the title "An Abrupt Climate Change Scenario and Its Implications for United States National Security."[59] Critical time frames as near as 2010–2020 were pondered; immediate crisis planning was recommended.

The fifth clock-watch, very different, was a matter of Christian faith, not scientific calculus. As the millennium itself came and went, 40 percent or more of American Christians continued to tell poll takers in 2000 and 2001 that they expected the biblical prophecies of Armageddon and the end times to come true. They saw day-to-day confirmation of their beliefs in the intensifying Middle Eastern wars, the battling over Israel and Persian Gulf oil, unusual natural disasters, and the rise of AIDS. By 2003 a popular Web site, Raptureready.com, listed the top four rapture signals as natural disasters, global terrorism, the formation of the European Union, and unrest in the Middle East.[60] Conservative politicians understood that for true believers their imminent rapture and the subsequent second coming of Jesus Christ were the *only* endgame. We can estimate that for 20 to 30 percent of Christians, this chronology superseded or muted other issues.

Because the national Republican coalition included some 70 to 80 percent of all three electoral constituencies—energy producers and conspicuous (mostly auto-driving) energy consumers; upper-bracket wealth holders and financiers; and fundamentalist, Pentecostal, and evangelical Christians—GOP strategists tended to be especially alert to their agendas. The tricky part was that the three groups responded to very different levels of candor, economic greed, and biblical preoccupation. Invading Iraq to secure oil supplies or help ExxonMobil might please the petroleum clubs of the urban Gulf Coast, but it would misfire in the nearby Pentecostal Assemblies of God and biblically intense Sun Belt suburban megachurches. Such preachers rarely read *Petroleum Weekly* or *The Wall Street Journal,* but some did a brisk side business in Sunday broadcast syndication and end-times videos.

Putting together an "Invade Iraq" domestic constituency was not easy for George H. W. Bush in 1990–1991, nor was it easy for George W. Bush in 2001–2002. However, Dick Cheney, who had been the elder Bush's defense secretary from 1989 to 1992, became The Man, thanks to his unusual combination of skills in military affairs, invading Iraq (1991), global petroleum issues, and U.S. domestic politics.

Some oil watchers later contended that Cheney let the cat out of the Iraqi-invasion bag in a 1999 speech to the London Institute of Petroleum. He observed: "By some estimates, there will be an average of two percent annual growth in global oil demand over the years ahead, along with conservatively a three percent natural decline in production from existing reserves. That means by 2010 we will need on the order of an additional fifty million barrels a day."[61] He did not mention Iraq or dwell on the mechanics of oil decline, but the heavy emphasis he placed on gas-resource development belied any upbeat expectations.*

These dour assumptions followed the analysis, without the professional jargon, of geological publications that had stirred sharp debate over the previous few years. British geologist Colin Campbell's book *The Coming Oil Crisis* came out in 1997; then a related article, "The End of Cheap Oil," by Campbell and fellow geologist Jean Laherrère, appeared in *Scientific American* in 1998.[62] More oil-peak expositions followed in 2000 and 2001. Like other senior oil executives, Cheney cut to the chilling bottom-line implications.

This peak-scenario pessimism squared with individual companies' oil and gas exploration reports. As we saw in chapter 1, by 2000 North America's aging resources were clearly depleting. More and more wells in Texas had to be drilled just to keep production constant. Reuters later reported the belief that Canadian gas output had peaked in 2001–2002.[63] Even as Cheney spoke in 1999, top executives at Royal Dutch/Shell and British Petroleum must have been hearing about shortfalls in exploration

---

*How much Cheney drew on this 1999 awareness in his 2001 task-force strategic deliberations over U.S. energy policy and the possible role of Iraq's oil fields may never be clear. The extent to which participants have remained silent is reflected in Texas investment banker Matthew Simmons's 2005 book *Twilight in the Desert: The Coming Saudi Oil Shock and the World Economy.* A sometime adviser to George W. Bush and a member of Cheney's task force, Simmons describes U.S. reliance on Saudi Arabia and the Saudis' claims of being able to increase their oil production to 15 million barrels per day and deliver them for fifty years as a pipedream. He says Saudi oil production has already peaked, and $100-per-barrel oil is on the way. His book does not even mention Bush, Cheney, Iraq, or any of their decisions, which may be appropriate, but there is one mention (p. 329) of Halliburton, Cheney's old company, and the ultra-sophisticated technology that it and Schlumberger have provided (Saudi) Aramco for recovering previously bypassed oil. This helps to support Simmons's point about Saudi weakness, but perhaps Cheney's own early sense of that potential exhaustion helped to spur a 2001–2002 U.S. targeting of Iraq as a successor to Saudi Arabia both in terms of oil and as a military platform for controlling the Middle East.

and reserves that became public knowledge in 2002. By 2003 experts had described ExxonMobil's production as flat since 1999.[64] The 1997–1998 reports of foreign rivals angling for Iraq concessions would have magnified the fears of U.S. and British oil executives who read or even half believed Campbell, Laherrère, and their colleagues. All of this would have backstopped a 2000–2002 sense of Iraq-as-solution.

Come the new administration, few energy insiders would have been surprised when Cheney took the point. By early 2001, the situation he had addressed in 1999 had substantially worsened. It was now known that in 1998 the United States for the first time had imported more than half of the petroleum it consumed. Data for 2001 showed the United States having surpassed Europe as an importer of Middle Eastern oil.[65] The winter of 2000–2001 had seen natural-gas prices spike in the United States, while oil prices jumped to thirty dollars per barrel.

Charged with interweaving energy policy and national security, Cheney's team ranged far afield. No transcripts exist, and few public explanations have come from those involved, but Paul Roberts, in *The End of Oil*, contended that in the spring of 2001 Cheney and other strategists

> pored over maps of Iraqi oil fields to estimate how much Iraqi oil might be dumped quickly on the market. Before the war, Iraq had been producing 3.5 million barrels a day, and many in the industry and the administration believed that the volume could easily be increased to seven million by 2010. If so—and if Iraq could be convinced to ignore its OPEC quota and start producing at maximum capacity—the flood of new oil would effectively end OPEC's ability to control prices. As supply expanded, prices would fall dramatically, and not even the Saudis with their crying revenue needs would be able to cut production deeply enough to stop the slide. Caught between falling revenues and escalating debts, the Saudis, too, would be forced to open their oil fields to Western oil companies, as would other OPEC countries.[66]

Naïve as this seems in retrospect, it may have been Cheney's hope. He certainly understood the U.S. oil industry's anxiety. Prime Minister Blair's government, ever intimate with British Petroleum and Royal Dutch/ Shell, would have had a similar set of concerns. BP, mindful of oil resource depletion, was already preoccupied enough with alternative fuels to take on yet another nickname: "Beyond Petroleum."[67] After the Iraq war, Blair's environment minister, Michael Meacher, who had resigned in protest, described the clouds gathering in British energy skies: "Four months ago [autumn 2003], Britain's oil imports overtook its exports, underlining a decline in North Sea oil production that was already well under way. North Sea oil output peaked at about 2.9 million barrels per day in 1999, and has been predicted to fall to only 1.6 million bpd by 2007."[68]

Like many others, Meacher also cited the estimates made by the Association for the Study of Peak Oil and Gas and was glum about the chance of meeting the expanded global need Cheney had cited in 1999. The former British minister summed up: "These [late 2003] calculations place the coming oil crunch some time between 2010 and 2015, perhaps earlier. The reserves in the world's super-giant and giant oilfields are dwindling at an average rate of 4–6 per cent a year. No more big frontier regions remain to be explored except the north and south poles. The production of non-conventional crude oil has already been initiated at enormous cost in Venezuela's Orinoco belt and Canada's Athabasca tar sands and ultra-deep waters. Yet no major primary energy alternative can replace oil and gas in the short-to-medium term."[69]

While the constituency pressures pushing Bush, Blair, Cheney, and Rumsfeld toward war were evident, the endgame urgings of the major U.S. oil corporations were less clear. Although the giant firms left many partial fingerprints on task forces and meetings later officially denied by the White House, even critics differed over what the corporations sought. The money, prestige, and reserves at stake were beyond dispute. Were ExxonMobil, ChevronTexaco, BP, and Royal Dutch/Shell to divide up Iraq, their receipts over several decades would be in the trillions of dollars.

Although no oil-company or government estimates were made public, James Paul of the Global Policy Forum offered these estimates: "Iraq's oil is the world's cheapest to produce, at a cost of only about $1 per barrel. The gigantic 'rent' on Iraq's oil, during decades of production, could yield company profits in the range of $4–5 trillion. . . . Assuming fifty years of production and 40% royalties, Iraq could yield annual profits of $80–90 billion per year, more than the total annual profits of the top five companies, even in the banner year of 2003."[70]

Such a windfall would have sent oil companies' stock prices soaring. In January 2004, when Royal Dutch/Shell had to reduce its worldwide reserve estimates by 20 percent—from 19.3 billion barrels to 15.4 billion—its stock and market capitalization immediately dropped by 7 percent. Were any of the giants to get long-term control of one of the 15- to 30-billion-barrel Iraqi megafields, even that large a company could roughly double its reserves.[71] That, in turn, could increase their market capitalization by 40 to 60 percent, obviously a boon to shareholders. No company management could do other than join in planning for such a possibility.

Iraq watcher Paul, from his perch near the United Nations, told a TV interviewer in 2004 that because the U.S. and U.K. oil giants were so worried about their futures, "it's really only through that lens that we can understand both the present situation and what's been happening in Iraq over quite a substantial period of time."[72] James Akins, the former U.S. ambassador to Saudi Arabia, likewise commented in early 2003 that "what they [the Bush administration] have in mind is denationalization, and then parceling Iraqi oil out to American oil companies. The American oil companies are going to be the main beneficiaries of this war."[73]

However, centrist commentators were more likely to describe the prewar viewpoint of big oil companies as "defensive." One progressive-tilting analysis concluded by citing the views of consultants, diplomats, and company executives that the large U.S. firms were torn between greed and fear. If all went well, they wanted to be at the table when the spoils were divided, but they feared that a fiasco could turn Middle Eastern opinion against the United States and the American oil companies.[74] Six months after the U.S. invasion, when Iraqi output shrank in the face of relentless sabotage of pipelines and facilities by Iraqi insurgents, Saudi Arabia stunned industry observers by giving a big gas-development contract to French Total instead of ExxonMobil. The Saudis, it seemed, were displaying their annoyance over U.S. behavior.[75]

The U.S. energy industry had given George W. Bush more money in 2000 than it had to all the previous 1992 and 1996 contenders combined because of the stakes and GOP responsiveness to the oil industry. But nothing about his career in the Texas oil industry suggested that he was a deep-thinking global strategist, a skepticism justified by the outcome of the 2003 invasion with respect to both Iraqi oil production (down) and global oil prices (up).

Despite the extent to which the fate of the U.S. dollar was also tied to the Iraqi oil showdown, and jeopardized by failure, it received little attention in the American mass media. A rare exception came shortly after the U.S. incursion, when *Newsweek* described the bad blood between American and European (French and German) policy makers in terms of currency and monetary rivalry. The real clash was not over weapons of mass destruction, wrote correspondent Howard Fineman, but over the dollar versus the euro—"who gets to sell—and buy—Iraqi oil, and what form of currency will be used to denominate the value of the sales. That decision, in turn, will help decide who controls Iraq, which in turn, will represent yet another skirmish in a growing global economic conflict."[76]

This, as noted earlier, was the third countdown. Major publications in Europe, much more candid, made frequent reference to the currency stakes, perceiving the U.S. dollar at loggerheads with the euro, in what the *Daily Telegraph* reported some observers calling "a global realignment stemming from the Iraq war, which threw Russia, Germany and France together into a new Triple Entente."[77] As we will see, Russian president Putin had already discussed pricing oil in euros, not dollars, with German chancellor Schroeder in 2002.

From the U.S. standpoint, Iraq by 2002 and 2003 was a rogue nation not just because of hidden weapons or attempts to undercut the United States in the oil arena but also because Saddam Hussein sought to unhorse the dollar in the global financial markets. Closely on the heels of the euro's 1999 introduction, Baghdad had started trading its oil for euros, not dollars, a policy that became official in late 2000. There are no records, but Cheney's reported early 2001 plotting against OPEC may well have touched on the related peril to the dollar. Indeed, shortly after Iraq was occupied, U.S. administrators put it back on the dollar standard for its oil transactions in June 2003. Moreover, had the hoped-for flooding of world markets by Iraqi production been able to weaken or break OPEC, that would simultaneously have undercut any chance that Iran, Venezuela, and Indonesia might convince the cartel to drop the dollar for the euro or a so-called basket of currencies.

Although the newly hatched European currency had lost ground against the dollar in 2000 and 2001 as rising U.S. interest rates drew foreign investors, the euro gained in late 2002 as U.S. rates fell and Washington mobilized against Iraq. Some currency analysts in Europe, however, preferred to credit OPEC members' antidollar machinations instead of the U.S. interest rate changes. Venezuela, for one, promoted barter arrangements instead of dollar transactions in selling its oil to Western Hemisphere nations, in response to the alleged 2002 U.S. coup attempt against Venezuelan president Hugo Chavez. Iran's central bank began shifting its reserves from dollars into euros.[78]

When in 2003 the U.S. takeover of Iraq bogged down in guerrilla warfare, attacks on oil installations, and escalating U.S. military casualties, those embarrassments spurred oil-related plans by some foreign nations to move into euros. Pertamina, the Indonesian state oil company, had announced that it was considering dropping the dollar even as the invasion occurred.[79] In June the prime minister of Malaysia publicly encouraged his country's oil and gas exporters to price in euros, while the Iranian central bank shifted more reserves and suggested to Asian traders that oil be paid for in euros.[80] Moreover, after encouragement by the European Union, Russian president Vladimir Putin announced, in a joint press conference with German chancellor Gerhard Schroeder, that Russia was considering selling its oil for euros.[81] Part 3 of this book, dealing with the U.S. debt and dollar predicaments, will extend and amplify the discussion of these challenges. For now, suffice it to say that in 2002 and 2003, dollar protection posed a serious problem. While the U.S. Navy could dominate the Persian Gulf or the waters off west Africa, its battleships were not free to train their sixteen-inch guns on foreign central banks.

Besides the oil-peak issue, U.S. oil company reserves, and the dollar's fate, the fourth endgame reflected climate-change fears ranging from sober to apocalyptic. Here environmentalists were beginning to see a countdown. The late-nineteenth-century West had suffered its own environmental fouling—the reeking smoke and haze of industrial Britain, the tons of horse manure dropped onto the streets of New York City and London. But the twentieth century, with its eightfold-greater consumption of hydrocarbons and thousands of new chemical syntheses, massively increased the atmosphere's carbon-dioxide content, which in turn trapped heat. One international response was the 1997 Kyoto Protocol, unacceptable to Congress and then the Bush administration because of the constraints it would have imposed on large-scale U.S. carbon-dioxide emissions, while leaving nations like India and China unaffected.[82] Climate change itself became a possible strategic and economic wild card, even though the 2003 report by the Defense Department's in-house think tank looking at a window of peril between 2010 and 2020 was dismissed by the

Bush administration. The constituency that elected the Bush regime all
but barred a serious response. Congressional Democrats had also doubted
Kyoto, but the Republican party's de facto hydrocarbon coalition gloried
in its SUVs and generally scoffed at switching to a conservationist or environmental mode. Even so, the entrenched petroleum and automotive interests of Houston and Detroit, as well as the combat-focused U.S. defense
industries, were relative sophisticates compared to the 30 or 40 percent of
the GOP electorate who believed in the inerrancy of the Bible.

By this point, the reader may find the notion of five countdowns hard
to follow. But the significance goes beyond the occasion of how oil geologists, "Big Oil" executives, currency watchers, climatologists, and evangelicals all had stopwatches ticking toward crises or great events, which
drove their biases and calculations. There is also the potential for an incendiary convergence if—a big if, to be sure—several of the worry-wart
camps prove to be correct. Geologists and investment bankers who
preach peak-oil timelines see per-barrel prices well above $100, and 2010
is a much-referenced date. As we will see in part 3, some who observe financial and currency markets see a speculative credit bubble, a housing
bubble, and $4 trillion of U.S. international indebtedness triggering a cri-
sis within much the same time frame. Particularly concerned climatologists talk about the 2010s. Federal-deficit watchers, in turn, cite the $30
trillion needed to fund the future of Medicare and the inability to be
completely sure of Social Security solvency past 2018. I can't remember
anything like this multiplicity of reasonably serious calculations and
warnings. It is as if the United States, like the poet Oliver Wendell
Holmes's "One-Hoss Shay," is about to lose all its wheels at once.

If one or two of the four are correct, major troubles lie ahead. True-
believing Christians, also convinced of a world entering the end times, at
least see a joyful ending for themselves, if not for everyone else. Lumped
together, these stressful time frames have to be taken somewhat seriously, even if most people would prefer not to put them all on one great
foreboding chart.

End-times prophecy fueled a fifth dynamic at work as the forces for
the Iraqi invasion gathered, because many Christian fundamentalists dismissed worries about oil or global warming out of belief that the end
times were under way. The Bible lands were what mattered. Events were
in God's hands. Even Senator James Inhofe, the Oklahoma fundamental-

ist chairing the Senate Environment and Public Works Committee, was reported saying, "I don't believe there is a single issue we deal with in government that hasn't been dealt with in the Scriptures," while declining to discuss his belief in the imminence of end times.[83]

Partly as a result, GOP political strategists had no desire for a far-reaching debate on either global warming or peak oil. The religious right had its own rapture chronometers and apocalypse monitors reporting how many months, days, and hours remained. Tom DeLay of Texas, the Republican majority leader in the House of Representatives and widely regarded as the most influential fundamentalist in Congress, had on his office wall a poster that read: "This could be the day."[84]

This true-believer endgame has been accelerating for many decades, especially since the creation of Israel satisfied the biblical prophecy of the Jewish return to Palestine. As we will see shortly, the growth during the 1970s, 1980s, and 1990s in the numbers of Protestant fundamentalists, evangelicals, and Pentecostals was explosive. Many became Republicans and helped to give the GOP an increasingly religious coloration. Although the stunning sales of the *Left Behind* series grabbed most of the cultural attention, other books and videos during the late nineties described how Saddam Hussein was rebuilding Babylon, the citadel of evil. Still others pondered whether the antichrist was already alive and who he might be. (Saddam himself was a frequent choice.) Nearly one-quarter of Americans polled in 2002 even believed that the Bible had predicted the events of September 11, 2001![85] While these beliefs were surely a factor in Republican invasion planning, they are difficult for politicians to acknowledge— and they are especially tricky to discuss publicly, so they are instead quietly promoted in clandestine briefings or loosely signaled by phrases and citations that reassure the attentive faithful.

The final chapters of this book will revisit the U.S. global overreach and the economic vulnerability writ large in White House willingness to remain aggressively but ineptly dependent on oil. The economic, military, and financial parallels between America today and previous leading world powers are eerie. However, we will first look at the evolution and politics of southern-dominated religious radicalism in the United States and then at the dangers that such excesses pose for America and the world.

Part II

TOO MANY PREACHERS

4

Radicalized Religion

As American as Apple Pie

Since at least 1776 the upstart sects have grown as the mainline American denominations have declined. And this trend continues unabated, as new upstarts continue to push to the fore.
— Roger Finke and Rodney Stark, *The Churching of America*, 1992

It is impossible to locate a period of American history when so-called small sects were not growing at a faster clip than denominations then viewed as large and stable.
— R. Laurence Moore, *Religious Outsiders and the Making of Americans*, 1986

The place of the United States as the world's only remaining superpower magnifies the importance of the Christian history of North America. The spread of American influence around the world has meant that American versions of the nature, purpose, and content of the Christian faith have also spread widely.
— Mark A. Noll, *The Old Religion in a New World*, 2002

FEW QUESTIONS WILL BE MORE IMPORTANT TO THE TWENTY-FIRST-CENTURY United States than whether renascent religion and its accompanying political hubris will be carried on the nation's books as an asset or as a liability. While sermons and rhetoric propounding American exceptionalism proclaim religiosity an asset, a somber array of historical precedents— the pitfalls of imperial Christian overreach from Rome to Britain—tip the scales toward liability.

Christianity in the United States, especially Protestantism, has always had an evangelical—which is to say, missionary—and frequently a radical or combative streak. Some message has always had to be preached, punched, or proselytized. Once in a while that excitability has been economic—most notably in the case of the Social Gospel of the 1890s, which searched through Scripture to document the Jesus who emphasized caring for the poor and hungry. In the twentieth century, though, religious zeal in the United States usually focused on something quite different: individual pursuit of salvation through spiritual rebirth, often in circumstances of sect-driven millenarian countdowns to the so-called end times and an awaited return of Christ. These beliefs have often been accompanied by great revivals; emotionalism; eccentricities of quaking, shaking, and speaking in tongues; characterization of the Bible as inerrant; and wild-eyed invocation of dubious prophecies in the Book of Revelation. No other contemporary Western nation shares this religious intensity and its concomitant proclamation that Americans are God's chosen people and nation. George W. Bush has averred this belief on many occasions.

In its recent practice, the radical side of U.S. religion has embraced cultural antimodernism, war hawkishness, Armageddon prophecy, and in the case of conservative fundamentalists, a demand for governments by literal biblical interpretation. In the 1800s, religious historians generally minimized the sectarian thrust of religious excess, but recent years have brought more candor. The evangelical, fundamentalist, sectarian, and radical threads of American religion are being proclaimed openly and analyzed widely, even though bluntness is frequently muted by a pseudo-tolerance, the polite reluctance to criticize another's religion. However given the wider thrust of religion's claims on public life, this hesitance falls somewhere between unfortunate and dangerous. Charles Kimball, a North Carolina Baptist and professor of religion, speaks very much to the point: "Although many of us have been taught it is not polite to discuss religion and politics in public, we must quickly unlearn that lesson. Our collective failure to challenge presuppositions, think anew, and openly debate central religious concerns affecting society is a recipe for disaster."[1]

Still, the challenge is gathering. Academic projects that spotlight the resurgence of religious fundamentalism around the world now routinely include the United States, along with India, Israel, and many Islamic countries. Scholars have always touched on "militantly anti-modernist Protestant evangelicalism," but there is a renewed focus.[2] Some moderate-to-liberal theologians have begun to challenge half-baked preaching about the rapture and the end times as "a toxin endangering the health—even the life—of the Christian churches and American society."[3] Suburban megachurches, in turn, find themselves explained as offering the spiritual equivalent of a shopping mall: would you like psychic healing today, Hindu breathing exercises, or just a little observant mood music?[4] Ultimately, the larger political resurgence of historically controversial religiosity is what demands attention.

Evangelical, fundamentalist, and Pentecostal denominations began the new millennium verging on juggernaut status. To the surprise of some observers, the sectarianism and fragmentation of American Christianity remained as visible at the turn of the twenty-first century as they had been one hundred years earlier. A consensus on this development is taking shape, as we will see. The old mainline churches have been culturally and institutionally displaced by a new plurality; yesteryear's supposed fringes are taking over American Protestantism's main square.

Documentation is far from perfect, and statistics can be as misleading or obscure in this realm as in any other. The half dozen or so periodic religious surveys, membership directories, and atlases of religion published in the United States are useful but incomplete, in part because of the unwillingness of many small and midsized denominations to participate in religious samplings. The *Atlas of Religious Change in America, 1952–1990* begins with several pages to explain its methodologies and omissions. In a nutshell, only 80 to 85 percent of religious adherents were included because scores of churches, mostly white conservative or black, did not cooperate or submitted unsatisfactory data.[5] Fully presenting them would only enlarge the biblical and conservative predominance.

In contrast to the secular and often agnostic Christianity dominant in Europe, Canada, and Australia, the American view encompasses a very different outlook—one in which a large minority is in key ways closer to the intensity of seventeenth-century Puritans, Presbyterian Covenanters, and earlier Dutch or Swiss Calvinists. As we will see, these are not comforting analogies. The world's leading economic and military power is

FIGURE 1

The American People: A Biblical Worldview

The Bible—A Literal Truth[a]

Is the Bible literally accurate?

National sample: Yes, 55%
Evangelical Protestants: Yes, 83%
Non-evangelical Protestants: Yes, 47%
Catholics: Yes, 45%

Christianity: In What Do You Personally Believe?

	Newsweek *Poll,* 2000	*Gallup Poll,* 2004	*Fox News Poll,* 2004
God	94%	80%	92%
Miracles	84	—	82
Heaven	—	81	85
Angels	—	78	78
Hell	—	77	78
Satan/the Devil	75	70	70

Belief in Highlights of the Bible[b]

Are these descriptions literally true?

Noah's Ark: Yes, 60%
God's creation of earth in six days: Yes, 61%
God parting the Red Sea for Moses: Yes, 64%

The Book of Revelation and the Coming of Armageddon

Will events in the Book of Revelation occur sometime in the future or not?[c]

All Christians: Yes, 59%; no, 33%
Born-again, fundamentalist and evangelical categories:
Yes, 77%; no, 15%

Will the world end in an Armageddon battle between Jesus Christ and the Antichrist?[d]

All Christians: Yes, 45%; no, 39%
Evangelical Protestants: Yes, 71%; no, 18%
Other Protestants: Yes, 28%; no, 54%
Catholics: Yes, 18%; no, 57%

---

[a] Source: *Newsweek* Poll, December 2004.
[b] Source: *ABC Prime Time* Poll, February 16, 2004.
[c] Source: CNN/*Time*, 2002.
[d] Source: *Newsweek*, October 1999.

also—no one can misread the data—the world's leading Bible-reading crusader state, immersed in an Old Testament of stern prophets and bloody Middle Eastern battlefields.

There is, to be sure, a large and growing secular culture in the United States. Among northern university graduates and cultural elites, it is dominant—stronger by far than that of the biblical and salvationist contingent. However, the Republican coalition and administration of George W. Bush is heavily weighted toward the 30 to 40 percent of the electorate caught up in Scripture and the prospect of being suddenly transported to God's side. This is enough to push the United States toward what chapter 6 will posit as a national Disenlightenment. Indeed, American foreign policy has its own corollary to the end-times worldview: the preemptive righteousness of a biblical nation become a high-technology, gospel-spreading superpower.

Figure 1 details several of the most striking public faces of this extraordinary American belief system. Against this backdrop, Christianity's unusual evolution in North America does indeed merit more attention, as religious historians such as Mark Noll contend, than sophisticated elites in London, Paris, Beijing, or New Delhi—or for that matter in New York, Washington, and Los Angeles—have so far extended. While American religious tendencies toward parochialism and moral or political crusades mattered little in 1890, 1914, or even during the Cold War, they take on much greater importance now as Christian, Jewish, and Muslim holy lands occupy absolute center stage in world politics and as sites of military confrontation.

The idea of the United States as a biblically spurred great power, which has been framed by historians such as Walter McDougall in *Promised Land, Crusader State* (1997), has had unforeseen relevance to the Bush administration and cannot be cavalierly dismissed.[6] Historically, great powers have too often gone out in blazes of religious invocation. The newly Christian fourth-century Rome of the emperor Constantine and his successors held up the cross as Rome faced military defeat and crumbling frontiers from Hadrian's Wall to Assyria. So did seventeenth-century Spain, the proud but ill-omened command post of the Catholic Counter Reformation. Vestments of crusaderdom also cloaked imperial Britain's overreach in World War I and its aftermath. Those uncomfortable precedents will be elaborated upon in later chapters. First, however, we will take on the prominence and many flavors of religious radicalism in the United States, truly as American as apple pie.

The Sect-Driven Dynamic of American Religion

Part of the unusual sectarian quality of U.S. Protestantism derives from its cultural parentage. Britain, itself once a biblical nation convinced it was God's chosen one, was unlike other European powers in a willingness to populate the American colonies with Scripture-reading religious dissenters. The resultant flow from Britain and Europe helped to stamp the North American colonies as a religious refuge—for English and Welsh Puritans, Baptists, and Quakers, Scottish and Scotch-Irish Presbyterians, Jews from many parts of Europe, French Huguenots, and a myriad of German speakers fleeing continental wars: Moravians, Palatines, Amish, Mennonites, Anabaptists, Dunkers, and Salzburgers. Especially in the middle colonies, New York and Pennsylvania, the result was a population that exhibited the religiosity of refugee faith across a kaleidoscope of denominations and sects. Following independence, this all but mandated tolerance and ruled out any official church in these states. Only relatively homogeneous New England kept official Congregational churches in three states: Connecticut, Massachusetts, and New Hampshire.

While many foreign visitors commented on this national trait—high religiosity and tolerance seemingly buoying each other—fewer remarked on a related belief pattern. With choice of worship permitted, late-eighteenth- and early-nineteenth-century American Protestants, among the world's most Bible-reading, flocked to the sort of individualist and anti-hierarchical faith that emphasized a personal relationship with God. This made them responsive to pioneering evangelists such as English visitor George Whitefield during the so-called Great Awakening of the 1740s and to others during the Second Great Awakening of the early 1800s.

Periodic revivalism, in turn, fed a still-resonant exodus of Americans from established churches that had given up emotion for respectability, turning instead to movements or sects that emphasized salvation, spirituality, physical displays, founders' claims to special revelation (Mormons, for example), faith healing, and "holiness upon the land." Over the years, new waves of fervor, zeal, and agitation—from quakes, shakes, and jerks to millennial watch keeping and speaking in tongues—have sparked almost continuous cultural and behavioral comment from domestic and foreign observers. In one of the latest nontraditional evolutions, "third wave" Pentecostalism, hundreds of churches have replaced organ music with guitars, drums, and synthesizers, some adding unusual new forms of personal expression and spiritualism.

Mark Noll, one of America's foremost religious historians, in 2002 wrote the book *The Old Religion in a New World,* explaining the differences in Christianity in Europe and in North America. The major divergences go to the heart of what is unusual about American religion. As might be expected, the United States has a superabundance of denominations and sects compared to Europe, as well as a far higher ratio of churchgoers. By one count, the United States in 1996 had 19 separate Presbyterian denominations, 32 Lutheran, 36 Methodist, 37 Episcopal or Anglican, 60 Baptist, and 241 Pentecostal.[7] Globalization and immigration have added to the proliferation in surprising ways. In *A New Religious America* (2001), Diana Eck pointed out that Muslims in America outnumber Presbyterians or Episcopalians, and that Los Angeles is the most varietal Buddhist city in the world.[8] Each Sunday the *Los Angeles Times* publishes a directory of services that includes more than six hundred denominations.

To add to the complexity, theological crosscurrents are sapping the old denominations and making their labels less meaningful. In Noll's words, "free-flowing Pentecostal and charismatic styles will go on spreading their influence far beyond the explicitly Pentecostal churches. The most important Christian schisms will increasingly follow theological-ideological lines rather than denominational lines. Especially as the historic Catholic-Protestant chasm continues to narrow, Christians will be linked to fellow believers from other denominations according to shared convictions."[9] Examples of this emerging transdenominationalism include the growth of the new suburban megachurches—some boasting congregations of ten to fifteen thousand—and the post-Pentecostal networks of Calvary Chapels and the Association of Vineyard Churches.

Also to the point, U.S. Protestantism uniquely abounds with what Noll terms "populist innovations," or forms of worship developed by laypeople. One is the widespread American embrace of "dispensational premillennialism"—a fervor launched in the nineteenth century around biblical passages interpreted to signal the second coming of Christ. A second, Pentecostalism, is based on the "latter rain" of revival in the Holy Spirit prophesied in Joel 2:23. To Pentecostals the defining sign of an individual's possession by the Holy Spirit is the gift of tongues—the ability to utter words and sentences intelligible only to God and those with the gift of interpretation.[10] Noll acknowledges that "neither dispensationalism nor Pentecostalism has ever appeared respectable in academic environs, but each has attracted far more adherents and driven far more practical religious activity than any academically respectable theology of the twentieth century."[11] Although survey results vary, some 7 to 10 percent of U.S. churchgoers appear to be Pentecostals, and perhaps a quarter of churchgoers are full-fledged end-times believers, as opposed to the 50 percent or so who relate to the symbolism when holy wars or tsunamis dominate the news.[12]

Conversion on the part of adults—the deep personal experience of being "born again" in Christ—is also far more important in the United States, with its emphasis on individual choice and personal experience, than elsewhere.[13] In the mid-1980s some 33 percent of respondents told the Gallup Poll they had been "born again"; by the early 2000s the number had climbed to 44 to 46 percent.[14] George W. Bush's own tale of coming to God struck a chord in the churchgoing United States that would have been impossible in less-observant Europe. Even in kindred Canada, supposedly no prime minister has ever claimed to be born again.[15]

Likewise notably American is the pervasive influence of the Bible, from the first English migrations a staple of belief and interpretation. Bible publishing in the new republic quickly became an industry—some 1,800 different English-language editions were published between 1777 and 1865—and remains one today, with more than seven thousand editions available as of 1990.[16] National attentiveness to Scripture, in turn, helps to explain the unusual popular commitment to biblical inerrancy, prophecy, and the supposed end times. A related topic, the recurrent conflict between religiosity and science, reflects how much American thinking has been steeped in both. Tensions between the Book of Genesis and Darwinian theories of evolution, brought to a theatrical and political head in 1925 in Tennessee's famous Scopes trial, still throb. "The result," concludes Noll, "has been a much greater salience in America concerning evolution and 'creation science' than in any other Western society."[17]

Sociologists Rodney Stark and Roger Finke, in their pioneering study *The Churching of America, 1776–1990,* provide a revealing explanation of America's religious idiosyncrasies. The religious history of the United States, they say, rests heavily on sectarian emotion and revival—a process under way since the eighteenth century, in which churches become establishmentarian, "compromise their 'errand into the wilderness' and then . . . lose their organizational vigor, eventually to be replaced by less worldly groups, whereupon the process is repeated."[18]

Even by the time of the American Revolution the old colonial elite denominations—Congregationalists in New England, Quakers in Pennsylvania, and Anglicans from Chesapeake Bay and to the south—were in places being challenged or overtaken by upstart Baptists and Scotch-Irish Presbyterians. By 1850 revival-minded Methodists and Baptists, with their itinerant preachers, circuit riders, and camp meetings, ranked first and second nationally. By the early twentieth century Baptists had pulled ahead, with Pentecostal, charismatic, "restorationist," holiness, and other sects gaining traction. The colonial-era elite denominations kept slipping down the list, holding ever smaller ratios of U.S. worshippers.

By the end of the twentieth century, the fundamentalist-leaning Southern Baptist Convention, wedded to biblical inerrancy, was by far the largest Protestant group. Indeed, as we will see in greater detail, the SBC, together with other once-peripheral sects, boasted some forty million adherents versus a combined fifteen million members of the four leading mainline churches (Methodist, Episcopal, Presbyterian, and Church of Christ Congregational).[19] Like Stark and Finke, historian Noll observed that "previously marginal groups have become larger and more important, while previously central denominations have moved toward the margins. . . . The Protestant bodies whose rates of growth in recent decades have exceeded general population increases—sometimes far exceeded—are nearly all characterized by such labels as Bible-believing, born again, conservative, evangelical, fundamentalist, holiness, Pentecostal, or restorationist."[20]

While avoiding judgmental descriptions, Stark and Finke did insist on "the primary feature of our religious history: the mainline bodies are always headed for the sideline."[21] Sectarianism keeps claiming center stage, reinforcing or reinventing the radical aspects of American religion.

The Ever-Expanding American Revival Tent

As the twenty-first century began, none of the western countries in which Reformation Protestantism bred its radical or anarchic sects nearly five hundred years earlier—England, Scotland, Germany, Switzerland, and the Netherlands—still had congregations of any great magnitude adhering to that theology. Even sympathetic commentators have described church attendance in England with phrases such as "catastrophic decline," and a recent survey of students at Belgium's ancient Catholic University in Louvain found only 16 percent crediting the resurrection of Christ and a mere 3 percent believing in the infallibility of the Pope.[22] The United States, religiously inspired and settled by some of those same radical Protestant sects in the 1600s and early 1700s, took a different course. Its religious revivals keep coming, now jumping from rural tents to the electronic podiums of televangelism.

At the close of the American Revolution, which began with only 15 to 20 percent of the population regularly attending church, Anglicans, Quakers, and even politically victorious New England Congregationalists found their strongholds besieged by Baptists and Methodists. Inspired by democratic rhetoric and opportunity, the insurgent denominations found the late 1780s and 1790s a fruitful time for promoting personal salvation and harvesting souls. In contrast to the staid services and educated clergy of the established denominations, Baptists and Methodists shared practices and techniques especially successful in remote or frontier areas—reliance on part-time or itinerant preachers who had little formal education and received minimal pay and, most of all, revivals and camp meetings.

It is an exaggeration to think of this as a largely American behavioral innovation. Princeton's Leigh Schmidt and other religious historians have located important roots in the seventeenth- and eighteenth-century Presbyterian "holy fairs" that developed in the southwest of Scotland and then in nearby northern Ireland. Sometimes involving many thousands of worshippers, these outdoor events were marked by swaying, crying, swooning, and the like—mockingly caricatured by the famous Robert Burns and others. Being much in the minds of Scottish and Scotch-Irish settlers in North America, their memories helped to inspire the similar revivals and camp meetings along the Appalachian frontier.

But if the Scottish ancestry is clear, the enthusiasm and lack of restraint does seem to have been greater in the New World. New physical ecstasies joined "Quaker" and "Shaker" in the religious lexicon. One Methodist recalled that "while I was preaching, the power of God fell on the assembly, and there was an awful shaking among the dry bones. Several fell on the floor and cried for mercy."[23] Cane Ridge, Kentucky, where on one evening in August 1801 twenty thousand sobbed, shrieked, and shouted themselves into near hysteria, gained particular fame as a revival ground. Between 1800 and 1850 the western half of New York became known as "the burned-over district" because of the emotional inflammations there that matched the searing heat of forest fires.[24]

Both evangelical insurgencies saw their flocks multiply. Between 1776 and 1806 Methodist ranks in the United States increased by 2,500 percent—from 4,900 adherents to 130,000—while Baptist membership ballooned from 35,000 in 1784 to 173,000 in 1810.[25] By 1850 populist outreach had made Methodists the largest U.S denomination, with 2.7 million members, the Baptists placing second, with 1.6 million.[26] Successful American Protestantism proselytized with an evangelical accent.

For both churches the burgeoning South (including the southern-settled Ohio Valley) had emerged as their principal center of gravity.[27] Nevertheless, before the Baptists and Methodists could make evangelical religion dominant below the Mason-Dixon Line, they had to—and did—shed notions that were perceived as radical, such as opposition to slavery and enmity to social hierarchies, as well as their early emphasis on self-revelation and church fellowship, which in some localities had been deemed harmful to family bonds. As one recent historian of the Bible Belt has pointed out, this meant "altering, often drastically, many earlier evangelical teachings and practices concerning the proper roles of men and women, old and young, white and black, as well as their positions on the relationship between . . . Christianity and other forms of supernaturalism. As a result, evangelism looked much different in the 1830s than it had in the 1790s."[28] In some poor, low-slaveholding areas, white dissidents did break away into minor sects.

Especially in the North, well-educated, established clergy often deplored the emotionalism, physical displays, and lack of erudition among the Baptists and Methodists. Those churches, said Connecticut Congregationalist Lyman Beecher, were "worse than nothing."[29] Critics also harped on the prurient incitements when baptism involved total immersion of girls wearing flimsy shifts, and they disparaged the liquor often sold in proximity to camp meetings. Barton Stone, later a famous evangelist, candidly described the "bodily agitations" seen at the Cane Ridge revivals of the early 1800s. They included "falling" (often with a piercing shriek), "the jerks" (often of the head), "dancing" (as an extension of the jerks), and "barking" (as an accompaniment to the jerks).[30] While opponents frequently exaggerated this behavior, they were hardly making it up.

Comparable insults had been leveled in the 1740s, when old-line Virginia Anglicans and New England Congregationalist leaders blistered evangelists like George Whitefield for emotionalism, enthusiasm, and threat to good order. Even so, the first half of the nineteenth century introduced a range of new denominations that made Baptists and Methodists look sedate.

The frontier-centered restorationist movement—by some also called "primitivism"—sought to recapture the pure, unencumbered Christianity of the New Testament by stripping away the imported corruptions of European ecclesiastical authority and practice. Labels such as Lutheran, Anglican, or Baptist—for that matter, even the term "reverend"—were to be cast aside. During the 1830s the several groups of dissidents cohered as the simply named Christian Church but later split into three separate networks—confusingly named the Churches of Christ, the Christian Churches, and the Christian Church, Disciples of Christ. Accepting no more than a bare-bones institutional framework, the three became significant sects in the upper South and Ohio Valley states during the decades before the Civil War.[31]

Greater flamboyance marked two other new sects, both enlivened by founders' claims of special divine revelation. After the failure of predictions by William Miller, a self-educated farmer from upstate New York, that Christ would return in 1843 and then 1844, elements of his following were reorganized by associates. They claimed that the return had indeed taken place, but only as a spiritual (and invisible) passage into the presence of the father.[32] A full return was still to come. One founder, Ellen White, claimed to have had a personal vision of creation. The Seventh Day Adventists, as they became known in 1860, worshiped on Saturday, kept awaiting the advent, and emphasized dietary practices that pioneered the role of grains as cold cereal. They, too, thrived and grew to count one million members in the United States by 2000.

Most provocative of all was the emergence of the Mormon faith in the 1820s under the messianic leadership of Joseph Smith, another New Yorker. In 1830 he published *The Book of Mormon,* explaining how God had prevailed on Christopher Columbus "to venture across the sea to the promised land, to open it for a new race of free men." Revelations to Smith by the angel Moroni told how the future United States had been occupied many years before Christ by several Hebraic peoples: the Lamanites (an ancestors of the American Indians) and the Nephrites. Mormon himself, the father of Moroni, was a Nephrite who recorded the story of his tribe on gold plates.[33] The New Jerusalem would be in America, and when Jesus returned it would be to the area near Independence, Missouri. No shrinking violet, Smith announced in 1844 that he was running for president. With his popularity as worrisome to the respectable as his beliefs—an early example of the political threat of populist religion—Smith was jailed in Illinois and then shot while incarcerated.

The Mormons had embraced polygamy, authorized by a revelation to Smith, while honoring both the Christian Bible and *The Book of Mormon.* After Smith was killed, they left their major settlement in Nauvoo, Illinois, and followed new leader Brigham Young west to Utah, establishing their New Israel around the Great Salt Lake, the River Jordan, and Utah Lake, a grouping that resembled an upside-down map of the biblical Galilee-Jordan–Dead Sea region. A century and a half later, more or less (but not entirely) shorn of polygamy, the Mormon religion dominated Utah and Idaho and constituted an influential regional force in six adjacent states. From under fifty thousand in 1850, the Mormon population of the United States expanded to 1.1 million in 1950 and 5 million in 2000.[34] In most surveys, however, Mormonism is still categorized as not quite Christian and not quite Protestant.

Jehovah's Witnesses were yet another of the militant denominations assembled in the nineteenth century to await a second coming. Founder Charles Russell, who rejected the doctrine of the trinity, proclaimed that Christ had returned to earth invisibly in 1874 preparatory to establishing a full presence. The cataclysm or advent was predicted for 1914. Over the years, Witnesses refused to serve in the military, vote, hold office, or salute the American flag, calling such practices the province of the antichrist.[35] As with the upsurge of the Seventh Day Adventists, part of the Witnesses' twentieth-century growth was international, resulting from missionary activities. In the United States alone, nearly one million witnessed the millennium.

Evangelism of the more prosaic sort also accelerated after the Civil War. This time, though, Methodism—now the nation's largest denomination, embracing a middle-class mind-set and edging away from earlier Wesleyan intensity—had become a religious establishment to be raided. The holiness movement, which had pre–Civil War roots, advocated a return to Methodist founder John Wesley's striving for Christian perfection as a gift of the Holy Spirit. As Methodism boasted more costly church buildings, seminaries, and a plentitude of bishops, breakaway movements proliferated. They included the Indiana-based Church of God in 1881, the Christian and Missionary Alliance in 1887, the Church of the Nazarene in 1895, and the Church of God in Christ in 1897.[36] Poaching-minded holiness preachers called on "all true holiness Christians to come out of Methodism's church of mammon."[37]

In the nineteenth century, as we have seen, religious historians tended to minimize fragmentation and downplay the sects. They preferred to emphasize eventual and ultimate Christian unity (and the fulfillment of America's divine mission). In his 1986 book *Religious Outsiders and the Making of Americans,* Cornell University's R. Laurence Moore explained that historians writing in the 1840s and 1850s also wanted to support the separation of church and state, in New England still politically controversial. (Massachusetts, the last New England state to disestablish Congregationalism, did so in 1837.) To that end, they argued that sectarianism had not run wild and that "many churches existed in America, but only a few were significant."[38]

That tenuous hope could still be justified during Methodism's mid-nineteenth-century heyday, but not for much longer. Too many Protestants, lacking priests to assure them of forgiveness, searched for God's grace in personal experience. By the 1890s holiness Methodists were defecting from their old church. Baptists were overtaking and passing Methodists in the South and overtook them in the nation as a whole around 1906.[39] As the twentieth century got under way, not only were the holiness churches thriving, but fundamentalism and Pentecostalism were beginning their own ascents. Mainline Protestantism fell behind the revival-minded denominations by World War I, if the restorationist and holiness churches are counted alongside the Baptists. However, religious historians of that era, mainline Protestants, were not eager to give them such credence and position. Moore quotes one respected chronicler, William W. Sweet, whose *Story of Religion in America* became a standard text in 1930, ridiculing the sects while matter-of-factly describing the recruits of the "great Protestant churches" as "sane Christians."[40]

Sociologists Stark and Finke, for their part, employed a new technique in their statistical trail blazing. Disregarding the actual head counts of individual churches—numbers that usually rose as population increased—they introduced a comparative calculus: the rise or fall of each denomination's share of the total sum of religious adherents in the United States. Middling membership gains, they argued, often disguised a relative decline. These mathematics shone a more negative light on the appeal of the established churches while spotlighting insurgent developments. For example, between 1776 and 1850 the Congregationalists dropped from 20.4 percent of all religious adherents to just 4.0 percent, and the Episcopalians from 15.7 percent to 3.5 percent, while the Methodists soared from 2.5 percent to a peak 34.2 percent.[41] Then between 1850 and 1980, in a different statistical format, the Methodists fell from 117 adherents per one thousand population to 74, a relative decline even though actual Methodist numbers rose over those 130 years.[42] Few of Stark and Finke's predecessors or colleagues swung such an iconoclastic ax, and so the rise of extreme sects was slow to be recognized.

Another explanation why the early-twentieth-century strides of the holiness, fundamentalist, and Pentecostal groups escaped emphasis for so long hangs on these unfashionable elements' much publicized embarrassment during the 1920s. Press and public mockery swelled after the evolution-centered 1925 Scopes trial, the foolish 1924 attempt of the Presbytery of Philadelphia to bring modernist Harry Emerson Fosdick to trial for heresy, and the 1927 publication of *Elmer Gantry*, novelist Sinclair Lewis's scathing portrait of a corrupt revivalist. As the fundamentalists reeled, pundits employed dismissive characterizations such as "split and stricken," saying such movements had "lost any semblance of unity or collective force."[43]

According to Calvin College historian Joel Carpenter in his book *Revive Us Again: The Reawakening of American Fundamentalism*, after "fundamentalism's fall from respect in the late 1920s," inward-turning adherents used the thirties and forties to "consolidate an institutional network, and rethink their mission to America," using Bible institutes, fellowships, and radio gospel hours.[44] As for Pentecostals, they were even more withdrawn civically. Their "journals that appeared between the early 1930s and the late 1940s, years of a catastrophic depression and war, [gave] no sense that events took place in the world other than the wonder working, soul-saving miracles of the Holy Ghost."[45]

Small wonder, then, that most observers, naturally unaware of what trends the late twentieth century would confront, glossed over any indications of mainline Protestant weakness—its public and social authority during the twenties remained unchallenged—and saw little future for primitive fundamentalism and revivalism. In fact, though, the actual statistics of the World War I years and the 1920s document their gains, not a retreat. Between 1916 and 1926, according to Stark and Finke, the Presbyterians (USA), Congregationalists, and Methodists retired or closed down a significant percentage of their denominations' individual churches. Yet during that same period unfashionable sects were recording huge expansions of churches: a 656 percent rise for the holiness Churches of Christ, 577 percent for the Church of the Nazarene, 553 percent for the Assemblies of God, and 442 percent for the Tennessee-based Church of God.[46]

Noll, too, concluded that "during the first half of the twentieth century, the fragmentation of Protestantism meant that the nation's historically most potent religious force became a declining influence in the nation as a whole."[47] He argued that "the 1930s marked the beginning of the relative decline of the older, mainline Protestant churches." Meanwhile, despite any lingering negative imagery, "for fundamentalist, holiness, Pentecostal, African American, and the new-evangelical churches and organizations, it was a time of expansion. The Southern Baptist Convention, the holiness Church of the Nazarene, the Pentecostal Assemblies of God, and the main black Baptist denominations all grew rapidly during this period."[48]

Acceptance of this thesis has been solidifying: sects up, mainline down. Carpenter also agrees that the religious crisis during this period was only among the "older or more prestigious denominations," some of which lost membership, baptisms, and revenues. At the same time, "fundamentalists' missions and ministries grew, Southern Baptists gained almost 1.5 million members between 1926 and 1940, and the pentecostal denomination the Assemblies of God quadrupled."[49] During the 1930s,

moreover, the middle-class Northern Baptist Convention and the Presbyterians (USA) were split by a fundamentalist exodus that launched new
conservative denominations: the General Association of Regular Baptist
Churches (1932), the Presbyterian Church of America (1936), and the
Bible Presbyterian Church (1937).[50] These multiple citations buttress a
different interpretation than the received wisdom: that evangelical, fundamentalist, and Pentecostal religion, far from evaporating or stagnating
in a backwater during the early twentieth century, seem to have been a
gathering force, like an incoming tide. No wonder the much-reported revival captained by the youthful Billy Graham in 1949–1950 could surprise
with such unexpected attendance—and bring in its wake a further conservative momentum throughout the sixties and seventies. An important
piece of missing U.S. religious history seems to be slowly, albeit belatedly,
reappearing.

By this point the reader may feel baptized by statistical and denominational total immersion. However, there is no other way to lay out the
foundations, crossbeams, and buttresses of the unusual American religious
structure that led to the rise of the religious right and to the related transformation of national politics, the consequences of which we face today.

By the 1950s even the mainstream media perceived the implications of
Billy Graham's fulsome public reception. A graduate of Wheaton College
in Illinois, the Harvard of American evangelicalism, Graham had roots in
born-again, biblically inerrant, premillennial Protestant fundamentalism.
His achievement, first in southern California, and then in bringing fifty
thousand listeners to Boston Common in January 1950, where the great
evangelist Whitefield had drawn twenty thousand or so in 1740, gave his
contemporaries pause about the real meaning of the supposed rout during the cynical 1920s.[51] Graham himself was wise enough to duck any
fundamentalist tag, embracing ecumenicalism and preferring the unelaborated label "evangelist."

In retrospect, the apparent seamlessness of holiness, fundamentalist,
and Pentecostal expansion from the 1880s and 1890s through Graham's
Christian crusade should focus our questions about the rise of today's influential sects. The mismeasurement after the twenties is not the only
one. We should be more broadly skeptical about the labeling of the several so-called great awakenings, which start to look less like sudden erup-
tions than high points in ongoing momentum. Based on the data now

available, the twentieth century saw sectarian gains and surges to match those of the eighteenth and nineteenth. Indeed, Stark and Finke match up the reasonably continuous revivalist tendencies of the public with a more or less steady rise in the percentage of Americans who stated some religious adherence—from 17 percent in 1776 to 34 percent in 1850 to 45 percent in 1890, 56 percent in 1926, 62 percent in 1980, and 63 percent in 2000.[52] Neither historical calculus has been seriously rebutted, although their calculation of religious adherents does not represent one uniform statistical series, and the new figure for 2000 is controversial.

A bit more history is in order to grasp the twentieth-century emergence of the fundamentalists. We have seen how the century began with the Baptists pulling ahead of the Methodists as the largest Protestant denomination. By one account, the impetus that became fundamentalism "began in the last quarter of the nineteenth century as an interdenominational revivalist network that formed around the era's greatest evangelist, Dwight L. Moody. This movement drew most of its constituents from the generally Calvinist wing of American Protestantism."[53] At this point, it was more northern than southern.

Between 1910 and 1915 Moody's conservative successors, alarmed at the growth of liberal theology and secular spirit, published a series of booklets called "The Fundamentals." These most basic of the basics, all beyond compromise, included an intense focus on evangelicalism; the need for an infilling of the Holy Spirit after conversion; belief in the imminent second coming of Christ; and the absolute, inerrant authority of the Bible.[54] In 1919 the hard-liners promoted the formation of the World's Christian Fundamentals Association, and in 1920 the new antimodernist faction was given the name "fundamentalist" by Curtis Lee Laws, editor of the Baptist paper *The Watchman-Examiner*.[55] To some religious historians, the rise of fundamentalism from the 1920s through the 1960s is now seen as the period's most dynamic and influential U.S. evangelical impulse.[56]

Joel Carpenter, in his profile of fundamentalism during those years, cites the interpretations of two principal authorities, Ernest Sandeen and George Marsden, that fundamentalism had serious roots in nineteenth-century religious ideas and so could not be dismissed as simply a revolt against modernism.[57] Of course, roots in nineteenth-century sectarianism, itself born amid the dislocating modernism of steamboats, railroads, and the telegraph, are not necessarily very different.

Pentecostalism, the faith many religious historians identify as Protestantism's late-twentieth-century populist innovation, emerged out of the late nineteenth-century holiness movement, updated in the sectarian pressure cooker of early 1900s California. It caught hold in the 1910s and 1920s, abetted by preachers in the black community and then by the flamboyant Aimee Semple McPherson, radio personality and founder of the International Church of the Foursquare Gospel, another fringe sect that has since climbed much higher in membership. McPherson, who sometimes rode a motorcycle down the aisle of her Los Angeles temple, thrived on publicity and even claimed to have been kidnapped in 1926 when she was actually hiding out with a new lover.[58] Like Baptism in its early form, Pentecostalism did not thrive by being respectable.

The movement's distinguishing characteristic, the practice of speaking in tongues, took its name from the New Testament. During the biblical celebration of Pentecost, when "the Holy Spirit descended in power upon the apostolic worshipers, one manifestation of that power was that those present 'began to speak in other tongues as the Spirit gave them utterance.'"[59] Today, only people with the "gift" could understand words and sentences of godly derivation that otherwise seem babbling and unintelligible. As with early southern evangelicalism, Pentecostalism, in order to take hold, was obliged to ease its initial egalitarianism and interracialism and become more acceptable to middle-class and commercial society.[60] Like the Baptists in the South, however, it prospered from some perceived moderation. Economic conservatives often warm to sects in which a preoccupation with personal salvation turns lower-income persons away from distracting visions of economic and social reform.

To return to the mainstream, observers have long identified the tumultuous 1960s as the decade when the mainline Protestant denominations declined, partly by taking cultural and political positions on war, society, and civil disobedience that were too liberal for their congregations. Religiously, though, the decade of Vietnam and Woodstock seems to have been less of a watershed than assumed. By the calculations of Stark and Finke, between 1940 and 1985 mainline Protestantism's share of all U.S. religious adherents was steadily plummeting. The largest group, the United Methodists, dropped from 124.7 adherents per thousand total church members in 1940 to 93.0 in 1960 and to just 64.3 in 1985. For the Presbyterians (USA), the simultaneous decline was from

41.7 to 36.4 to 21.3, while the Episcopalian fall was from 30.9 to 28.6 to
19.2. Meanwhile, the United Church of Christ (Congregationalists) slid
from 26.5 to 19.6 to 11.8. In mid-twentieth-century cultural and political
terms, these denominations, seats of relative theological centrism, had
been home to a disproportionate share of the nation's college graduates,
business elites, and elected national officeholders. Changes in theological
dominance thus proved to be harbingers of broader political and societal
changes.

The ascendant Southern Baptists, during the same period, climbed
from 76.7 adherents per thousand total church members in 1940 to 85.0
in 1960 and to 101.3 in 1985. The Pentecostal Assemblies of God vaulted
from 3.1 in 1940 to 4.4 in 1960 and to 14.6 in 1985.[61] These, in the 1940s
and 1950s, were national outsider denominations, found more often
in unfashionable locales than in wealthy ones. Nonestablishment Protestantism were moving to the fore.

Wheaton's Noll dates the gathering mainline slump from the thirties
but acknowledges that "the public turmoil of the 1960s accelerated that
decline."[62] For the nearly four-decade period between 1960 and 1997—
and taking denominational mergers into account—the Presbyterian
Church, the Episcopal Church, the United Church of Christ (including
the Congregationalists), and the Methodists lost between 500,000 and
2 million members each, the last being the Methodist slippage.[63] In the
meantime, the Southern Baptist Convention added 6 million, the Mormons
3.3 million, the Pentecostal Assemblies of God 2 million, and the Church
of God (Tennessee) some 600,000.[64] The direction in these several tabulations is clear: the sectarian gains race across the decades like an express
train, another hint of the changes to come.

Taken together, Starke and Finke, Noll, and Carpenter concur that in
recent decades American Protestantism, through itself slowly ebbing in
relative adherence, has increasingly leaned toward the Pentecostal and
charismatic movements and churches.[65] The two categories are hardly
monolithic. The more numerous Pentecostals of the older Assemblies of
God are fundamentalist and Scripture-minded, epitomized by former attorney general John Ashcroft, who on being sworn into office also had
himself anointed with cooking oil in the biblical manner of King David.
A nondancer and disbeliever in frivolity, Ashcroft, on becoming attorney

general, covered the bare breast of the Justice Department's large statue of the Spirit of Justice.

In a vivid contrast, the small but fast-growing Vineyard Churches and Calvary Chapels—California-born, charismatic, and third wave—mix informality, unchurchly language, and soft-rock music with what skeptics call the "spiritual smorgasbord" of charismatic experience from physical healing to speaking in tongues. Their story has been told sympathetically in *Reinventing American Protestantism: Christianity in the New Millennium.*[66] However, critics have noted that the "holy laughter" cultivated in some Vineyard churches can degenerate. In 1995 the Toronto Airport Vineyard Church was booted out of the Association of Vineyard Churches for allowing it to include animal noises—barking like dogs, oinking like pigs, roaring like lions, and so forth.[67] Some sociologists assert that elements of West Coast Pentecostalism, very much a minority nationally, have made a liberalizing cultural accommodation to the loose and mellow Pacific Coast culture—a so-called Californication of conservative Protestantism.[68]

By a careful synthesis of polling results, we can affirm that "about one in four Americans (or 25 percent) are now affiliated with a church from this network of conservative Protestant churches (that is, fundamentalist, evangelical, holiness, or Pentecostal). Not quite one in six (around 15 percent) are affiliated with the older denominations that used to be called the Protestant mainline."[69] Still, the conservative ratio may be understated by leaving out America's million Mormons and million Jehovah's Witnesses, and perhaps also by pegging Pentecostals at a cautious ten million adults rather than in the sometimes suggested twenty-million range. On the other hand, the so-called third wave may be misplaced in the conservative category.

This is no abstract inquiry. The fundamentalist, evangelical, and sectarian head count helps to explain the poll findings in figure 1 of such widespread popular belief in matters ranging from biblical inerrancy to the imminence of the end times. The national population does appear to be more sectarian and movement driven, with a lower proportion of mainline Christians and fewer secular nonbelievers than common wisdom has assumed.

Because these pages are principally concerned with the radicalization of U.S. Protestantism, they touch only lightly on overlapping phenomena within American Catholicism. However, Noll and Stark and Finke see the church of Rome as caught by some of the same trends that have sapped the mainline Protestant denominations, principally inroads by charismatic movements, widespread nonattendance, and rising losses to Pentecostalism. The Roman Catholic Church claims some sixty million members, but only half are frequent churchgoers. The sharp decline from 1965 to 1990 in church ability to recruit priests, nuns, and seminarians in the United States has been charted from the *Official Catholic Directory* by Stark and Finke. From 10.6 enrollments in seminaries for every ten thousand U.S. Catholics in 1965, the number plummeted to 1.1 in 1990.[70]

Until the last generation or two, their argument goes, the Catholic Church in the United States was an amalgam of outsider ethnic factions and parishes—Irish, Italian, French, Serbian, Polish, Hungarian, et al. For this reason Catholicism as an institution behaved more like a group of sects than an established church. Outsider psychologies and distinctive ethnic nationalisms were supporting pillars for the church, not debilitating weaknesses. As these were lost, and as the U.S. Catholic hierarchy followed the papacy's Vatican II liberalizations in the 1960s—ending masses held in Latin, voiding the prohibitions against eating meat on Fridays, removing impediments to Protestant-Catholic marriages, promoting Christian unity—the old Catholic hold weakened. Not everyone agrees, but Stark and Finke cite these changes to explain why, between 1964 and 1978, the percentage of U.S. Catholics regularly attending services dropped from 71 percent to 50 percent.[71]

Although Stark and Finke do not hypothesize the "Protestantization" of American Catholicism, they do promote an analogy between weakening faiths.[72] Because Catholics can marry non-Catholics, can set foot in other churches, and can miss mass without thereby committing a sin, less is being demanded of them, and less loyalty is being returned. As with Protestants, more decision making and interpretation is being left to individuals and consciences. Many Catholic organizations and universities have measurably secularized. Pentecostal and other Protestant inroads among Hispanic Catholics have been described by theologian Andrew Greeley as an "ecclesiastic failure of unprecedented proportions," trends that lead Stark and Finke to doubt that "the American Catholic Church will be able to halt its transformation from an energetic [nineteenth-century] sect into a sedate mainline body."[73]

The point here is less to survey the various denominations—in examining the GOP electorate, we will revisit aspects of their size, ideology, and political geography from several perspectives—than to sketch the revival-prone sectarian and radical side of American religion. Its increasing presence is breeding a politics of cultural narrowness, moral and biblical bickering, revivalism in the White House, and international warfare to spread the gospel, fulfill the Book of Revelation, or both. Yet far from being a sudden national departure, religion's powerful role in U.S. politics and warfare goes back to the seventeenth century.

Religion, Politics, and War

We can begin by describing the role of religion in American politics and war with two words: *widely underestimated.*

To be sure, forces that once impelled twentieth-century sophisticates and academicians to minimize the role played by religion—Marxist economics, scientific modernism, market determinism, Enlightenment fashion, secular humanism, and dismissive sociology—are giving ground. The resurgence of faith is too clear, not least in Islamic, Christian, and Jewish fundamentalism. Pentecostalism is turning parts of Latin America into "burned over" districts like that in New York in the nineteenth century. Dismissals of worship as the mere opium of the people are today running up against hypotheses that humankind may have something like a "God gene" that breeds religious impulses.[74]

From colonial days to the present, war and politics in the United States have borne a heavy imprint of church leadership and denominationalism, the latter frequently overlapping with racial, regional, and ethnic self-identifications. Economics has been subordinate in this basic framework, more of a separate cross-hatching that becomes increasingly important during downturns and panics. My own research into U.S. voting patterns over five decades beginning in the mid-1950s turned up regional, racial, ethnic, and religious factors as the most frequent and best explanations of why State A or County A differed from State B or County B. To find out how people in a particular neighborhood or apartment building in New York City, for example, were likely to vote, your first question should be ethno-religious: are the residents Irish, Jewish, black, white Anglo-Saxon Protestant, or what? Incomes would tell you less. In Greenville, South Carolina, especially in a Republican primary, you would want to identify various Protestant evangelical, fundamentalist, and separatist factions. Despite its importance, religion remained an underappreciated factor in U.S. politics well into the 1960s.

To suggest the depth of religion's political influence, an examination of the historical and political dynamics of the three principal civil wars among English-speaking peoples—the English Revolution of the 1640s, the American Revolution, and the 1861–1865 War Between the States—will show religion as a major factor, often the decisive one, in how individuals and communities chose sides.* Moreover, in these cases the clergy were commonly among the most prominent drumbeaters. This involvement has also been documented in less significant combats—notably, the War of 1812 and the Spanish-American War—and in the two U.S. military engagements in Iraq. Unfortunately, relatively few Americans know what to watch for. Ignorance is not bliss.

So, too, for religion's role in electoral patterns. In 1990, Oxford University Press published *Religion and American Politics,* a volume that assembled distinguished contributors. Its purpose was trenchantly described in a chapter by editor Mark Noll and contributor Lyman Kellstadt: "Social scientists studying twentieth-century politics have assumed, until quite recently, that religion in America is a private affair of little public influence. From this assumption, the conclusion followed that it was not worth studying religion with the same care that sociologists and political scientists devoted to race, income, education and other important social variables. Scholarship on nineteenth-century America should have shaken these assumptions, but it took the surge of the Religious Right to alert academics to the continuing salience of religion in political life."[75]

Consider: America's founding event, the Revolution, was in many ways a religious war, reiterating some of the cleavages found 130 years earlier in the English Civil War. Two major religious denominations, Congregationalist and Presbyterian, furnished the highest ratios of patriots in 1776, just as their antecedent groups had been leaders on the parlia-

---

*This subject is treated at length in my book *The Cousins' Wars: Religion, Politics, and the Triumph of Anglo-America* (New York: Basic Books, 1999).

mentary side in the England of the 1640s. Meanwhile, colonial parishioners of the Church of England—Anglicans then, Episcopalians now—divided in fair measure along high church–low church lines. High Anglicans, especially in New England, New York, and New Jersey, supported the Crown, as their forebears had in 1642. Low-church Anglicans—the Enlightenment-oriented vestrymen planters of Virginia and the Carolinas who read John Locke and wanted bishops in America no more than Massachusetts Puritans did—supported the Revolution.[76]

Much more supporting detail exists, as well as the inevitable exceptions. Suffice it to say that when Federalist and Jeffersonian political-party lines began to emerge in the late 1790s, religious divisions again bulked large. The depleted ranks of Anglicans joined New England Congregationalists on the conservative (Federalist) side, whereas the anti-ecclesiastical Baptists of the southern backcountry were ardent Jeffersonians.

In *Religion and the American Civil War,* another useful volume, Randall Miller, Harry Stout, and Charles Wilson waited barely a page into their introduction before instructing that "the United States was the world's most Christian nation in 1861 and became even more so by the end of the war. In the late 1830s, Alexis de Tocqueville had remarked on the pervasive influence of religion on American private and public life, and swelled by revivals during the 1830s and again during the 1850s, membership in churches rose dramatically."[77] During the 1830s and 1840s, when U.S. national politics matched Democrats against Whigs, religious divisions were central enough that most denominations could be assigned to one camp or the other.[78] Religious cleavages remained central when the Republican party replaced the Whigs in the mid-1850s.

Organized amid the slavery crisis, the Republican party enjoyed lopsided support from members of those northern Protestant churches that took strong antislavery positions and also from free blacks in states where they could vote. Before and after the War Between the States, the Democrats could count on the southern churches that defended slavery and split away from their national organizations. That party also commanded usual majorities among members of the two major faiths—Catholic and Lutheran (particularly Missouri Synod)—that took no position on slavery. With some variations, these divisions lasted into the 1890s.

So clear was the religious imprint that historian James McPherson argued in the 1990s that "because the American Civil War was not a war of religion, historians have tended to overlook the degree to which it was a religious war. Union and Confederate soldiers alike were heirs of the Second Great Awakening. Civil War armies were, arguably, the most religious in American history."[79] Indeed, as we will see, the major Protestant denominations split along geographic lines before the nation as a whole did along political ones. And in the case of the Confederate flag–waving Southern Baptist Convention, the consequences of that separation still resonate.

By most criteria the cleavage of U.S. politics left by the Civil War lasted through World War II, only beginning to shift in the 1940s and 1950s. During these transitional years, one could still cite the old alignments in religious divisions. Mainline Protestantism was Republican and centered in the small-town and suburban North. Catholics clustered in ethnic and industrial areas and voted Democratic disproportionately. Members of black churches usually couldn't vote in the South and rarely had much influence in the North. Southern white Baptists and sects were still heavily Democratic, especially in local elections.

Over the four decades beginning in the 1960s, new alignments slowly emerged in which religion played a new kind of central role, as chapters 5 and 6 will pursue. In the 1990s pollster George Gallup stated that "religious affiliation remains one of the most accurate and least-appreciated political indicators available."[80] By 2004, as religiosity became the key to how Americans voted for president, USA Today led off a lengthy analysis by labeling the "religion gap" as the clearest divide in U.S. politics.[81]

However, with religion also playing so much of a role in the 2002–2003 buildup to the U.S. invasion of Iraq, in which George W. Bush proclaimed America's commitment to upholding liberty and freedom, it is well to note important antecedents: among Anglo-American Protestants these twin threads of justification for wars hark back to the Reformation. As detailed in The Cousins' Wars, these themes can be traced from the English Civil War through the American Revolution to the American Civil War, but they always applied to internal freedoms and jeopardies. That U.S. Protestant theology has now refocused itself on the biblical holy lands as a battleground is just another of the extraordinary transformations taking place on account of the influence of religion on American politics and war.

American Self-Perceptions of Being a Chosen People and Nation

This national self-importance is no secret, at home or abroad. For centuries Americans have believed themselves special, a people and nation chosen by God to play a unique and even redemptive role in the world. Elected leaders tend to proselytize and promote this exceptionalism—presidential inaugural addresses are a frequent venue—without appending the necessary historical cautions. Previous nations whose leaders and people believed much the same thing wound up deeply disillusioned, as when Spanish armadas were destroyed while flying holy banners at their mastheads, and when World War I German belt buckles proclaiming "Gott Mit Uns" became objects of derision in the Kaiser's defeated army.

Millennial prophecies have fared no better. They conspicuously failed in the fourth century, at the millennium in 1000, amid the tumult of the medieval Crusades, during the savage seventeenth-century European religious wars, in prerevolutionary New England, in the U.S. Civil War period, during World War I, and in 2000. In consequence, believers have time and time again had to work out elaborate explanations for why Jesus did not appear, why premillennial claims had not been borne out. Books and videos detailing and amplifying these relentless embarrassments and disappointments —as far as I know, few such exist—might offer a useful counterpoint to the end-times and second-coming materials marketed in such profusion by current fundamentalist drummers.

Subsequent chapters will return to the high stakes of contemporary religious politics. However, one corollary—the importance of supposed biblical covenants with God in shaping self-perceived national identities as a New Israel—must be raised here. The relevance is that such peoples tend to be zealous, driven by history—risky leadership for a great power. The pertinence of this self-image to the United States is visible from the first settlements through the nineteenth century, drawing upon the importance the public attached to Scripture. The South, as we will see, long ago passed New England as the region most caught up in manifest destiny and covenanted relationships with God. It has become the banner region of American exceptionalism, with no small admixture of southern (they'd prefer a capital "S") exceptionalism.

Identification of the English colonies in North America as a New

Israel enthused not only John Winthrop in New England but the earlier settlers of Virginia. Seventeen years before Winthrop set down the Puritan covenant with the God of Israel on board the *Arbella* en route to Massachusetts in 1630, Anglican clergyman Alexander Whitaker, a founder of Virginia's Jamestown, penned "Good Newes from Virginia." It assured Protestant England that "fortie yeares were expired before Israel could plant in Canaan, and yet God had called them by the word of his mouth, had led them himself by an high hand. Yet may you boldly look for a shorter time of reward."[82]

Besides the British Isles, the post-Reformation geography of the New Israel aspiration also included the Puritan and Calvinist Netherlands. The embattled Protestant city-states elsewhere on the continent were all too small to think nationally—and we are talking about national psychologies. To historian Simon Schama, a specialist in both Britain and the Dutch Republic, the latter's "Hebraic analogy" was weightier than the former's "Puritan Zion-Albion." With vivid description, he envisions how "every Sunday (at least) a cascade of rhetoric would crash down from the pulpit, invoking the destiny of the Hebrews as though the congregation were itself a tribe of Israel. Lines dividing history and scripture dissolved as the meaning of Dutch independence and power was attributed to the providential selection of a new people to be as a light unto the nations. In this Netherlandish addendum to the Old Testament, the United Provinces featured as the new Zion, Philip II [who sent the Spanish Armada] as a king of Assyria and William the Silent [the Dutch liberator] as a godly captain of Judah."[83]

Anthony Smith, professor of ethnicity and nationalism at the London School of Economics, in *Chosen Peoples: Sacred Sources of National Identity*, agrees in limiting this post-Reformation syndrome in Europe to the British Isles and the Netherlands.[84] Outside Europe, he includes the United States, Afrikaner (Dutch) South Africa, and the latter-day Zionist reprise of ancient Israel.[85] A third scholar, Canadian historian Donald Akenson, in *God's Peoples*, concentrates on the force of covenant and land in South Africa, Israel, and Ulster.[86]

We should note a coincidence—or is it one? The three Protestant "Hebraic analogy" and covenanting cultures—Dutch, British, and then American—just happened to produce the three successive leading world economic powers of the seventeenth through twenty-first centuries. All opened their doors to religious refugees and their commercial skills— Protestant French Huguenots and Flemings, as well as Jews—an inflow that fertilized local economies and reinforced already strong national interests in the holy lands. Obviously, claiming covenant has been a potent self-conception. If any unusual lobby has guided Dutch, British, and U.S. attentions, clergy and readers of Scripture must have been in the van.

The disseminating nations were England, Scotland, and Holland. The Boers of colonial South Africa, in turn, drew on the seventeenth-century Dutch Reformed psychologies explained by Schama, which were reconfigured by nineteenth- and twentieth-century geography and events. The 1834–1838 Great Trek took the Boers away from the British-ruled Cape of Good Hope and northward to independence in the soon-to-be Orange Free State and Transvaal. This exodus, to Smith, "became the central myth and epic of later generations of Afrikaans-speakers, particularly among adherents of the Dutch Reformed Church. The wanderings of the Boers from British oppression to the freedom of a promised land on the high veldt echoed, indeed re-enacted, it seemed, the biblical story of the deliverance of the Israelites from Egypt. Just as the Lord had saved the Israelites from Pharaoh's hosts, and from Midianites and Amalekites, and caused them to cross the Jordan, so had he miraculously delivered the Boer *voortrekkers* from danger and defeat at the hands of the British imperialists, and the Ndebele and Zulu warriors."[87] The "covenant" made in 1838 was celebrated, repeated, and commemorated by Afrikanerdom at various later dates—1864, 1881, 1903, 1910, 1938, and so on. That renewal has lapsed, to be sure, because of the collapse of South Africa's white politics and apartheid regime beginning in the late 1980s.

Historic Ulster, the onetime Irish province now embattled Northern Ireland, took its Protestant Calvinism and covenanting memory from Scottish settlers who crossed the Irish Sea to settle there during the seventeenth and early eighteenth centuries. In Ulster, these Scotch-Irish, as they were later named in America, fought indigenous Irish Catholics with the same Old Testament self-congratulation that the Dutch marshaled against their Spanish occupiers and the Boers directed against both nearby Zulu tribesmen and would-be British colonial rulers. Harking back to

Scottish Presbyterian national covenants in 1557, 1590, 1638, and 1643, as well as to the Scotch-Irish triumph of 1689–1690, the Ulstermen, too, became a people driven by sacred memory and biblical analogy.

In Akenson's words, "On 23 September 1912, more than 218,000 men—virtually the entire adult male Protestant population of Ulster—signed 'Ulster's Solemn League and Covenant.' This Ulster covenant was modeled on a Scottish Presbyterian original of the late sixteenth century which, in its turn, took its doctrine of the reciprocal responsibilities of God and a righteous civil polity directly from the Hebrew scriptures."[88] In 1969 British troops were again deployed on Ulster streets, and the bloody sectarian conflict they have since policed, recently fading, has diminished the perception of Ulster as a militant Protestant polity based on Hebrew Scripture.

The reason for spotlighting history's relative handful of covenanting cultures is the biblical attitudes their people invariably share: religious intensity, insecure history, and willingness to sign up with an Old Testament god of war for protection. To use a modern-day analogy, these are proud, driven peoples, not ones who would find it easy to get risk insurance. Besides comparing the Boer, Ulster, and Hebrew covenanting mentalities and histories, Akenson finds other parallels in their shared Old Testament moralities of tribal purity and sacred territoriality. The reasons for the elaboration in these pages have less to do with Ulster and South Africa and more to do with the United States and particularly the South. Israelis and, to an extent, Scripture-reading Americans are on their ways to being the last peoples of the covenant.

Some of the attendant psychologies involved may be cause for worry. Akenson brushes by comparisons between South Africa and the American South or between the Ulster Scots and their cousins below the Mason-Dixon Line. In footnotes, however, he lists several such studies.[89] Smith diplomatically confines his American promised-land and chosen-people discussions to nineteenth-century art—the grandiose "Promised Land-scapes," he calls them, of Thomas Cole and Albert Bierstadt.[90]

By contrast, in 1971 Conrad Cherry, later the director of the Center for the Study of Religion and American Culture, grappled with the American self-perception head-on in his book *God's New Israel: Religious Interpretations of American Destiny*. Time after time, images from the Bible have been used to translate bits of American history into scriptural challenges and analogies: a grateful nation hailing George Washington as the American Moses (or Joshua); the 1776 portrait of King George III as Pharaoh in his chariot; and the no-longer-downtrodden South of 1876 claiming "redemption" from northern (read: Egyptian) occupation and Reconstruction. We might even add the image building circa 2002 of Saddam Hussein as another Nebuchadnezzar and Baghdad as the second Babylon. As chapter 7 will show, religious allies of the Bush administration voiced these and other scriptural analogies.

To Cherry, the American Revolution and the Civil War were the principal revelatory building blocks: "The first was a moment when God delivered the colonies from Pharaoh Britain and the 'evils' of the Old World, revealed the purposes of the nation, and adopted the Young Republic as an example and instrument of freedom and republican government for the rest of the world. The Civil War was the nation's first real 'time of testing' when God tried the permanence of the Union or, in some interpretations, brought judgment upon his wayward people."[91] Blended with American exceptionalism, subsequent variations of this national self-assuredness have transcended church or creed. "Beheld from the angle of governing mythology," says Cherry, "the history of the American civil religion is a history of the conviction that the American people are God's New Israel, his newly chosen people. The belief that America has been elected by God for a special destiny in the world has been the focus of American sacred ceremonies, the inaugural addresses of our presidents, the sacred scriptures of the civil religion. It has been so pervasive a motif in the national life that the word 'belief' does not really capture the dynamic role that it has played for the American people, for it passed into the 'realm of motivational myths.'"[92]

Indeed, as religion extends its sway over U.S. politics, "theology" may be the better word. To be sure, the contemporary United States hardly claims the covenant relationship with God that Israel still does, and which remained real to the Afrikaners and Ulster Protestants well into the late twentieth century. Still, Puritan and then Congregationalist New England did so up through the Revolution, and even the men from Scotch-Irish towns in revolutionary Pennsylvania and the Carolinas marched off to fight the British in 1776 with the memories of covenanting Scottish and Scotch-Irish Presbyterian forebears in their minds.[93] The Mormons in the American West of the 1840s and 1850s likewise immersed themselves in self-proclaimed chosen nationhood. Utah was colonized as New Zion, and July 23, the date of Mormon entry into the promised land, became their principal holiday and their occasion for celebrating their own exodus and triumph.[94]

More to the point, as the next chapter will amplify, the New Israel Protestantism established by Yankee New England generations earlier passed, figuratively at least, to the true-believing South during the Civil War era. Religion thrived and intermingled with a new history. After the Confederacy's defeat, southern churchmen routinely sermonized that God had chastened his beloved South between 1861 and 1865 but had not abandoned it. Suffering as the South did under Reconstruction, ministers argued, could be redemptive. Thus, when the last Yankee troops withdrew from the South in 1877, in the wake of considerable northern popular disenchantment, God was proclaimed to have kept faith with a South that had kept the covenant. Dixie's victorious white conservative politicians were duly named "Redeemers."

One southern historian has further enlarged the analogy: "The New South promoters reveled in the Resurrection story. The South, paralleling Jesus, had risen from the dead of Reconstruction to the living Redemption. The southern economy could sustain that story and repeat it again and again. As Virginian Philip Alexander Bruce wrote in 1905, the story of the New South is 'a vital narration of the progress of a mighty people, who, from adversity which as no other section of North America has ever experienced,' had risen and 'won the race with adverse fate and become the pride of the Union.'"[95]

Such boasts from southern nationalists in 1905 were romantic fiction. The North had the power and pride of victory. A century later, however—after great religious and political transformation in both the South and the nation as a whole—the evidence of ascending southern political and religious influence is substantial. From presidential-election dominance to military adventurism and Southern Baptist expansion to become the leading U.S. Protestant denomination, more Dixie ambitions have been fulfilled than any Confederate war veterans' convention could ever have contemplated. And as W. J. Cash wrote in The Mind of the South, that region is "not quite a nation within a nation, but the next thing to it."[96]

The outlook that Israel, Ulster, and South Africa supposedly had in common—the sense of a biblical nationhood bathed in blood and tribulation—closely resembles the scriptural fidelity and religious nationalism forged by the South but too little understood beyond its bounds. This mentality now has an unprecedented influence in the United States as a whole. Well may Americans—and the rest of the world—ponder what William Faulkner said about the land of his birth: "The past is never dead. It's not even past."

5

Defeat and Resurrection
The Southernization of America

There is a war going on here. It is an ancient conflict, as war and time go in this country. The Civil War is like a ghost that has not yet made its peace and roams the land seeking solace, retribution, or vindication. It continues to exist, an event without temporal boundaries, an interminable struggle that has generated perhaps as many casualties since its alleged end in 1865 as during the four preceding years when armies clashed on the battlefield. For the society that became the South after 1865—and, truly, one could not speak of a distinct South before that time—the Civil War and the Reconstruction that followed shaped the form it takes today.

—David Goldfield, *Still Fighting the Civil War:*
The American South and Southern History, 2002

The primary duty of southern ministers and editors in 1865 and 1866 was to convince themselves and their congregations that God had not deserted the South: the righteousness of the southern cause, the Justice of God, and Confederate dead could and would be reconciled. Even before the war ended, some ministers were developing a framework within which they could accommodate both the assurance of God's continued favor and the military defeat of the South.

—Daniel W. Stowell, *Rebuilding Zion: The Religious Reconstruction*
of the South, 1863–1877, 1998

In the twentieth century, with the SBC becoming the largest Protestant denomination in the United States, it became increasingly apparent that white southerners had lost the war but won their peace.

—Paul Harvey, *Redeeming the South,* 1997

NO LONGER CAN AMERICANS DISCUSS THE BATTLE OF GETTYSBURG AS THE high-water mark of southern advance and ambition. Over the last quarter century, the onetime Confederacy has seen the population center of the United States march southwest across Missouri toward the Arkansas state line. This while the expansion-minded Southern Baptist Convention made itself into one of the top four denominations in a dozen *northern* states. A born-again Texan, in turn, became the first U.S. president to be hailed by Gary Bauer, Ralph Reed, and other Dixie-flavored Christian-right stalwarts as that movement's national leader. Even Gettysburg has been rewritten as a Confederate victory by the pen of a former Republican Speaker of the House from Georgia turned historical novelist.[1] From the Pentagon to Congress and the White House, the South, more than the North, speaks with the voice and carries the insignia of national command.

In the weeks after the 2004 presidential election, a redrawn map of North America circulated on the Internet, prompting wry amusement along the northern rim of states that had opposed George W. Bush. The various Canadian provinces, joined by the regions that had voted for John Kerry, were renamed the United States of Canada. To the south, the pro-Bush states congregated in another new geopolitical entity: Jesusland.

It was in fun, but not entirely, given the ratio of persons in California, in Connecticut, and on Cape Cod who had enlivened summer and pre-election parties with remarks about attractive real estate in Vancouver or hints of relocation to Nova Scotia in the event of a Bush victory. Among geographic divisions in the United States, after all, the religious and political chasms between greater New England and the South rank as the oldest and deepest. Under cultural pressure, these stress lines frequently reappear—as in 1775–1776, 1814, 1860–1861, 1968–1972, and 2000–2004.

Indeed, the 2004 contest marked a historic electoral first: never before had all nine northeastern states—Maine, New Hampshire, Vermont, Massachusetts, Rhode Island, Connecticut, New York, New Jersey, and Pennsylvania—voted against the winning presidential candidate. Resentment ran high. For all that flippancy about a second civil war reeked of convenient hyperbole, the sectional tension was familiar enough.

The North-South Axis of American Cultural Conflict

To colonial officials in Oliver Cromwell's London, the cultural polarization in America would have been visible enough. The Puritans and Pilgrims of New England supported Parliament in the English Civil War, while the two plantation colonies to the south, Maryland and Virginia, took the king's side. This now all-but-forgotten split was the forerunner of many others.

Several generations ago, the cleavage was dismissed as a myth, a pre–Civil War striving by both North and South to find deep-seated antecedents for reemerging mutual disdain. In 1961, as society in the television-era United States supposedly moved toward homogenization and smoothed its regional disparities, the notion of remote divisions over the English Civil War was described as "fictional sociology" by historian William R. Taylor in his study *Cavalier and Yankee*.[2]

Alas, for today's riven America, that cultural requiem turned out to be sounded prematurely. For one thing, the South's sectional consciousness was resurging by the last half of the twentieth century, not fading. For another, scholars began to mine newly accessible resources for evidence of seventeenth- and eighteenth-century regional rivalry and awareness. Far from being geopolitical fiction, the Cavalier/Roundhead divisions were heartfelt: hundreds of men from Massachusetts and Connecticut sailed back to England in the 1640s to fight on the Puritan side against Charles I, while Royalist Virginia welcomed Cavalier emigrés and expelled its Puritans. Fighting took place in the colonies themselves as well. In 1655 Anglican-Catholic forces in Maryland were defeated by Puritan foes at the battle of the Severn near Annapolis, Maryland.[3]

A century later, persisting distrust almost undercut the American Revolution. Archival gleanings from the 1775–1777 squabbling inside Congress, within the military, and over the Articles of Confederation establish the geography. The Second Continental Congress had "sectional prejudice running from North to South as well as from South to North. While John Adams castigated southerners for their alleged fear of New England's 'Designs of Independency—An American Republic—Presbyterian Principles—and twenty other things,' he nevertheless admitted his own 'local Attachment . . . hardness . . . Prejudice in favour of New England . . . [where] the People are purer English Blood less mixed with Scotch, Irish, Dutch, French, Swedish than any other.'" According to one historian, "Southern fears of northern domination were strengthened by suggestions that Congress move northward from Philadelphia. The distrust ran so deep in 1775 that some at least considered the creation of 'two grand Republics' by Congress—one southern and one northern—as a real possibility."[4]

Fear mingled with dislike. In 1777 Edward Rutledge of South Carolina objected to the first draft of the Articles of Confederation because its terms would subordinate the South to "the Government of the Eastern [New England] Provinces."[5] A decade later, negotiation of the federal Constitution nearly failed because of bipolar rivalry. Some participants doubted that the South and North could ever work out a union. Alexander Hamilton opined that if a split came, New York and Pennsylvania would be drawn to each other and then to New England. James Monroe, in turn, worried that if Pennsylvania took the northern side in a split, proximity to the new border would endanger his home state of Virginia.[6]

From the constitutional deliberations of 1787, James Madison distilled a political essence: "The great danger to our general government is the great southern and northern interests on the continent, being opposed to each other. . . . [T]he states were divided into different interests [at the Constitutional Convention] not by their difference of size, but by other circumstances; the most material of which resulted partly from climate, but principally from the effects of their having or not having slaves."[7] Hamilton appended other occupational differences: northerners were more commercial and "navigating," southerners more agrarian and equestrian.

To explain southern distinctiveness, latter-day scholars have dissected federal census data for the 1790–1860 period. Three-quarters of the pre-1845 New England population was of lowland English extraction, while some three-quarters of the white southerners hailed from Britain's Celtic fringe—Scotland, Ireland, Wales, and Cornwall—or from the kindred uplands of northern and western England. These disparate origins, the argument went, explained much of the culture—unlearned, hot-blooded, combative, warlike—prevalent below the Mason-Dixon Line.[8] Frank Owsley, in his well-known *Plain Folk of the Old South,* argued that these distinctions made the southern people "a genuine folk long before the Civil War."[9]

While not everyone accepts the thesis, it has some merit. North Carolina sociologist John Shelton Reed has ventured a related explanation. To him, southerners are a "quasi-ethnic group"—indeed, Reed wrote the "Southerners" entry in the *Harvard Encyclopedia of American Ethnic Groups*. Thus, in his view, "the South remains as much a sociological phenomenon as a geographical one," with a strong separate, historically shaped identity.[10] According to Reed's measurements, anti-South sentiment in the United States is greatest among New Englanders, which is fitting. Persisting animosities between the two regions have sparked secession movements on *both* sides.

Keeping in mind that the South rather than the "eastern" or New England states controlled the youthful federal government between 1800 and 1824, the first actual grousing about possible secession had a nasal Yankee twang. Even as colonies, the New England areas had periodically been grouped together—in John Winthrop's New England Confederation of 1643 and again in the short-lived Dominion of New England ordered by London in 1686. After Virginian Thomas Jefferson succeeded John Adams of Massachusetts as president in 1801, separatism became a semipublic conversation in Hartford and Boston. By 1804 regional politicians led by Massachusetts senator Timothy Pickering talked of a northern confederacy that would include the New England states, New York, and New Jersey.[11]

War with Britain in 1812, crippling to New England commerce, rekindled enough sectional tension that Jefferson wrote to Adams in 1813—the two ex-presidents were now friends and correspondents—that "rivalry between Massachusetts and Virginia had the makings of a civil war, 'a La Vendée.'" Virginia was agricultural; Massachusetts depended on its exposed maritime economy. In late 1814 New Englanders gathered at the Hartford Convention to mull separatism and other antisouthern measures—inept and embarrassing timing because General Andrew Jackson was about to ignite war-related public euphoria by defeating a British invasion at the battle of New Orleans. As late as 1820 President James Monroe worried that Senator Rufus King of New York, one of the few Federalists still in office, hoped to lead a confederation of that state and New England.[12]

The Missouri Compromise of 1820, however, allowed Maine to enter the Union as a free state while Missouri joined as a slave state, maintaining the critical North-South balance in the U.S. Senate and the Electoral College and refocusing the political centrality of slavery. Some early-nineteenth-century observers, idealizing the rapid rise of the trans-

Appalachian new West, pictured it transcending and chastening the old Atlantic seacoast division so visible since 1787. However, that turned out to be a cultural mirage, just as the more observant founding fathers had feared. Jefferson, Madison, Monroe, Charles Pinckney, and others all foresaw that fights over new states would unfold around electoral balance and the geography of slavery.[13]

Between 1787 and 1848 westward movement from the old South filled in population as far as Missouri, Arkansas, and Texas (with a southward leg into Florida), while Yankees, whose great emigration awaited canals and railroads, reached Michigan, Iowa, and Wisconsin. The contest between the North and South to populate their western hinterlands engendered political jockeying over new state admissions. This persisted until the Mexican War ended, and California's admission as a free state in 1850 tipped the balance. No more plausible territories for slave states remained.

By then, southern leaders, seeing the predominantly northern handwriting on the westbound railroad tickets, understood their imperative to look farther afield—adding Cuba, say, or three or four states in northern Mexico. Less plausibly, they could open up the territories of Kansas and Nebraska (under the act of 1854) to "popular sovereignty," workable only if enough proslavery men could move in. Ambitions south of the border lingered through the late 1850s. The two U.S. senators from Mississippi, Jefferson Davis and Albert Gallatin Brown, openly pointed to Cuba and the Mexican states of Yucatán, San Luis Potosí, and Tamaulipas.[14]

When these alternatives stalled or unraveled in the late 1850s, secession or confrontation grew more likely. This Cook's tour of North-South rivalry should underscore why the political, religious, and cultural mobilizations preparatory to open combat in 1861 were steeped in such acrimony. Long-standing frustrations, hopes, and disdains were coming to a head. Among them, as we will see, were specific religious concerns, including divergent interpretations of what the Bible said about slavery. These helped to precipitate the Civil War, then infused its conduct on both sides with righteousness, a quality reheated after 1865 across a South subjected to military-backed Reconstruction. With little exaggeration, these vitriolic clashes of scriptural interpretation and denominational fratricide could be called a Hidden Civil War.

Most historians agree that the accumulated prewar, wartime, and

Reconstruction enmities polarized sectional memories, and with particular bitterness in the South. Because the intensities involved may ring false at first reading, multiple descriptions seem in order. To Samuel S. Hill, editor of *The Encyclopedia of Religion in the South,* the South's response "is singular in American history, religious and otherwise, and is seen quite clearly in its religious life. A region became a culture, constructively and defensively, creatively and reactively. . . . Many interpreters of southern history have penetrated the subject of the mythic South to tell us that 'the South' is a function of the Civil War and its aftermath more than it is of the antebellum period. 'The Confederacy became immortal' is the way that Robert Penn Warren expressed it."[15]

To North Carolina historian David Goldfield in *Still Fighting the Civil War,* "it is this continuing historical consciousness, particularly how southerners have interpreted the Civil War and Reconstruction and then implemented that vision, that has set the South apart from the rest of the nation, though not apart from the world."[16] Paul Harvey, a historian of southern religion, explained how "white southerners after the war created their own civil religion, featuring its own theology, myths, rituals and saints. . . . According to the tenets of Lost Cause theology, God's chosen people (white southerners) had been baptized in the blood of suffering and thus had been chastened and purified."[17]

To sharpen regional sentiment, southerners for generations used every opportunity and locale—from cemeteries, pulpits, and war memorials to parades and Confederate veterans' events—to promote their interpretation-cum-theology. Confederate memorials and statues spread even across border states that had sent more men to the northern armies that to the southern.[18] Memory itself became a battlefield.

Ever vigilant, the South kept muskets and remembrance at the ready through the first half of the twentieth century, even while racial segregation in the South continued with the judicial and political acquiescence of the North. Then, in the civil rights debate of the 1950s and 1960s, the old racial and sectional mistrust burst into flames again, blazing across decades that pundits and scholars have called a second conflict or Reconstruction. Goldfield's assertion that Dixie never stopped fighting is also apt.

Ironically, when national observations of the Civil War centenary began in 1961, bland words from an official commission sought to put any unpleasantness in the past. Historians Maurice Isserman and Michael

Kazin, in their book *America Divided: The Civil War of the 1960s,* recalled how the official brochure avoided the words "Negro" and "slavery." Indeed, Civil War Centennial Commission director Karl Betts had told one interviewer: "The story of the devotion and loyalty of Southern Negroes is one of the outstanding things of the Civil War. A lot of fine Negro people loved life as it was in the old South."[19]

However, only months after the centenary commemorations began, new racial clashes across the South put mass confrontation back in the headlines—in what one writer called "The Battle of Oxford, Mississippi," and then in Montgomery and Birmingham.[20] "To its northern and southern supporters," wrote Isserman and Kazin, "the civil rights movement was a 'second Civil War,' or a 'second Reconstruction.' To its southern opponents, it was a second 'war of northern aggression.' Civil rights demonstrators in the South carried the stars and stripes on their marches; counter-demonstrators waved the Confederate stars and bars."[21]

The wartime analogies still fascinate. In 1998 I moderated a thirtieth-anniversary panel on 1968's significance that included conservative commentators Robert Novak and Patrick Buchanan, along with Jules Witcover, the author of *The Year the Dream Died: Revisiting 1968 in America.* Asked whether the 1960s had elements of a civil war, all three agreed it had. During the 1970s two veterans of sixties activism on the left, Kirkpatrick Sale and Carl Oglesby, published the books *Power Shift* and *The Yankee and Cowboy War,* respectively, portraying the Dallas-to-Watergate period as a desperate struggle between the Yankees of the northeastern Establishment and the Sun Belt cowboys of Lyndon Johnson, Richard Nixon, John Connally, and Ronald Reagan.[22]

Attention to the South's importance was also growing. John Egerton, a southern writer, began a new genre in 1974 with his book *The Americanization of Dixie: The Southernization of America.* Describing how southern culture, especially populism and evangelical religion, was beginning to influence the rest of the country, Egerton argued that Billy Graham "has taken the old-time religion of his native South out into the nation and the world. . . . In doing so, he has firmly established himself as the single most influential figure in what can fairly be called the Southernization of American religion."[23] Two decades later, Peter Applebome, a *New York Times* correspondent based in Atlanta, extended Egerton's thesis in *Dixie Rising* (1996). He identified the southern roots not just of country music but of the nation's conservative tide, the salience of race in national politics, the rise of states' rights groups, and the spread of Southern Baptists into the North. "Only the blind could look at America at the century's end," wrote Applebome, "and not see the fingerprint of the South on almost every aspect of the nation's soul."[24]

If the events of 1861–1865 have some of the characteristics of a Rorschach blot, so does the debate over the existence and longevity of any second civil war. Before the 2004 election, former ambassador Richard Holbrooke identified the lingering disagreement over Vietnam as such a war.[25] Political commentator William Schneider perceived a deadlocked national politics, the roots of which "go back to the great civil rights war of the 1960s, a cultural civil war in which a New Left and a New Right emerged to challenge the country's post–World War II consensus."[26] Electoral demographer Michael Barone hypothesized a civil war between the two ideological wings of the baby-boom generation.[27] Commentator George Will observed some years back, "So powerful were—are—the energies let loose in the sixties that there cannot now be, and may never be, anything like a final summing up. After all, what is the 'final result' of the Civil War? It is too soon to say."[28]

In 1986 a quartet of academics, anticipating tensions that have since grown, published a volume entitled *Why the South Lost the Civil War*. Part of their argument, though, was that "in some respects the South did not lose the Civil War. Southerners eventually resolved the dissonance between the world as it was and the world as they had wanted it to be by securing enough of their war aims—state rights, white supremacy and honor—to permit them to claim their share of the victory."[29] Obviously, the subsequent decades have been even more encouraging for southerners.

Indeed, southerners have bred a new cultural and political phenomenon: neo-Confederates. This upsurge goes beyond mere nostalgia. In *The Memory of the Civil War in American Culture* (2004) authors Alice Fahs and Joan Waugh point out that "the Civil War has never receded into the remote past in American life. The most momentous conflict in American history, it had a revolutionary social and political impact that continues to be felt today. The political firestorms of the 1980s and 1990s over the appropriateness of the Confederate battle flag flying over statehouses in Georgia, Mississippi and South Carolina, for instance, demonstrate how deeply meaningful Civil War symbols remain in politics, especially racial politics." As evidence, they add that "the unveiling of Richmond's first and only statue of Abraham Lincoln in 2003 brought forth a bevy of protesters. Although supporters of the life-size bronze sculpture of Lincoln and his son Tad emphasized the statue's symbolism for reconciliation, neo-Confederates waved signs bearing the slogan 'Lincoln: Wanted for War Crimes.'"[30]

In 2002 two cultural geographers, Edward Sebesta and Euan Hague, ventured onto some unusual terrain with an article titled "The U.S. Civil War as a Theological War: Confederate Christian Nationalism and the League of the South."[31] During that war, a minority of southern Presbyterian clergymen had insisted that the conflict was ultratheological—a fight between southern true Christianity and Yankee heresy—and this interpretation, still alive on the margins of Dixie culture, has been raised again, say the two authors. Activists grouped around the nine-thousand-member League of the South, the Institute for the Study of Southern Culture and History, the Sons of Confederate Veterans, the Dixienet Web site, and the Christian Reconstructionist movement have reiterated the old verities in support of a new Confederacy. Largely mirroring the League of the South's ninety-six chapters, its proposed polity would include the eleven states of 1861–1865 plus Oklahoma, Missouri, Kentucky, and Maryland.

Peripheral as these events may seem, they flesh out the image of a region still immersed in its own exceptionalism, often at loggerheads with the North and driven by a unique history toward self-justification and expansion. And a very important part of that compulsion is religious.

The Civil War Forge of Southern Resurrection, Redemption, and Revival

If southern memory is indeed "haunted by God," to quote a favorite caution of native sons and daughters, the sermons of southern clergymen during the Civil War period were haunted by apparitions of Hebraic heroes, analogies, and Old Testament place-names: Nehemiah and Moses, of course, as well as Josiah, king of Judah, Job and his burden of righteous suffering, and the inspirational secession of the Israelites from the Jewish nation under Rehoboam.[32] From Montgomery to Richmond, few even half-plausible biblical analogies were left undrawn.

As we have seen, the post-1865 embrace of the lost cause put a power-ful imprint on the southern culture and politics that ultimately marched triumphant into the twenty-first century. Little could the gaunt, aged Jefferson Davis released from prison in 1867 have guessed that in the 1990s Southern Baptists would dominate Washington, or that in 2002 a Republican Senate majority leader from Mississippi would publicly wax nostalgic about the segregationist Dixiecrat presidential campaign of 1948. Or, for that matter, that a Republican Speaker of the House, Newt Gingrich—a onetime Pennsylvanian turned Georgian and Southern Baptist—would wind up as a historical novelist, crafting epics of south-ern battle flags sweeping victorious across his state of birth.

The intensity of southern devotion to the literal Bible, steeped in the veneration of Iron Age Judea and Samaria, is another necessary real-ization. Since the emergence in the 1980s of the religious right and the Washington ascendancy of southern Republican politicians, dozens of historians have pored through the churchly annals of the 1850s, 1860s, and 1870s, publishing their findings under a host of evocative titles: *Gos-pel of Disunion: Religion and Separatism in the Antebellum South* (1993), *Religion and the American Civil War* (1998), *Still Fighting the Civil War: The American South and Southern History* (2002), *Rebuilding Zion: The Religious Reconstruction of the South, 1863–1877* (1998), and *Redeeming the South: Religious Cultures and Racial Identities Among Southern Baptists, 1865–1925* (1997).[33] What these and other kindred volumes document is the story of a self-identified chosen people—for now, at least, one more successful than most previous covenant makers—who simply wouldn't let them-selves be beaten, religiously or politically.

By the 1830s, as we have seen, evangelical Protestantism had won the soul count below the Mason-Dixon Line. Repentance of sin, born-again conversion, and biblical inerrancy soon became regional foundations of faith. When Yankee abolitionists escalated their attacks on slavery, south-ern clergymen marshaled their own scriptural defense—taken from Exo-dus 20–21, Matthew 10:24, Ephesians 6:5–6, and others—with passages from the Bible that acknowledged or even supported slaveholding.[34] These biblical citations were frequently accompanied by dismissals of abolitionism as wickedness and heresy.

This interpretive combat raised the religious stakes in both regions. As we have seen, the United States of the mid-nineteenth century, from

North to South, was arguably Christendom's most churchgoing nation, bristling with exceptionalist faith and millennial conviction. Thus, doctrinal disagreements helped to define regional distinctiveness. This folk geography fed the separatism that eventually shouted for secession.

Historian Mitchell Snay parsed these events in his book *The Gospel of Disunion:*

> The way Southern clerics understood the relationship between religion and politics is key to understanding the role of religion in the development of Southern separatism. . . . They sanctified slavery with an elaborate scriptural justification of human bondage, a slaveholding ethic to guide the conduct of Christian masters, and a program to bring the Gospel to the slaves. They transformed the meaning of the sectional controversy into a larger struggle between orthodoxy and infidelity. Through clarifying the boundaries between religion and sectional politics, Southern clergymen essentially translated the political conflict into religious terms.[35]

Similar language can be found in other volumes.

As this disagreement over Scripture festered, the three major U.S. Protestant denominations were pulled apart. An 1844 debate, joined over whether a slaveholding clergyman could become a Methodist bishop, split that church, then the nation's biggest, into two branches, largely along sectional lines. The Baptists followed suit in 1845, and the Presbyterians divided in two stages, 1837 and 1857. Following the schisms of 1844 and 1845, politicians such as Henry Clay and John C. Calhoun wondered, all too prophetically, how long Americans would share a political union when they were no longer willing to share religious pews.[36]

Before the war, citizens on both sides had proclaimed America to be God's vehicle for the redemption of mankind, glorifying the tale of biblical Israel and the postindependence United States as "strikingly similar and analogous." However, once division came, according to chronicler Snay, "the appeal to Old Testament history and the analogy between biblical Israel and the United States was far more prevalent in the writings of the Southern clergy during the secession crisis." Examining both Confederate and federal fast-day sermons, he found only one explicit northern invocation of God's New Israel, a theme common among southerners.[37]

Southerners, in particular, identified with Israel because of their self-image as a more prayerful people than northerners—and because they shared Israelites' consciousness of being the people of a beleaguered small nation surrounded by enemies.[38] Scripture, the Confederate clergy advised, even justified secession. The Rev. Lucius Cuthbert Jr. of Aiken, South Carolina, reminded his flock that "when Rehoboam placed heavy burthens upon his people, God sent Jeroboam to head the secession of the ten tribes."[39] The *Central Presbyterian* of Richmond elaborated that the dissolution of the Hebrew tribes "came, not as a sudden and abrupt schism, but, as the inevitable result of these chafing and loosening causes, that had been acting for years"—in short, just like supposed Yankee provocation.[40] Ministers also argued that if defensive war by Israel had been justifiable in the Bible, it must be justifiable again.

Because of its theological weight, Scripture could not be abandoned when the Confederacy experienced disheartening reverses, as with the death of Stonewall Jackson in 1863 or Lee's defeat at Gettysburg. Searching again, southerners opened their Bibles to different passages. In the words of James McPherson, "Like Job, many southerners concluded that God was testing their faith as a preparation for reformation and deliverance; as a southern woman put it, 'The Lord loveth whom he chasteneth.' "[41]

Besides, God's chosen people had been led into captivity before—by the Egyptians and Babylonians—only to eventually triumph. In *Still Fighting the Civil War,* David Goldfield concluded that "southerners not only accepted adversity; they wore it as a hair shirt of faith. . . . As white evangelicals restored southern pride and dignity, they convinced themselves that the war had been part of a grand design, as one minister noted in 1866: 'God is working out larger ends than those which concern us as a people.' God controlled southern history now, and as long as southerners followed Him, they and their region would achieve salvation."[42]

To reinforce their self-esteem, southerners recast their lost war using half-truths and exaggerations. They had the best generals and soldiers, rarely beaten by equivalent forces. The Confederacy was defeated only because of the effectiveness of Washington's naval blockade and foreign politics, combined with the North's lopsided strength in manpower and industrial production. A memorial statue put up by the United Daughters of the Confederacy in 1909 bore the proud boast: "As at Thermopylae, the greater glory was to the vanquished." North Carolinian Goldfield observed: "the generic portraits of Confederate soldiers, wan and doomed,

that graced white southern homes in the decades after the war resembled Jesus in gray. As medieval townspeople erected statues to the
saints, . . . scarcely a southern town existed without a statue or memorial
to the Confederate soldiers as a permanent reminder of the heroic conflict."[43] A new gospel was being compiled.

Only in recent years, according to historian Reid Mitchell, have researchers begun to peel away myth, querying the case for the greater religiosity and superiority of the southern soldiery, with its self-reinforcing
post-1865 disdain for supposed northern foreign mercenaries, paid substitutes, and house-torching marauders.[44] Another southern historian,
Charles Reagan Wilson, has detailed the foundations of "the lost cause"
southern civic religion—an architecture of Christian and Confederate
symbols held together by the clergy's postwar theology that reconciled
defeat with the will of God and Confederate righteousness.[45]

Self-deception or not, what actually happened and what southerners
thought happened ultimately became a single historical process, not unlike the Bible's own origins.[46] In introducing their anthology *Religion and
the American Civil War,* historians Miller, Stout, and Wilson concluded:
"Thus, in the mythology of Lost Cause, the southerners became like the
Israelites of the Old Testament. They remained God's people, who
would enter the promised land if they kept His commandments and covenants, among which was fealty to their noble cause."[47] Baptized in
blood, the South would be redeemed if it kept faith and walked the old
ways, which it determined to do.

In the pantheon of Protestant chosen peoples, southerners seem to
have more than matched the Ulstermen and Afrikaners, whose fealty to
territory, tribe, and covenant has claimed so much attention. Their edge
derives from the comparative importance of the United States. By the
early twenty-first century, avid southerners could claim apparent redemption and seeming triumph in geopolitical power that utterly dwarfed that
of Northern Ireland or South Africa. Whether this eased frustration or
whetted ambition remains to be seen.

Under its own interpretation, the South was "redeemed" by 1877, when
the last northern troops withdrew following the stalemated 1876 presidential election. Politics and religion both played vital roles—politics because northern public opinion became disheartened with Reconstruction,
and the Republican White House had to broker an election compromise

by agreeing to troop withdrawal, and religion because of the extraordinary anti-Reconstruction determination and persistence displayed by Southern Baptists, Methodists, and Presbyterians. Refusing to reunite with their erstwhile northern co-religionists, they instead embraced and kept alive what can only be called southern nationalism.[48]

Between 1865 and 1877 continuing Yankee/ex-Confederate competition over Reconstruction below the Mason-Dixon Line involved three principal constituencies: southern white, southern black, and northern white, each holding strong beliefs. The ex-Confederate worldview, which took full control in 1877, merits recognition as an extraordinary venture in successful mythmaking, but it is important to bring up northern religious overreaching during and after the war.

Zealous northerners, who looked back on prewar southern secession from national church bodies as simply another dimension of Confederate sinfulness, sought to reconstruct the South's tainted churches along with its tainted politics and government. The fierce response of most southern churchmen, in turn, rested on "the adamant conviction that God still favored the South and its churches. Slavery as an institution and secession were not sinful, though most admitted that some abuses had existed in the practice of slavery. Since northern denominations were hopelessly political and radical, the southern denominations had a duty to preserve the Gospel untainted." Moreover, because "northerners and freedpeople controlled much of the political and economic life of the [Reconstruction] South, southern evangelicals had to maintain their churches as bastions of regional identity."[49]

Southern unwillingness to make any apology or compromise had been hardened by wartime excesses. In *Rebuilding Zion,* Daniel Stowell described how "federal forces destroyed twenty-six Baptist churches in Virginia alone. Between ninety and one hundred Presbyterian churches were seriously damaged or entirely destroyed throughout the South; approximately one half of these were in the Synod of Virginia. . . . All of the churches in Pine Bluff, Arkansas, Knoxville, Tennessee and Fredericksburg, Virginia, were damaged or destroyed by Federal armies."[50] Other indignities included the so-called invasion of the South by northern denominations, especially Methodists. They sought to take over church buildings and recruit local congregations, aided by federal War Department orders permitting seizure of southern church properties.[51] Even Lincoln had difficulty halting these practices.

Angry memories, old and new, spurred white membership in the ex-Confederate Baptist, Methodist, and Presbyterian denominations. During the late 1860s and 1870s, by Stowell's calculations, these three churches experienced "dramatic increases in membership" well in excess of overall white population growth. This provided "a unique glimpse of how average white southerners reacted to competing visions of religious reconstruction."[52] New Sunday schools, seminaries, religious publications, and denominational colleges further supported the white conservative movement.

By the mid-1870s northern denominations and missionaries looking to reconstruct Dixie religiously knew they faced defeat. "In the contest for white Christians," by one assessment, "the southern churches won an overwhelming victory as they grew far more rapidly than the northern churches [proselytizing] in the South."[53] Recruitment by northern denominations among whites was successful only in bitterly divided eastern Tennessee and another dozen counties elsewhere in southern Appalachia. Overall the centrality of the religious factor suggests a second informal ballot conducted in church pews: on whether southern "theopolitik" would sustain its antebellum hold. By and large, the southern clergy prevailed, effectively employing their pulpits, church media, and educational institutions. In the eyes of southern true believers, a defeated country recast itself as righteous republic.

Northern pressures on behalf of freedpeople slackened. By 1875 Walt Whitman, the poet and wartime Lincoln supporter, had come to view racial relations through an essentially southern lens. The "black domination," he argued, "but little above the beasts—viewed as a temporary, deserv'd punishment for their [southern whites'] Slavery and Secession sins, may perhaps be admissable; but as a permanency of course is not to be consider'd for a minute."[54] Critiques of the corruption in some Reconstruction governments that were imposed on the South likewise weakened national support, as did hostile depictions of the evils of Yankee money chasing and the northern cities full of immigrants, crime, and tenements.[55]

As southerners reentered their unreconstructed churches and rejected the party of abolitionism and Reconstruction, ex-Confederates recaptured control of their state governments—Tennessee in 1869, Virginia in 1869, North Carolina in 1870, Georgia in 1871, Alabama and Arkansas in 1874, Mississippi in 1876, and Florida, South Carolina, and Louisiana in 1877. True believers compared the reprieve to the redemption God granted to Israel, an analogy infuriating to northerners aware how much the outcome also owed to violence, lynchings, and the Ku Klux Klan. Historian Stowell has traced the terminology:

> White southern evangelicals described the end of Reconstruction as a "redemption," a term that evoked a sense of regaining control of their political destinies, which had for too long been in the hands of usurpers. This "favorite euphemism of the white Democrats," as Kenneth M. Stampp described it, had distinctively religious overtones. . . . Although the first usage of the term remains obscure, southerners were employing it at least from the time that the first southern state, Tennessee, was redeemed in 1869–70.[56]

After "redemption," mythmaking moved toward a mock zenith, which probably came in 1915, when a pro–Ku Klux Klan movie—D. W. Griffith's *Birth of a Nation*—enjoyed a special showing in the White House. It reportedly gained praise from President Woodrow Wilson, who had attended Johns Hopkins University with the book's author, Thomas Dixon Jr.[57] However, even critics of the southern record, such as David Goldfield, cite the favored biblical analogies in their analyses without sarcasm, because that was how the majority of white southerners spoke and thought, wrongly or otherwise.[58]

No one should be surprised, then, that Dixie has bred so many historians. It is said that when southerners aren't going to church, they're cherishing old grudges, burnishing Civil War statues, or remembering something. The Southern Baptist Convention, in particular, has been shaped by what local people call "the backward glance."[59]

The Southern Baptist Convention: State Church of the Ex-Confederacy?

Normally it would be presumptuous to single out one church in a region, but in today's South there is no choice. The Southern Baptist Convention— its official name, not merely a reference to its annual meeting—is preeminent in the South, an eight-hundred-ton dinosaur in the parlor of American Protestantism, and over the last century the fastest-growing major church in the United States. To read about the SBC is to experience an impressive flow of adjectives: distinctive, unique, fundamentalist, missionary, independent, imperial, uncompromising. The church is also, as we will see in chapter 6, the increasingly political institution that in the 1990s cemented the Republican hold on the South and kept the party positioned to win the White House.

One description rarely ventured is "mainline." To quote Richard Hutcheson in *Mainline Churches and the Evangelicals,* "The Southern Baptist Convention, the Lutheran Church, Missouri Synod, and some of the major black Baptist groups, are certainly large denominations with deep roots in American history, but they would be omitted from many 'mainline' lists. Why? Because they are strongly conservative and are not part of the ecumenical movement."[60] The SBC is also, in considerable part, populated by fundamentalists.

Baptists in the South, however, have always been distinctive. At first they shocked colonial-era Anglicans with their exuberance, physical convulsions, and adult baptism. Then more numerous Baptists annoyed the gentry of the new southern states circa 1790 by their occasional biracialism, opposition to hierarchy, and disrespect for patriarchal authority. Thereupon, as we have seen, to gain community acceptance for their evangelical mission, denominational leaders made accommodations on prickly issues. By 1830 "white Baptists who had questioned slavery in late-eighteenth-century Virginia were defending it as a divinely sanctioned social order."[61] In place of frontier one-room meetinghouses, Baptists in some towns opened colleges, ran newspapers, and built impressive churches, although too few to change the denomination's overwhelmingly rural nature.

By rallying around regional culture, hierarchy, and slavery, antebellum southern Baptists did alienate considerable numbers of co-religionists, mostly poor whites unsympathetic to urban fashion, schools, costly good works, and support for the local power structure. These discontented folk turned away to become the "primitive" and "antimission" Baptists of the Appalachian upcountry and Texas hills, so labeled because they opposed missionary efforts as middle-class, expensive, and, by the Calvinist doctrine of predestination, a waste of time. According to the *New Historical*

Atlas of Religion in America (2001), these primitive or "hard-shell" Baptists grew to number a half million or so, white and black, by the end of the twentieth century.[62] Other small sects are numerous. Even in Dixie, many conservative white Baptists belong to denominations less fashionable or sophisticated than the SBC.

As noted earlier, the national Baptist movement of the mid-nineteenth century seethed with sectionalism. In 1845, after northern Baptists told southern compatriots that Yankeedom could "never be a party to any arrangement that would imply approbation of slavery," irate southerners decamped to Augusta, Georgia. There, eight states led by Virginia formed their own regional bloc, the Southern Baptist Convention, which from the start wore its regionalism with pride.[63] A century and a half later, the SBC would be the only American Protestant denomination to still retain the word "southern" in its name, a badge of its origins and commitment.

Antebellum northern and southern Baptists differed over more than slavery. Despite alliances with the local establishment, those in the South "tended to be of lower social and economic status, exhibited much less interest in an educated ministry, and extended westward by means of farmer-preachers." Northern Baptists, by contrast, "tended to be middle class, tended to think in terms of an educated ministry, and expanded westward by way of missionaries."[64]

After war broke out in 1861, a flag-waving SBC inundated the Confederate Army with uplifting pamphlets. One such, entitled "A Mother's Parting Words to Her Soldier Boy," penned by Jeremiah Jeter, a Virginia newspaper editor and Baptist minister, supposedly was the most popular single piece of religious literature in Confederate camps, with more than 250,000 copies handed out. By 1864 Baptists had provided the southern army with more than one hundred different tracts totaling some fifty million pages, while also vending Bibles, hymnals, and religious miscellany. Not long after the war, Baptists in Virginia preened that "the history of the world, we presume, reports no instance of an army so thoroughly under the influence of the gospel as was our noble Southern army."[65]

When Reconstruction followed, the Southern Baptist Convention remobilized, despite wrecked churches, impoverished congregations, and lack of funds. These years put a strong psychological imprint on its future as well as the region's—akin to the intense Boer experience with the

Great Trek and Ulster Protestant immersion in the do-or-die confrontations of the late seventeenth century. No other religious subculture in the United States bears any similar stamp.

To religious historian Paul Harvey, "white Baptists viewed political and religious reconstruction as the same process in different institutional settings," and from the start "prominent Virginia Baptists portrayed white southerners as victims of northern marauders." In Georgia federal troops shut down the *Christian Index and Southwestern Baptist* for its "advocacy of disloyalty as a moral and religious duty of the white South." Moreover, "churches expressing sympathy for the Union or for Republicans found themselves booted out of Baptist associations and other religious organizations."[66]

By reiterating prewar views, including Dixie righteousness and black incapacity for self-government, the SBC pitched a popular tent. In *Rebuilding Zion,* Daniel Stowell concluded that

> the speedy restoration of southern denominational institutions and religious newspapers gave Confederate Christians a distinct advantage over northern missionaries who came south seeking Unionists and penitent rebels. Southern ministers preached a different version of God's purposes in the war, and once denominational mechanisms were again in working order, southern churches began to receive thousands of new members. Denominational periodicals zealously guarded against laxity among southern Christians and mercilessly attacked northern denominations and their missionaries.[67]

"By the 1870s," according to Stowell, "southern churches were virtually bereft of black members, and many of those members had joined northern biracial denominations. . . . Although they continually voiced their commitment to black evangelization, southern Baptists refused to allow blacks the full privileges of membership."[68] The ultimate irony is that separate, black-controlled Baptist congregations thrived, providing training grounds for self-government, through which black Baptists attained an equal or greater depth of religious and political commitment that was to serve them well in the civil-rights struggle a century later.

Not surprisingly the postbellum legacies of white southern separatism and ecclesiastical warfare all but ruled out a reunion with northern Baptists. For the SBC, sectional feeling and theology blended into a "sense of holy separation," a commitment to remain free of northern "contamination" because southern religion was more virtuous and biblically sound.[69] One North Carolinian put matters bluntly in 1899: "we are a different people, a different blood, a different climate, a different character, different customs, and we have largely a different work to do in this world."[70]

"By the late nineteenth century," according to Miller, Stout, and Wilson, "ministers with the Southern Baptist Convention controlled much of the religious life of their region. They had grown in numbers after the war, and despite the individual poverty of many congregations, by sheer numbers they had consolidated a hegemonic position within the South. A growing racial consensus among whites North and South allowed southern whites to manage their own race relations, and Southern Baptists participated fully in mythologizing the Lost Cause. . . . Southern Baptist ministers were now leading cultural figures throughout the South."[71]

After it became clear that Baptists could not reunite nationally, the two camps did manage to agree on who would operate where. The Southern Baptist Convention, increasingly expansion minded, got its requisite franchise, first to control missionary work in the South, then after an 1894 agreement the opportunity to proselytize in the West.[72] In 1895 the separate, all-black National Baptist Convention, ultimately to become the nation's second-largest Baptist denomination, was organized as the culmination of three decades of work toward self-government.[73]

During this same period, while other large denominations lost members to Pentecostal and holiness sects, the SBC did not. Predominantly rural, lost cause–dedicated, unsophisticated, revivalist, and evangelical— but not yet fundamentalist—the turn-of-the-century SBC gained from populist and revivalist currents. Membership in convention-affiliated churches reached just over one million in the early 1870s, rising to nearly two million in 1910 and three million by 1920.[74] One observer noted that "while to this day there are Evangelical Presbyterian denominations (EPC), an Evangelical Methodist denomination (EMC) and two Evangelical Lutheran denominations (ELCA; EL Synod), there is no Evangelical Baptist church. Beginning during this era [1890–1910], Southern Baptists made the term redundant."[75]

With little to dilute its appeal, the SBC consolidated strength in the ex-Confederacy, aided by its postwar role as a bulwark of sectional identity and its unique mixture of biblical conservatism and revivalism.[76] Between 1870 and 1916, according to the *New Historical Atlas of Religion in America,* the number of counties in Virginia, Kentucky, Georgia, Alabama, Mississippi, and Texas in which Baptists of all kinds predominated over any other denomination doubled or tripled. More than half of the counties marked as having Methodist or Presbyterian margins in 1870 were converted, and by World War I, only a few ex-Confederate states retained significant clumps of Methodist counties.[77]

By 1910, as revivals filled SBC pews, some 40 percent of white southern churchgoers and 60 percent of black southern churchgoers were Baptists, for a total of some five million. The Southern Baptist Convention became the nation's largest Protestant denomination, while the National Baptist Convention took pride in identifying itself as the largest black religious organization in the world.[78] However, big as the SBC had become, it was still the church of the plain-folk, country South. Some 80 percent of Baptist church members were farmers (35 percent of them tenants), and as late as the 1920s some 86 percent of the SBC-affiliated churches stood in rural areas. Of congregations with meetinghouses, 85 percent met in cabinlike one-room structures.[79] Substantial SBC congregations were uncommon outside city limits.

This helps to explain why, in the first quarter of the twentieth century, the fast-growing congregations of the Southern Baptist Convention became important nurseries of American fundamentalism. The scriptural crisis surrounding the Civil War had nurtured biblical literalism, the 1890s had seen a reemphasis on revivalism, and in the decade after World War I a conservative and biblical counterreaction to the culture shock of radio, automobiles, short skirts, and the jazz age was unleashed. For the SBC, venting cultural antimodernism was as comfortable as Br'er Rabbit found the briar patch.

Southern Baptists, as we have seen, were front and center in drafting "The Fundamentals"—the 1910–1915 compilations that soon gave fundamentalism its name. But if the SBC still prioritized winning souls and sought to eschew political stumping, it did not entirely succeed. The convention was at the fore during the 1920s in promoting Prohibition and in helping the anti-evolution movement to convince state legislatures to ban the teaching of Darwinian theory in Oklahoma, Florida, North Carolina, Texas, Tennessee, Mississippi, Louisiana, and Arkansas.[80]

Many annals of the twenties hold that southern fundamentalists and Pentecostals, embarrassed by national ridicule, faded back into Appalachian hollows or coastal piney woods. But as we have seen, they did not retreat in numbers. Their network of seminaries, Bible fellowships, and radio gospel hours expanded, enabling them later to reenter the national stage with considerable muscle.

At midcentury, SBC conservatism—satisfaction with the cultural status quo, well flavored with patriotism and anticommunism—rested comfortably on a theological framework that remained essentially evangelical and mission minded. From 1940 to 1960—in decades when segregation and civil-rights demonstrations were roiling the South—the SBC saw the number of its adherents nearly double from just over five million to just under ten million.[81] (The significant expansion brought by these gains in northern and western states will be pursued shortly.) These SBC missionary achievements, moreover, took place while more staid northern Baptists—shorn of fundamentalists who split off in the 1930s and again in the 1940s—underwent decline. On racial issues specifically, the SBC of the 1950s cannot fairly be caricatured because in 1954 its Christian Life Commission disregarded political and white-congregation sentiment to issue an endorsement of the Supreme Court's *Brown v. Board of Education* school-desegregation decision.[82] Many, if not most, white Southern Baptists would have disagreed, but the SBC colleges and seminaries had an influential progressive element.

Still, the interplay of culture, biblical inerrancy, and racial circumstances during the 1960s began to move the SBC toward the aggressive political conservatism it would embrace in 1979 with the election of a new presiding officer and then entrench during the 1980s. For decades the leadership of the convention, men who eschewed open politicking in favor of bringing converts to Jesus and saving souls, had cut some slack to moderates on social themes to keep the internal peace. The sixties and seventies, however, saw that truce crumble as moderates and liberals in the SBC infrastructure of agencies and commissions pushed increasingly controversial positions.

Disagreement over evolution and racial desegregation stood out. Convention theologian Ralph Elliott's book *The Message of Genesis* (1961), doubting the existence of Adam and Eve and questioning Jonah's survival in the whale, caused a ruckus. So did the moderate faction's orchestration of the SBC's 1968 "Statement Concerning the Crisis in Our Nation," a call for social action in race relations and antipoverty efforts, which included a confession of complicity in the injustice done to blacks.[83] To opponents, such controversies got in the way of the SBC's primary mission: spreading the gospel. Not a few conservatives became convinced of the need to regain organizational control.

In his 1997 book, *The Rise of Baptist Republicanism*, South Carolina conservative Oran Smith contended that by the 1970s the gospel-spreading priority had supplanted attention to policy: "What began simply as natural brand loyalty and confidence evolved into a dangerous hubris, and out of church-building megalomania and a creeping belief that the SBC had a particular 'divine mission' came a certain presumption."[84] One moderate leader suggested that "in the 1950s through the 1970s, the SBC reflected the culture. Baptists were 'in denial,' they wanted *peace* not *admonition*. . . . The attitude was 'anything that takes away from building the church is anathema.'"[85] In fact SBC statistics showed its membership share peaking among whites in half of the ex-Confederate states in 1960, then losing a little ground by 1970 and more by 1980. Controversy may have taken some toll.[86]

As SBC affiliation peaked in the southeastern states where Baptist momentum reached back to eighteenth-century evangelism but where northerners were now moving in, convention missionaries recorded better 1960–1990 results in the south-central and border states: Alabama, Mississippi, Louisiana, Arkansas, Oklahoma, Missouri, Tennessee, and Kentucky. There, SBC ratios either expanded or stabilized.[87] That the biggest strides came in Oklahoma and Missouri reflected another trend with notable political implications: how Southern Baptist expansion was moving north and west, albeit most pronouncedly in areas of original southern settlement or later migration from the former Confederacy.

Beyond the Civil War border states, the national church-membership survey for 1990 found impressive increments for the SBC in southern Ohio, Indiana, and Illinois, southeastern Kansas, and eastern New Mexico, as well as in scattered rural counties in Nevada, Colorado, Wyoming, and Idaho. Forty years earlier, Southern Baptists had not led other Protestant denominations in a single county in Ohio, Kansas, Nevada, or Wyoming; by 1990, they led in seventeen such counties.[88] As we will see in chapter 6, this expansion became a major benefit to the Republican party as its leadership southernized and took up a de facto political partnership with the SBC.

The Texans who led the conservative takeover of the convention were initially aroused by, of all things, the supposed modernism creeping into Old Testament classes at Baptist-supported Baylor University in Waco. After consultations, they developed a plan to take over the SBC presidency at the 1979 annual meeting and employ that office to appoint true believers to the SBC's quasi-independent agencies, boards, and commissions. By the late 1980s, after ten years of conservative appointments had remade the bureaucracy, the eighteen-million-member Church of the Southern Cultural Memory was on its way to becoming a newly fledged Church of Biblical Inerrancy and Republican Ascendancy—an extraordinary metamorphosis full of national and even global implications.

Before we shift to the church's political heft, two aspects of this portrait require further clarifying brushstrokes. First, can the SBC of the late twentieth and early twenty-first centuries be fairly described as fundamentalist, given the pejorative and antimodern implications of that dour image? And second, more portentously, can the Southern Baptist Convention be considered the de facto Church of the South—the closest approximation to an official church in the United States since the disestablishment of Congregationalism in New England almost two centuries ago?

"Historically, fundamentalism referred to those 20th century American Protestants who reacted negatively to science and acted militantly against any reading of the Bible other than a wooden literal reading," contends Robert Parham, director of the Baptist Center for Ethics in Nashville. "Today, fundamentalism is a description applied to militant extremists who demand that others embrace their way or hit the highway."[89] Clearly, there is disagreement over this, and, practically speaking, the definition is in flux. Nevertheless, the majority view among religious scholars is that yes, the term "fundamentalist" does fit the latter-day SBC viewpoint; witness the comments of prominent figures such as Martin Marty, Scott Appleby, and Charles Kimball.[90] The dissident moderate faction of Southern Baptists, based in organizations such as the Alliance of Southern Baptists and the Cooperative Baptist Fellowship, routinely and unhesitatingly labels the controlling conservatives fundamentalists. Self-proclaimed fundamentalist Jerry Falwell saluted the SBC in his co-edited history, *The Fundamentalist Phenomenon*.[91]

In *The Rise of Baptist Republicanism*, Oran Smith, after loosely locating evangelical religion between mainline belief and fundamentalism to the right, concluded that the SBC was already on the rightward fringe of evangelicalism during the sixties and seventies, slipping into overt fundamentalism after its conservative faction took over in 1979.[92] Political chronicler Smith took his criteria from *Defenders of God: The Fundamentalist Revolt Against the Modern Age* (1989), a comparative study of religions and cultures by Bruce Lawrence, a prominent Duke University theologian.[93] Lawrence's main yardsticks—creedal belief, Scripture as the fount of legitimacy and ideology, an attraction to charismatic leaders and preachers, self-perceptions of embattled purity and righteousness, tendencies toward opposition and separatism, and domination by male elites—all seem to apply to the SBC. There is no doubt about its reliance on Scripture, biblical inerrancy, disdain for ecumenicalism, and refusal to let women serve in positions of authority.[94]

The quibble, ironically, comes from the fringe right. South Carolina's separatist fundamentalists centered at Bob Jones University reserve true fundamentalism for themselves; they reject the SBC as too ecumenical and doctrinally impure. Theological beauty is also apparently in the eye of the beholder.

The case for the Southern Baptist Convention as a sort of state or "established" Church of the South—touched upon, at least, by many regional historians—may seem far-fetched given its fundamentalism. However, the two are not necessarily incompatible. Most characterizations of the SBC identify it, quite plausibly, as a "folk" church determined to keep its relationship with southern farmers and country people.[95] Religious historians have also profiled a commitment to Scripture and sacred territory and a past of upholding and intensifying Confederate identity, comforting fighting men in the field, and serving after the war as a keeper of the flame of myth and history.[96] This could fittingly be called quasi nationalism.

Indeed, these past identities also uphold the considerable analogy to the covenanting God and the biblical, prefundamentalist churches of the *other* New Israels. All were actual or de facto state churches: in the sixteenth- and seventeenth-century Netherlands, the Dutch Reformed

Church, and then the successor Dutch Reformed Church of nineteenth- and twentieth-century South Africa; for Ulster, its pair of combative an- cestral kirks, the Reformation (Presbyterian) Church of Scotland and its heir, the Presbyterian kirk in Northern Ireland, the de facto church of the Scottish settlers. To extend the parallel, the heavy Scotch-Irish influence on the eighteenth- and nineteenth-century South is well documented. U.S. historian George Frederickson, a Civil War expert, has also found some similarity between how southerners and Afrikaners experienced frontier circumstances and racial tensions.[97] The partial SBC parallel to the circumstances and churches of other covenanting peoples deserves some attention in its own right.

To chronicler Smith, the "most evident feature" of Southern Baptists is their very southernness, along with their role in the South's folk reli- gion, a case also framed by Southern Baptist academician Norman Vance in *Religion Southern Style.*[98] "Baptist exceptionalism," in turn, thrives on the evangelical link between cultural domination and pursuit of mem- bership growth: "Eventually, the notion of a Christian or even Baptist re- gion becomes a civic religion, a mentality so binding that Southern Baptists begin to think of themselves as the cultural majority with the goal not of rejecting society (as some small, sect-like religious conserva- tives have done), but of absorbing it. In such a world, Baptist clergy and lay leadership have no interest in taking stands against Southern cultural norms. They are not motivated to oppose the culture or appear unpatri- otic about the region, for to a greater and greater extent, they *are* the cul- ture, they *are* the region."[99]

In 1996 they were also the nation—or at least the nation's Washing- ton leadership. The president, vice president, Senate president pro tem, and Speaker of the House were all Southern Baptists, an absolutely unprecedented foursome that would have stunned the eighteenth- and nineteenth-century southern-born presidents, who were Episcopalians or Presbyterians. Baptists were not the southern leadership class. In 1861 the president of the Confederacy, Jefferson Davis, was an Episcopalian. In a sense, this was Washington's second upheaval during the 1990s.

But surprisingly little attention was paid to the regional role of the church to which Bill Clinton, Albert Gore, Strom Thurmond, and Newt Gingrich all belonged. Few descriptions of the SBC go beyond historians' acknowledgments or explanations of how it is *unique* (in success and folk regionalism), *distinctive* (huge, fundamentalist, and biblical), *independent* (opposed to ecumenicalism), *separate* (a sense of apartness), *expansionist* (missionary and territorial), and a *keeper of the regional and cultural flame* (steeped in southern history and memory). But these characteristics do seem to combine in a way that bespeaks the greater role that the SBC has played.

The Greater South and the Future of the Republic

The Confederacy defeated in the Civil War was only the heart of a larger cultural or geographic region that geographers circa 1860 could fairly have mapped as southern. Before the eleven Confederate states could be subdued by the wealthier, more entrepreneurial, and industrial North, the Lincoln administration had to contain a potentially larger rebellion. From downstate Delaware to Missouri to southern California, portions of the Greater South decided against secession or were blocked from attempting it.

For some eighteen months in 1861 and 1862, the federal government critically improved its odds for victory by (1) applying military power to keep the border areas of Maryland, western Virginia, Kentucky, and Missouri in the Union; (2) supporting local Republican politicians in the 1862 elections, in which voters in southern-settled sections of Ohio, Indiana, and Illinois gave the Democrats congressional gains and in two states nearly captured governorships that might have shut down war commitment; (3) blocking a Confederate invasion of what is now New Mexico and Arizona (by a Texas column aiming for California) with a military victory at La Glorieta Pass in March 1862; and (4) suppressing secessionist sentiment and activities by southern sympathizers in California and Oregon, as well as in mining camps from Nevada and Idaho east to Colorado. By 1863 and 1864, with these problems relatively contained, federal forces were able to take the offensive in Confederate territory, and even then victory was long in doubt—Lincoln himself was worried well into the summer of 1864.

While the ups and downs of 1861 and 1862 may be of interest to armchair generals, for the purposes of this chapter (and for twenty-first-century political strategy) suffice it to say that the Greater South, united against Yankeedom, might have won back then. Today's Greater South, in turn, deploys an even larger share of the nation's population and political and economic power.

Maps 1 and 2 are attempts to portray the boundaries of the cultural Greater South, one by geographer Raymond Gaskil and the other by sociologist John Shelton Reed. The first is Gaskil's portrait based on cultural and linguistic regions. The second, by Reed—his other boundary criteria, not entirely serious, have ranged from kudzu to outdoor toilets to the states and cities mentioned in country-music hits—represents an unusual departure. In it, he maps the locales where people *perceive themselves* to be southern, based on the ratio of telephone-directory business listings that begin with "Southern" as opposed to "American."[100] Like Gaskil's, this map takes the South into Kansas and the Ohio Valley, while also nudging into Pennsylvania.

Instructive as these contours may be, though, even they fail to measure the considerable southern cultural and religious influence through both the Midwest and West. The Ohio Valley portions of Ohio, Indiana, and Illinois, well understood to have been settled from the South and border states, are hardly the only southern cultural outliers. A fuller look at the extended 1861–1865 geography of secessionist sentiment and Confederate flag-waving is a necessary but still only preliminary introduction to the reach of the present-day southern coalition.

Both of the two western states newly admitted to the Union, California (1850) and Oregon (1859), had substantial southern and secessionist populations. Abraham Lincoln later admitted that his pair of narrow victories there had come by the "closest bookkeeping that I know of."[101] Oregon, settled by Yankees in Portland and the nearby Willamette Valley, also had southerners and border staters in its southwest, central, and northeastern counties, enough to briefly hatch a plan for an independent slaveholding republic under Oregon's southern-born senator, Joseph Lane.[102] Lincoln barely won in 1860, taking 36 percent of the votes to 34 percent for John C. Breckinridge, the southern Democrat, and 28 percent for Stephen Douglas, the northern Democrat.[103] Many pro-secessionists had traveled west from Missouri, the jumping-off point for the 2,100-mile Oregon Trail.

In California the population center of San Francisco was Yankee-dominated, while southern and secessionist elements clustered in the thinly populated Los Angeles area, in the Central Valley, and in forty-niner mining districts. South Carolina palmetto banners and Confederate

Map 1: The South as a Cultural Region

● Nonconforming metropolitan area

After Raymond Gaskil, *Cultural Regions of the United States* (Seattle: University of Washinton Press, 1975).

Map 2: "Southern" Listings as a Percentage of "American" Listings in Telephone Directories, ca. 1975

After J. S. Reed, "The Heart of Dixie: An Essay in Folk Geography," *Social Forces* 54 (June 1976).

flags flew in Stockton, San Jose, Visalia, Santa Barbara, San Bernardino, and Los Angeles. More tangibly, proposals were made for reinstituting the Bear Republic of the 1840s or for launching a new Pacific republic including California and Oregon; and a short-lived training camp for Confederate recruits was set up in El Monte.[104] On the federal level, California's Tennessee-born senator William Gwin supported the South's secession, as did the state's all-Democratic House delegation.[105] Strategists in Confederate Texas hoped to reach California by an invasion corridor through the New Mexico Territory, and Texas cavalry did get as far as Tucson. Indeed, a new Territory of Arizona, spanning the invasion corridor and with Tucson as its capital, was claimed as part of the Confederacy in 1861.[106]

Another soon-to-be-admitted state, Kansas, teetered for a while in the late 1850s, as northern emigrants vied with proslavery forces from adjacent Missouri to pass a suitable constitution. The first version, the so-called Lecompton Constitution, favorable to slavery, was accepted by President James Buchanan but disdained by Congress because of fraud. A second popular vote, held in 1858, rejected the proslavery agreement, 13,088 to 11,300. Finally, in 1861, after secession, when southern senators and representatives had gone home, the new northern Congress admitted Kansas as a free state.[107]

The last group of eventual states caught up in the western side currents of the Civil War held only territorial status at the time: Colorado, Utah, Nevada, Idaho, and Montana. Utah was Democratic leaning, hostile to New Englanders who damned its controlling Mormons for their proslavery and polygamist inclinations. Elsewhere in the Rocky Mountains, immigrants by the tens of thousands clumped around the only destinations lucrative enough to outweigh Indian perils: rich veins of gold, silver, copper, and lead. The 1850s had seen gold strikes in Oregon, and 1859 brought a bigger one in Colorado, centered on Denver. More rich lodes were found in 1860 in Idaho's Clearwater and Salmon valleys, followed by even richer ones in western Montana, where creeks such as Grasshopper, Stinking Water, and Alder Gulch became legendary and notorious: "In 1863, the 17-mile length of Alder Gulch's gravel bars [was] reported to have 10,000 miners and on its steep banks were four 'cities' with names famous in mining history: Virginia, Nevada, Central, and Summit."[108]

Besides gold and silver, a further opportunity lay in fleeing the hazards of Bull Run, Shiloh, and Antietam: "The mining camps had their Unionists, but they also had their southern sympathizers and Democrats were in the majority. Many miners from both sides in the Civil War had come to the mines to escape military conscription, but they gallantly defended their homelands and causes with toasts, torch-light parades and fist fights on Saturday night."[109] So substantial were the numbers that the governor of Iowa called for patrols at the Missouri River crossings to catch evaders fleeing west.[110]

Although the western territories were under nominal Washington control, law enforcement was slack, especially in the rowdy mining camps. "During the war," wrote historian Earl Pomeroy, "the Lincoln administration treated the Far West as tactfully as it had treated the border states early in 1861. The President never applied the draft west of Iowa and Kansas, apparently considering that it was not expedient to draw more men from the [West] coast than had volunteered. The army feared it would waste its strength tracking draft-dodgers and deserters through the back country, and Western businessmen repeatedly expressed fear of secessionist uprisings."[111]

Montana and Idaho (part of Washington Territory until 1863) and Colorado had large southern populations. Virginia City, in present-day Montana, had at first been called Varina City, after Jefferson Davis's wife, but a local judge changed the name. Other sites included Dixie, Fort Sumter, and Confederate Gulch, the mining center of the Big Belt Mountains. By one estimate, nearly 80 percent of the population had secessionist sympathies, and Republicans in the territorial administration brought in wagon trains of emigrants from St. Paul, Minnesota, to help maintain control.[112] One particular fear was of plots to ship gold to the South.

In Colorado, Republican governor William Gilpin, charged with keeping Colorado loyal to the Union, wrote to authorities in Washington that 7,500 people, almost one-third of the population of Denver and the mining camps, were Confederate sympathizers.[113] "In addition," noted historian Alvin Josephy in *The Civil War in the American West*, "Colorado was stirred constantly by reports of pro-Confederate plots, many of them real. Several well-known Southern sympathizers organized bands of followers to try to join the Confederates in Texas. . . . Still another group of secessionists congregated secretly at Mace's Hole, a hideout south of the

Arkansas River, and tried to organize themselves into a Confederate regiment."[114] Had the Confederate troops won at La Glorieta Pass in 1862, they might have continued on to the Colorado goldfields.

Josephy's book probes one of the least-known and most fascinating sidebars to the general history of the Civil War. However, the current-day reason to underscore how portions of the early West mixed northern and southern politics and population strains is that in many important ways—substantial born-again evangelicalism or fundamentalism, sectarian rather than mainline religion, political conservatism, and cultural individualism—the blending is ongoing. Responding to many different lures, southerners and southern inclinations and affinities continued to move westward during the late nineteenth and twentieth centuries.

Indeed, mining was the original draw for some southerners, because the Dahlonega district of northern Georgia held the nation's best-producing goldfields at the period prior to the California Gold Rush. At its peak in the 1830s, fifteen thousand miners were on hand there.[115] By the forties and fifties, they were looking for new opportunities. Indeed, Georgians from Dahlonega—meaning "yellow money" in Cherokee—discovered the gold in both the Cherry Creek and Leadville districts of Colorado. In Montana, Georgians striking it rich named Last Chance Gulch near Helena, and another, John Bozeman, blazed the trail bearing his name to the Montana goldfields.

After 1865 southerners took jobs not only in mining but on the transcontinental railroads. Enough worked on the Union Pacific as it crossed Wyoming in 1867 to keep the pro-Confederate *Frontier Index* popular as the railroad's house organ.[116] But the preeminent influx, by the late 1860s and 1870s, came with the cattle drives, mostly north from Texas, following the Chisholm, Goodnight-Loving, Great Western, and other trails into Kansas, Nebraska, Montana, and Wyoming. These movements brought the cattle culture not just to the railheads but into valleys near the Oregon Trail and the mountain pastures of the Rockies. Texans and Missourians came, too. According to one regional history, "Many men who came up the Texas trail [to Montana] during the great years of the Long Drive brought with them both longhorn cattle and their political allegiances."[117] By the mid-1870s Montana ranges were being grazed by once-southern cattlemen, all the way to the Canadian border.

The Oregon Trail itself kept bringing Missourians to the Rockies and the Pacific Northwest. After 1863 pro-secessionists from a strip of western Missouri counties, put under martial law because of guerrilla strife and northern retribution, began heading west in large numbers. Of roughly forty thousand emigrants traveling west on the Platte River Road in 1864, about half were Missourians, many of them Confederate sympathizers.[118] At the trail's end, draft dodgers and Missouri Democrats were conspicuous enough to make one Republican remark that " 'the left wing of [Missouri Confederate general Sterling] Price's army' was still encamped in [the eastern] part of Oregon, and that the Oregon democracy generally were only a step removed from Price and Jefferson Davis."[119] Within another decade, many Oregonians were joining the Southern Alliance, an agrarian radical group that operated through secret societies, excluded blacks, and used Klan-like rituals and paraphernalia.[120]

Toward the end of the nineteenth century, as the timber business began to migrate west to the spruce, cedar, Ponderosa pine, and Douglas fir forests of the Pacific Northwest, eastern loggers came along. "A substantial immigration from the southern Appalachian Mountains into the Northwestern lumber districts had begun in the 1880s, reinforcing the southern and border stock of the earlier years."[121] Logging centers in southwestern Oregon, Idaho, and Washington State were favored destinations.

The twentieth century saw the extension of the movement. Missouri and Texas became the second- and third-ranking states in number of migrants sent to California during the 1920s, and these inflows continued during the 1930s alongside Oklahoma and Kansas residents fleeing parched farms in the Dust Bowl. Giant federal works projects such as the Grand Coulee, Bonneville, Fort Peck, and Hoover dams also beckoned the unemployed westward, as did the war industries and military installations that ballooned between 1941 and 1945. In *Dixie Rising,* Peter Applebome profiled the huge migration out of the South between 1910 and 1960. Besides 4.5 million blacks, mostly bound for the urban North, some 4.6 million whites also left the South, principally for the Midwest and the West.[122]

So many Kentuckians, West Virginians, and Tennesseans went northward to the automobile and rubber plants of the Great Lakes states that most factory cities had their hillbilly hollows and Little West Virginias.

Ypsilanti, Michigan, close by Ford's huge Willow Run facility, was known as Ypsitucky. In Ohio, Dayton and Columbus had Appalachian neighborhoods, but the fiddle-and-revival capital was rubber-making Akron. In 1940 the *Ohio Guide* noted that over 60 percent of its people were of southern origin.[123] Plants in southern Ohio brought in large numbers of strikebreakers from the Tennessee and Kentucky mountains, who grouped together in shantytowns named Happy Top and Gobbler's Knob.[124]

Along the Pacific and in the Rocky Mountain states, chroniclers of the emigration from below the Mason-Dixon Line generally emphasize the huge draw of the 1941–1945 war industries and military installations. From Puget Sound to San Diego, Phoenix, and Los Alamos, the histories of local SBC area associations typically mention the southern-bred population influx that began after Pearl Harbor.

The tale of this demographic extension of the South has been told elsewhere—although perhaps without the detail that befits a discussion of the consequences for early-twenty-first-century U.S. politics. We must now turn to a less-discussed but related corollary: the piggybacked extension of southern culture and evangelical, fundamentalist, and Pentecostal religion.

The historical mythmaking of the lost cause did not simply intensify southern and border-state memories; it also recast them. States where most men serving in Civil War armies had fought for the Union—Maryland, Kentucky, and Missouri—wound up with a disproportion of southern memorials and museums. James Loewen profiled this Confederate *reconquista* in his book *Lies Across America,* which describes inaccurate historical sites. What the Confederates did not win on the 1861–1865 battlefields, they achieved on historical markers and the inscriptions on veterans' memorials. Tributes to the boys in gray turned up as far north as Helena, Montana, while Kentucky—a state that sent ninety thousand soldiers to Union armies and just thirty-five thousand to southern units—wound up with seventy-two Confederate monuments, compared with just two for the Union side.[125] The Confederate monument in Montana, put up by the Daughters of the Army of the Confederacy in 1916, commemorates the southerners of Last Chance Gulch, now Helena's Main Street. Perhaps these unsung heroes smuggled more gold back to the South than historians believe.

The proliferation of southern religion, however, greatly exceeded that of Confederate memorials. By the 1930s the SBC missionary effort in the West had begun, and the migrations from the South during World War II provided a major boost. A later history, *Southern Baptists in the Intermountain West,* credited the buildup of military bases and war industries, noting that between 1940 and 1974 SBC western membership grew from "two small state conventions in New Mexico and Arizona to ten state conventions, 145 associations, 2,210 churches, 35,387 baptisms, and 689,139 members."[126]

The county-by-county maps of the influence of religious denominations during this same period show a steady SBC advance, on one hand consolidating within the boundaries of the old Confederacy, and on the other chalking up inroads in the border states, as well as in eastern New Mexico ("Little Texas"), Oklahoma, southeastern Kansas, and southern Illinois. By 1990 and 2000 the expansion was wider still. The greatest concentrations in western states were often in rural counties, but sometimes they were in metropolitan areas with a country-music presence (Wichita, Kansas, and Bakersfield, California), ties to oil (Casper, Wyoming, and Fairbanks, Alaska), or prominence as a Christian evangelical mecca (Colorado Springs, Colorado). In any event, map 3 on p. 169, which displays not only the Southern Baptist Convention–dominated states of the Greater South but also the outliers where the SBC was one of the top four religious denominations, clearly establishes the West as the principal adjunct to the South.

Historian Edwin Gaustad, in his *New Historical Atlas of Religion in America,* underscored the contrast between the SBC and the less effective northern Baptists: by 1990, he wrote, "the 'southerners' found themselves in Pennsylvania and New York, in the Old Northwest, in the Great Plains, and ultimately in California, Oregon, Washington, and even Alaska. 'Southern' no longer referred to a region but to a culture and an evangelical mode. Given the enormous size of the Southern Baptist Convention, this shift represented something of a thrust in the direction of the 'southernization' of American religion as a whole."[127]

Journalist Applebome, in *Dixie Rising,* made a related but larger point: "In a way that once would have seemed a contradiction in terms, Southern Baptists were no longer geographically Southern Baptists. Beginning in 1942, when they spread to California, Southern Baptist congregations have set up shop in every state in the Union; now there are 1,900 black congregations, 3,000 Hispanic ones, and 800 Korean ones, a denomination speaking 101 languages endlessly morphing and reproducing itself across the country, like a Southern gene, bringing both the Good News of Jesus and the conservative values of the small-town South with it."[128]

In the states of the old Confederacy, most of the SBC churches are English speaking, but this is not the case in the West. Almost any metropolitan area could illustrate the point; the Sacramento Association of Southern Baptist Churches includes the following ethnic congregations: Chinese (1), Vietnamese (1), Mien/Laotian (1), Hmong (1), Russian (3), Romanian (1), Korean (3), Hispanic (4), and Filipino (1). Black SBC churches are also many and increasing. In discussing Southern Baptists, then, clearly we are not talking just about WASPs. Nationally, ever more importance is also attaching to ASPs (Asian Protestants) and LAPPs (Latin American Pentecostal Protestants). However, the SBC can fairly be said to constitute a white conservative southern sphere of influence.

Here a brief return to the religious politics of race is in order. The SBC's cultural conservatism is not of the sort that inhibits nonwhite conversion and enlistment. What it does propound, though, is a conservatism of evangelical theology preoccupied with saving souls and dismissive of other designs—whether liberal sociology or government-run social-welfare programs—to ameliorate the ills of society. The answers, say SBC preachers, lie in the Bible and in coming to Jesus; government social-welfare planning and programs, in this view, only get in the way of individuals' assumption of personal responsibility and salvation.

In *Divided by Faith: Evangelical Religion and the Problem of Race in America,* two southern sociologists, Michael Emerson and Christian Smith, make a compelling case that evangelical beliefs support the status quo when they lead white southerners to insist that persons of both races are masters of their own fates and salvation. White evangelicals lopsidedly believe that if blacks don't get ahead, it is because of black culture or lack of initiative, explanations that pivot on individual responsibility. Under evangelical theology, social structures are not the real problem, and government action and involvement are rarely the solution—or so white true believers usually conclude.[129] To Emerson and Smith, these attitudes work to maintain racial divisions.[130] However, although such beliefs make southern whites unsupportive of legislation that many southern blacks favor, they do not seem to turn conservative black congregations away

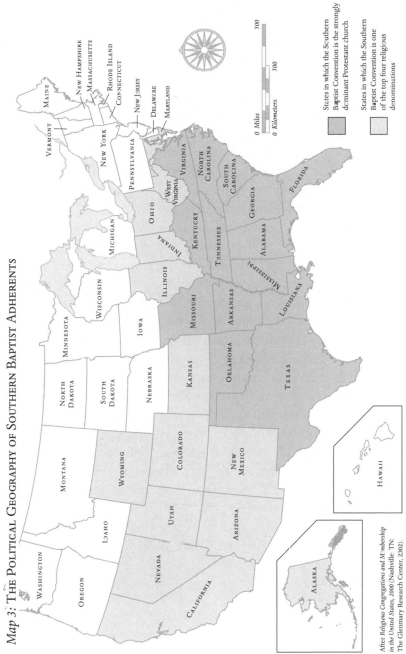

Map 3: THE POLITICAL GEOGRAPHY OF SOUTHERN BAPTIST ADHERENTS

States in which the Southern Baptist Convention is the strongly dominant Protestant church

States in which the Southern Baptist Convention is one of the top four religious denominations

0 Miles   500
0 Kilometers   500

After *Religious Congregations and Membership in the United States, 2000* (Nashville TN: The Glenmary Research Center, 2002).

from the SBC. On the contrary, their numbers have grown from virtually none in 1890 to eleven hundred in 1990 and twenty-seven hundred in 2000.[131]

Still, whether we look at Southern Baptists or other denominations sprung from eighteenth- and nineteenth-century roots in the South or border states, their original imprint in the West and Midwest, if not the recent ethnic embroidery, essentially came from white migration from below the Mason-Dixon Line. Billy Graham wasn't the only southerner who spread Dixie's evangelical faith. This case has been documented in detail by Oregon sociologist Mark Shibley, who penned the "Southernization" entry in the *Encyclopedia of Religion and Society*.[132] There, Shibley described his own research: "He showed that virtually all the membership growth in evangelical churches during the 1970s could be attributed to growth in historically southern evangelical churches. Moreover, Shibley found that the growth of southern-style religion was especially marked outside the South and corresponds with regions that experienced high levels of in-migration from the South during the same period. Shibley's book, *Resurgent Evangelicalism in the United States*, . . . showed that the pattern held through the 1980s."[133] However, along the Pacific, especially in California, the eighties saw local culture start to reshape conservative southern evangelical religion toward a more relaxed and liberal outlook.

A further point, of course, is that the southern-sprung religion spread across the West and Midwest was not all brought in by the SBC. Emigrants from the South and border states also brought restorationist or primitive denominations (Churches of Christ, Christian Churches, and Churches of God), as well as holiness, Pentecostal, and charismatic sects. While map 3 portrays the importance of the West as a lesser Southern Baptist outpost, chapter 6 will expand the portrait of conservative religion.

One is partly reminded of how much ethnic maps of Europe had changed between 1871 and 1919. New ethno-religious lines and borders often mean new political battlegrounds. And it is that uncertain clash to which we now turn.

6

The United States in a Dixie Cup

The New Religious and Political Battlegrounds

George Bush is an evangelical Christian, there is no doubt about that. The president's evangelicalism means he believes in the truth of the Bible, with a capital T: the virgin birth, the death of Christ on the Cross for our sins, the physical resurrection, and most important, a personal relationship with Jesus.

—Richard Land, chief Washington representative of the
Southern Baptist Convention, 2003

The religion gap is the leading edge of the "culture war" that has polarized American politics, reshaped the coalitions that make up the Democratic and Republican parties and influenced the appeals their presidential candidates are making. . . . Voters who say they go to church every week usually vote for Republicans. Those who go to church less often or not at all tend to vote Democratic.

—Susan Page, *USA Today*, 2004

For the first time since religious conservatives became a modern political movement, the President of the United States has become the movement's de facto leader.

—Dana Milbank, *The Washington Post*, 2001

The Bush administration's worldview is one grounded in religious fundamentalism—that is, it emphasizes absolutes, authority, and tradition, and a divine hand in history and upon the United States. Such a worldview is disastrous for a democratic system.

—David Domke, *God Willing*, 2004

171

172 TOO MANY PREACHERS

———

PLEASE REREAD THE FOUR EPIGRAPHS ABOVE. FOR THE FIRST TIME, THE
United States has a political party that represents—some say over-
represents—true-believing frequent churchgoers. And theocracy, a subject
once confined to the history books, has crept into current-affairs journals.

The southernization of U.S. politics and the growing, glaring reorga-
nization of the Republican party around religion are like the chicken and
the egg: which came first is hard to say. The more crucial question for us
today is how far the two interrelated processes can proceed.

This is not the first time such a troubling confluence has occurred.
Once before, when a U.S. political party in control of the White House
became captive to an excessive southern ideology and hawkishness laced
with fundamentalism and adherence to Scripture, national governance
was transformed and the Republic thrown off course. War became inevitable. No matter that the same party three decades earlier had scored
a notable success by knitting a less-belligerent South into a new and dominant electoral coalition—there seems to be a fundamental drive rooted
in the South's haunted history, regional religion, and combative tem-
perament.

That earlier ill-fated political coalition was forged by the seventh U.S.
president, Democrat Andrew Jackson. When he unseated President John
Quincy Adams of Massachusetts in 1828 by sweeping the South, the border states, and Pennsylvania, Jackson initiated a cycle of Democratic White
House domination that lasted until the great sectional crisis of 1860. As
president from 1829 to 1837, he squelched South Carolina's attempted
"nullification" of federal law in 1832, an early harbinger of disunion. But
Jackson died in 1845, before the excesses of the cotton states precipitated
a fierce national debate.

In northern eyes, the slaveholding hauteur of the South was becoming
unacceptable, touching old regional and cultural divisions still with us
today. Martin Van Buren, originally Jackson's secretary of state and later
his vice president, became the northern spoiler for Democratic White
House hopes in 1848 by running as an independent antislavery (Free Soil)
candidate, fatally splitting the old coalition in pivotal New York. Two of
Jackson's former attorneys general shifted parties during the 1850s: one
of them, Supreme Court Justice John McLean, received 197 delegates at
the 1856 Republican presidential convention. Francis P. Blair, a leader of

Jackson's Kitchen Cabinet, helped organize the GOP that year. Lewis Cass, once Jackson's secretary of war, resigned from the Democratic administration of James Buchanan in 1860 because of its prosouthern excesses.[1] Two of Abraham Lincoln's new cabinet members in 1861—Treasury Secretary Salmon P. Chase of Ohio and Navy Secretary Gideon Welles of Connecticut—had earlier been Jacksonians. Rekindled sectionalism scripted new alignments.

That was a long time ago, to be sure. No comparable party tremors shook the first administration of George W. Bush, save briefly in 2001, when Vermont senator Jim Jeffords decided to leave the GOP, costing the party control of the upper chamber. Besides which, the twenty-first-century Greater South commands a much bigger share of the nation's population and resources than did the ill-fated Confederate states. The North no longer has its former advantage. Unlike members of the latter-day League of the South and other neo-Confederates, few New Englanders do more than joke about their own region's secession, although some might applaud a southern departure.

In this twenty-first century, of course, the North and South are no more likely to have a civil war than are Scotland and England or Ontario and Quebec. Even so, both of these quite relevant comparisons remind us how much ill will can endure in politics. Some contemporary U.S. tensions, moreover, do resemble those of the antebellum years: sharp national divisions between the red and blue (instead of the blue and gray), war hawks shrilling from a perch in Dixie, Bibles being brandished as public policy guides, pompous sermons proclaiming a chosen nation obliged to redeem the world, and fire-eyed preachers counting down to Armageddon (albeit in the holy land, not along the Potomac or Rappahannock). Too few of these symptoms, all in evidence before September 11, 2001, have been fully analyzed. Political hypotheses offered during 2004 about a "metro"/"retro" cleavage ignored the more significant historical precedents. And unfortunately, with respect to both southern belligerence and the dangers of crusading religion, this historical dimension suggests the need for great caution.

The second Bush term did provoke more candor among critics than the first had, especially with respect to the Republican party's emergence as the political vehicle of the scripturally zealous and religiously observant. Some of the implications for national policy making could hardly be ignored. The Middle East imbroglio was center stage, as was Washington's visible hostility toward the United Nations and its persistent difficulty in collaborating with international organizations. On another, related front, the government began to defy science, notably biotechnology, climate studies, and straight-talking petroleum geology. As chapter 7 will describe, there was theology (or pseudotheology) motivating elements of the new politics.

Those theological mainsprings, in turn, are substantially southern. As W. J. Cash argued more than half a century ago in *The Mind of the South,* the problem is that while "there are many Souths, the fact remains that there is also one South."[2] As we have seen, its regional commitment is strong. Moreover, if John Shelton Reed is likewise correct about the cultural persistence of an "enduring South," then its achievement of national leadership—census projections for population growth by 2020 and 2030 only underscore the new tilt—may ensure an enduring regional and religious tension. As we will see, religious excess and global crusaderism have fed off each other in prior leading world powers, and with dire results. To understand how these forces might impact America in the future, we must examine the extraordinary transformation of the Grand Old Party.

Southerners and Republicans: The Great Reversal

Back in 1860, who could have guessed? Very few southerners that year ever got a chance to vote for or against Abraham Lincoln and the Republican party. In the eleven states that shortly raised the Confederate flag, the nominee and his party—quite often equally despised—were simply not on the ballot. These states, for the most part, featured three-way races between the southern Democratic contender (John Breckinridge of Kentucky), the northern Democratic nominee (Stephen Douglas of Illinois), and the Constitutional Union choice (John Bell of Tennessee). The South Carolina legislature, uncommitted to any popular participation in choosing presidents, picked state Breckinridge electors itself. Missouri, Kentucky, and Maryland were scarcely less dismissive of Lincoln and the GOP.

This makes the turnabout of the last century and a half especially stark. The Republican presidential nominee took all eleven ex-Confederate states in both 2000 and 2004. Under George W. Bush, the rural and small-town Greater South became what GOP leaders reverently called "the base."

Party politics in the major Western nations offers no parallel to this great reversal. It is understandable only in light of one phenomenon: the transfer, over five decades, of deep-seated fealty to southern folkways and sectionalism from the Democrats to the Republicans. So what psychology reversed, how, and why?

When postwar reconstruction took the form of military rule in 1867, the Republican party, having no prior electoral relationship to the ex-Confederate states, established one with the working end of a bayonet. Former slaves would be enfranchised, and biracial coalitions orchestrated by northern advisers and expanded by white southern unionists—carpetbaggers and scalawags, in the lexicon of white ex-Confederates—would elect Republicans to state and national office. In the end, that political reconstruction fared little better than the parallel northern bid to reconstruct southern religion. The Democratic party's defense of southern white society would win it nearly a century of regional gratitude and fidelity. After a congressional commission gave Republicans the electoral votes of three disputed southern states in 1876's stalemated presidential contest, no state in Dixie supported another GOP presidential nominee until 1920, when semi-isolationist Tennessee voted Republican largely to protest Woodrow Wilson's war policies and involvement in Europe. Then 1928 saw southern Protestant objections to the Catholicism of the Democratic nominee, New York governor Alfred E. Smith, produce Republican successes in Tennessee, Florida, and Texas. No other victory would follow until Dwight Eisenhower's breakthrough in 1952.

Aroused by hostility to Franklin D. Roosevelt and the New Deal, upper-income whites from Houston to Palm Beach and the Virginia hunt country had started voting Republican for president by 1940. But while this had significance in parts of the outer South, it counted little in states such as Alabama, Arkansas, and Mississippi, where truly upper-income whites could be outvoted by a half-dozen fair-sized Baptist churches. Racial tensions broke away more voters in the late 1940s and 1950s. In 1952 Eisenhower carried three southern states, followed by five in 1956. Richard Nixon took three in 1960. Then conservative strategists let their ambitions below the Mason-Dixon Line get out of hand.

In 1964, by opposing civil-rights legislation, Barry Goldwater carried the five states of the Deep South, but lost in the outer South—and almost everywhere else. This electoral miscarriage inhibited future Republican strategies, demanding greater wisdom. After 1968, when Richard Nixon, making his second presidential bid, carried five southern states, Republicans held the White House for twenty years out of the next twenty-four. The GOP enforced basic civil-rights laws but emerged as the party willing to appoint Dixie conservatives to executive and judicial positions and to oppose unpopular desegregation remedies, such as the busing of pupils to promote racial balance.

In January 1972, Alabama governor George Wallace's third-party candidacy—strong enough in segregationist sentiment and populist rhetoric in 1968 to garner electoral votes in Georgia, Alabama, Mississippi, Louisiana, and Arkansas—slipped into the past tense when he decided to run only in that year's Democratic presidential primaries. Wallace's appeal played havoc in North and South alike. However, northern Democrats, firmly in control of the party's 1972 delegate-selection and nomination processes, responded to grassroots disarray by shifting leftward to nominate South Dakota senator George McGovern.

But even before that selection, the Washington rumor mill hummed with a related possibility. Just as the Republicans newly arrived in the capital in 1861 had been unable to control Congress until its southern Democrats went home to put on Confederate gray, breakthrough in 1972 required another big fix, some kind of new double harness. Southern politicians interested in an overt alliance included ex-governor John Connally of Texas, Senator Harry Byrd of Virginia, Mississippi senator James Eastland, and Congressman Joe Waggonner of Louisiana, leader of the southern conservative bloc in the House.

National GOP strategists devoutly hoped—and national Democrats mightily feared—that under the right circumstances, the conservative Democratic southern officeholders and influence-mongers of congressional Washington would join up. Figure 2 displays the electoral momentum hurtling the South toward presidential Republicanism, which Dixie Democrats well understood. After World War II, the slow emergence of the "second reconstruction" of the South, in this instance implemented by federal courts and U.S. marshals, covered that same, tense quarter century.[3] Historians using that term included C. Vann Woodward, Eric Foner, Dan T. Carter, Manning Marable, and Richard Vallely.

The enormity of southern support for Nixon in the 1972 presidential

FIGURE 2

The Dixie Presidential Shift: 1944 to 1972

Southern States Giving a Major Party Landslide Support (60% or over)	1944	1948*	1952	1956	1960	1964	1968*	1972
Over 60% GOP	None	None	None	None	None	Miss. Ala.	(Other states diverted by Wallace) None	Ala. Ark. Fla. Ga. La. Miss. N.C. S.C. Tenn. Tex. Va.
Neither Party over 60%	None	8 States	8 States	10 States	10 States	8 States	11 States	None
Over 60% Democrat	Ala. Ark. Fla. Ga. La. Miss. N.C. S.C. Tenn. Tex. Va.	Ark. Ga. Tex. (Other states diverted by Dixiecrats)	Ala. Ga. Miss.	Ga.	Ga.	Tex.	None	

*Most of the 1948 Thurmond vote would have stayed Democratic in a two-way race; 1968 polls showed that most of the Wallace vote would have gone to Nixon in a two-way race.

Source: Kevin P. Phillips, *Mediacracy* (New York: Doubleday, 1974), p. 112.

election is still inadequately understood, mostly because its fruition between 1973 and 1976 was reversed by the Watergate scandal. I can remember being flabbergasted as I read the county-by-county figures
weeks after the election. Two decades later, in *The Vital South: How
Presidents Are Elected,* political-science professors Earl and Merle Black
looked back on those dimensions as "astonishing . . . the most overwhelming southern white vote—79%—ever won by a Republican presidential candidate," a peak that still stands.[4] The University of Michigan's
National Election Studies for 1972 put Nixon's share even higher, at
82 percent.[5] Ronald Reagan, George H. W. Bush, and George W. Bush
never matched these levels. Nixon's shortfall was in not being able to enlarge the opportunity to include major congressional gains.

Absent Watergate, some fusion of southern Democrats and Republicans
would almost surely have taken place. An unsullied Nixon would have
claimed 62 to 63 percent of the presidential vote instead of 61 percent,
avoided a stay-at-home moderate GOP protest movement, and pulled in
twenty to thirty new Republican senators and congressmen instead of
the net ten seats actually gained. That increment, along with the omission
of what by early 1973 became a blighting scandal, would have consummated high-level negotiations with thirty to forty amenable southern
Democrats. As several accounts have rightly described, both the executive and legislative branches would have been reconfigured under some
power-sharing arrangement.[6]

With Nixon destroyed, any hope of cross-party alliance fell apart, enabling the Democrats to narrowly win the 1976 presidential election.
They did so with a born-again, Southern Baptist ex-governor of Georgia,
Jimmy Carter, who took ten of the eleven ex-Confederate states, losing
only Virginia. The role of the South in national politics was thrown back
up into the air—or it appeared to be.

On the day of Carter's inauguration in January 1977, Democrats controlled nine of the eleven ex-Confederate governorships, sixteen of the
twenty-two southern U.S. Senate seats, and almost three-quarters of the
region's seats in the House of Representatives. The hemorrhage feared in
1972 had been avoided, and Carter's election pushed glum Republicans in
Washington farther to the sidelines. The reduced percentage of Senate
and House members from the South who were Republican in 1977 cut

short the rise from just a handful in 1953, to not quite a quarter in 1969, and over 30 percent in 1973, postponing the sharp gains that early 1970s fusion would have brought until 1994. For a few years Democrats dreamed of renewing their southern and evangelical support, but in 1980 those hopes collapsed.

Let me suggest an unacknowledged influence for the hiatus of the 1970s. Much of the short-lived post-1973 liberal renaissance produced by Watergate marshaled behind issues ultimately tied to religion: the Supreme Court's 1973 *Roe v. Wade* decision opening up the Pandora's box of legalized abortion, the secular campaign against school prayer, the excitement of women to put the Equal Rights Amendment into the Constitution (especially unpopular with religious conservatives committed to women's traditional role), and various aspects of the sexual revolution (gay rights, women's liberation, mainstream acceptance of pornography, and school or government distribution of contraceptives). All of these new issues surging to the fore angered conservative family-values advocates. A 1972 fusion, by contrast, might well have reduced both the secular liberal pressure and the powerful countermobilization of the religious right. In retrospect, besides stalling electoral history, the delay ensured that the battle march would be "Onward, Christian Soldiers," not an occasional stanza of "Dixie." As the new agenda led to culture wars, the Carter administration, despite its southern accent, became an ambuscade for Democratic hopes below the Mason-Dixon Line.

Before further amplification, a central premise must be introduced. Among the vital, albeit unwilling, architects of the Republicans' southern gains were the four southern Democratic presidents of the second half of the twentieth century. Three were Southern Baptists (Truman, Carter, and Clinton) and one belonged to the Disciples of Christ (Johnson). Over five decades, each pursued policies sought by national Democratic constituencies that strenuously contradicted traditional southern stances on cultural, religious, foreign-policy, and states'-rights issues. Truman's desegregation of the military, his executive order prohibiting discrimination in federal employment, and other civil-rights proposals spurred the 1948 revolt of the Dixiecrats, many of whom then took up GOP presidential voting in 1952. Johnson, in turn, alienated the core South with his advocacy of civil-rights legislation and portions of the Great Society.

Carter managed to annoy even his fellow Southern Baptists with his positions; and Clinton, despised in many of the region's churches, consummated the cultural and moral disenchantment.

Racial policy, to some the obvious and all-encompassing explanation, in my opinion probably accounted for one-third to one-half of the white voter exodus that took place. Foreign policy, especially bungled war mismanagement, also offended the South—then and now America's most hawkish region. Truman and Johnson presided over the U.S. military embarrassments in Korea and then Vietnam. Carter often looked weak and in 1980 flubbed the rescue of the fifty-three Americans held hostage in Iran. Clinton's military image, in turn, took three wounds: from his youthful anti–Vietnam War stance, his impolitic emphasis during his first week in office on permitting gays to serve in the military, and the analogy posed by the Hollywood movie *Wag the Dog,* which caricatured a president who waged war in the Middle East to take Americans' eyes off a sexual liaison.[7] Clinton profited on the economic front, but Truman, Johnson, and Carter all lost support by appearing to abet inflation, and the last of these suffered also from a reelection-year recession. But if liberals tend to overstate race as the be-all and end-all, there is no doubt about its importance.

The Democrats' crowning problem lay in a deepening mismatch with the cultural and religious viewpoints of their erstwhile bastion, the white South. When Democratic administrations were in office, Washington authorities were as much at odds with the southern white majority as the carpetbaggers of old, which helps to explain the resentments unleashed. The centennial of the first reconstruction, unpopular below the Mason-Dixon Line, helped turn memory into working analogy. How many white southerners, with their famous "backward glance," perceived the essential role reversal: that over the years the northern-run *Democratic* party, albeit only informally, was the one using southern-born presidents to implement a second reconstruction and to build biracial coalitions along the lines pursued one hundred years earlier by GOP firebrands such as House Speaker Thaddeus Stevens and Senate president pro tem Benjamin Wade?

One hundred years of "lost cause" worship had turned this regional sensitivity into a political nerve ending. In retrospect, the Democratic party by the mid-1960s could elect no one but southerners to the presidency, a tricky requirement that the nominees sensed. Even Johnson, the Texan who generally emphasized his home state's western roots, deepened his drawl when he visited the South.[8] However, all four were obliged to implement northern liberal cultural agendas. By the 1990s neo-Confederates were nicknaming them scalawags.

The contemporary parallels cannot be ignored. In *The Vital South,* the Black brothers pointed out that "the Reagan campaign [of 1980] also criticized Carter as a betrayer of southern values." Wallace had made some of that case against Johnson, and southern Republicans belabored Clinton with it.[9] The president from Arkansas later chuckled about southerners calling him a "scalawag" in the nineteenth-century sense: "They see me as an apostate. . . ."[10] Conservative Democrats who had switched parties wielded this rhetorical saber with particular enthusiasm. In Mississippi, former governor John Bell Williams told a 1980 crowd that "Jimmy Carter took us down the boulevard of broken promises." Ridiculing Democrats who urged support for Carter because "he's a Southerner born and raised in the South," Williams asked, "Do you see any indication of it in the last four years?" The assembled Mississippians roared, "No."[11]

Both Nixon and Reagan sharpened their appeals to the South with tangible policies as well as federal nominations. However, much of what they offered was symbolic: Nixon's rhetoric on busing and law and order, Reagan's 1980 embrace of states' rights in a visit to bloodstained Neshoba County, Mississippi (where three civil-rights workers had been killed in 1964), his appearances with Jerry Falwell, and his jokes about "welfare queens." Republicans knew now they had to sidestep the Goldwater trap of actual opposition to black civil rights.

In fact, most of the great GOP advances below the Mason-Dixon Line came from angry white responses to southern and border-state Democratic presidencies. As noted, Eisenhower's southern breakthroughs in 1952 followed the Dixiecrat revolt of 1948 and the ensuing shifts of many Dixiecrat supporters—in low-country South Carolina, the Mississippi Delta, and bayou and northern Louisiana—to GOP presidential voting. Reactions against Lyndon Johnson's policies fueled the next big cluster of GOP southern breakthroughs: Goldwater's sweep of the Deep South in 1964, the sizable congressional gains in 1966 (including the South), the Democrats' 1968 loss of ten of the eleven ex-Confederate states to Nixon and Wallace, and the Republican presidential crest of 1972, when the

1968 Wallace vote went to Nixon. Dissatisfaction with Carter fueled the next sequence: GOP midterm gains in 1978 (including the Texas governorship), followed by the Reagan sweep in 1980, with its attendant major southern congressional gains and capture of the Senate.

Following these, the next big inroads—the fourth such sequence in the South—began in 1994, when a so-called midterm "negative landslide" against Clinton swung both the House and the Senate to the Republicans. By the end of 1995, the new leaders of the Senate were Majority Leader Trent Lott of Mississippi and Senate president pro tem Strom Thurmond of South Carolina, the Dixiecrat presidential nominee of 1948. The strong Dixie follow-up in the presidential election of 2000 and the 2002 congressional races also seems, as we will see, to hark back to the southern-led 1998 impeachment of Clinton, with its accompanying revelations of immorality and Bible Belt outrage.

Can these incremental southern shifts be said to flow from the second reconstruction? In considerable measure, but especially in the sixties, seventies, and eighties, they can. By the 1990s, first under George H. W. Bush, then under Bill Clinton, and finally under George W. Bush, the mainsprings of U.S. politics were shifting from economics, race, and cultural symbolism to a new set of divisions rooted in beliefs and theology that transcended the simplistic "values" label left over from prior culture wars. Talk about the Republicans becoming a religious party akin to the Italian or German Christian Democrats began in 1988, grew in 1992 and thereafter, and caught hold in the George W. Bush years.

The First American Religious Party

Since its founding, the United States has never had a national religious party of any kind, either one that was denominational or one that collected the religious of all faiths to fight secularism. Europe and Asia, of course, have had religious parties aplenty specifically aligned with Catholic, Protestant, Jewish, Hindu, Islamic, or Buddhist interests. These have principally marshaled one faith rather than mobilized religious intensity on a multidenominational basis. By the second administration of George W. Bush, the Republican party in the United States was on the road to a new incarnation as an ecumenical religious party, claiming loyalties from hard-shell Baptists and Mormons, as well as Eastern Rite Catholics and Hasidic Jews. Secular liberalism was becoming the common enemy.

In the late nineteenth century, religion played a large enough role in voter choice of parties that many denominations displayed lopsided loyalties. In the Midwest circa 1884, for example, the Yankee Congregationalists, Swedish Lutherans, and Welsh Methodists were overwhelmingly Republican, while German and Irish Catholics, Wisconsin Synod Lutherans, and Southern Baptists were lopsidedly Democratic.[12] Conceivably the most devoted worshippers were especially strong in their partisanship, but no survey takers left records. Among current-day Americans, however, polls and experts identify persons with the most intense religiosity and greatest frequency of attending services as the most Republican. Among Jews, the Orthodox—with their large families, somber clothing, and Old Testament mind-set—take the Republican side, while secularized Reform Jews are heavily Democratic. Even with respect to Bible believers, though, quibbles arise. Religiosity often makes blacks, especially SBC adherents, more conservative, but it doesn't make black churchgoers as a class Republican. Nor does deep-seated liberal Christian theology make Episcopal or Unitarian feminists potential recruits for GOP women's groups. And theologians for the moderate-liberal faction of the Southern Baptist Convention tend to be Democrats.

Exceptions prove the rule summed up by political analyst William Schneider: "Since 1980, religious Americans of all faiths—fundamentalist Protestants, observant Catholics, even Orthodox Jews—have been moving towards the Republican Party. At the same time, secular Americans have found a home in the Democratic Party. This is something new in American politics. We have never had a religious party in this country."[13] The United States, to be sure, is also the only major Western nation to be caught up in a powerful conservative religious tide.

As recently as the early 1960s, national politics still operated in the lingering sunset of the Civil War–era denominational alignments. Mainline Protestantism was the central and sedately respectable image of the GOP, and there were jokes about the Episcopal Church being the Republican party at prayer. The Democrats, for their part, still enjoyed lopsided support from northern Catholics and Southern Baptists. By 1972, however, when the conservative counterattack against secularism and social liberalism registered its first great triumph, new cracks were visible in the old cement. According to a 2004 review of Gallup/CNN/ *USA Today* polls, "The religion gap didn't exist before 1972. Voters who said they went to church every week didn't vote any differently than those who did not. But after the tumultuous 1960s, President Nixon appealed to the traditionalist views of the nation's 'silent majority.' A significant gap, 10 percentage points, opened in the 1972 election."[14]

That Republican ten-point edge among churchgoers has been ascribed to the fact that Nixon's opponent, George McGovern, came from the liberal activist wing of the Democratic party, prompting Republican campaigners to label him "the triple-A candidate—Acid, Amnesty and Abortion." More recently, analyses by Geoffrey Layman of Vanderbilt University and Louis Bolce and Gerald De Maio of the City University of New York provided a more measured explanation. Comparing national convention delegates and activists from 1972 to 1992, Layman found that in 1972, secularists—atheists, agnostics, religious "nones," the unchurched, and the self-identified "irreligious," most of them McGovern supporters—constituted the largest "religious" bloc among Democratic delegates.[15] To Bolce and De Maio, the 1972 Democratic convention was tantamount to a "secularist putsch," after which the party began driving out traditionalists with its ever more secularist positions.[16]

Nixon's support in 1972 among white, southern regular churchgoers, most of them still registered Democrats, reached a stunning 86 percent, as measured by the American National Election Study. He drew 76 percent among members of SBC congregations, the latter being a somewhat lower-income slice of southern voters.[17]

Elections analyst Samuel Lubell, in his prescient book *The Future While It Happened* (1973), called Southern Baptists the "group having the most explosive impact," who "may have emerged holding the balance of voting power in the South and perhaps in the whole country. Nixon's speeches, in fact, seem designed to appeal to the traits which characterize Baptists—an ingrained individualism, suspicions of government and resentment of taxes. Baptists generally do not hold society responsible for man's failings, but believe that each man must find personal salvation by mastering his own inner soul and coming to know Jesus personally. They seem less concerned with changing society than with changing oneself."[18] Largely unheralded, this was the debut of the Southern Baptists as a Republican electoral force. A still grander overview of the forces active in 1972 came from futurist Herman Kahn: "The biggest movement in America in the 70's is the counter-reformation. Religions such as the Baptists, Church of Christ, Pentecostals, Jehovah Witnesses and the Jesus freaks are all on the same rise. I want to emphasize this because the United States is the only Western country that seems to be going through this counter-reformation on a large scale."[19]

But the Watergate scandal, besides destroying Nixon's presidency and the near-term Republican ability to capitalize on favorable trends, gave the Democrats the brief chance for a regional comeback in the election of Southern Baptist Jimmy Carter as president. The GOP's edge among churchgoers shrank, as Southern Baptists in 1976 gave 51 percent of their votes to Carter, whose credentials ranged from teaching Sunday school to fluency in the convention's figurative language of Zion. The SBC had even published Carter's campaign biography, *Why Not the Best?*, through its Boardman Press in 1975.[20]

Carter's misfortunes in the White House, while most glaring in the economic and foreign-policy arenas, also had a powerful but less obvious religious component. Watergate's revitalization of liberal activism, as we have seen, escalated issues—from the Equal Rights Amendment to renewed efforts to take religion out of public schools—that were simultaneously provoking a religious countermobilization. Between 1977 and Ronald Reagan's first year in office, a half-dozen new national organizations linked to religious conservatives emerged: the National Federation for Decency (1977), evangelist Jerry Falwell's Moral Majority (1979), the Religious Roundtable (1979), the Christian Voice (1979), the National Affairs Briefing (1980), the Council on Revival (1980), and the Council for National Policy (1981).[21]

By 1980 the president from Plains, Georgia, found himself in a crossfire akin to that which in 1979 had defeated his moderate-faction allies in the Southern Baptist Convention. Grassroots sentiment had shifted to the right. Carter's own positions on the new religious agenda now displeased SBC adherents and pastors, 60 percent of whom approved of Falwell's Moral Majority.[22] The Georgian never broke with the Southern Baptist Convention while president, but its earlier support of him chilled. In 1980 it passed a resolution calling Carter's White House Conference on the Family "a general undermining of the biblical concept of family." Other resolutions opposed abortion and the Equal Rights Amendment.[23]

Surveys showed Carter handily surpassing Reagan in public perception as a religious person and man of high moral principles, but such abstractions seemed not to matter.[24] The incumbent's Christianity was glum and quirky. Liberal Georgia historian Dan Carter later recalled the luckless president as a man who "talked of limits and self-denial, of aggression and pain. At its heart, the science of governing was a willingness to engage in an endless struggle to control man's sinful nature."[25] Under these circumstances, victory went to Reagan and his ability to mirror regional viewpoints and evoke the optimism of Southern Baptist evangelism and exceptionalism. Whereas Jimmy Carter had taken ten of the eleven southern states against Gerald Ford in 1976, Reagan won ten in 1980, leaving Carter only his home state.

Another significant change emerged in that year's U.S. Senate races. Catholic Republicans Don Nickles and Jeremiah Denton, both staunch conservatives, won seats in Oklahoma and Alabama, two states where anti-Catholicism had been visible in the presidential elections of 1928 and 1960. In 1980, with conservative, traditional Catholics such as Paul Weyrich, Richard Viguerie, and Phyllis Schlafly captaining the religious right, that no longer mattered. Humanism and irreligion had become the common foe, another milestone in the emergence of an American religious party.

Seeking reelection in 1984, Reagan took all eleven ex-Confederate states, winning percentages higher than any Republican nominee save Nixon. He, too, garnered a majority among Catholics. Even so, the former Hollywood actor was an unlikely president to orchestrate an across-the-board GOP appeal to church attendance and nuclear-family togetherness. He and his wife didn't usually go to church, something he had acknowledged years earlier, although during his White House years he explained that his security arrangements would disturb worshippers. Clearly religious in his way but also molded by Hollywood, Reagan was the only divorced president in U.S. history—let alone the only one to have been married to two movie stars. He had also had his share of family problems; one dysfunction came to light when his adopted son, Michael, raised a complaint: the then-president had never bothered to see his grandchild, Michael's daughter, who was two. Further, the Reagans' daughter, Patti, eventually spited them by posing nude for *Playboy*.

Nancy Reagan, in turn, had a long-standing interest in astrology, using it in planning her husband's activities and ultimately in checking the timeliness of his presidential schedule. This did not go unnoticed by religious traditionalists. In 1988 the Southern Baptist Convention had considered canceling a Reagan speech to their annual meeting following the revelation of how much attention the Reagans paid to the planets and stars.[26]

That same year, with U.S. evangelical and charismatic membership surging, the Christian broadcaster Pat Robertson, a Southern Baptist turned Pentecostal, decided on a bid for the Republican presidential nomination opened up by Reagan's retirement. Part of Robertson's assumption was that Vice President George H. W. Bush, as an Episcopalian and erstwhile Planned Parenthood and Equal Rights Amendment supporter, was too weak among true believers to win the nomination. When the dust settled, however, Bush had consolidated his Christian-right support not just for the nomination but for the November general election.

In itself, this was a watershed of sorts. The elder Bush was ready to court the conservative Christian electorate in a way that Reagan had never found necessary. In 1988 Bush published *Man of Integrity*, a book detailing his own born-again status and close ties to leading evangelical leaders. His son became a key liaison. According to *Newsweek*, "as a subaltern in his father's 1988 campaign, George Bush the Younger assembled his career through contacts with ministers of the then-emerging evangelical movement in political life."[27] Nor did the southern and religious emphasis end there. As his chief political aide Bush Senior chose Lee Atwater, a South Carolinian who specialized in go-for-the-jugular cultural politics; for vice president, he selected Indiana senator J. Danforth Quayle, a conservative ally of the Christian right.

The unusual religiosity of the 1988 campaign drew some well-deserved attention. For the first time in U.S. history, two prominent presidential candidates were clergymen: Robertson and Jesse Jackson for the Democrats.[28] Southern historian C. Vann Woodward found the year memorable because "it was so thoroughly saturated with religious issues, conflicts, personalities, fanatics, candidates, scandals and demagogues."[29]

Robertson's presidential bid led the Pentecostal Assemblies of God, his new army of foot soldiers, into Republican politics. They helped him to win caucuses in Hawaii, Alaska, Nevada, and Washington State and to make respectable caucus showings in Minnesota, Iowa, and Michigan.[30] By the general election, the Robertson organizers and Pentecostal rank and file had been recruited en masse by Bush, and surveys showed Assemblies of God ministers and activists as more than 90 percent Republican.[31] The SBC, unsupportive of Robertson and his practice of speaking in tongues, had stuck by Bush in the nomination drive.

State Republican parties were also moving to the right. In Oklahoma the 1988 GOP state platform read like a Pentecostal critique of U.S. society: opposition to homosexual marriage, New Age influence in education, abortion, surrogate motherhood, sex education, school-based health clinics, and such.[32] In Arizona, Robertson colluded with backers of ultra-conservative ex-governor Evan Mecham to write a Christian Reconstructionist state platform that declared the United States a "Christian nation" and asserted that the Constitution had created "a republic based upon the absolute laws of the Bible, not a democracy."[33] By the end of the 1990s more than half of the fifty Republican state committees had been taken over by the religious right at least once.

The Democrats, for their part, nominated Massachusetts governor Michael Dukakis, whose technocratic demeanor—commentator Garry Wills called him "the first truly secular" candidate for president in U.S. history—made George H. W. Bush look like a down-home Baptist deacon.[34] The Republican nominee also adopted Robertson's indictments of Dukakis—his membership in the "antireligious" American Civil Liberties Union, refusal to endorse the religious language in the Pledge of Allegiance, and imputed tolerance of child pornography—and found them effective. In a nutshell, Bush's courtship of the Christian right paid off.

Some of this benefit drained away by 1992, after the name-calling Republican primary campaign waged against Bush by Patrick Buchanan over cultural issues. In the general election, independent presidential nominee H. Ross Perot diverted secular Republicans from Bush, and the Democrats put part of the old Confederacy back in play by selecting Arkansas governor Bill Clinton, a Southern Baptist, albeit one allied to the moderate-liberal faction that was anathema to the SBC's ruling fundamentalists. Doubling his bet on the upper South, Clinton selected another moderate-liberal Southern Baptist, Tennessee senator Albert Gore, as his running mate. Thus, after carrying all eleven ex-Confederate states against Dukakis in 1988, Bush held only seven—Virginia, North Carolina, South Carolina, Florida, Alabama, Mississippi, and Texas—while Clinton took Arkansas, Tennessee, Louisiana, and Georgia.

The Southern Baptist Convention, fighting its own factional civil war, stuck with the GOP incumbent. Bush had spoken to the SBC's national meeting in 1991, tearfully reassuring the audience that the Gulf War had overcome his Episcopalian inhibitions about praying in public. Quayle addressed another national meeting in 1992, attacking abortion, homosexuality, and sex education and characterizing the 1992 campaign as a war between traditional values and the agenda of the liberal cultural elite.[35] The upshot, among white SBC voters, was a 49 percent to 37 percent Bush-Quayle lead over the all-Baptist Democratic team, in comparison to the 43 percent to 38 percent margin for Clinton over Bush in the nation as a whole.[36] Even more revealingly, the Republican presidential edge among frequent church attenders jumped to 14 percent, four points higher than Nixon's breakthrough numbers twenty years earlier.

In 1992, according to Vanderbilt University's Layman, the religion gap had become unmistakable. Bolce and De Maio, in turn, reported that "by the first Clinton election, divisions among party elites spilled into the general election and were so apparent in exit poll and public opinion data that one team of academic researchers identified 1992 alternatively as the 'Year of the Evangelical' and the 'Year of the Secular.' The vote distribution of white respondents who indicated that they had backed a major party candidate . . . support[s] this assertion. Clinton carried three fourths of the secular vote, while George H. W. Bush won two-thirds of the traditionalists."[37] Data from Gallup and the Voter News Service likewise confirmed 1992 as an inflection point for religious frequent attenders. Most of us, myself included, paid too little attention to this sea change, now startlingly clear in hindsight.

Within weeks of Clinton's 1992 election, unfriendly state SBC conventions had passed resolutions recommending that the president-elect be guided by prayer and biblical principle. Floridians urged him to stop supporting abortion and homosexual rights, and delegates to the national SBC meeting in 1993 passed a resolution combining the two themes.[38] Churchgoer dissatisfaction with Clinton boiled over by 1994, helping to bring about the southern-led GOP takeover of Congress. Regular church attenders polled eight points more Republican than other voters in the 1994 elections, the highest disparity in congressional contests to date.

On the GOP side, party gains below the Mason-Dixon Line in 1994 once again drew on local dissatisfaction with a southern Democratic presidency. This was the first, however, to result in a takeover of Congress led by *southern* Republicans. In 1953, when the GOP House of Representatives elected with Dwight Eisenhower convened, the geography of Republican control was still as northern as a blue Yankee uniform. The northeastern delegation was lopsidedly Republican (64 percent), while members from the South were almost solidly Democratic (92 percent). Even in 1973, when Watergate aborted GOP-Dixie fusion, the old blue-gray division still prevailed.

The southern upheaval in 1994 was the key to the congressional revolution. Even in 1997, as Congress remained Republican despite Clinton's reelection, the South sent the most Republican (61 percent) of regional delegations to the House of Representatives, while the Northeast chose the most Democratic (59 percent).[39] Nearly a quarter century after George McGovern's defeat in 1972, the great reversal had finally come to Congress.

The election of 1996 requires no great attention because a voter backlash against new House Speaker Gingrich and the shrill GOP Congress countered some of the negative focus on Clinton, who won easy reelection. The president from Arkansas carried four southern states (his home state, Florida, Tennessee, and Louisiana), even though the GOP maintained its sway over southern House seats. However, the next great cultural and religious catalyst—Clinton's affair with White House intern Monica Lewinsky and his subsequent impeachment—was not far away.

In retrospect, considerable attention has justifiably focused on the apparent 1998–2002 influence of Bill Clinton. In their pre-2004 election analysis of what they called "The New Religion Gap," John Green and Mark Silk, director of the Center for the Study of Religion in Public Life, found "one possible explanation" of the 1998–2002 trend arising out of the tawdry impeachment sequence: "Although the country as a whole did not favor removing Clinton from office, a sizeable number of frequent worship attenders may have been sufficiently distressed by the affair to change their voting habits. . . . It is conceivable that, in the late 1990s, an increasing number of frequent attenders transferred their moral disapproval of Clinton on to his party as a whole."[40] An analysis by Zogby International of its own polling data struck a similar note: "On the political, economic and social values espoused by [the Clintons] . . . a solid majority of Red State

FIGURE 3

Faith, Religiosity, and Partisanship, 2000–2004

Voter News Service exit polls, 2000

Group	% for Bush
Frequent-attending white religious right	87
Frequent-attending white Protestants	61
Frequent-attending white Catholics	57
Other white Christians	57
Less-attending white religious right	56
Less-attending white Protestants	51
Latino Protestants	48
Less-attending white Catholics	46
Other non-Christians	36
Latino Catholics	30
Secular	27
Jews	20
Black Protestants	9

Gallup/CNN/*USA Today* polls, 2003–2004

Frequency of religious attendance	% for Bush
More than once per week	68
Once per week	58
1–2 times per month	41
Few times a year	40
Seldom	39
Never	35

Note: 2003–2004 Gallup polls are for the preelection period.

voters reject the Clintons' values (56%) while 34% agree." Blue-state voters split almost evenly: 45 percent favorable, 47 percent unfavorable.[41]

Early in the 2004 election campaign, an analysis by *USA Today* of that newspaper's shared Gallup Poll data also touched on the Clinton effect: "Bill Clinton, dogged by rumors that he dodged the draft and cheated on his wife, won the [1992] election because of his promise to address voters' concerns about the economy and health care. But those who attended church each week were much less likely to support him than others. In 2000, [George W.] Bush emphasized the role that his born-again faith had played in turning around his life. The gap got bigger."[42]

In some ways George W. Bush had approached the 2000 election as a cross between political project and biblical mission. In 1999 he told an assemblage of Texas pastors that he believed God had called him to run. That same year he spoke to the Council for National Policy, a group that included religious-right leaders and some Christian Reconstructionists. No text of that meeting has ever been released. In one televised debate in 2000 with his rivals for the GOP nomination, Bush, upon being asked to identify the thinker who had most influenced him, stunned viewers with his answer: Christ.[43]

If the elections of 1988 and 1992 had unusual religious components, the election of the millennium had even more, although once again hindsight provides illumination. Well before September 11, 2001, religion and intensity of faith and worship were emerging as the principal dividing lines in national politics. The "religious party" that Ohio political scientist John Green and others had tentatively discerned in the 1988 electoral tea leaves was becoming a reality, as poll data proclaimed.

From ten points in its unheralded 1972 debut, the religion gap dropped to single digits for two decades. Then it jumped back into prominence (fourteen points) in 1992, expanding eight years later to a record twenty points. Although legitimate doubts were raised about frequency of attendance at services being the best measure, the basic thesis of religiosity's importance gained wide acceptance. The whys and wherefores were clear enough. To Geoffrey Layman, "the two parties' positions on issues, especially moral issues like abortion, gay marriage and prayer in schools, have grown increasingly polarized, and it's these issues that are the key to the religious split between the parties. This is something we're seeing across the country."[44] Religion watcher John Green explained that "once

social issues came to the forefront—abortion, gay rights, women's rights—
it generated differences based on religious attendance."[45] Theology was
beginning to exert real electoral influence.

Although the 2002 midterm elections were influenced by the memory
of September 11 and saber rattling over Iraq, they also extended the 2000
pattern, which was shaped by religion, morality, and anti-Clinton sentiment. In the 2000 congressional races frequent attenders at religious services were eighteen points more Republican than the overall electorate,
and in 2002 the congressional "religion gap" widened to twenty points.[46]
According to Green, "frequent attending white Protestants turned out in
significantly higher numbers in the South than in other regions of the
country—and that fueled impressive GOP victories south of the Mason-
Dixon Line."[47]

The election of 2004 did not greatly change the alignments of 2000.
But it did highlight small trends and offer clarifications—the fallout of
September 11 on religious voters, for example—of the forces redefining the
national Republican electorate. It is to these contours that we now turn.

Born-Again Republicans: 2004 and the New Religiopolitical Map

By 2004 some 43 to 46 percent of Americans described themselves as
born again in Christian faith, although perhaps half of those would not
have passed a strict set of three or four follow-up criteria.[48] At the same
time, some 40 percent of Americans said they frequently attended religious services, although some academics thought 30 percent would be a
more truthful figure. Combining both groups, with their admittedly
large overlap, reasonably religious voters cast close to half of the nation's
votes. Among whites, some 70 to 75 percent supported George W. Bush
and represented by far the largest portion of his electoral coalition. As
USA Today said in introducing its poll analysis, "Forget the gender gap.
The 'religion gap' is bigger, more powerful and growing."[49]

If the religion gap has indeed become the most important denominator of American voting patterns, then we ought to be able to draw a
good map of what happened in the Bush-Kerry contest using religious
data and denominational concentrations. And, indeed, we can. The map
of red Republican states facing blue Democratic states—between 2000
and 2004, two (Iowa and New Mexico) shifted to the red side and

one (New Hampshire) to the blue side—suffices to begin the conversation.

Before the 2004 ballots were cast, pollster John Zogby took the red-blue divisions of four years earlier and explained their most revealing components. In the red states collectively, 57 percent of the voters were Protestant, 23 percent were Catholic, and 1 percent was Jewish; those in the blue states were 37 percent Protestant, 33 percent Catholic, and 4 percent Jewish. More red-state voters were married (64 percent) than were blue-state voters (56 percent). In the blue states 20 percent were single as opposed to 10 percent in the red ones. Urbanites, college graduates, younger voters, Catholics, Jews, and union members were more numerous in the blue states, while the red bloc had the edge in born-again Christians, gun owners, rural dwellers, conservatives, and military veterans.[50]

What slowly became clear about the 1994–2004 decade was that different denominations, theologies, intensities of faith, and secularisms bred disparate viewpoints on issues such as abortion, family roles, prayer, the definition of marriage, and gay rights. Banners of the so-called culture wars for a quarter century, the salience of these concerns to fast-growing conservative Christian denominations, in particular, helped to make religiosity, biblical fundamentalism, and theology increasingly vital keys to U.S. electoral behavior.

Talk about supposed "values" had long muddied the underlying divisions. In the 2004 exit polls, values meant one thing to supporters of Ralph Nader and a very different set of topics to conservatives. For true believers, commitment to biblical inerrancy is a theological mandate. The belief that society can be seriously reformed only by saving souls, not by embracing government welfare or manipulation, has become a tenet of evangelical religion, not just a mere "value." Values are what *society* holds; what *churches* hold is theology and belief.

Figure 1, on page 102, profiled some of the disparate views substantially shaped by religious intensity and denomination. Much in electoral politics, in turn, can be clarified by identifying the concentrations of key denominations and theologies in different sections of the United States. Viewed through that lens, the outcomes make more sense.

To begin with, the 2000 and 2004 elections narrowly won by George W. Bush constitute an uncommon pairing—unusual because presidents who get elected in close races and then go on to obtain a second term usually do so by opening up broad support, thus winning that race handily (Jefferson in 1804, Lincoln in 1864, McKinley in 1900, Nixon in 1972). Bush's 50.7 percent share in 2004, by contrast, was the weakest for an incumbent since Woodrow Wilson in 1916. (And even Wilson raised his vote share by nearly eight points between 1912 and 1916.) What this suggests—and what the voting data amplifies—is that his presidency rested on an uncommonly narrow base. Part of the explanation lies in the increasingly narrow, even theocratic, sentiment among Republican voters displayed in figure 4.

Among religions and denominations, Bush had both gains and losses. White evangelicals increased their support from 72 percent in 2000 to 78 percent in 2004. John Green, the religious-voting expert, hesitated about overcrediting evangelicals. He noted that "religious conservatives were absolutely critical to President Bush's re-election, . . . but it was a broader coalition of religious groups. Central to that group were evangelical Protestants, but it also included Catholics, black Protestants, and other groups as well."[51]

The influence cut across racial and cultural lines. Black support for Bush, up from 8 percent in 2000 to 11 percent in 2004, was greatest (22 percent) among frequent church attenders. Much of this gain pivoted on the gay-marriage issue, which was emphasized by many black pastors.[52] Among Jews Bush's support jumped from not quite 20 percent in 2000 to about 25 percent in 2004. Well below what his advisers hoped for, the improvement largely depended on Jewish groups associated with Israel's religious right. According to the Israeli newspaper *Haaretz,* "approximately a quarter of American Jewish voters cast their votes for Bush this time, as opposed to 18.5% four years ago. Experts calculated that about 85% of Orthodox Jews and about 95% of Haredi Jews voted for him. The high birthrate in these two communities helps to explain the significant rise in Jewish votes that went to the Republicans."[53] The Orthodox group, 8 percent of all U.S. Jewish voters, included both Hasidic and Haredi Jews, the latter being the ultra-Orthodox, including Lubavitchers, whose small, independent Israeli party in 2005 belonged to the governing right-wing Likud coalition in the Jerusalem parliament that was closely tied to the Bush administration.

On the other side of the demographic ledger, Republican support from the U.S. Muslim population of some four million plummeted from a solid majority in 2000—credited in some quarters with helping to carry

FIGURE 4

The Theocratic Inclinations of the Republican Electorate

Should a political leader rely on religion when making policy decisions?[a]

	Yes	No
Conservatives	63%	32%
Republicans	62	35
National sample	40	55
Independents	38	59
Moderates	36	58
Democrats	27	65
Liberals	20	77

Which worries you more, politicians inattentive to religion or politicians too close to religion and its leaders?[b]

	Inattentive	Too close	Depends/unsure
Republicans	53%	30%	17%
National sample	35	51	14
Independents	29	53	18
Democrats	25	65	10

Should religious leaders try to influence politicians' positions on the issues?[c]

	No	Yes
White conservative evangelicals	37%	62%
White churchgoing evangelicals	46	53
Conservatives	49	49
Republicans	50	48
White evangelicals	53	46
Catholics	65	34

continued

FIGURE 4 (*continued*)

	No	*Yes*
National sample	64%	35%
Independents	67	32
Moderates	69	29
Democrats	71	28
Nonevangelical Protestants	70	27
Seculars	77	22

Do you think religious leaders should try to influence government decisions?[d]

	Yes
United States	37%
Italians	30
Canadians	25
Australians	22
Koreans	21
Germans	20
British	20
Spanish	17
French	12

[a] Source: ABC/*Washington Post*, April 2005.

[b] Source: CBS News/*New York Times*, Nov. 2004.

[c] Source: ABC News/*Washington Post*, May 2004.

[d] Source: Associated Press/Ipsos Poll, International Comparisons, June 2005.

Florida for the party—to between 10 and 20 percent in 2004.[54] Muslim majorities in urban southeastern Michigan, Islam's largest U.S. population concentration—in Dearborn, local McDonald's even have halal Chicken McNuggets—helped Kerry carry that state.

Among U.S. Protestants, Bush paid for gains on the right by losing some mainline Protestants, once the Republican base. Analyst Green told a television interviewer that in 2004 "Bush got a majority of mainline Protestants. But his support was down a little bit from the 2000 election, particularly among the regular[ly] attending mainline Protestants. . . . This was one real bright spot for the Kerry campaign among religious groups. A lot of those regularly attending mainline Protestants have a somewhat more liberal theology and care about issues like the environment and poverty."[55]

To map the conservative Republican victory coalition, let us start with map 3 on page 169. This showed the Southern Baptist Convention core states in the old Confederacy, plus the adjacent layer in the old border (West Virginia, Kentucky, Missouri, and Oklahoma) and beyond these the SBC's twentieth-century extension into western states where by 1990 it had become one of the top four religious denominations. The national SBC provides the most important color base of the red-state map.

Map 4 adds the rest of the GOP's critical religious geography. The small circles indicate the Mormon concentration, which is centered on Utah and southern Idaho but also extends into Oregon, Nevada, Montana, Arizona, and New Mexico. In the 1890s and 1900s, when the Republicans controlling Washington finally came to terms with the Church of Latter Day Saints—making Utah a state (1896) and later seating Reed Smoot, a Mormon apostle, in the U.S. Senate (hearings stretched between 1904 and 1908)—part of the motivation was electoral. GOP strategists had literally drawn a map. Of the eleven states or territories along or west of the Rockies, seven had significant Mormon populations, making the church a potential broker in national politics.[56] The calculus—partly that of President Theodore Roosevelt—was sound. In 2004 U.S. Mormons—now ten times more numerous—gave almost 90 percent support to George W. Bush, and their western concentration underpins the GOP domination in Utah and Idaho and assists in the other Rocky Mountain states.[57]

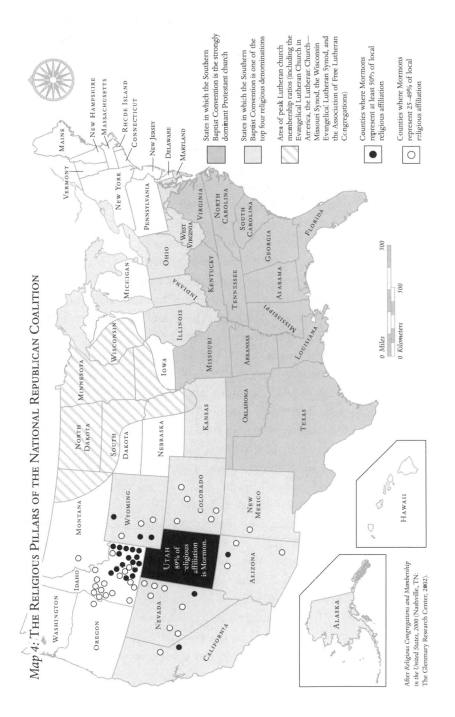

Map 4: THE RELIGIOUS PILLARS OF THE NATIONAL REPUBLICAN COALITION

States in which the Southern Baptist Convention is the strongly dominant Protestant church

States in which the Southern Baptist Convention is one of the top four religious denominations

Area of peak Lutheran church membership ratios (including the Evangelical Lutheran Church in America, the Lutheran Church—Missouri Synod, the Wisconsin Evangelical Lutheran Synod, and the Association of Free Lutheran Congregations)

● Counties where Mormons represent at least 50% of local religious affiliation

○ Counties where Mormons represent 25–49% of local religious affiliation

UTAH 89% of religious affiliation is Mormon.

0 Miles 500
0 Kilometers 500

After *Religious Congregations and Membership in the United States, 2000* (Nashville, TN: The Glenmary Research Center, 2002).

200 TOO MANY PREACHERS

The next group, too scattered to effectively display on map 4, involves the leading restorationist, or "primitive" denominations (Churches of Christ, Christian Churches), the top holiness groupings (Church of the Nazarene, the Indiana-based Church of God), and the conservative Pentecostals (Assemblies of God, Pentecostal Assemblies, and the Tennessee-based Church of God). Most of these had southern or border-state origins, and their highest ratios are still concentrated in the South, the border states, the Ohio Valley, the lower Great Plains, and the West.[58] Most of the states in which these denominations concentrate are part of the red bloc, with the principal exceptions of Oregon and Washington, which in addition to major concentrations of holiness and Pentecostal denominations also have unusually high secular ratios.

To round out map 4's portrait, the striped area represents four Lutheran denominations, most notably the archconservative Missouri Synod Lutherans (2.5 million strong) and the moderate-conservative Evangelical Lutheran Church in America (4.5 million). The latter took shape in 1988 from a merger of three midsized denominations, themselves formed by the earlier amalgamation of dozens of small German and Scandinavian ethnic Lutheran denominations.[59] Although Lutherans dominate in a number of Pennsylvania, Ohio, Indiana, Illinois, and Missouri counties, their overwhelming population ratios and regional dominance concentrate in the upper Midwest.[60] Missouri Synod Lutherans appear to have backed Bush by about four to one in 2004, and his overall 55 to 60 percent support among more centrist ELCA voters clearly varied by ethnic group and degrees of individual church attendance.[61]

Along with churchgoing Texas and Utah, the Lutheran strongholds of the northern prairie display some of the nation's highest ratios of church membership as a percentage of total population.[62] Conservative, pro-religious politics in these areas are intense, just as secularism and nonaffiliation reach their highest ratios along or near the East and West Coasts in technology, university, and counterculture centers such as San Francisco, Silicon Valley, Seattle, and Boston.[63]

From southern fundamentalists and midwestern Germans to Rocky Mountain Mormons, this religious geography helps to explain the deep-hued scarlet of the core red states. On the periphery, Wisconsin and Minnesota are the swing states of eastern Lutherdom. What was once "the border" in post–Civil War U.S. politics—from Maryland through

West Virginia and Kentucky westward through Missouri to Oklahoma—lost that status in 2000 and 2004. Overwhelmingly urban and suburban Maryland has been absorbed into the northeastern megalopolis that runs from Washington to Boston, while the remaining four states are sufficiently influenced by Southern Baptists, other conservative Baptists, restorationist and holiness denominations, and Pentecostals to qualify as traditionalist redoubts.

Religiopolitically the new "border" runs from southern Pennsylvania across Ohio through southern Indiana and Illinois to Iowa. In 2000 and 2004 Pennsylvania, Ohio, and Iowa were all battlegrounds. Rural and small-city southern Pennsylvania has the Northeast's closest approximation of a Bible Belt. In the West, presidential showdowns over the religion gap took place in Oregon and Washington, where Pacific Coast secularism, the nation's height of irreligion, meets the westward flow of Mormons, Southern Baptists, Assemblies of God, and Nazarenes. A second set of western battlegrounds lies in the Southwest: Nevada, Arizona, New Mexico, and Colorado. Here, emigration and influence from California, northern retirees, Hispanic Catholics, and artistic, resort, and vacation-home communities bump into large Mormon, conservative Baptist, evangelical, and Pentecostal contingents, some of them Latino, as well as the "Little Texas" conservative cultural extensions in New Mexico and Colorado.

As we will pursue further in the afterword, demographics favor the conservatives because the evangelical, Pentecostal, and fundamentalist denominations ranked as the fastest-growing ones at the turn of the century, outweighing the expansion of the secular, unaffiliated, or nonreligious element. The politics, however, are more problematic.

Theories of how the forty-third president takes after the ideology of Reagan, not of his father, the forty-first president, generally ignore a third alternative: the younger Bush's considerable echo of the conservative political fundamentalism displayed by Barry Goldwater. In the annals of late-twentieth-century American conservative strategy, the 38.5 percent of the national electorate won by Goldwater in 1964 stands as the nadir while the 59 percent won by Reagan in 1984 is the apogee. George W. Bush's 50.7 percent support in 2004 falls in the middle statistically. However, the gaps between Reagan's level of support and Bush's jump out of the electoral details. Figure 5 distills the state-by-state performances of Reagan and Bush the Younger. In the perceived cosmopolitan

FIGURE 5
George W. Bush and Ronald Reagan: A 1984–2004 Comparison

Worst Bush Declines

State	Bush Share of Total Vote for President, 2004	Percentage Point Decline Compared to Reagan, 1984
New Hampshire	49%	20
Vermont	39	19
Connecticut	44	17
Maine	45	16
Nevada	51	15
New Jersey	46	14
Massachusetts*	37	14
New York	40	14
Rhode Island	39	13
California*	45	13
Florida	52	13
Illinois	44	12
Arizona	55	11
Michigan	48	11
Colorado	52	11
Washington	46	10

Smallest Bush Declines (or Gains)

State	Bush Share of Total Vote for President, 2004	Percentage Point Decline (or Gain) Compared to Reagan, 1984
Alabama	63%	+2
West Virginia	56	+1
Kentucky	60	0
Tennessee	57	1
Mississippi	60	2
Georgia	58	2
Wyoming	69	2
Indiana	60	2
Minnesota*	48	2
Texas*	61	3

*A presidential nominee from these states was on the ballot in either 1984 or 2004, in several cases creating some distortion.

states of the Northeast, Great Lakes, Pacific, and Southwest, mostly blue but some red, Bush in 2004 trailed Reagan's 1984 showing by twelve to twenty points, a large and revealing shrinkage. The upper half of the figure lists the sixteen states that saw the steepest Bush decline relative to Reagan. We tend to forget how well Reagan did in this part of America. The bottom half, by contrast, shows the ten states where Bush ran close to Reagan's percentage or even ran ahead. The top four—Alabama, West Virginia, Kentucky, and Tennessee—are fundamentalist and evangelical strongholds notable for their unimpressive rankings in education, mental health, child poverty, and homicide rate. These are places where church drives have been strongest, where the new fundamentalist conservatism has been most appealing. Liberals even brandish unflattering data on red-state IQ measurements. In a number of West Virginia, Kentucky, and Tennessee Appalacian counties notable for high ratios of conservative Protestant sects, Bush gained five to ten points between 2000 and 2004.[64] Part of this increment reflected two additional decades of local spade-work by church and religious-right groups. In years to come, when academics complete their research, the sectarian tide in places such as Appalachia and the Ohio Valley should take on sharper definition.

Both geographically and ideologically, then, the younger Bush displayed much less outreach than Reagan. This also registers in a second portrait when the state-by-state support for George W. Bush in 2004 is compared with the particulars of the 1964 Goldwater debacle. Bush's national gain of twelve points over Goldwater was unevenly arranged. In bellwethers such as Illinois, Ohio, and Pennsylvania, Bush's gains were merely average: eight to twelve points, in line with his overall improvement over Goldwater. Where Bush built most successfully on Goldwater (gaining twenty points or more) was in the conservative "old border" and small-town interior West: in Kentucky, West Virginia, Missouri, and Oklahoma; in Utah, Idaho, Wyoming, Montana, North Dakota, and South Dakota; as well as in Alaska and Hawaii.[65]

Most of these states are culturally conservative. In the unusual circumstances of 1964, they had been scared away by Goldwater's hawkishness, economic conservatism, and Dixiecrat-seeming opposition to civil rights. By 2000 and 2004, however, they were far more amenable to an updated mixture of religious populism and political fundamentalism. In 2004 it helped that the sort of politics seeking approval already controlled the

White House, with its access to money and media (and control of the national-security dialogue), and simultaneously enjoyed massive support from a well-organized network of religious organizations and churches, principally SBC, Mormon, and Pentecostal. Goldwater had nothing similar.

In the early 1960s, before civil-rights stridency narrowed the appeal of the Goldwater campaign, conservative strategists striving for national realignment hoped to exploit roughly the geopolitical terrain that Bush did in 2000 and 2004. While the ability of Reagan—an ex-Democrat and four-time voter for Franklin D. Roosevelt—to win Massachusetts, New York, and Hawaii was centrist icing on the Electoral College cake, only the cake itself (baked by a bare majority of electoral votes) was constitutionally necessary. Bush did not dilute his conservatism or religiosity in search of a much larger margin.

Of course, by 2004 Bush had another advantage, a politico-moral platform that neither Goldwater nor Reagan could have remotely contemplated. The 2001 attacks on Manhattan and Washington touched the national psyche in a way that created a textbook opportunity for a response rooted in the conjunction of religious and political fundamentalism.

9/11: Seizing the Fundamentalist Moment

For months after the surprise attacks of September 11, the public's initial panic, anomie, and fear lingered. Sleeplessness and stress faded, but even a year later 50 percent of U.S. adults surveyed by CBS News felt "somewhat uneasy" or "under danger from terrorist attacks," and 62 percent said they still thought about September 11.[66] As national attention turned to the probability of a preemptive U.S. attack on Saddam Hussein's Iraq, a few pundits and scholars began to raise a further concern: had the public's apprehension and anxiety been molded into a new politics of good-versus-evil—"if you're not with us, you're against us"—rigidity, a crisis-forged, red, white, and blue ideology of religion, patriotism, and respect for authority?

Let me call some expert witnesses. Over several years, I've built a framework of explanation derived from the work of respected experts and authors: Martin E. Marty and R. Scott Appleby, editors of the multischolar Fundamentalism Project; Charles Kimball, professor of religion at Wake Forest University and author of *When Religion Becomes Evil: Five Warn-*

ing Signs (2002); Bruce Lincoln, professor of religion at the University of Chicago and author of *Holy Terrors: Thinking About Religion After September 11* (2003); David S. Domke, associate professor of communication at the University of Washington and author of *God Willing? Political Fundamentalism in the White House* (2004); and Bruce B. Lawrence, professor of religious history at Duke University and author years earlier of *Defenders of God: The Fundamentalist Revolt Against the Modern Age.* They found much to worry about.

In *Fundamentalisms Observed,* Marty and Appleby had explained the "family resemblances" between the different strong religions around the world. To begin with, *"Fundamentalisms arise in times of crisis, real or perceived.* The sense of change may be keyed to oppressive and threatening social, economic or political conditions, but the ensuing crisis is perceived as a *crisis of identity* by those who fear extinction as a people."[67] In the early nineties, the two had hypothesized that a public perception of moral unraveling in the United States was spreading such fear, but the events of September, alas, fit their definition far better.

Bruce Lawrence emphasized five symptoms of fundamentalism. Among them were a predilection to impose God's will—the one true faith—on other peoples, an intolerance of dissent, and a central reliance on inerrant scripture for ideology and authority. These, too, seemed characteristic of the post–September 11 White House.

Charles Kimball identified five principal perverse fundamentalist tendencies: (1) claiming absolute truth (when "people presume to know God, abuse sacred texts and propagate their particular versions"); (2) seizing upon an "ideal time," as in claims for imminent cataclysms or fast-approaching end times; (3) fostering blind obedience; (4) using ends to justify means (as in deaths or acceptance of collateral damage); and (5) pursuing "holy war" as in the Crusades (and to some extent the 1991 Gulf War).[68]

"Inauspicious" describes their applicability. Marty, Appleby, and Lawrence, writing years before September 11, 2001, had unknowingly anticipated traits of the Bush administration that were magnified in its responses to that traumatic event. In 2004 Kimball told a Baltimore interfaith meeting that he had become concerned about the indicators of a claim to absolute truth and George W. Bush's apparent belief in having a mission.[69]

Taking a second approach, Professors Lincoln and Domke analyzed the 2001–2005 speeches of top administration officials—for the most part those of George W. Bush himself—from the standpoint of what was said and with what apparent religious and political goals. In 2002 Lincoln had dissected Bush's October 2001 speech to the nation about his planned military response to the events of September 11. He found the president's rhetoric to be not unlike Osama bin Laden's own statements in that "both men constructed a Manichean struggle, where Sons of Light confront Sons of Darkness, and all must enlist on one side or the other, without possibility of neutrality, hesitation or middle ground."[70] While the American chief executive's words were less overtly religious than bin Laden's, Lincoln described a "double-coding" through which Bush signaled attentive Bible readers that he shared their private scriptural invocations— using phrases from the revelation of St. John (6:15–17, about the wrath of the lamb) and Isaiah (about evildoers hiding in caves and the lonely paths of the godless).[71]

Later, the Chicago theologian subjected the text of Bush's 2004 acceptance speech to the Republican National Convention to the same kind of double-coding analysis. In addition to a single paragraph on abortion and gay marriage, "early on, Bush spoke of 'hills to climb' and 'seeing the valley below,' an allusion to Israel's escape from slavery and Moses's vision of the Promised Land as described in Deuteronomy 34." Then, with respect to Afghanistan, Iraq, the war on terror, and the economy, he "described losses overcome through hope, steadfastness and faith." Only in Bush's culminating example, said Lincoln, "did he name what he saw in them all. 'For as long as our country stands,' he [Bush] proclaimed, 'people will look to the resurrection of New York City, and they will say "Here buildings fell, and here a nation rose."' *Resurrection.* Lower Manhattan may be a case in point, but it was not the point of the story."[72] The president used the phrase "I believe" twelve times, added Lincoln, and two of the references "were meant to justify his wars as holy. The first—'I believe that America is called to lead the cause of freedom in a new century'— prompts a question: called by whom? The second helps answer that query: 'I believe freedom is not America's gift to the world. It is the Almighty's gift to every man and woman.'"[73] The man in the White House was becoming America's preacher in chief.

Domke, in *God Willing?* and subsequent comments, flatly contended that Bush had pulled together "a religious fundamentalist worldview with political language to create a political fundamentalism" acceptable to Americans "in the aftermath of September 11."[74] Liberty and freedom, Domke interpreted, were set out as the God-defined norm for which Americans were fighting, both in Iraq and in the war on terror, and which Bush propounded as the ultimate remedy against both fear and terror.[75] To Domke, the White House marketed "the universal gospel of freedom and liberty" as a blessing that the president attributed to God, therefore in effect sending an implicit message—sometimes almost explicit—that he and the U.S. government were carrying out God's own wishes.

In a later analysis of Bush's September 2004 speech accepting the GOP nomination, Domke found the same clarion: "I believe that America is called to lead the cause of freedom in the new century."[76] Four months later Domke noted that in Bush's January 2005 State of the Union speech the president had used the words "freedom" and "liberty," in some form, thirty-four times, following forty-nine citations in his second inaugural address two weeks earlier. "The president's linkage of freedom and liberty with divine wishes," Domke concluded, "is indicative of how central an evangelical worldview is to his conception of the United States' role in the post-9/11 world. . . . [T]he U.S. government is doing God's work."[77]

As expert testimony, these remarks cohere powerfully around discomfort over Bush's sense of religious mission and seeming presumption that God speaks through him. Martin Marty commented in 2003 that "after September 11 and the president's decision to attack Iraq, the talk that other nations found mildly amusing or merely arrogant has taken on international and historical significance."[78] Appleby worried that Bush's global gospel of freedom and liberty was "a theological version of Manifest Destiny."[79] Kimball expressed concern about Bush's sense of mission, and Lincoln regretted that "George W. Bush believes God has called him to be president. You won't hear him say so openly, of course, but he regularly conveys this to a core constituency—the religious right."[80] Domke also elaborated that "Bush's fusion of a religious outlook with administration policy is a striking shift in rhetoric. Other presidents petitioned for blessings and guidance. Bush positions himself as a prophet, speaking for God."[81]

In mid-2004, when George W. Bush was campaigning among the Old Order Amish in south-central Pennsylvania, the *Lancaster New Era* ran a report that he told one gathering, "I trust God speaks through me. Without that, I couldn't do my job."[82] That same summer, *Time* commented that "however often Bush defends Islam as a religion of peace, his case for war now rests less on high-fiber geopolitical arguments than on the suggestion that the 3rd Infantry Division be used as an instrument of God's will to share the gifts of liberty with all people."[83] No analysis of the intertwining of Bible and state in Washington can ignore this kind of accumulating evidence and interpretation.

Initially, this twinning of religion and politics paid major political dividends in the public-opinion polls. So did maintaining the public's dual fear and belligerence with presidential orations about "evil ones," reports of new leads on this or that investigation, and upward and downward revision of the color-coded terror-threat levels: yellow, orange, then yellow again. Rhetoric from Washington so frequently interspersed sentences about Islamic terrorism and Osama bin Laden with references to Saddam Hussein and Iraqi evil that much of Bush's religious electorate muddled them into one dire threat and danger to the United States, as we will see. By 2004 and 2005 the presidential-campaign dialogue, the deterioration of the American position in Iraq, and the White House intervention prompted by the religious right in the Terri Schiavo "right to die" case began to clarify the sea change under way in the United States. Besides changing the nature of the Republican-Democratic party competition, the southernization of American governance and religion was abetting far-reaching ideological change and eroding the separation of powers between church and state. The theology soaking into U.S. politics was also bringing hints of theocracy, to which we now turn.

The Emerging Republican Theocracy?

Theocracy—some degree of rule by religion—has been an anathema in the modern United States. But the confusion over early-twenty-first-century trends can be clarified, although not resolved, by trying a simple multiple-choice question: Is theocracy in the United States (1) a legitimate fear as some liberals argue; (2) a joke, given the rising secular population, the continuing obscenity and violence from Hollywood, the brothels and gambling in Nevada, and the gay-marriage services in San Francisco; (3) a worrisome bias of several major GOP constituencies and pressure groups; or (4) all of the above? The answer, of course, is all of the above. Conservatives fixate on the provocations and ignore the excesses visible in the neo-puritan and rightist countertide, and liberals have reversed the error, keening over the religious threat while ignoring the secular provocation. The balance of danger, however, has been redefined by the momentum of the Bush-era counterattack.

To be sure, any incipient theocracy in the twenty-first-century United States would bear little resemblance to the stereotypical precedents: John Calvin's sixteenth-century Geneva or John Winthrop's seventeenth-century church-run Massachusetts Bay Colony. Those, as suggested earlier, were the products of small but intense religious migrations. In a nation approaching three hundred million in population and stretching between the Atlantic and Pacific, diversity alone ensures major differences. However, we can all too plausibly contemplate a recent watershed in which fundamentalist and evangelical churches play the dominant organizational role in supporting the Republican party that other groups—business, labor, farm, pro- and antislavery—enjoyed in earlier presidential cycles. This could induce red-state Republican conventions to proclaim the United States a Christian nation, endorse antihomosexual and antiabortion amendments to the Constitution, and urge that the United States withdraw from the United Nations, which they see as an auxiliary of the antichrist. Indeed, all of this has happened.

In such a milieu, not only would the major parties group around religious attendance or secularism, but they would emphasize issues with theological importance. Public schools and textbooks would be pressured toward prayer and theological correctness on matters ranging from science and evolution to sex education, family life, and foreign policy. Governments would be urged to restrain public morality at odds with interpretations of the Bible, shifting their regulatory preoccupation away from business, the economy, or the environment to issues of life and death, sex, and family.

Candidates for Republican presidential or U.S. Supreme Court nominations would be vetted by little-known private groups like the Council for National Policy, the Family Research Council, and the Federalist Society. Senior Pentagon generals, in turn, would tour friendly churches in uniform, advancing thinly disguised endorsements of holy war in the Middle East. Books about end times and Armageddon would surge to the top of the bestseller lists and convince the television networks to under-take similar dramatic programming. U.S. delegates to global AIDS and women's conferences would oppose contraception, offering abstinence as Washington's solution. Fewer foreign scientists and professionals would come to the United States, while some already resident would leave. Demographers might report signs of gay influxes–cum-ghettoization in blue states like Massachusetts, New York, and California.

While it sounds a bit like political science fiction framed this way, the evidence everywhere was well in hand by 2005. Even while Democrats left in place a three-decade secularist trend in the makeup of their party cadres and conventions, Republican efforts to mobilize churches and churchgoers reached new fervor during the 2004 election campaign. According to Mark Silk, "White conservative evangelical churches have become across the South the organizational engine for the Republican party the way labor unions became the organizational engine for the Democratic party in the industrial heartland during the 1930s."[84] Others likened the constituency benefits of the Bush administration's faith-based initiatives in funding public services through church-related groups to the advantages Democratic constituencies enjoyed from the Works Progress Administration outlays of the New Deal years or the war on poverty under Lyndon Johnson.[85]

Activists on both sides see political culture wars turning into theolog-ical soul wars. Liberal evangelist Jim Wallis commented in 2004 that "we're now in a debate for the heart and soul of what it means to be reli-gious and political."[86] Richard Land of the Southern Baptist Convention observed that "a fault line ran through the denominations . . . with moral absolutists on the one hand versus those who see shades of gray on the other. Religion's role is increasing and will only continue to increase."[87] To conservative Dr. Janice Crouse of Concerned Women for America, the religious gap "really is a divide along faith lines, I think. It's a divide that says there are human solutions to our problems and there are faith-based solutions."[88]

Under Bush, this new political theology also began to reshape America's dialogue with the rest of the world. Jacques Delors, the former European Commission president, added that "the clash between those who believe and those who don't believe will be a dominant aspect of relations [between the United States and Europe] in the coming years." Dominique Moisi, another well-known commentator, shed light on the U.S.-European divergence: "The combination of religion and nationalism in America is frightening. We feel betrayed by God and by nationalism, which is why we are building the European Union as a barrier to religious warfare."[89]

Within the United States, the religious mobilization of 2004 was extraordinary. In the South voting by regular church attenders soared, partly because Republicans sought high November turnout among the faithful to ensure against another failure to carry the national popular vote as in 2000.[90] Supposedly tight states, such as Florida, Tennessee, and Arkansas, turned out not to be. However, in the spring, as tight races became likely between Bush and Kerry in Pennsylvania and the Midwest, the Bush campaign and its religious allies had stepped up their efforts. In June GOP e-mails leaked to the press describing how Bush forces planned to enlist churches around the nation in distributing political information and registering voters. In Pennsylvania the Bush-Cheney campaign sought "to identify 1,600 friendly congregations where voters friendly to President Bush might gather on a regular basis."[91] Even Richard Land thought that went too far, and the Reverend Barry Lynn, executive director of the liberal Americans United for Separation of Church and State, observed, "I never thought that anyone could so attempt to meld a political party with a network of religious organizations."[92]

However, this was only the tip of a large iceberg, and the administration's religious allies were often out in front rather than waiting for instructions. According to a postelection analysis by *The Washington Post*, "national religious leaders, and their lawyers, also made a concerted effort to persuade pastors to disregard the warnings of secular groups about what churches can and cannot do in the political arena."[93] Jay Sekulow, chief counsel of the American Center for Law and Justice, which was launched in the 1990s by Pat Robertson, advised in a mailing to forty-five thousand churches that "short of endorsing a candidate by name from the pulpit, they were free to do almost anything," and he later told the *Post* that "thousands of clergy members gave sermons about the election, and that many went further than they ever had before."[94]

Catholics were a particular target across several states in the industrial belt. Overall, the GOP campaign appointed fifty thousand Catholic "team leaders" at the local level, and while meeting with the Pope in June "Bush asked the Vatican to push the American Catholic bishops to be more aggressive politically on family and life issues, especially a constitutional amendment that would define marriage as a union between a man and a woman."[95] During the summer, the *National Catholic Reporter* posted a story on its Web site that the Republican National Committee had asked pro-Bush Catholics to provide its Catholic outreach unit with copies of their parish directories to help identify potential supporters.[96]

In Ohio Bush's share of the Catholic vote rose from 50 percent in 2000 to 55 percent in 2004.[97] The jump was greater still in rural and small-town German Catholic centers, a century ago Ohio's top Democratic strongholds. Mercer and Putnam, the state's two most heavily Catholic counties, went three to one for Bush in 2004, his top percentages.[98]

Warren County, in southwest Ohio, touted for its outer-suburban GOP gains, also had a religious factor at work. According to a 2000 religious census, Southern Baptists were the most numerous Protestant denomination there, one of only six such Ohio counties.[99] (The six were Butler, Greene, Montgomery, Pike, Preble, and Warren.) Traditional Catholics, conservative Protestant evangelicals, and fundamentalists were vital in Ohio to offset the Democratic gains from high black turnout in the Cleveland area and from uneasy mainline Protestants and Yankee suburbanites in the Cleveland metropolitan area. The GOP weakness in Greater Cleveland—the onetime "Western Reserve" of Connecticut—and reliance on the German and southern-settled areas reversed the geography of Ohio's post–Civil War party coalitions.

John Green, the Ohio-based religious-voting expert, explained the centrality of the Midwest as a religious crossroads and melting pot: "One reason why Ohio, Michigan, Wisconsin and Pennsylvania are so competitive is that they . . . have a lot of 'centrist' groups." Groups that he puts into this category include Catholics, Lutherans, and Methodists.[100] Green also explained Iowa's shift from Gore in 2000 to Bush in 2004 by indicating that "close to a third of the voters this time were white born-again Protestants," reflecting their large turnout.[101] Bush's big gains over 2000 came in western Iowa, mostly in counties with unusual concentrations of holiness or German-Dutch Reformed denominations.[102] Not coincidentally, Iowa is where Pat Robertson surprised and beat the elder George Bush in the 1988 GOP presidential caucuses. In 2004, the Bush family profited from the high churchgoer participation so discomfiting sixteen years earlier.

Nor did the politico-religious mobilization end there. New plans were quickly afoot in pivotal Ohio. By early 2005 the Southern Baptist Convention, already a force in southwestern Ohio, announced that metropolitan Cleveland had been selected as its one national "Strategic Focus City" for 2006–2007. Backed by a budget of $2.5 million, thousands of volunteers from all over the country would converge to help win converts and start new churches.[103] Before long, local Christian conservatives announced the Ohio Restoration Project, a plan to marshal evangelical, Baptist, Pentecostal, and Roman Catholic leaders as so-called Patriot Pastors to take control of the Republican party and elect a born-again governor in 2006.[104]

While this stops short of a merger of church and state, the potential for important constituencies to nudge the Republican party in a theocratic direction has a little-heralded historic dimension. Several of its vital denominational allies exemplify a political closeness to government. The Southern Baptist Convention, as we have seen, is regarded by some as more or less the unofficial state church in Dixie. Indeed, studies suggest that northerners moving to the South frequently join it, not least Newt Gingrich, the former Pennsylvanian.[105] Moreover, since the 1990s the SBC's moderate-liberal opposition faction has criticized the dominant conservatives for getting too close to Washington and soft-pedaling the church's historic commitment to separation of church and state.[106] One SBC moderate-liberal, Will D. Campbell, wrote a novel—*The Convention* (1988)—"in which the SBC is renamed the Federal Baptist Church and is by the end of the book indistinguishable from a political party."[107]

The major Pentecostal denomination, the Assemblies of God, has worked closely with the Republicans ever since the Robertson presidential campaign, perhaps reflecting Robertson's own disdain for church-state separation. His Pentecostal allies, as noted earlier, pushed blatantly theocratic resolutions at state Republican conventions. John Ashcroft of Missouri, a dedicated Assemblies of God layman, became a particular target for proponents of strict church-state separation because of the new Justice Department units and policies he developed as George W. Bush's first attorney general.

The church history of the Mormons, in turn, could fill a book—and often has—with what one chronicler summed up as "its polygamous family structure, ritual worship practices, 'secret oaths,' open canon, economic communalism and theocratic politics."[108] The Church of the

Latter Day Saints was the last U.S. regional theocracy, continuing that way into the early twentieth century, and the title of its president—officially "President, Prophet, Seer, and Revelator"—still reflects that heritage. Philip Goff, director of the Center for the Study of Religion and American Culture, emphasizes that over the last hundred years the Mormons did much more than survive: "The Latter-Day Saints created a de facto establishment of religion in the inner mountain West that continues to this day."[109] The Mormon analogy that Baptist-watching historian Paul Harvey sees, not surprisingly, is to the parallel accomplishments of the Southern Baptist Convention.[110]

Finally, the two major Lutheran denominations also tap a tradition of accommodating state power. The Missouri Synod Lutherans, arch-conservative and "corporatist," regarded theirs as the one true church, followed the word of the Bible, upheld male authority, kept the German language as long as they could, and separated themselves from other faiths through parochial schools and church-related organizations.[111] The evangelical Lutherans, as we have seen, came together in several stages from the multiplicity of German, Danish, Norwegian, Swedish, and Finnish Lutheran churches of the upper Midwest, many of which were offshoots of state churches in the old country. Door County, Wisconsin, has enough of an Icelandic fishing community to support an Icelandic Lutheran church.

The SBC, Mormon, and Lutheran churches are the three Protestant denominations in the United States with the sort of strong regional preeminence that in itself breeds a powerful clerical closeness to everyday community governance and political authority. It is in their core strongholds—places like the west Texas Bible Belt, Greater Utah, and the northern plains—that U.S. churches have their highest ratios of adherence.[112] Community pressure and conformity would be substantial. It is no coincidence that the geography of the three denominations is also a religious map of the Republican party's churchgoing ascendancy, as displayed in map 4.

The rise of the religious right has been yet another force for potential theocracy. Its intense political motivation pivots, in part, on genuine belief that religion must regain the place in the public life that it enjoyed in the early days of the Republic, when Connecticut, Massachusetts, and New Hampshire lawfully maintained established (Congregational) churches.

But the challenge of such a restoration, many feel, is so huge that gaining sway over government is necessary to rebuild that religious component. This, in one of its harsher forms, is the premise of Christian Reconstructionism, a radical theology that will be examined in chapter 7.

While most religious-right leaders have given lip service to church-state separation, many have periodically let the mask slip—and sometimes slip badly. Jerry Falwell has said, "I hope I live to see the day, when, as in the early days of our country, we won't have any public schools. The churches will have taken them over again, and Christians will be running them."[113] Bob Jones III, president of the politically attuned university bearing that name, opined that "the so-called 'wall of separation' between church and state is a liberal fabrication to try to put churches out of a place of influence in political life."[114] In 2004 he congratulated George W. Bush on his reelection, urging him to press profamily legislation in keeping with Scripture.[115]

The Reverend Sun Myung Moon, the owner of the *Washington Times* and the head of the well-funded Unification Church, said that "we must have an autocratic theocracy to rule the world. So we cannot separate the political field from the religious. My dream is to organize a Christian political party including the Protestant denominations, Catholic and all religious sects. We can embrace the religious world in one arm and the political world in the other."[116] Moon, somewhat surprisingly, has been close to the Bush family, having been praised by the senior Bush in a 1996 speech. Then in 2001, Moon cohosted George W. Bush's inaugural prayer lunch.[117]

To Pentecostal Pat Robertson, ever blunt, "there is no way that government can operate successfully unless led by godly men and women under the laws of the God of Jacob." For all practical purposes, Robertson is a Christian Reconstructionist. His Virginia educational complex bears the name Regent University, because a regent is one who governs in the absence of a sovereign, and Regent University is a "kingdom institution" for grooming "God's representatives on the face of the earth" to serve until the return of Jesus.[118]

However, as political operators like Georgia's Ralph Reed acknowledged years back regarding the tactics of the Christian Coalition, stealth is a major premise, furtiveness a byword. The Christian right usually does not like to acknowledge what it is doing or where.[119] The point is to minimize public attention to its influence and back-stairs power.

A half century ago, before the election of John F. Kennedy as president, many Americans feared—in a carryover of nineteenth-century tensions and suspicions—that Roman Catholicism might someday threaten America with church power and theocracy. Especially since the Vatican II reforms of the 1960s, that psychology has reversed, with current theocratic inclinations in the United States concentrated among conservative Protestants. Pew Center polls found that while majorities of Protestants, particularly evangelicals, acknowledged that their personal religious views and faith influenced their voting, only 32 percent of Catholics did.[120] Polling by ABC News in May 2004 found the following rank order of support for religious leaders trying to influence politics: white conservative evangelicals 62 percent, white churchgoing evangelicals 53 percent, white evangelical Protestants 46 percent, evangelical Protestants 43 percent, Catholics 34 percent, nonevangelical Protestants 27 percent, persons with no religion 22 percent.[121]

To amplify this point, in 2004 rank-and-file Catholics, by 72 percent to 22 percent, opposed Roman Catholic bishops' denying communion to politicians who supported abortion rights.[122] Gary Bauer, a leader of the religious right, captured the irony: "When John F. Kennedy made his famous speech that the Vatican would not tell him what to do, evangelicals and Southern Baptists breathed a sigh of relief. But today, evangelicals and Southern Baptists are hoping that the Vatican will tell Catholic politicians what to do."[123]

As for the leanings of key GOP leaders, much of the attention focused on George W. Bush and Tom DeLay, the Republican House majority leader, who openly said, "God is using me all the time, everywhere, to stand up for a biblical world view in everything that I do and everywhere I am. He is training me."[124] However, the larger tale lies in data showing that in 2004 all seven of the top Republican leaders in the U.S. Senate, starting with Majority Leader Bill Frist of Tennessee and working down to Senator George Allen of Virginia, chairman of the National Republican Senatorial Committee, boasted 100 percent ratings from the Christian Coalition, founded by Pat Robertson in the wake of his 1988 presidential bid.[125]

As of this writing, none of the half-dozen pieces of quasi-theocratic legislation drafted by the religious right and introduced in Congress by its supporters—bills like the House of Worship Free Speech Restoration Act, the First Amendment Restoration Act, and the Constitution Restoration

Act—had achieved passage, but the time could come.[126] (These and others are glowingly described on the Web site of the Christian Coalition.) Political correctness on the left has been surpassed by its theological equivalent on the right, and 2005 saw the first Republican member of Congress stand up and say so. Congressman Christopher Shays of Connecticut in late March 2005 sadly declared that "the Republican Party of Lincoln has become a party of theocracy."[127]

A cultural adjunct to these ambitions, end-times theory and literature, with its audience of fifty to one hundred million Americans, emerged as a big business in the United States during the 1990s, turning dozens of fundamentalist and charismatic preachers into multimillionaires, thanks to their bestselling books, videos, televised sermons and Bible hours, TV stations, and broadcast networks. Not surprisingly, most are ardent supporters of tax cuts and reduced economic regulation, as their faithful flocks concentrate on morality, salvation, biblical guidance, a possible rapture, and the countdown to Christ's return. These believing constituencies, in turn, want more of their "government"—over whatever time may be left—to come from religious institutions, with the imprimatur of a president who openly favors at least some transfer of power.

Such mingling of theology, popular culture, and theocracy has already brought about aspects of an American Disenlightenment, to employ a descriptive antonym. Effects can be seen in science, climatology, federal drug approval, biological research, disease control, and not least in the tension between evolution theory and the religious alternatives—creationism and so-called intelligent design. Some commentators have pictured the greatest religious threat to science since the Catholic Church in 1633 put Galileo under house arrest for heresy in stating that the earth revolved around the sun. But we are getting ahead of ourselves. The religious hawkishness, substitution of faith for reason, and missionary insistence increasingly visible in the United States have plagued leading world economic powers from Rome to Spain to Britain. It is time to turn to the theologization of American politics and the unfortunate historical precedents it calls to mind.

7

Church, State, and National Decline

One of the biggest changes in politics in my lifetime is that the delusional is no longer marginal. It has come in from the fringe, to sit in the seat of power in the Oval Office and in Congress. For the first time in our history, ideology and theology hold a monopoly of power in Washington.
—Bill Moyers, 2004

Liberals regularly contend that one of America's two great parties is bent on creating a theocracy—backed by a solid core of somewhere between a quarter and one-third of the population.
—*The Economist*, 2005

By a series of recent initiatives, Republicans have transformed our party into the political arm of conservative Christians. The elements of this transformation have included a constitutional amendment to ban gay marriage, opposition to stem cell research involving both frozen embryos and human cells in petri dishes, and the extraordinary effort to keep Terri Schiavo hooked up to a feeding tube.
—Episcopal minister and former Republican senator John Danforth, 2005

RELIGIOUS, SECULAR, OR SOMEWHERE IN BETWEEN, MOST AMERICANS OF the early 2000s shared some concern about a broad range of threats to the nation's future: immorality, decadence, crime, terrorism, private and public corruption, moneyed politics, greed and luxury, and the stratification of wealth and power. But how they defined them or what they chose to emphasize varied greatly.

Conservatives saw a threat that was predominantly religious and moral, and the gloomy, neo-Calvinist preoccupation of important elements of the religious right emerged all too clearly in their leaders' immediate, unthinking interpretation of the meaning of September 11. Jerry Falwell and Pat Robertson agreed that the United States had been attacked because of God's displeasure with secular immorality. Their comments, although quickly retracted, painted a picture of the stern Old Testament God hurling thunderbolts and death at his wayward chosen people.

Secular Americans and those who only occasionally attended religious services had a somewhat different point of view. Their fears had more to do with economics, society, and the successes or failures of U.S. foreign policy. Not a few worried about the excesses of organized religion and the influence of the Christian right. Between 2001 and 2005, after the Terri Schiavo episode, national polls showed such concern doubling. Among secular voters a startling two-thirds expressed antipathy to evangelicals.[1] To many of the born-again, "secular"—as in secular humanist – was an expletive to be culturally deleted.

Controversy also began to collect around the fundamentalist pulpiteers' prophecies of rapture, end times, and Armageddon. By 2005 a counterattack was apparent in mainline religious responses, Catholic and Protestant alike. This was exemplified by publications such as *The Rapture Exposed,* Lutheran theologian Barbara Rossing's contention that rapture theology was little better than a racket, and comparable works on the Catholic side, replete with charges that what was really left behind in Tim LaHaye's series was biblical truth.[2] Polls are few, but those taken showed that majorities of Catholics, Lutherans, Episcopalians, Congregationalists, Presbyterians, and Methodists disbelieved in the event so central to the *Left Behind* books and fundamentalist jeremiads.[3]

The historical dilemma is that while religion has generally served humankind well, certainly in framing successful societies around the world, there have been conspicuous exceptions—bloody religious wars, malevolent crusades, and false prophecies. Indeed, the precedents of past leading world economic powers show that blind faith and religious excesses—the rapture seems to be both—have often contributed to national decline, sometimes even being in its forefront.

As with Charles Kimball's five criteria for the mutation of religion, I believe that a yardstick can be set up for Rome, Hapsburg Spain, the Dutch

Republic, Britain, and the United States that isolates and profiles five critical symptoms of decline in the past leading world economic powers. Just as Kimball's five criteria are broadly framed and need not all be present simultaneously—one or two, he says, can be enough to suggest trouble—likewise for these five symptoms of a power already at its peak and starting to decline. These broad categories are mine, in no firm order and based on research for several of my books over two decades. However, the relevant history has many sources and confirmations.

One symptom is widespread public concern over cultural and economic decay, with its many corollaries. The second is a growing religious fervor, church-state relationship, or crusading insistence. Next comes a rising commitment to faith as opposed to reason and a corollary downplaying of science. Fourth, we often find a considerable popular anticipation of a millennial time frame: an epochal battle, emergence of the antichrist, or belief in an imminent second coming or Armageddon. Last, empires are prone to a hubris-driven national strategic and military overreach, often pursuing abstract international missions that the nation can no longer afford, economically or politically.

I have not included high debt levels in this set of symptoms, partly because it seems a familiar facet of great-power economic aging, but principally because it is the subject of part 3 of this book. In its most deadly form, debt accompanies corrupt politics, hubris, and international overreach and then—as we shall see—becomes crippling in its own right.

The second half of this chapter will examine the five basic symptoms in the present-day United States. All are present to at least some extent. However, before we turn to these indicators, it is essential to describe how these vulnerabilities and perils made themselves felt in the past. All four nations and empires I will discuss believed in their own exceptionalism, a wellspring of encouragement and reassurance for early and middle generations but a source of strategic blindness during the last years of illusion.

Exceptionalism: The Delusion That the United States Is Different

The four empires in question—Rome, the Spanish-centered Hapsburg empire, the Netherlands, and Great Britain—were each, in its day, the leading world economic power and the principal naval or military power.[4]

Rome's triumph spanned many centuries before clear decline set in during the fourth and fifth centuries. Spain's global heyday began in the 1490s, spanning the sixteenth century before crumbling during the seventeenth. Spain, in this imperial context, goes beyond the Iberian Peninsula because of the sixteenth-century Hapsburg dynastic tie to Italy, Austria, and Burgundy.* The Dutch empire, built on the maritime piers and pilings of global commerce, rose during the seventeenth century and eroded during the eighteenth. Great Britain emerged in both industrial and naval might during the eighteenth century, dominated the nineteenth, and lost its broad hegemony during the early decades of the twentieth. The symptoms analyzed here are those seen during each power's notable period of decline. No nation escaped the processes and subsequent disillusionment.

Historians of great-power decline do not emphasize religion, save with respect to Rome, but it has also played important roles elsewhere. These pages put religion first less because of preeminent causation—economics and warfare have played equal or greater roles—than because of this book's larger focus on the reemergence of faith-driven politics.

Edward Gibbon, in his 1776 masterwork *The Decline and Fall of the Roman Empire*, pointed to an overconfident and intolerant Christianity as the cause of imperial decline. The English historian's basic thesis was that after the late-fourth-century Roman Empire made a state religion of Christianity, which until then had been just a minor sect, that combination of church and state became crippling and divisive, so that religious excess helped to bring down an already weakening empire.[6] Other historians have agreed. Michael Grant in *The Fall of the Roman Empire* has suggested that, by contrast, the previous polytheism had been versatile and relatively tolerant. Christian Rome, however, withdrew tolerance and pressured its regions and peoples on behalf of the one true religion. This worsened Roman relations with allied German tribes practicing a some-

---

* In *Empire* Henry Kamen, a prominent historian of Spain, underscores better than most how Hapsburg "Spain" was much more than the Iberian Peninsula. A rare coincidence of inheritance brought together under the elected Holy Roman Emperor Charles V, also known as Charles I of Spain (1516–56), not just the peninsula but also Italy, the Low Countries, Austria, and part of Germany. The four-decade union of crowns was not a full economic or political union, but it enriched the power of a Spain also lucky enough to be welcoming gold and silver fleets from the Americas.[5]

what different, even heretical Christianity, Jews unhappy with a rival monotheism, and adherents of the old gods that were so much a part of Roman history. In consequence, concludes Grant, "what contributed above all to this decline was the application of religious coercion; for it achieved precisely the opposite of its unifying aims, powerfully accelerating the forces of disintegration and dissolution."[7] The emperor Constantine, the great Christian advocate, weakened Rome by splitting it into separate eastern and western empires, the latter soon untenable. Like Gibbon, Grant goes into considerable detail.

As for Spain, its late-fifteenth- and sixteenth-century ascent had been closely tied to Catholic faith and expansionism: the reconquest of the Iberian Peninsula from Islam (completed in 1492), the overseas missions of conquistadores, Jesuits, and priests carrying the cross to the New World, and at home the forced full conversion or expulsion of Spain's nominally converted Jewish and Muslim populations (from 1492 into the early 1600s). However, further extensions of these narrow psychologies helped to bring about the nation's seventeenth-century decline. Religious excess and the Crown's preoccupations with advancing Catholicism globally are widely agreed upon as contributing factors.

For one thing, Spain's religiosity deepened in the late 1500s after the conversion or expulsion of its Jews and Muslims emphasized the national commitment to Catholicism. The faith militant became the faith triumphant. New religious orders proliferated—seventeen were founded in Madrid during the reign of Philip II—as did almshouses and hospitals run by groups such as the Hospitaller Brothers of St. John. Inward piety and direct communion with God increased among those in monasteries and convents, turning their faith away from church teachings. These practices and literature, although in ways heretical, were accepted as a form of mysticism.[8]

The emphasis on missionary work in the new empire—from Santo Domingo and Mexico City to Argentina and Peru—was so widespread that as late-seventeenth-century Spain lost its great-power status, many churchmen consoled themselves by claiming that "the spiritual conquest succeeded and the Catholic identity was Spain's greatest colonial legacy."[9] Militant Catholicism had drained Spain in Europe, but Catholic growth in Spanish and Portuguese America continued. If one counts the cardinals from the Western Hemisphere involved in the selection of recent popes, this contention is not easily dismissed.

But at home the Spanish Inquisition, the epitome of religious coercion, helped breed a climate of orthodoxy and fear, and by the early seventeenth century Spain was sagging under the weight of church bureaucracy. Between the sixteenth-century reign of Philip II and the kingship of Philip IV, ending in 1665, the count of regular and secular clergy in Spain doubled to some two hundred thousand while the population as a whole did not increase. Castile itself had nine thousand religious houses just for men.

Faith also took an economic toll. In the words of one prominent historian, "religious festivals in some places occupied a third of the year, . . . and the dead weight of a vast apparatus of ecclesiastical bureaucracy lay heavily on Castile."[10] For religious reasons having to do with usury, Spanish authorities prohibited the execution of interior bills of exchange, which limited credit arrangements.[11] Although later kings and their advisers were concerned enough to try to limit the wealth and expansion of the church, including a 1677 proposal to curb the number of the clergy, the vested interests were by then too powerful and embedded.[12]

Thus, in 1621, after multiple bankruptcies, talk of reform, and two decades of intermittent truces with the English, French, and Dutch, King Philip III effectively went back to imperial principles resembling those of his father, Philip II, whose belief in his role as God's viceroy had sent the unsuccessful armada against England. The entrenched militant Catholicism was beyond reform. In the words of historian Paul Allen, "For the remainder of the century, then, Spain's monarchs and ministers would steadfastly reject . . . reason-of-state approaches to policy in favor of providing solid support for the Catholic cause, even at the expense of Spain's empire. In so doing, they fulfilled to the letter Philip II's pious vow to Pope Pius V that 'rather than suffer the least damage to the Catholic church and God's service, I will lose all my states and a hundred lives if I had them.'"[13] What Spain did lose was worldly power and hegemony.

The Dutch nation, in addition to the resources of wind and water, also drew on the power of fierce religion: the Calvinist fervor of the Dutch Reformed Church, so prominent in the long war to break free of Spain. Militant, scriptural, and little more tolerant than Spain's Catholicism, it

gained official status following the 1618 Synod of Dordrecht despite adherence by no more than half of the Dutch people. This percentage rose
in the seventeenth century, but then ebbed again. By the 1730s and 1740s,
after Dutch trade, wealth, and power had passed their peaks, a growing
influx of Catholics, Lutherans, and Jews, mostly from neighboring German
territories, reduced the Dutch Reformed share of the population back
toward the 50 percent mark.[14]

These changes angered Reformed Church preachers (*predikants*), who
ranted over the nation's immorality and lost greatness. Simon Schama
noted how for prominent Orangist thinkers, "it had been the reformed
religion which had blessed the war against the Spanish Anti-Christ with
victory and had appointed the princes of the House of Orange to be its
Godly captains." Between 1747 and 1751, what historian Jonathan Israel
calls a "Second Orangist Revolution" restored to power the Dutch political faction (the quasi-royal House of Orange) long allied with the fundamentalist *predikants*.[15] As revolutionary ideas spread, the Prussian army
restored the Orangists again in 1787.

During the second half of the century, as the Dutch people watched
their cities, industries, and maritime capacity continue to decline, religious
divisions fed two separate movements, each urging a brand of political
and moral renewal. The Orangist faction, grouped around the heirs of
William the Silent, hero of the sixteenth-century Dutch revolution, had
long been loosely allied with churchmen whose agenda was to suppress
Catholics, deepen church-state collaboration, and restore the nation's
fading Puritan morality. The rival "Patriot" faction—in background and
sentiment somewhat akin to the revolutionaries developing nearby in
France—was reformist, more secular, and more toleration minded,
drawing substantially on Catholics, Lutherans, Mennonites, and moderate Reformed Church elements. Civil war broke out again during the
1780s and 1790s, and in 1795 French forces empowered the Patriots, who
proceeded to disestablish the Dutch Reformed Church.[16] The church was
already much less important than its equivalent was in Catholic Spain,
but the divisive legacy of early Dutch religious zealotry crippled any
chance of an ecumenical national renewal.

The contributions of British religious enthusiasm to the country's
years of decline in the early twentieth century are more straightforward.
A wave of missionary and evangelical religion pushed the old England of

Anglican squires and cathedrals toward a new middle-class moralism during the Victorian era, following on the heels of the eighteenth-century rise of nonconformists—Quakers, Methodists, Independents, and Jews—which had spurred so much innovation in finance, commerce, and industry. However, the evangelical wave was especially influential, as summarized by historian R. C. K. Ensor in *England, 1870–1914*: "No one will ever understand Victorian England who does not appreciate that among highly civilized countries . . . it was one of the most religious that the world has ever known. Moreover its particular type of Christianity laid a peculiarly direct emphasis on conduct. . . . [I]t became after Queen Victoria's marriage practically the religion of the court and gripped all ranks and conditions of society. After [Prime Minister] Melbourne's departure [1841], it inspired nearly every front rank public man, save Palmerston [prime minister for all but one year between 1855 and 1865] for four decades."[17] Moral pretension became a second British flag, just as it later became a second American flag.

Between 1850 and 1914 the percentage of people in England attending church or chapel declined somewhat, from the 40 to 50 percent range to 25 to 35 percent, largely because of disaffiliation as the population became concentrated in large cities like London, Manchester, and Liverpool.[18] Attendance remained higher in Scotland, Northern Ireland, and Wales, all largely nonconformist Protestant rather than high-church Anglican. Wales, in particular, underwent a major revival as late as 1904 to 1907—a paroxysm of revelation and ecstasy so powerful that for a while crime slackened and Welsh liquor consumption fell by half, bankrupting a considerable share of tavern owners.[19]

Besides inner conversion, evangelicalism also emphasized outward conversion efforts by its adherents. As a result the nineteenth century saw a huge increase in foreign missionary activity, along with an upsurge of moral imperialism—belief in Britain's duty to save the world—that abetted and reinforced the everyday patriotism of parades, naval reviews, music-hall songs, and saber-rattling literature. Initial public enthusiasm for World War I, as we will see, marched in part to the stirring cadences of "Onward, Christian Soldiers." When postwar disillusionment took over, few British institutions paid a higher price than the war-drumming denominations, led by the Church of England.

To summarize: religion, while not routinely cited as a significant factor in Dutch and British decline, did play a considerable part and had also played a central role in the downfalls of Rome and Spain. Fervent religion feeding into national hubris late in an imperial trajectory is a particularly worrisome historical sign that should summon caution for the present-day United States.

Symptom number two, related to the first, involves the interplay of faith and science. What might be called the Roman disenlightenment has been well dissected in Charles Freeman's *The Closing of the Western Mind* (2002).[20] He dwells on how Rome's fourth- and fifth-century Christian regimes closed famous libraries like the one in Alexandria, limited the availability of books, discarded the works of Aristotle and Ptolemy, and embraced the dismissal of Greek logicians set forth in the gospel of Paul. To Freeman, the elevation of faith over logic stifled inquiry in the West—leaving the next advances to Arab mathematicians, doctors, and astronomers—and brought on intellectual stagnation: "It is hard," he wrote, "to see how mathematics, science or associated disciplines that depended on empirical observations could have made any progress in this atmosphere." From the last recorded astronomical observation in 475, "it would be over 1,000 years—with the publication of Copernicus's *De Revolutionibus* in 1543—before these studies began to move ahead again."[21]

Hapsburg Spain, a second empire immersed in Catholic theology, was equally hostile to scientific inquiry. The eminent British historian of Spain, J. H. Elliott, recounted the seventeenth-century episode when the Spanish government, deliberating over a vital canal project, assembled a junta of theologians who advised that if God had intended the rivers Tagus and Manzanares to be navigable, he would have made them so.[22] Another historian of Iberia, Henry Kamen, quotes a visiting Italian nobleman in 1668 as saying that "the ignorance is immense and the sciences are held in horror."[23] Detailing how Spain relied on Italian and other foreign scholarship while importing needed technicians from other Catholic parts of Europe, Kamen summed up, "Spain remained prominent by its absence from the European intellectual and scientific scene. When the Royal Society of London in the 1660s began to organize its scientific links with European intellectuals, Spain did not feature. The puzzle, which still eludes any easy explanation, is why the most universal society of the globe, was unable, after centuries of imperial experience, to discourse on equal terms with other European nations that shared the same background."[24]

Parenthetically, this is the same time period in which the papacy found Galileo guilty of heresy—and placed him under house arrest for seven years until he recanted—for propounding the Copernican argument that the earth revolved around the sun. David Landes, in *The Wealth and Poverty of Nations,* points out that in 1600 philosopher Giordano Bruno had been burned in Rome for much the same offense, by which "the church proclaimed its intentions of taking science and imagination in hand and leashing them to Rome."[25] Spain was even more dogmatic and medieval.

That could not be said of the discovery-minded Netherlands. In the seventeenth century their scientific and technological knowledge had impressed all Europe, and even in the early eighteenth century the Dutch Enlightenment was the "instructor of Europe" in microscopic science, botany, anatomy, and medicine.[26] But by the mid-eighteenth century, the republic's science was fading and its universities were losing prestige and enrollment. Most of the difficulty had to do with the general ebb of the nation's industry and economy, which shrank educational outlays and funding of facilities. Even so, after the Orangist Revolution of 1747–1751, the ability of the Dutch Reformed Church to influence university appointments was a damper.[27] The scientific side of the Dutch Enlightenment withered.

The impact of British evangelicalism on science was largely cultural, not heavy-handed or political. Science, as opposed to industry and exports, was not much of a cause or priority in the last decades of the nineteenth century. The preoccupation of Britain's elite with moral imperialism, global finance, colonial administration, foreign missions, and the Great Game in India, Persia, and central Asia—to say nothing of the glamour of the Household Cavalry, Bengal Lancers, and the world's greatest navy—had shaped upper-tier education in a different vein. Its dominant preoccupations were with gentlemanly conduct, sportsmanship and playing fields, moral principles, religion, classics, history, Athens and Sparta, Locke and Blackstone, Drake and Wellington, not engines and test tubes. After Charles Darwin published his theories of evolution, many churchmen became prominent critics of scientific inquiry.

At Rugby, the famous headmaster Matthew Arnold commented that "rather than have it [science] the principal thing in my son's mind, I would gladly have him think that the sun went around the earth and that the stars were so many spangles set in the bright blue firmament. Surely the one thing needed for a Christian and Englishman to study is a Christian and moral and political philosophy."[28] Just as the battle of Waterloo a hundred years earlier had been won on the playing fields of Eton, the technological naïveté writ large in initial British enthusiasm coupled with unreadiness for World War I had at least some connection to the sort of elite curriculum at Rugby. But as World War I lengthened without British success, the nation's lack of adequate scientific and technological preparation became a scandal—the stuff of irate speeches in Parliament and appalled acknowledgments by government commissions charged with investigation.

In *The Closing of the Western Mind,* Freeman suggested that late Roman faith began to "create the barrier between science—and rational thought in general—and religion that appears to be unique to Christianity."[29] If so, perhaps latter-day evangelical Protestantism exemplifies this tendency, given how American sects of the 1920s and again in the early twenty-first century challenged the science of Charles Darwin in much the same way that so many religious Britons had during the Victorian years.

A third common litmus test—the economic and social polarization and decay common to the late years of our four world powers—is probably their most commented-upon characteristic. Brevity, then, seems in order, and readers interested in fuller detail will find some in chapter 4 of my book *Wealth and Democracy* (2002). Rome's multifarious decay, in fact, has become a stereotype—a Hollywood drama of epicene emperors lolling on purple couches stuffing and amusing themselves as the poor starved and Goths and Vandals crossed the Rubicon. But this characterization should not be mistaken for fantasy or fiction: the decay was real.

Spain's decline has also become a caricature, especially in history books that quote the *arbitrista* reformers of the early seventeenth century. One of them, González de Cellorigo, summed up that Spain "has come to be an extreme contrast of rich and poor, and there is no means of adjusting them one to another. Our condition is one in which we have rich who loll at ease, and poor who beg, and we lack people of the middling sort, whom neither wealth nor poverty prevents from pursuing the rightful kind of business enjoined by natural law."[30] Most scholars cite his views. Spanish morale was dulled by *desengaño,* a national disillusionment, vast bureaucracy, upper-class luxury, immorality, and political corruption. These were targeted—without any notable success—by sumptuary decrees restricting attire, by curbs on prostitution, and by abolition of unnecessary government positions and receiverships. Then as now, such reforms rarely succeed.

So, too, for mid-eighteenth-century Holland, about which the famous description came from visiting traveler James Boswell: "Most of their principal towns are sadly decayed, and instead of finding every mortal employed, you meet with multitudes of poor creatures who are starving in idleness. . . . Were Sir William Temple [a seventeenth-century chronicler] to revisit these provinces, he would scarcely believe the alteration which they have undergone."[31] Dutch Reformed pastors called for national renewal and incessantly attacked laziness, prostitution, French fashions, immigrants, and homosexuals.

The British example, of course, is the freshest. Winston Churchill in 1908 expressed gloom that "the seed of imperial ruin and national decay—the unnatural gap between the rich and the poor, . . . the exploitation of boy labor, the physical degeneration which seems to follow so swiftly on civilized poverty, . . . the swift increase of vulgar, jobless luxury—are the enemies of Britain."[32] In *The Strange Death of Liberal England, 1910–14,* George Dangerfield described 1911 as a year of London "climbing towards its peak of plutocratic splendor, and tales of ballrooms banked high with the loot of hothouses, of champagne flowing like a sea, or bare backs, jeweled bosoms and fabulous expenditure."[33] Cultural historians have dwelt on the other upheavals and tensions of the fin de siècle: the "decadence" movement among literary Londoners epitomized by Oscar Wilde and Aubrey Beardsley, the estimates of sixty thousand or so prostitutes in the capital, occultism, and the suffragette campaign for women' votes and women's rights.[34]

"Decay" always has two faces: the one displaying economic and social polarization and injustice, which always stirs complaint among progressives, and the second representing moral and cultural decadence-cum-sophistication, which invariably stirs conservative and fundamentalist outrage. The focus of criticism can run the gamut from haute cuisine and fashion to prostitution, effete art, and homosexuality. Here, too, as we will see, the early-twenty-first-century United States is repeating portions of a familiar pattern.

Our fourth hallmark involves the widespread perception of a premillenarian time frame, as when preachers talk of a war to end all wars, of Armageddon, or of Christ's imminent return. This is another way in which the influence of religion feeds a willingness for war. Late-fourth-century Roman Christians thought the end times might come when Rome fell to the barbarians. Spain's confidence cracked somewhat after the defeat of the armada in 1588, when Spanish leaders had to answer English, Dutch, and Lutheran taunts that King Philip II was the antichrist. Part of Spain's response was to captain the Counter Reformation and the Catholic side in the draining Thirty Years War (1618–1648). As the Netherlands in turn embarked on a costly quarter century of alliance with England and war with France in 1689, Dutch Reformed *predikants* had identified their own new antichrist: Louis XIV, the king of France.

But the most disturbing late-imperial premillennial focus is that of Britain from 1900 into the early years of World War I, until the national trauma of the 420,000 British casualties on the Somme in 1916. As we have seen, Britain in the second half of the nineteenth century was fired by evangelical religion, global missionary instincts, and the "white man's burden" identified by Rudyard Kipling. "Onward, Christian Soldiers," the great martial hymn published in 1871, boasted triumphal music by Sir Arthur Sullivan (of Gilbert and Sullivan fame). Something of an imperialist, Sullivan in 1900 composed a Te Deum to celebrate the imminent victory in the Boer War, but it could not be played until 1902, after his death.[35]

Music-hall jingoism, militant Protestant hymnology, and queen-and-country literature converged. Much as the male population of the United States rose during the 1980s and 1990s to the excitement of renewed gunboat diplomacy (the 1986 bomber strike on Tripoli, Libya) and invasions (Grenada, Panama, and the Gulf War), as well as endless fictional high-tech combat thrillers of the sort pioneered by Tom Clancy, British males did much the same thing between 1890 and 1914. Cecil Eby, an American professor, has tabulated the drumrolls and bugle calls: by 1889 forty thousand brass bands existed in Britain, playing more military marches than anything else; five hundred music halls in London alone belted out patriotic choruses.[36] Between 1871 and 1914, in addition, English fiction writers turned out sixty books about foreign invasions of Britain (forty-one German, eighteen French). In none of these volumes was Britain the aggressor, but even in Boy Scout and cricket uniforms young British males were preparing for the great match to come.

Preachers and prophets also had their eyes on the clock. Charles T. Russell, leader of the U.S.-based Jehovah's Witnesses, had earlier forecast Armageddon in 1914, and the word was on many European lips.[37] However, instead of being the war to end all wars, the great match became the war to end the British Empire. Its conclusion in the cynical Peace of Versailles in 1919 set the scene for a follow-up twenty years later that finished off what was left of British overseas investment and the reveries of nineteenth-century headmasters.

A fifth bellwether of imperial decline, already suggested in part 1, lies in the seeming inability of leading powers to avoid dangerous overreach in international commitment, and in foreign military involvement and its cost. These decisions can seem necessary or at least plausible at the time, with hubris helping. The unwise economic, political, and military overstretch usually becomes entirely clear only in retrospect, although sometimes it does not take long.

Rome, for example, was obliged to defend some far-flung frontiers in North Africa and along the Rhine and Danube. However, historians fault both the choice of perimeters and the draining expense of large armies and extravagant frontier defensive systems, most of which were never attacked as the empire rotted from within and foes came from unexpected directions.

For the Spanish, Dutch, and British, the costs of war and empire became problems within a generation or two of their imperial zeniths. The economic impact—in trade and debt—will be discussed in part 3, but it is appropriate here to note the conflicts that did so much damage. For Spain, the eighty years of off-and-on war in the Netherlands (the Dutch Revolution) beginning in 1570 took on a European and even global breadth in the Thirty Years War, which broke the back of Spanish power. The Dutch, in turn, were obliged to fight France in 1672, when Louis XIV invaded with a huge force, although the results were surprisingly inconclusive. However, the subsequent quarter century of Anglo-Dutch war with France was hard on the United Provinces, not least because their hereditary *stadtholder,* William of Orange, had also become king of England. The Dutch assumed a larger role than they could afford—and paid the price. In retrospect, these wars facilitated England's political and economic emergence at Dutch expense.

The next example is all too familiar. Two centuries later, the first and second world wars led to the end of the British Empire and announced the arrival of the United States as the new leading world economic power. The subsequent Cold War led to a contest between the two military superpowers, the United States and the Soviet Union, which the United States won in the late 1980s. One unfortunate result was hubris and triumphalism. The obvious question of the twenty-first century is whether oil- or religion-based conflict in the Middle East or some broader resource war may punish American overstretch.

For such powers past their zenith, religion, our subject in these chapters, is usually one of a larger set of interconnected factors. The need to condense this discussion into a dozen pages results in descriptions and citations that can make these analogies seem too pat. Nevertheless, I have not found any contrary arguments—typically that these declines have been exaggerated—at all convincing. Suffice it to say that even at considerable discount, these precedents should unnerve readers weaned on American exceptionalism and unaware of how much doubt prior history casts on that uniqueness.

A Twenty-First-Century American Disenlightenment?

The frequent by-products of religious fervor in the later stages of the previous powers—zealotry, exaltation of faith over reason, too much church-state collaboration, or a contagion of crusader mentality—shed light on another contemporary U.S. predicament. Controversies that run the gamut from interference with science to biblically inhibited climatology and petroleum geology and demands for the partial reunion of church and state have accompanied the political rise of Christian conservatism. Such trends are rarely auspicious.

The essential political preconditions fell into place in the late 1980s and 1990s with the emergence of the Republican party as a powerful vehicle for religiosity and church influence, while state Republican parties, most conspicuously in the South and Southwest, endorsed so-called Christian-nation party platforms.[38] These unusual platforms, as yet nationally uncataloged, set out in varying degrees the radical political theology of the

Christian Reconstruction movement, the tenets of which range from using the Bible as a basis for domestic law to emphasizing religious schools and women's subordination to men. The 2004 platform of the Texas Republican party is a case in point. It reaffirms the status of the United States as "a Christian nation," regrets "the myth of the separation of church and state," calls for abstinence instead of sex education, and broadly mirrors the reconstructionist demand for the abolition of a large group of federal agencies and departments, including the Energy Department and the Environmental Protection Agency.[39]

George W. Bush's election to the presidency and his unusual choice of former Missouri senator John Ashcroft to head the Justice Department were true milestones. We have already seen Bush's involvement in intensifying the religiosity of the Republican party and in linking White House policy statements to Scripture and prophecy. When Ashcroft, a longtime favorite of the religious right, had explored seeking the presidency in 1997 and 1998, most of his financial support came from Christian evangelicals such as Pat Robertson.[40] Conservatives subsequently mobilized in favor of his selection as attorney general. Son and grandson of Pentecostal preachers, Ashcroft, more than any previous attorney general, viewed law and politics through a religious lens. He made no effort to shade this connection. In Ashcroft's memoirs, explained one critic, "he describes each of his many electoral defeats as a crucifixion and every important political victory as a resurrection, and recounts scenes in which he had friends and family anoint him with oil in the manner 'of the ancient kings of Israel' with each new public office."[41] While in the Senate, Ashcroft enjoyed a 100 percent approval rating from both the Christian Coalition and the National Right to Life Committee, pleasing the latter by sponsoring a constitutional amendment that extended protection to the "unborn" at "every stage of their biological development, including fertilization," a breadth that might have criminalized birth control.[42] As attorney general, the Missourian was accused of dragging his heels on the prosecution of abortion-clinic bombers.[43]

Earlier in his political career, Ashcroft had decried the barrier between church and state as "a wall of religious oppression." Midway through the first Bush administration Americans United for Separation of Church and State, a liberal group, condemned his actions as attorney general: "Whenever cases deal with government funding or promotion of religion," said its spokesperson, "the Justice Department under Ashcroft is always on the side of bringing church and state together."[44] Perhaps, but it is also fair to say that Bush's religious constituencies thrill to the criticisms of such hostile groups.

During Ashcroft's time in the Senate, he had also authored successful legislation to let states turn over welfare and other social services to religious providers, a program that George W. Bush embraced as governor of Texas and which helped to inspire his 2001 proposal for federal faith-based initiatives.[45] Where possible, religious agencies would take over the provision of federal social services. When Bush's legislation stalled in the Senate, he used a federal executive order to establish faith-based-initiative units in six departments (Justice, Education, Health and Human Services, Housing and Urban Development, Labor, and Agriculture), as well as in the Agency for International Development. At the General Services Administration, the office-maintenance arm of the federal government, Bush appointees held lunch-hour revival meetings in the front hall, making it seem, in the words of The Washington Post, "more like the foyer of a Pentecostal storefront church."[46]

The House and Senate lobbies had some of that same look. House Majority Leader Tom DeLay and Oklahoma senator James Inhofe, chairman of the Senate Committee on Environment and Public Works, were two who insisted that all the answers were in the Bible, and two-thirds of Republican House and Senate members enjoyed 80 percent or better voting ratings from groups such as the Christian Coalition, the Traditional Values Coalition, the National Right to Life Committee, and the Family Research Council.[47] Dozens of legislators anxious to be theologically correct competed to maintain perfect ratings.

As for the interaction of church and state in the White House, two characterizations peculiar to George W. Bush—his salute from several religious-right leaders in 2001 as the national head of their movement and his seeming self-image as someone who spoke for God—added to the perception of a unique presidency. That a chief executive could be described in these ways without sparking a heated national debate bespoke the public's willingness to accept religion and authority in the aftermath of September 11.

The way in which Bush White House policies were the application of hard-line, preformed doctrine rather than the results of evidence seeking was explained by two departing and disillusioned officials. Former trea-sury secretary Paul O'Neill recalled his dismay that ideology dwarfed real-world analysis: "Ideology is a lot easier, because you don't have to know anything or search for anything. You already know the answer to everything. It's not penetrable by facts."[48] John DiIulio, the first head of the White House Office of Faith-Based and Community Initiatives, rue-fully described "the complete lack of a policy apparatus" or "meaningful, substantive policy discussions" because everything was political, with much of the policy coming from right-wing think tanks and the Christian right.[49]

The president was most comfortable with black-and-white, good-versus-evil portraiture, acknowledging that nuance was not in his play-book.[50] Anti-intellectualism, which profited George Wallace so much in his 1968 presidential campaign, became a Bush prop, too, as in his mock-ery of high grades during a visit to Yale, his alma mater, to receive an honorary degree in 2002.[51] An unidentified senior administration official dismissed the intellectual elites, "what we call the reality-based commu-nity . . . [people] who believe that solutions emerge from your judicious study of discernible reality."[52] In the Oval Office, instinct, prayer, and faith took precedence.

Several cartoonists went so far as to draw Bush in robes like those worn by the Iranian ayatollahs, and as we saw in chapter 6, portraits of funda-mentalist movements around the world displayed considerable resem-blance to those of the George W. Bush administration. Nor was that behavior governed simply by deep commitment to religion and religiosity. Esther Kaplan, in her book *With God on Their Side*, identified a much narrower worldview:

> He really isn't interested in faith in general. The president didn't flick an eyelash when the National Council of Churches and the U.S. Council of Catholic Bishops opposed his war on Iraq. He didn't listen when the Council on American-Islamic Relations filed a suit chal-lenging the constitutionality of the Patriot Act. When the Union for Reformed Judaism announced that an antigay marriage amendment would "defile the constitution," the president took no notice. Nor did Bush respond to a joint call, signed by fifty prominent Christian lead-ers, including Richard Cizik of the National Association of Evangelicals and Jim Wallis of Call to Renewal, for policies that promote "quality

health care, decent housing and a living income for the poor." His is not an embrace of spirituality or ethics broadly speaking, or of faith as an important voice among many in the national debate. It is, instead, an embrace of right-wing Christian fundamentalism.[53]

Even more to the point, many of Bush's views exuded a theological correctness that was almost a mirror image of the political correctness displayed by secular liberals in discussing minority groups, women's rights, and environmental sanctity. By 2005 words such as "theocrat" and "theocon" were gaining traction in political journalism, and with cause. As religious conservatives became the dominant Republican constituency in the 1990s, their tune became the essential party dance music. Swings to the right and then bows to various church-related partners took over conservative choreography.

In Republican politics theological correctness—call it TC—became a policy-shaping force in determining Middle Eastern geopolitics, combating global AIDS, defining the legal rights of fetuses, pretending that oil was not a cause for the invasion of Iraq, and explaining geological controversies in language compatible with the Book of Genesis. As church congregations became GOP auxiliaries and a host of religious-right organizations provided essential scorecards of senators and congressmen up for reelection, the nature of constituency pressure changed from share our values to support our doctrine—or else.

A few Republican centrists became openly critical of this juggernaut. Arizona senator John McCain had criticized the Jerry Falwells, Pat Robertsons, and Bob Joneses during his confrontation with Bush in the 2000 Republican presidential primaries. In 2004 Rhode Island senator Lincoln Chafee suggested that Bush's "I carry the word of God" posture warranted voter attention. In 2005 Connecticut GOP congressman Christopher Shays, as we have seen, sparked attention simply by describing the Republican party as a "theocracy."[54]

As public skepticism grew, even one-third of self-identified Republicans found themselves critical when poll takers queried whether the religious right had too much or too little influence in Washington.[55] But they were too late. Theology had moved from church pulpits into the decision-making circles of the nation's capital.

The Theologization of American Politics: Symptoms and Prescriptions

In the last three chapters, we have seen how the intensity of religion in the late-twentieth-century United States was transforming national politics. By 2001 theology —the yardstick of belief, not judgment—began to displace logic and realpolitik in official Washington, especially within the Republican party. The impact of conservative religion on national policy making, which burgeoned under Bush the Younger, is striking and documented, but its effects were so widespread that we need to look at its different components.

Several principal areas highlight the extent to which constituency politics began to compel TC. First and foremost were the issues involving birth, life, death, sex, health, medicine, marriage, and the role of the family—high-octane subject matter since the 1970s. These are areas where perceived immorality most excites stick-to-Scripture advocates and the religious right. Closely related is the commitment by the Bush White House and the religious right to reduce the current separation between church and state. In the 1960s and 1970s, to be sure, secular liberals grossly misread American and world history by trying to push religion out of the public square, so to speak. In doing so, they gave faith-based conservatism a legitimate basis for countermobilization. But in some ways the conservative countertrend itself has become a bigger danger since its acceleration in the aftermath of September 11.

Topics such as natural resources, climate, global warming, resource depletion, environmental regulation, and petroleum geology—all surprising targets for religious attacks—mark out a third important arena. Such debates draw in the energy industry, automobile producers, utilities, industries that pollute, and the environmental movement, as well as the forces battling for so-called intelligent design, creationism, or the literal interpretation of the Book of Genesis. Major business lobbies, all too aware of the GOP's religious blocs, harness their biases where possible and avoid trespassing on matters of theology. However, governing conservatives in Washington look foolish because of their inability to discuss problems such as global warming and the probability that global oil production is not far from its peak, a silence that goes against the national interest.

Chapter 2 has noted the attempt since 1999 of religious conservatives to cloak their side's environmental and energy policy—hitherto largely a matter of property rights, tax incentives, and minimal regulation—in a theology more sophisticated than the brusque Christian Reconstructionist demands for the abolition of the EPA and true-believer statements about Genesis 1:28 empowering developers to bring forth the earth's mineral fruits.

Organizations such as the Interfaith Council for Environmental Stewardship (ICES) and the Acton Institute for the Study of Religion and Liberty have enlisted a fair amount of conservative religious and corporate support for preparing what amounts to a pro-business, pro-development explanation of Christian stewardship.[56] The Acton Institute, aided over several years by ExxonMobil, for some time published the *Environmental Stewardship Review,* given to emphasizing market mechanisms and private property rights.[57] Besides endorsing corporate and development-oriented positions, Acton condemned supposed environmental extremists theologically. The institute's director, Roman Catholic Father Robert A. Sirico, contends that left-tilting environmentalism is idolatrous in its substitution of nature for God, giving the Christian environmental movement a "perhaps unconscious pagan nature."[58]

In 2005 a group of theological moderates and liberals convened by the National Council of Churches issued a statement, "God's Earth Is Sacred," that indicted the conservative credo as "a false gospel . . . that our human calling is to exploit earth for our own ends alone." One participant, Father Charles Bender, an Orthodox priest, contended that "some people say the environment doesn't matter" because the second coming of Christ will end the world as we know it. But he called that view "the height of arrogance" because each person will have to stand before God and account for his actions.[59] Although few political officeholders are involved in this debate, it suggests how theology is imposing itself on or becoming a necessary appendage to more and more elements of national policy making.

Then there is the subject matter of business, economics, and wealth, where the tendency of the Christian right is to oppose regulation and justify wealth and relative laissez-faire, tipping its hat to the upper-income and corporate portions of the Republican coalition. Christian Reconstructionists go even further, abandoning most economic regulation in order to prepare the moral framework for God's return. These extremes obviously represent instances of theology—biblical interpretations and priorities—trumping what most would regard as practicality and self-interest.

The last arena of theological influence, almost as important as sex, birth, and mortality, involves American foreign policy, bringing us to the connections among the war on terror, the rapture, the end times, Armageddon, and the thinly disguised U.S. crusade against radical Islam. Here the forty-third president has often coded his remarks to heighten biblical resonance for believers listening for it. A related and important practice—at least an apparent one—is the blurring or avoiding of positions that might contradict the worldview promoted by fundamentalist preachers, inasmuch as senior officials cannot explicitly endorse it.

National opinion surveys and the priorities expressed since the late 1970s by church, religious-right, and Republican grassroots organizations give precedence to the life-and-death, sex-and-family issues over any others. Endless confrontations have arisen over abortion, women's rights, assisted death and the right to die, the promotion of sexual abstinence, contraception, and the question of gay marriage. The spur is the scriptural belief patterns that significantly influence 60 to 65 percent of Americans and appear to dominate the views of roughly half that number. As figure 1 on p. 102 shows, viewpoints on these issues closely reflect the influence of religious denominations, not just religiosity in general.

By 2006 more than a half-dozen life-and-death issues—from a vegetative patient's right to die and stem-cell research to the question of "crimes against fetuses"—were grouped in a face-off involving medical and biotechnological criteria and intense theological pressure from religious conservatives to define life (or the right to life) as beginning under the most remote and attenuated circumstances. Conflicting federal and state judicial rulings and legislation on abortion only multiplied the confusion, and the related battle over the use of embryos for stem-cell research became incendiary. Citing his reverence for life, George W. Bush blocked federally supported embryonic stem-cell research on all but a dozen or so existing cell lines, close to a de facto prohibition. In the House of Representatives, Republican Majority Leader DeLay, a Texan proponent of a biblical worldview, castigated stem-cell research that used blastocysts (early embryos of only one hundred or so cells) as "the dismemberment of living, distinct human beings."[60] That belief prevails among Republican core voters, but the overall electorate—and many elected Republicans—supported stem-cell research in order to advance medical and scientific discovery.

Foreign policy also found itself in the theological arena. The State Department and other federal agencies took action to block needle-exchange and other harm-reduction programs in United Nations drug-control efforts, to suppress foreign efforts to extend civil rights to sex workers (Brazil persisted in doing so), to defeat international women's treaties, and to keep federal funds from being used to support any international program that funds contraception efforts.[61] Although critics condemned what one called "Bush's devotion to his right-wing Christian base," most took hardly any note of one particular theology: the extent to which Christian Reconstructionists supported a move toward biblical law, including the death penalty for homosexuals, adulterers, prostitutes, and drug users.[62] Moderate reconstructionists, as we will see, support only jail sentences for such people, but still call for punishment of transgressors, not succor.

The Terri Schiavo case, in which George W. Bush as president and Jeb Bush as governor of Florida attempted to intervene, pivoted on the right for a patient in a vegetative state to die—in this case after she had allegedly asserted that choice beforehand to her husband. Voters were offended not by the rulings of the courts and doctors involved, which approved the removal of life support, but by the actions of the Congress and the president in trying to pass special legislation to enable a federal instead of state trial. Some 65 to 70 percent of the public objected.[63] Belief that politicians had responded to outside pressure focused popular resentment on the religious right, and many congressmen backed off as the unpopularity of their intervention became clearer.

Controversies over life and death—often pivoting on precise definitions of each—can only continue to burgeon. When life begins is a particular pivot. In a federal Food and Drug Administration debate over fertility drugs, Kentucky gynecologist David W. Hager, a Bush appointee to a key advisory committee, prevailed in changing the clinical end point in these drug trials from live birth to "fetal heart motion."[64] The federal Unborn Victims of Violence Act, for its part, declared fetuses—defined as a child in utero (attached) at any stage of development—to be fully protected persons for the purposes of criminal prosecution. This act paralleled a state statute used by Utah prosecutors to charge a woman with murder when one of her twins was stillborn because, they said, the mother had caused the death by delay in having a C-section.[65]

These are not social or "values" judgments. The arguable rights of women (or parents) are being displaced by the rights of embryos or by the prerogative of sperm and egg to join, decisions rooted largely in theology, not science. Perhaps the preoccupation involves maximizing the potential soul count for the hereafter, in the manner of sixteenth- and seventeenth-century inquisitors who ordered that heretics must die even if they repented, yet pursued repentance to save their souls first.

Within the Republican party's most loyal denominations—Southern Baptists, Mormons, and Missouri Synod Lutherans—overall theology accords women secondary status. The essential female role is biblical and familial. Church hierarchies must be male—and not just in these three sects but in the Assemblies of God (in which women can be ministers but not members of the hierarchy), Roman Catholicism, and the Orthodox Jewish community.[66] Catholics decline to ordain women as priests, and many Orthodox Jewish females cannot even study the Torah. In traditionalist constituencies, support for changes like the proposed Equal Rights Amendment of the 1970s has been minimal, opposition to abortion high, and the rights of the unborn weightier than women's rights.

In a related vein conservative publications emphasized the importance in the 2004 election of the "baby gap"—the data showing that pro-Bush voters have more children than do Democratic voters. The states where white fertility rates were high went conservative, while the states where they were low—most notably Massachusetts, Vermont, and Rhode Island— preferred liberal politics.[67] Conversely, the states where abortion rates were highest supported Kerry. Culturally the Kerry states ranked higher— in number of symphonies or universities, and even intelligence quotients— hints that the kind of single people and couples drawn there would put less emphasis on families than did the religious citizenry, more caught up in fecundity and the idea that children are gifts of the Lord.

To religious traditionalists, homosexuality threatened the institutions of family and marriage. Eleven states held November 2004 referendums to ban gay marriage. In the seven states where conservative denominations are strong, the propositions carried by huge majorities: 86 percent in Mississippi, 77 percent in Georgia, 76 percent in Oklahoma, 75 percent in Kentucky and Arkansas, and 66 percent in Utah and Montana. Churchgoing black voters, principally Baptists and Pentecostals, supported the curbs by lopsided margins, increasing the antigay margins in the Deep South (and accounting for much of the small 2004 Republican increase in black support). Secular voters were the principal upholders of gay marriage, which made the balloting much closer in Oregon, for example. Theologically the conservatism at issue contends that homosexuality is not inherited (or God given) but taken up volitionally—and a sin. Thus true believers liken practicing homosexuals to adulterers, drug users, or alcoholics, insisting on the individuals' ability to make a different choice and rehabilitate themselves. Contrary biological evidence could become as divisive as Darwinism.

In all of these matters, the need of Republican officeholders and party conventions to be theologically correct puts them through all sorts of contortions. At first George W. Bush was uncertain about supporting a federal constitutional amendment to prohibit gay marriage. Then pressure from the religious right forced the issue, and he endorsed it on February 24, 2004. When the proposed amendment died in the Senate weeks later, the GOP obtained a small but significant Election Day wedge issue. Ironically, in January 2005, after Bush said there was no need to keep pushing the ban, annoyed religious conservatives threatened to refuse to back his Social Security program unless he changed his mind. He thereupon repeated his support for the constitutional amendment in his February 2 State of the Union message.

The theology of death is cloudier and also riskier politically. Although Bush took a bold and ultimately unpopular stand in the Terri Schiavo case, bending over backward to insist on continuing her life support, blocking death is not the theological equivalent of enabling birth. The Bible abounds with the killing of those already born, both by God and by lawful authorities. Bush himself, as governor of Texas, sent hundreds of prisoners to the electric chair. Nor has collateral damage to civilians in a "just war" been a problem. The Lord of Hosts also struck out broadly and bloodily. Donald Akenson, in his study of the peoples of the covenant, cites biblical example upon example: 120,000 men killed in one day and 200,000 women and children carried away captive (2 Chronicles 28:5, 6, and 8); 185,000 Assyrian warriors killed (2 Chronicles 32:21); 42,000 Ephraimites put to death because of a minor dialectic variation (2 Judges 12:6).[68] Against this backdrop, a couple of thousand Babylonian children killed in what is now Iraq wouldn't have made it into Scripture any more than such possibilities seem to have inhibited the Pentagon in 1991 or 2003. In the Bible death comes lightly.

The next throbbing cluster of issues involves church-state relations. The nonradical theocon wing of the GOP demands a more conservative judiciary and an expanded role for religion in education, social services, and the constraining of immoral behavior—abortion, homosexuality, pornography, and contraception—but avoids spelling out any grand revolutionary mandate. The Christian Reconstructionist movement, by contrast, proclaims ambitions that range from replacing public schools with religious education to imposing biblical law and limiting the franchise to male Christians.[69] Since not many people identify openly as Christian Reconstructionists, the movement's ability to influence U.S. politics in these radical directions is unclear.

Most Americans, having never heard of Christian Reconstructionism, likely assume it has only fringe status. The groups that monitor such activists—Theocracy Watch, the Public Eye, the First Amendment Foundation, *Church & State* magazine, Americans United for Separation of Church and State, and others—take the movement more seriously, however. Their contention is that the reconstructionists exercise a great deal of indirect influence through the Southern Baptist Convention, the Assemblies of God, Promise Keepers, the Christian Broadcasting Network, the Christian Coalition, the conservative Council for National Policy, and other groups that share many of their less radical perspectives.[70] That is plausible, given the array of lesser Christian-right figures who, while denying they are reconstructionists, admit to agreeing with some of their positions.

Journalist Frederick Clarkson quotes reconstructionist theoretician Gary North, for many years a member of the Council for National Policy, claiming that his element's ideas "have penetrated into Protestant circles that for the most part are unaware of the original source of the theological ideas that are beginning to transform them." The "three major legs of the Reconstructionist movement" are "the Presbyterian-oriented educators, the Baptist school headmasters and pastors, and the charismatic telecommunications system."[71] North refers here not to mainline Presbyterianism but to several independent fundamentalist denominations—the Presbyterian Church of America and the Orthodox Presbyterian Church—that broke away from the national church over doctrinal differences.

The connection with the Southern Baptist Convention is difficult to measure. In 2004 Clarkson alleged that "the Reconstructionists have taken over the Southern Baptist Convention's national leadership." An SBC spokesman, John Revell, acknowledged that his denomination and the theocrats agree on many issues—from biblical infallibility to male primacy in family and church governance—but that only "a small minority" of SBC adherents supported theocracy. Clarkson countered that the SBC backs a politics of "majoritarianism"—popular political mobilization behind an essentially religious agenda.[72]

On the other hand, reconstructionist ties to the Assemblies of God have been important since Pat Robertson mobilized their superchurches for his 1988 presidential campaign. Attorney General John Ashcroft, son and grandson of AOG preachers, was perhaps the best example of a high Bush administration official whose policies had some reconstructionist coloration. Robertson himself was an open advocate of the so-called restoration acts cited in chapter 6, and Herb Titus, the onetime dean of the law school at Robertson's Regent University, was involved in crafting them.[73] At the very least, all three legislative proposals are building blocks for ending the separation between church and state; if ever enacted as a group, they would signal a far-reaching upheaval in U.S. politics and government.

Parenthetically, both George W. Bush and Florida governor Jeb Bush drew on thinkers and administrators with ties to reconstructionism in their implementation of faith-based social services. Marvin Olasky, a major architect of this plan and coiner of the term "compassionate conservatism," was influenced by prominent reconstructionists and cited many in his books.[74] In Florida Jerry Regier, appointed in 2002 by Jeb Bush to head the state's Department of Children and Families, was identified by *The Miami Herald* as having drafted a reconstructionist manifesto for the Christian right's Council on Revival in 1989.[75] On this dimension, at least, the two men have been willing to turn to reconstructionists.

Three national organizations, influential but hardly household names—the Council for National Policy, the Council on Revival, and the Committee to Restore American Values—were established in the 1980s, with Tim LaHaye and others sharing Christian-right or John Birch Society backgrounds taking a role. All three have had a considerable number of reconstructionist members and board members. In a 2002 report ABC

News described the CNP as "the most powerful conservative group you've never heard of."[76]

Let me stipulate: reading about the webs and connections between reconstructionism and the rest of the religious right set out in progressive and liberal publications calls to mind the exposés published by conservatives fifty or sixty years ago that linked various progressive organizations to Communist front groups and fellow travelers. The release in recent decades of old Soviet files has confirmed some of what the conservatives were charging, and today's liberal and progressive muckrakers are probably just as accurate in suggesting a larger-than-realized influence of Christian Reconstructionists.

As George W. Bush's second term began in 2005, religious issues from abortion to the First Amendment underpinned conservative desire to take over as much as possible of the federal judiciary. That April columnist Frank Rich quoted Tony Perkins, the president of the Family Research Council, telling a Washington conservative assemblage that the judiciary poses "a greater threat to representative government" than "terrorist groups."[77] While Perkins's analogy seems radical, others on his side have been just as aroused, just as belligerent. The federal judiciary is the arena in which the battles most critical to incipient theocrats—those over sex, life, and death issues, church-state separation, and the global contest between good and evil—will be fought out judge by judge, court by court.

Indeed, in their anxiety to control the federal judiciary Christian conservatives have matched or exceeded the efforts of Franklin D. Roosevelt and the liberal Democrats to control it on behalf of the New Deal when FDR submitted his famous proposal to pack the U.S. Supreme Court in 1937. Signs of that anxiety burst into view in an early 2005 meeting at which conservative evangelical leaders were addressed by Tom DeLay and Senate Majority Leader Bill Frist. The focus of the strategy session was how to strip funding or jurisdiction from federal courts, or even eliminate them. James Dobson of the California-based Focus on the Family named one target: the Ninth Circuit Court of Appeals. "Very few people know this, that the Congress can simply disenfranchise a court," Dobson commented. "They don't have to fire anybody or impeach them or go through that battle. All they have to do is say the 9th Circuit doesn't exist anymore, and it's gone."[78] A spokesman for Frist said he did not agree with the idea of defunding courts or shutting them down, but DeLay, who had once said, "We set up the courts. We can unset the courts," declined to comment. The battle, clearly, is only beginning.

Beyond the judiciary, pressure for theological correctness became overt in federal government relationships with the varieties of science—from climatology to geology, and even entomology—that can conflict with the Book of Genesis, scriptural home to Adam, Eve, Noah, and the animal-laden ark and fount of authority for God's creation of the earth in more or less a week some six to seven thousand years ago. For the growing number of elected officials who uphold Genesis—Southern Baptist Convention leaders say that George W. Bush believes the Bible is the truth with a capital "T"—the Almighty, not carbon dioxide, brings about climate change. Global oil resources date back only to the creation, not to the Jurassic Age.

The consequences here go far beyond the evolution-doubting books being sold by the National Park Service or inconvenient information about contraception, climate change, or caribou habitats in oil lands being deleted from government Web sites. The implications also go far beyond the Tennessee school texts that William Jennings Bryan and Clarence Darrow fought over in the Scopes trial. Eight decades ago the federal government was not involved in the controversies. Nor did the geography of the Republican electoral coalition require President Calvin Coolidge to worry about offending the Southern Baptist Convention or the Assemblies of God—or to risk making the United States look foolish in the eyes of the international scientific community.

Today the SBC and the Assemblies of God are Washington power brokers, and much of the U.S. scientific community is up in arms. In 2001, when the National Academy of Sciences presented the new president with a study laying out the perils of global warming, he paid no attention. The administration's preferred HIV treatment, abstinence-only sexual education, has been identified as medically unsound by the National Institutes of Health, the American Medical Association, and the American Academy of Pediatrics. Hearings by a Food and Drug Administration panel on a pregnancy pill snubbed the forty-five-thousand-member American College of Obstetricians and Gynecologists in order to hear from the American Association of Pro-Life Obstetricians and Gynecologists, with one-tenth the membership.[79] The examples in this vein are many.

Michael Mangiello, a leader of the Coalition for the Advancement of Medical Research, backers of stem-cell research, told an interviewer that at a major hearing "the prestige gap between our scientists and their scientists was overwhelming," but religious forces had the president's ear. In late 2003, when the Grand Canyon bookstore began selling a creationist interpretation of the canyon's origin, seven national geological organizations wrote to caution the National Park Service against "giving the impression that it approves of the anti-science movement known as young earth creationism or endorses the advancement of religious tenets as science."[80] Against the recommendation of the Park Service's senior geologist, the book remained on sale.

In a 2003 controversy over Bush-administration pressure on the Environmental Protection Agency, Russell Train, its director under Republican presidents Nixon and Ford, wrote, "I can state categorically that there was never such White House intrusion into the business of the EPA during my tenure."[81] The 2004 election year saw the issuance of a statement on "Restoring Scientific Integrity in Policymaking" by sixty-two preeminent scientists, including Nobel laureates and former advisers to administrations of both parties, which charged the administration with widespread and unprecedented "manipulation of the process through which science enters into its decisions." As an adjunct, the Union of Concerned Scientists released detailed documentation of alleged suppression and distortion of scientific findings and manipulation of the government's scientific advisory system.[82]

Observers noted that the credentials or motivations of Bush's allies were often religious. *The New York Times* observed that David W. Hager, then one of Bush's nominees to the influential Food and Drug Administration panel on women's health policy, "had a resume more impressive for theology than gynecology."[83] Former Republican senator John Danforth of Missouri commented that "the only explanation for legislators comparing cells in a petri dish to babies in a womb is the extension of religious doctrine into statutory law."[84]

In Texas, where the cotton industry is plagued by a moth that has evolved an immunity to pesticides, a frustrated entomologist commented that "it's amazing that cotton growers are having to deal with these pests in the very states whose legislatures are so hostile to the theory of evolution. Because it is evolution they are struggling against in their fields every season. These people are trying to ban the teaching of evolution while their own cotton crops are failing because of evolution."[85]

Opponents of evolution—successful so far in parts of the South—are indeed busy trying to ban the teaching of it and textbooks that support it in many northern conservative or politically divided areas, including large states such as Michigan, Missouri, Pennsylvania, and Ohio.[86] However, the latest effort is more than a replay of the Scopes confrontation. Creationism now shares its "educational" stage with a slick city cousin, so-called intelligent design, hypothesizing simply that some intelligence produced the universe. The latter is a tactical response to a major court case in 1987, *Edwards v. Aguilard,* which found that creationism promoted a religious viewpoint, not a scholarly one. Intelligent design, seeking classroom acceptability, has kept vague enough about its religious motivations to avoid the *Edwards* yardstick, but its lack of serious science is a significant handicap.[87] Some of its founders also have ties to Christian Reconstructionism. Still, public opinion is certainly open to the theory of intelligent design, so the battle is far from over.

Meanwhile, the bigger message—depressingly reminiscent of our imperial predecessors—is that science in the United States is already in trouble. Money is draining out, with dire consequences. Intel chairman Andrew Grove says critical scientific-infrastructure spending is being neglected, and the premier research universities are losing their edge. Susan Hockfield, the president of MIT, says, "We're falling behind. We're not keeping up with other countries. The science and math scores for our high school graduates are disastrous. We're underfunding research in the physical sciences and lagging seriously on publications in these sciences."[88] Stanford professor Irving Weissman, a stem-cell researcher, told *The Boston Globe,* "You are going to start picking up *Nature* and *Science* and all the great journals, and you are going to read about how South Koreans and Chinese and Singaporeans are making advances the rest of us can't even study."[89]

In 2005 the Business–Higher Education Forum released new data showing that fifteen-year-old Americans are worse at problem solving than their peers in twenty-five countries.[90] Something else young Americans don't seem to understand—perhaps not surprisingly—is evolution. In 1993 an international social survey ranked Americans last—behind Bulgaria and Slovenia—in knowledge of the basic facts of evolution.[91]

Part of the explanation involves the religious right's larger view of economic matters and the dismantling of government. In the radical Texas Republican platform adopted in 2004, the Lone Star GOP was not content to call for abolishing the Environmental Protection Agency and the Department of Energy; it also demanded the abolition of the Internal Revenue Service and the elimination of the income tax, the inheritance tax, the gift tax, the capital-gains levy, the corporate income tax, the payroll tax, and state and local property taxes. Apparently the White House was not embarrassed.

We have seen in previous chapters that evangelicals, Southern Baptist Convention adherents, and others oppose government social and economic programs because they interfere with a person's individual responsibility for his or her salvation. One recent scholarly analysis updated evangelical economic thinking to include the role of televangelists, specifically Falwell and Robertson, in upholding "a marriage between religion and American capitalism" during the 1980s. It further elaborated on "theology increasingly espoused by Pentecostal and charismatic preachers: . . . that God's blessings are not confined to the next life. Indeed, God desires to bless his children materially in this world. By naming what you want (a new car, better job, good health), claiming it in the name of Jesus, and living in the faith that it will come to you, these believers no longer tied private property to the notion of hard work."[92]

The permissive theology involved—known as Name It and Claim It— originated with Oklahoma televangelist Oral Roberts but crested under the aegis of Bruce Wilkenson, founder of the Atlanta-based Walk Thru the Bible Ministries. According to historian James German,

> this movement reached its apex at the end of the [twentieth] century with the immensely popular 92-page book *The Prayer of Jabez*. Heretofore an unknown character in the Old Testament, Jabez became the hero for many (more than five million books were sold) who daily repeated his simple prayer: "Oh, that You would bless me indeed, and enlarge my territory, that Your hand would be with me, and that You would keep me from evil, that I may not cause pain." Tying the ancient supplication to modern life, author Bruce Wilkenson claimed that "If Jabez had worked on Wall Street, he might have prayed 'Lord, increase the value of my investment portfolio.'"[93]

Others were diverted by rapture and end-times possibilities. "Overall, this kind of teaching has certainly stifled social consciousness among evangelicals," said Tim Weber, professor of church history at Northern Baptist Theological Seminary. "If Jesus may come at any minute, then long-term social reform or renewal are beside the point. It has a bad effect there."[94] Peter Peterson, a lapsed Republican who had earlier been secretary of commerce, could also plausibly blame GOP "tax-cut theology" for his bête noire, federal deficit spending. Tax reduction, he said, had become a matter of "faith."[95] All kinds of quasi-religious explanations were converging in the makeup of party policy, leaving faithful economic stewardship the loser.

In the Crusaders' Footsteps: The Anglo-American Achilles' Hubris?

Since Islam and Christianity began fighting in the seventh century, the holy land has often brought disillusionment: after the Crusades (all nine of them), after the fall of Constantinople in 1453, and five centuries later for the British, in particular, after World War I. Unmindful Western nations may still be playing out the Crusader hand. As we will see, in the months before George W. Bush sent U.S. troops into Iraq, his inspirational reading each morning was a book of sermons by a Scottish preacher accompanying troops about to march on Jerusalem in 1917.

One of the more chilling themes of world history is the relationship between great wars and religious ambition. Holy war inflames religion into arrogance; and as all four of the nations we have examined were passing their apogees, there was talk about the antichrist and Armageddon, one of Christendom's familiar mass excitements. Fifth-century Romans whose forebears had cursed Nero now damned the Vandals and Huns. After the Reformation, popes and Spanish kings became the antichrist to Protestants. Then when France emerged as the major threat to Dutch power in 1672 and thereafter, the Netherlands named Louis XIV the antichrist. The papacy, in turn, gave crusadelike status to the Hapsburg Spanish battle against Protestant heresy.

Although the Europe of 1900–1914 represented the world's most advanced civilization, talk of Armageddon and crusadership flourished. By 1914 military recruiting posters showed St. George, St. Michael, angels, and even Christ in the background. When hostilities began, German churchmen preached holy war in the east against Russia and in the west against "atheistic" France.[96] Kaiser Wilhelm himself also pretended to be a Muslim sympathizer to bolster his alliance with Turkey and ambitions in the Middle East.[97] Britons, however, singled out the Kaiser, and became almost manic over the return of the "Hun" and the threat to world civilization, against which God had marshaled his chosen island people. The most extreme blessing of the cannons came from the bishop of London, A. F. Winnington-Ingram, who called the war "a great crusade— we cannot deny it—to kill Germans." He advised *The Guardian* that "you ask for my advice in a sentence as to what the church is to do. I answer MOBILIZE THE NATION FOR A HOLY WAR."[98]

We have seen that between 1870 and 1914 the British developed a "national psychosis" of war expectation, and the United States displayed a lesser version in 1917–1918. Several books have been written about the U.S. churches' militance, for the rhetoric among U.S. clergy was as overblown as any in Europe.[99] The fuller U.S. parallel developed out of the Cold War with the Soviet Union. In the late 1970s and 1980s, the nascent religious right became a vocal participant, with prominent evangelical ministers arguing that Christianity could not convert the world for Christ with Soviet atheism in the way. From Ronald Reagan's White House down to grassroots congregations, the Soviet Union—the "evil empire"— became a biblical as well as ideological foe. Struck in the early 1980s by world turmoil seeming to match the prophecies of the Bible, Reagan brought up the a-word: Armageddon. In those years, end-times preachers named the USSR as the evil confederation supposedly referred to in the Bible.[100]

When the Soviet Union collapsed between 1989 and 1991, U.S. religious conservatives quickly identified a roster of replacements: Islam as the primary evil force and Iraq and Saddam Hussein, respectively, as (1) the reembodiment of the evil Babylon; and (2) the leading new contender for the role of antichrist. While few U.S. officeholders indulged any candor, many evangelicals and fundamentalists did. In 2003 Richard Cizik, vice president of the National Association of Evangelicals, told *The New York Times* that "evangelicals have substituted Islam for the Soviet Union. The Muslims have become the modern-day equivalent of the Evil Empire."[101]

This gains plausibility if we think about how the U.S. enthusiasm is at least partially replicating the evangelical, crusading, and Armageddon-flavored floundering in the British Empire during and just after World War I. Then as now British and American sanctimony reinforced each other, and the naïveté and global moralizing that Woodrow Wilson added to British posturing and misjudgment would be equaled in 2003 by British prime minister Tony Blair's reinforcement of Washington's missteps in Iraq.

The U.S. political backdrop to post–September 11 involvement in the Middle East also involved the biblical lens that much of Bush's constituency uses to view events in the holy land. As I detailed earlier, the 65 to 70 percent of the 2004 Bush electorate that are born-again or that believe in Armageddon represent the party's essential constituency.

Thus, just as scholars of the British war mentality in the years prior to 1914 do well to study the patriotic bombast of the music halls, the stanzas of "Onward, Christian Soldiers," and the endless books predicting German invasions, fathoming the Bush electorate requires its own study materials. In communications terms the White House has depended on what Bruce Lincoln, David Domke, and other experts have called double coding—the biblical allusions that cluster so thickly in some speeches that the faithful among his listeners respond warmly. With so many liberty-and-freedom, good-versus-evil speeches year after year, Bush made himself a bridge between politics and religion for a large percentage of his electorate, cementing their fidelity.

Meanwhile, portions of the Christian-right message—too radical and divisive to be voiced directly from the Oval Office—went out through a network of preachers with whom Bush and his advisers kept in touch, could not endorse, but conspicuously never disavowed. These, of course, are stalwarts of the rapture, end times, and Armageddon such as Tim LaHaye, Jerry Falwell, John Hagee, and Jack Van Impe, whose books and television ministries reached half of the Bush electorate. Their radical—and overimaginative—interpretation of the Bible relentlessly magnified that of a defrocked Anglican priest, John Nelson Darby, who visited the United States eight times during the 1860s and 1870s, and ultimately gained far more adherents in the New World than he ever did in his native British Isles.

In a nutshell, what Darby proclaimed—and what spread like wildfire through the hugely successful books of Cyrus Scofield (the 1909 *Scofield Reference Bible*), Hal Lindsey (*The Late Great Planet Earth,* fifteen million sales through many editions since the 1960s), and Tim LaHaye (the *Left*

Behind series, with multimedia sales in the sixty-million range)—is a world of turmoil now in the last of seven periods (dispensations) that will end with the rapture of true believers suddenly pulled into the sky to be with Christ. Next follows the seven-year tribulation, when the satanic antichrist will arise in Europe and seize world power. At its end Christ and his armies will triumph in a great battle in Har-Megiddo, near Haifa in what is now Israel. From Jerusalem Christ will proclaim the start of a one-thousand-year reign of peace.[102]

Through the 1990s, at least, most serious commentators ignored these books and broadcast ministries. But the election of George W. Bush, followed by the nation's post–September 11 responsiveness to a religious dialogue of good versus evil, sparked growing attention to LaHaye's series. In 2003 University of Wisconsin historian Paul Boyer, an expert on religious prophecy, estimated that "upwards of 40 percent" of Americans "believe that Bible prophecies detail a specific sequence of end-times events."[103] To Boyer, religion's huge and unrecognized role in policy formation was on display in "the shadowy but vital way that belief in biblical prophecy is helping mold grassroots attitudes toward current foreign policy. As the nation debates a march toward war in the Middle East, all of us would do well to pay attention to the beliefs of the vast company of Americans who read the headlines and watch the news through a filter of prophetic belief."[104] The Bible includes no specific sequence of end-times events, as most theologians point out, so belief that it does is largely a product of a century of amplified Darbyism, which is consummated in the *Left Behind* series.

Boyer's thesis is true enough. Similarly liberal observer Esther Kaplan analyzed the *Left Behind* series' themes and arguments and concluded that "Bush's Middle East policy perfectly aligns with the religious worldview of LaHaye and his millions of readers."[105] My own analysis, after reading several of his novels, is comparable. It was eerie, especially in the first few volumes published in the 1990s, to see so many Bush administration foreign-policy qualities anticipated: a global tribulation of good versus evil, the falsity of the United Nations, the emergence of an antichrist from Europe, the complicity of the French, the building of the second Babylon in Iraq, and its emergence as the headquarters of the antichrist.

Theologian Barbara Rossing, a professor of New Testament studies at the Lutheran School of Theology in Chicago, argues that "the Rapture and the dispensationalist chronology is a fabrication. . . . [T]he dispensationalist system's supposedly clear-cut answers rely on a highly selective biblical literalism, as well as insertion of non-existent two thousand year gaps and obvious redefinition of key terms. The system is not true to a literal reading of the Bible, as they claim."[106] Not only is this "a dangerous and false view of God and the Bible," but "the events where dispensationalists identify the Bible's cosmic plan coming to life are most of all world wars, bloody crashes, earthquakes, diseases and other violent cataclysms. Disasters of sickening magnitude are welcomed by prophecy buffs because they evoke feelings that God is present and alive."[107] Regretting how "Rapture and Armageddon scenarios tap into Americans' love for disaster films and survivalist plot lines," Rossing posits the ultimate *Left Behind* message: "God so loved the world that He sent World War Three."[108] Still, for many of LaHaye's readers the events of September 11 squared with the series' cultural and political message. Small wonder that, according to a *Washington Post* poll in September of 2003, some 70 percent of the population thought that Saddam—as "the evil one"—was involved in that day's attacks.

Three Catholic authors contributed rapture critiques that were well received in the Catholic press and elsewhere. Carl E. Olsen's study *Will Catholics Be Left Behind?* appeared in 2003, Paul Thigpen's *The Rapture Trap* was published in 2001, and David Currie's *Rapture: The End-Times Error That Leaves the Bible Behind* came out in 2003.[109] Compared with these, the mainline Protestant rebuttal was sparse. Still, the theological dismissals of the rapture certainly represent the view of mainline U.S. Protestantism, as well as most of the U.S. Catholic hierarchy.

An ounce of prevention, in a theological sense, would have been worth a pound of cure. In explaining readers' reactions to the series, Amy Johnson Frykholm reported that women in particular said over and over that the novels "bring the Bible to life." For many, the dispensational script brought these images "into a scheme of logic, assimilating them into a cosmic story they can understand."[110] Because mainline Christianity had not paid serious attention to the Cyrus Scofield–Hal Lindsey–Tim LaHaye viewpoint during the 1970s and 1980s when the Christian right was resurging, no contradictory theological foundation had been laid. As a result, the *Left Behind* message flooded persuasively into the thought processes of a considerable segment of American Protestants.

The rapture is just one dubious element of so-called dispensational premillennialism. However, before we look at premillennialism's impact on U.S. policy in the Middle East, it is useful to recall the calamitous pre–World War I legacy of British evangelicalism, moral imperialism, and religious hawkishness. In some ways, although certainly not all, the United States picked up the evangelical baton Britain dropped nearly a century ago—and ironically, few Americans were more aware of Britain's 1917 invasion of the Turkish-controlled holy land than George W. Bush. Just before the U.S. attack on Iraq in 2003, *Newsweek* ran a cover story on Bush's "defining [religious] journey: from reveler to revelation." In it, Howard Fineman described the president's immersion each morning in a book of evangelical sermons by Scottish Baptist Oswald Chambers. An itinerant preacher, Chambers spent his last days bringing the gospel to Australian and New Zealand soldiers massed in Egypt in late 1917 for the invasion of Palestine and the intended Christmastime capture of Jerusalem.[111]

The Britain that let itself drift into the First World War was caught up in many psychologies relevant to early-twenty-first-century America. The tide of evangelical, largely noncomformist Protestantism, despite important left-leaning and antiwar currents, was even more powerfully associated with the moral and political aura of the empire—witness the evangelicals who became imperialist symbols: David Livingstone, the explorer; General Charles Gordon, slain in Khartoum; and General Sir Henry Havelock, hero of the relief of Lucknow in the Indian Mutiny.[112] The same moral insistence also spurred the nineteenth-century British Christian foreign-missionary movement.

By 1914 many British churches were all but draped in flags. According to historian Arthur Marwick,

> Ministers of religion had embarked with enthusiasm upon the "Holy War." "The Church," as the minister of St. Giles Cathedral, Edinburgh, later recalled, "to an unfortunate degree had become an instrument of the State and in too many pulpits the preacher had assumed the role of a recruiting sergeant. Almost every place of worship throughout the length and breadth of the land displayed the Union Jack, generally placed above the holy table, while some had great shields carrying the flags of all the allied nations. . . . I said many things from my pulpit

during the first six months of my ministry that I deeply regret. It is no
excuse to say that many preachers were doing the same thing."[113]

Apart from any immediacy of Armageddon, wartime involvement in
the Middle East had its own biblical dimension. More than any other
European people, nineteenth- and early-twentieth-century Britons spoke
of resettling Jews in the historic land of Israel. This inclination dated
back to the seventeenth-century rule of Oliver Cromwell, whose Puritan
belief in Scripture led him to readmit Jews to England (they had been expelled in 1290) and to express hope for their eventual return to Judea.
Two imperially minded nineteenth-century prime ministers were also
well disposed: Benjamin Disraeli (who promoted the idea in a book) and
Viscount Palmerston (who thought a British client state in the Middle
East would be geopolitically advantageous).[114] By 1915 the subject came
before the British war cabinet, at this point unsuccessfully, where its principal supporter was Chancellor of the Exchequer David Lloyd George, a
Liberal whose poor Welsh constituency had been part of the great
1904–1907 revival. Moreover, as one historian has noted, he "had been
brought up by his uncle, who had been a preacher in a fundamentalist
Welsh Baptist sect with a tradition of interpreting the Bible quite literally."[115] As prime minister from 1916 to 1922, Lloyd George would be a
key to British focus on the Middle East.

The increasing familiarity of conflict with Islam was a further barom-
eter of London's thinking. After the 1857 mutiny in India, as British occupation moved northwest toward the Khyber Pass, the foes were Muslim
khans and tribesmen. The Great Game itself was played in a Muslim
arena—Afghanistan, Persia, India's North-West Frontier Province, and
Russian central Asia. So, too, for the military expeditions of Generals
Kitchener and Gordon in Egypt and the Sudan, as well as the outposts of
empire in northern Nigeria, Aden, Zanzibar, British Somaliland, and the
Malayan Straits Settlements. As the Ottoman Empire tottered, Muslim
lands became the next arena of European imperial ambition.

Britain's Armageddon rhetoric had a broader origin. In *The Road to
Armageddon* Cecil Eby summarized that "increasingly, in England, 'Armageddon' became a popular catchphrase referring to an apocalyptic
war that would be fought at some time in the future. Thus, when war finally broke out with Germany in 1914, H. G. Wells's famous phrase, 'the

war that will end war,' caught the public fancy because it appeared to fulfill St. John's prophecy of the war between the legions of God and Satan, conveniently defined as England and Germany, respectively."[116]

In later years the war's extensions into the Middle East and reconquest of Jerusalem in 1917, proximate to the old Megiddo battlefield, added force. The poet Rupert Brooke had written in the early days, "Well, if Armageddon's on, I suppose one should be there."[117] By the time Sir Edmund Allenby took Jerusalem in late 1917, an additional analogy was being superimposed. Major Vivian Gilbert's narrative *The Romance of the Last Crusade: With Allenby to Jerusalem* took its title from Allenby's supposed remark on entering the holy city, "Now the crusades have ended."[118] On the other hand, when Allenby was advanced to the peerage he became Viscount Allenby of Megiddo and Felixstowe.

The romance of the Crusades was alive and breathing strongly. As French and British imperialism moved into the lands of Islam during the nineteenth century, both nations turned out books with titles like *The Cross and the Crescent* and art like Delacroix's painting *The Entry of the Crusaders into Constantinople.*[119] When plans to carve up the Middle East took shape during the war, the French evoked the old crusader kingdoms of the twelfth and thirteenth centuries ruled by Frenchmen such as Godfrey de Bouillon. The British, having the legends of Richard the Lionheart but no actual crusader kingdoms to evoke, more or less decided to put their chips on a Jewish Anglo-American client state within the same boundaries.[120]

In his memoirs Lloyd George recalled being "brought up in a school where I was taught far more about the history of the Jews than about the history of my own land."[121] During the course of the war, he called Britain's role that of the Good Samaritan and enjoyed discussing the names and places in the holy land. He also provided critical support for a postwar Jewish homeland under British auspices and for the late-1917 British invasion of Palestine.[122]

British policy makers closed out the war in 1918 with a rising conviction that the Middle East was where Britain would find its postwar imperial expansion. German East Africa had been captured, Egypt became a formal British protectorate in 1919, and Persia became an informal one, leaving the holy land—Palestine, Jordan, and Mesopotamia—as the missing link in complete British dominance from Cape Town to Burma.[123] Pushed by Lloyd George, Britain had by the end of 1918 sent 1,084,000

British and Commonwealth troops into Ottoman territory to control the carving up, and the so-called settlement of 1922 fulfilled British ambition.[124]

Nevertheless, by 1922–1923 British policy makers knew that the foundations of these ambitions had collapsed. Many troops had been withdrawn in 1919, and then Britain's economy fell into a deep downturn in 1920 and 1921. Mesopotamia (Iraq) was restive, shrunken budgets forced cutbacks in imperial ambition, and Lloyd George's coalition government was defeated in the 1922 general election. As this took place, Palestine, Jordan, and Iraq became dusty way stations of an empire in decline, not one still cresting toward a greater future. As early as 1919 Britain urged the United States to take up a peacekeeping role in Constantinople and Armenia, but Congress declined.[125]

Slippage at home was visible in the inability of British churches to command their former respect and Sunday attendance. The Church of England lost public confidence through its thoughtless wartime flag-waving, and the largely evangelical nonconformists lost ground because their war support—many had been caught up in the drumbeat of moral imperialism by 1914—mocked their earlier peacetime priorities and preoccupation with social progress.[126] Churchgoing lost its quasi-obligatory status for middle- and upper-class Britons, reducing attendance to only 15 to 20 percent of the population in the 1940s.

How much of this misfortune might repeat in the even more evangelical and morally assured United States during the twenty-first century can be no more than a matter of speculation. But while the lessons of Rome and Spain are distant and only minimally relevant, that is not true of evangelical, Protestant Britain, marching proudly—and naïvely—to war under the same hymns still sung at Iowa church suppers. British observers were appalled, in March 2003, to find that George W. Bush had been transporting himself back to the Allenby years through his Oswald Chambers readings. In a column for *The Times* of London, Ben McIntyre regretted that Bush's focus was not "the grimly inspired ironies of Siegfried Sassoon and Robert Graves, nor the poignant painful questioning of Wilfred Owen." Instead he was absorbed in the 1917 advice of evangelical war chaplain Chambers, whose counsel was to put aside any consideration other than God's will, to "surrender your will to him absolutely and irrevocably" and "become more and more ablaze for the glory of God." For Chambers, said *The Times*, "the enemy was 'evil,' religious duty was clear, and Christian soldiers marched onwards in a straight line."[127]

Events in the Middle East had been part of Britain's post–World War I debacle. Nearly a century later, the error was about to be blindly repeated by a president of the United States who shared Lloyd George's biblical frame of reference, thought the enemy was "evil," and failed to profit from the larger lesson taught by history.

Since the collapse of the Soviet Union, America has taken up the war whoops of militant Protestantism, the evangelical Christian missionary hopes and demands, the heady talk about bringing liberty and freedom to new shores, the tingle of the old Christian-Muslim blood feud, the biblical preoccupation with Israel, and the scenarios of the end times and Armageddon—the whole entrapping drama that played in British political theater a century ago. American evangelical, fundamentalist, and Pentecostal churches, in turn, have become the new flag bearers of crusades against Islam's "evil ones." According to national public-opinion polls, evangelicals and their leaders far exceed other Americans in their disapproval of Islam. Two-thirds of these leaders consider Islam to be dedicated to "world domination" and a "religion of violence."[128] The anti-Muslim comments of prominent leaders of the Christian right such as Falwell, Robertson, Franklin Graham, and former Southern Baptist Convention president Jerry Vines confirmed evangelical leader Richard Cizik's contention about antagonism to Islam replacing hatred of the Soviet Union.

Yet much of their activity purports to be missionary. Instead of British church people and Bible societies accompanying Queen Victoria's soldiers to India, we have U.S. missionaries following the flag to the Middle East. Prior to World War II the mainline U.S. churches led missionary work, but today, says historian Paul Harvey, "American foreign mission efforts are dominated by conservative evangelical groups (the Southern Baptist Convention and the Assemblies of God, the largest Pentecostal denomination, are the two largest senders of career missionaries) and Mormons (by far the largest sender of non-career missionaries)."[129] Indeed, after the prophecy wave of the early 1990s the Southern Baptist Convention and other evangelicals reorganized their missionary activity to focus on

Islam in the Middle East and North Africa, and in 2003, *The New York Times* reported that the number of U.S. missionaries in Islamic countries had doubled since 1990.[130]

By 2003, after a decadelong drumbeat by religious organizations urging the United States to defend foreign Christian populations—another page taken from British nineteenth-century experience—the principal evangelical churches were not just war supporters but active mission planners. A year after the military took Baghdad, a survey by the *Los Angeles Times* found thirty evangelical missions in the city. Kyle Fisk, executive administrator of the National Association of Evangelicals, told the newspaper that "Iraq will become the center for spreading the gospel of Jesus Christ to Iran, Libya and throughout the Middle East."[131] John Brady, head of operations of the Southern Baptist Convention International Missions Board in the Middle East and North Africa, said in a fund-raising letter that events in Iraq represented a "war for souls." Within two years seven new evangelical Christian churches had been launched in Baghdad alone.[132] Some credited their humanitarian efforts, but the Roman Catholic archbishop claimed they "seduced" Christians from other churches, and some Muslims complained about the proselytization. Whatever the effect, many in the Christian right appear to have a larger purpose, perhaps related to preparation for the rapture, the tribulation, and Armageddon. Some 40 percent of Americans, as we have seen, believe that the antichrist is alive and already on the earth.

Paul Boyer dates evangelical preoccupation with the Middle East back half a century, stirred by the creation of Israel in 1948, then by the recapture of Jerusalem's Old City in 1967, and then again by the expansion of Jewish settlements in Gaza and the West Bank, all key end-times signs. They further ballooned during the years surrounding the Gulf War and the demonizing of Saddam Hussein. Islam's evil role, says Boyer, is an ancient view in Christian eschatology: "As Richard the Lion-Hearted prepared for the Third Crusade in 1190, the famed prophecy interpreter Joachim of Fiore assured him that the Islamic ruler Saladin, who held Jerusalem, was the Anti-Christ and that Richard would defeat him and recapture the Holy City." Later, even during World War I, the Ottoman Empire was cast in the antichrist role, and by the 1970s fundamentalists were transferring that evil to the Arab world.[133]

"Anticipating George W. Bush," Boyer adds,

> prophecy writers in the late 20th century also quickly zeroed in on Saddam Hussein. If not the Anti-Christ himself, they suggested, Saddam could well be a fore-runner of the Evil One. . . . Prophecy believers found particular significance in Saddam's plan, launched in the 1970s, to rebuild Babylon on its ancient ruins. The fabled city on the Euphrates, south of Baghdad . . . owed its splendor to King Nebuchadnezzar, the same wicked king who warred against Israel and destroyed Jerusalem in 586 B.C.[134]

Evil Babylon, the antithesis of Jerusalem, the good city, prompted its own literature in the 1990s, and LaHaye's tens of millions of readers praised his series as making the Bible and its supposed predictions "come alive." Like Boyer and other critics of LaHaye, I cannot help but think that by the early 2000s—certainly by September 11—the *Left Behind* series provided an extraordinary context for a president with a religious mission. Its biblical framework already bundled together the terrorism of September 11, the oil politics of the Persian Gulf (oil itself being, in the LaHaye books, a strategic calculus of the antichrist, it could not be a White House focus), and the invasion of Iraq-cum-Babylon. The distinctions that mattered to secular Americans—that Saddam was not involved in the September 11 attacks and that the weapons-of-mass-destruction excuse for invading Iraq was specious—would have mattered less to the tens of millions of true believers viewing events through a *Left Behind* perspective. They simply embraced Bush's broad good-versus-evil explanation.

Ultimately polling projects have suggested that Bush backers were uniquely muddled in their perceptions. One special survey undertaken by the Center for International and Security Studies at the University of Maryland found three-quarters of Bush backers still convinced in autumn 2004 that Iraq did have weapons of mass destruction or a development program and was also aiding al-Qaeda, despite well-publicized official reports to the contrary. As part of their worldview, these people simply refused to disbelieve Bush's original weaponry assurances or implications—a case of "cognitive dissonance."[135]

Unfortunately, the international consequence of U.S. misjudgment in the Middle East—from the loss of American prestige and rising oil prices to occupied Iraq's role in breeding, not relieving, Islamic terrorism—could not be so easily ignored. The military casualties and the budgetary deficit effects of the imbroglio in Iraq rose together. And if the disarray was far short of anything in World War I, some of the message was similar. As in Britain nearly a century earlier, evangelical religion, biblically stirred foreign policy, and a crusader mentality ill fitted a great power decreasingly able to bear the rising economic costs of strategic and energy supply failure.

If anything, the United States of the early 2000s, for all that it lacked Britain's established church, was under George W. Bush in the grip of a considerably more powerful religiosity, constituency pressure, and biblical worldview.

Part III

BORROWED PROSPERITY

8

Soaring Debt, Uncertain Politics, and the Financialization of the United States

Thirty years ago, neither firms nor politicians used (or could use) massive in-
debtedness to justify their actions or inaction. Since 1980, firms, politicians and
others have regularly used debt to rationalize conduct that has been damaging
to workers and to the poor. . . . Debt, directly or indirectly, has decayed the very
soul of America.

— James Medoff and Andrew Harless, *The Indebted Society*

IT'S FINALLY HAPPENED: MOVING MONEY AROUND HAS SURPASSED MAKING things as a share of the U.S. gross domestic product. But while the explo-sion of debt and credit is well acknowledged—in this context *The New York Times* in 2005 employed the term "borrower-industrial complex"— the benign phrase "financial services" still dominates the discussion. Even so, the armchair detective can easily figure out that we are approaching a national transformation in economic vitality that past world powers al-lowed to their peril.

In official statistics, the finance, insurance, and real estate (FIRE) sector of the U.S. economy swelled to 20 percent of the gross domestic product in 2000, jumping ahead of manufacturing, which slipped to 14.5 percent.[1] Since the 1980s financial deregulation has encouraged these three related vocations to interweave in so many holding companies and financial groups that their identification as one sector has become routine. In a revealing introduction to the *Financial Services Fact Book for 2005,* Gordon Stewart, president of the cosponsoring Insurance Information Institute, noted that a new chapter on mortgage finance and housing offered "a fascinating glimpse into home ownership demographics in the U.S. and recent refinancing activity."[2] Insurance, the investment business, and mortgage finance have become teammates. In this extended fraternity, the assets of the financial-services sector rose from $37.9 trillion in 2002 to $42.0 trillion in 2003 and $45.3 trillion in 2004.[3] The United States has a new dominant economic sector.

Debt was a critical enabler. Its huge expansion, especially in the 1980s and 1990s, paralleled—and helped to bring about—the growth in U.S. financial services. This has become one of the most underresearched and underanalyzed dimensions of late-twentieth-century U.S. economic transformation. As the collective weight of public and private debt ballooned between the Vietnam War years and 2000, the financial-services sector essentially accompanied debt up the staircase. In the words of investment strategist Stephen Leeb, "one key word says it all: debt . . . is behind the pulsating growth in financial services. . . . [O]ver the past fifty years, they have moved in lockstep as a percentage of GDP."[4]

Earnings added a further exclamation point. Financial-sector profits shot past those of manufacturing in the mid-1990s, thereafter moving farther ahead. By 2004 financial firms boasted nearly 40 percent of all U.S. profits.[5] The financial sector commanded a quarter of America's stock-market capitalization that year, up from just 6 percent in 1980 and 11 percent in 1990.[6] Historically this transformation is as momentous as the emergence of railroads, iron, and steel and the displacement of agriculture during the decades after the Civil War. Because several recent snapshots of financial services make a kindred point—that finance now outweighs, outmuscles, and outlobbies goods production—figure 6 combines them.

However unhealthy the financial-services relation with debt, the explanations are straightforward. American financial-services firms conduct much of their business in managing, packaging, or trading debt and credit instruments, as well as handling debt-related corporate restructurings. Lucrative returns have flowed from government and corporate bonds, asset-backed securities, credit cards, mortgages, and home loans, as well as financial and credit derivatives (like credit-default swaps), leveraged buyouts, and a plethora of other gambits and gambles. Much as railroads pro-

FIGURE 6

The Rise of Financial Services and the Decline of Manufacturing

The Mega-Leap of Finance, 1974–2004:
Data for quarter ending Dec. 31 of the year in question[a]

Manufacturing and Financial Services: Changes in Percentage Share of
U.S. Gross Domestic Product, 1950–2000[b]

	1950	1960	1970	1980	1990	2000	2003
Manufacturing	29.3	26.9	23.8	20.8	16.3	14.5	12.7
Financial Services	10.9	13.6	14.0	15.0	18.0	19.7	20.4

The Reversing Origins of U.S. Corporate Profits, 1950–2004[c]

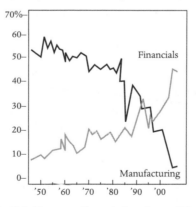

[a] Source: Goldman Sachs Global Investment Research, *Sector Strategy: Where to Invest Now*, Nov. 2005.
[b] Source: "Gross Domestic Product by Industry," Bureau of Economic Analysis, Nov. 11, 2004. For historical data, see Table B-12, Gross Domestic Product by Industry, 1987–2003, *Economic Report of the President, 2005;* and Table B-38, Manufacturing Output, 1943–1971, *Economic Report of the President, 1972.*
[c] Source: Ray Dalio, Bridgewater Associates.

liferated needlessly and recklessly in late-nineteenth-century Britain and
the United States, finance has done likewise in the 1980s, 1990s, and 2000s.

Part of what propelled financial services were the profits gained from
providing American households with artificial purchasing power —the
loans that many took out to splurge on consumption or to restore income levels they could no longer attain from shrinking manufacturing or
back-office wages. Financial firms in the credit business—and few major
companies were not in it—generally marketed their credit cards through
solicitations that held out low costs and instant gratification. By 2003
many were imposing fees and interest rates on unpaid balances that critics compared to loan-sharking.[7]

These 19 percent and 25 percent interest charges might be a sweet spot
on the ledgers, but anyone taking a larger perspective had cause for alarm.
Historically, top world economic powers have found "financialization" a
sign of late-stage debilitation, marked by excessive debt, great disparity
between rich and poor, and unfolding economic decline.* Ordinary citizens suffer most, but they usually lack the expertise to fully comprehend
the changes under way. The thesis of part 3 of this book is simple: this
debt and credit revolution constitutes the third major peril hanging over
the future of the United States.

Debt has long been a tool of economic and political management.
However, during its first century and a half the American Republic confined serious borrowing bouts to meeting the demands of major wars:
the Revolution, the Civil War, and World War I. The debt was often paid
down quickly, sometimes abetting a major postwar economic contraction. Large-scale expansion of public debt was rare in peacetime. The U.S.
shift to fiscal permissiveness came in two stages in the twentieth century:
in the 1930s, when the federal government accepted large-scale deficit
spending in peacetime to fight the Great Depression; and then in the
wake of World War II, when Washington decided against risking another

---

*"Financialization" can be defined as a process whereby financial services, broadly con-
strued, take over the dominant economic, cultural, and political role in a national economy.
In his book *In Praise of Hard Industries,* British journalist Eamonn Fingleton deplores "finan-
cialism" as "the increasing tendency by the financial sector to invent gratuitous work for itself that does nothing to address society's real needs but simply creates jobs for financial
professionals."[8] My term describes only the broader cultural and national transformation.

postwar contraction. Instead, policy makers let most of the wartime inflation and debt expansion stand. Accepting a national debt that had risen to more than 100 percent of GDP seemed the lesser evil.

Happily, that ratio fell rapidly. Prosperity expanded the economy, reducing debt's relative burden. Real problems held off until the late 1960s, when President Lyndon Johnson accelerated federal spending to pay for both a widening war in Vietnam and pursuit of what he called the Great Society at home. The sixties were the first-named "go-go" years, and White House economists, convinced that sophisticated new management could transcend the business cycle, shrugged off the guidelines of careful accountancy and bet that the country could afford "guns and butter" simultaneously.[9] These plans miscarried, and in a hint of worse to come the federal budget deficit in 1968 climbed to $25 billion or 2.9 percent of GDP, the largest since 1946.

Foreigners became distrustful, especially after the United States in 1971 stopped letting foreign central banks redeem dollars for gold, as they had long been allowed to do. Senior U.S. economic officials were thereafter obliged to seek the tolerance of international and domestic lenders for large U.S. budget deficits, creeping inflation, or a combination of both. Their forbearance allowed American voters and major business interests to sidestep some of the unpleasant choices—most notably tax increases or benefits cuts—forced on unluckier fiscally loose nations. By the eighties Democrats opposed serious spending reductions, while Republicans wanted to cut rather than raise taxes—and deficits rose accordingly.

During the early 1970s the budget shortfalls had been closer to 1968 dimensions. In the 1980s they reached critical mass: $208 billion and 6.1 percent of GDP in 1983, $184 billion and 4.9 percent of GDP in 1984, $212 billion and 5.2 percent in 1985, and $221 billion and 5.1 percent in 1986.[10] This time Republicans rather than Democrats were seduced into permissiveness, by supply-side economics and theories along the lines of the Laffer Curve.

Normally, domestic fiscal laxity on this scale has painful consequences. However, because the dollar was the world's reserve currency, the United States usually could more or less print the money it needed—and the rest of the world, after grumbling, would acquiesce. Many nations went along in part because they relied on the United States for other protection, military and economic. Washington's success helped to breed a policy and mind-set that could be described as *debtsmanship:* how big a deficit could the United States get away with, and for how long?

By the 1980s the fiscal cauldron boiled as the Reagan administration, shedding the familiar Republican green-eyeshade conservatism, began to employ economic strategies that went beyond debt tolerance to outright indulgence. Political as well as corporate wheeler-dealers perceived benefits: could a bigger deficit be shrugged off if it enabled tax cuts? Might that deficit, having been enlarged for tax cuts, then be turned around to compel reductions in federal programs? In 1980 George H. W. Bush had famously described this thinking as "voodoo economics," but he soon gave in. Old ideologies were metamorphosing.

Religion, of course, has its born-again dimension, and sometimes economics gets entangled with it. As conservative politics accepted debt, elements of the population were embracing born-again Christianity: evangelical, fundamentalist, and Pentecostal denominations that drew ever more of the population into a preoccupation with personal salvation. Some preachers even promised economic fulfillment along with salvation. George W. Bush, struggling with his succession of debt-ridden or nearly insolvent Texas oil businesses, had found alcohol first but then turned to God in 1986 as oil prices slumped to their ten-dollar-per-barrel nadir. It may not be irrelevant to wonder how many other Americans took similar refuge, comfort, or inspiration as economic or cultural nooses seemed to tighten.

The Precarious Trajectory of American Debt

As conservatives embraced new forms of economic stimulus in the 1980s, new genres of supportive economic literature found an audience. Some thinkers equated capitalism with quasi-religious gift giving, others perceived hitherto-unappreciated civic virtue in earlier ages' robber barons. Still others extolled the virtues of deficits that could curb taxation and debt that could unlock corporate assets for more profitable deployment. After a while, economic vice became economic virtue. Fiscal gunslingers became paladins of the new debt frontier. Novelist Tom Wolfe cast a Wall Street bond trader as a Master of the Universe, self-imagined, at least, in his bestseller *Bonfire of the Vanities.* By mid-decade the high-interest junk bonds pioneered by Michael Milken were being hailed as constructive levers of a more democratic capitalism. Liberal economist Robert Reich countered that "paper entrepreneurs" who reshuffled money and debt were replacing those who made actual goods.

To some conservative economists, wealth inequalities could be ignored because what ordinary Americans truly cared about was consumption: their own ability to participate in the endless television advertising and credit-card offers pouring out of Madison Avenue's American dream machine. "I shop, therefore I am" became a suburban motto and also a bumper sticker. The amount of consumer credit outstanding more than doubled between 1980 and 1990. Indebtedness flourished on many fronts: as a government artifice, a corporate tactic, an investment-firm underwriting bonanza, and, for many ordinary citizens, a household indulgence or sheer economic necessity. The foundations of the twenty-first-century borrower-industrial complex were being poured.

Although some federal-deficit apologias had merit, more were flawed, often by their insufficient attention to the maturity of the U.S. economy. Historically debt is constructive in emerging and adolescent nations but perilous in those beginning to age or contemplate retirement. Take, for example, Alexander Hamilton's timely 1781 notion of a funded public debt as a fiscal boon—a "national blessing." For a new nation with commercial aspirations, it might well be. The Dutch in the early seventeenth century and the English in the 1690s had pioneered funded national debts and found them essential for borrowing at reasonable rates of interest during wartime. Many generations later, however, as their public debts bloated and their national trajectories turned downward, Dutchmen and Britons in turn staggered under their heritage of lending, borrowing, and cultivating reliance on finance and rentier cultures. Debt ceased to be a blessing. Even Hapsburg Spain had its own unique economic system that used gold and silver bullion from the New World to support bond issues and underwrite extravagant foreign wars. We will revisit those unhappy precedents in the next chapter.

As the twenty-first century began, the United States was well into the dangerous part of the leading-economic-power trajectory. Finance had displaced manufacturing, despite Washington ploys to redefine and overstate the latter by including the output of hamburger emporiums and computer software.[11] As the Federal Reserve Board pushed down interest rates between 2001 and 2004, consumer debt psychologies became increasingly reckless. One economist lamented that "we're a what's-my-monthly-payment nation. The idea is to have my monthly payments as big as I can take. If you cut interest rates, I'll get a bigger car."[12]

At $7.8 trillion in 2004, although computations vary, the national debt—the amount owed by the United States to holders of its sovereign debt—was the largest ever measured. The credit-driven economy of 2003–2004, for its part, in turn provoked dismissal as a "phony recovery" because of U.S. dependence on "possibly the biggest fiscal and monetary stimulus in history."[13] In the meantime, yet another measurement, net *foreign* indebtedness—$3.3 trillion by 2004, up from roughly zero in 1987—confirmed the United States as the world's principal debtor. Yet the borrowing continued. Cynics joked about Washington having to wheedle $2.5 billion per day.

Corporate debt was another mirror. Many companies used the deep Federal Reserve interest-rate reductions completed in 2003 to refinance their debt. Even so, the quality ratings issued by Moody's, Standard & Poor's, and Fitch were lower and overall corporate debt levels higher than they had been in 1999, not a good sign.[14] By 2005, leveraged buy-outs, the great corporate-debt ploy of the eighties, were back in the news and fattening the risky loan totals. Record issuance of low-rated bonds prompted David Hamilton, director of corporate-bond default research for Moody's, to observe that "this percentage of really risky debt is unprecedented."[15]

Household debt, which includes credit-card balances, mortgages, and other loans, was also of growing concern. By 2005 it had reached levels that made toughening of federal bankruptcy law, enacted that April, a high financial-services-industry priority. Courtesy of economists at Northern Trust, Goldman Sachs, and elsewhere, a few voters in 2004 had heard fleeting references to the "household deficit," an unnerving portrait of how much more American households were spending each year than they earned. In 2004 they had laid out $1.04 for every $1.00 of income, falling in total some $400 billion in the red.[16]

That red ink, of course, required households so burdened to make it up by taking out loans or drawing down assets. To find comparable examples, Paul Kasriel, chief economist at Northern Trust, had to go back to 1946–1950, a period during which Americans spent pent-up savings left from the shortage years of World War II, when stores had offered little for sale.[17] The twenty-first-century pattern, by contrast, was better explained by the unprecedented decline of the U.S. personal savings rate over a quarter of a century.*

Figure 7 sketches not only the looming mass of the entire current U.S. mountain of debt but its accretion over regular intervals since the 1950s. The first steep rise came in the 1980s. The 1990s then carried what economists call total credit-market debt—government, business, financial, and household—above its previous top (287 percent of GDP) in the era surrounding the 1929 crash. The transition from the stock-market expansion of 1997–2000 into the subsequent credit and housing expansion raised the peak higher still. By 2004 total credit-market debt reached 304 percent of GDP, the sort of Himalayan altitude generally associated with dizziness and nosebleeds.[18] Just how worried the average American was remained unclear.

Robert Marks, an enterprising New York economist, devoted a page in *Barron's* to an intriguing and disconcerting thesis: that by 2004, the unprecedented magnitude of credit and debt in the United States had made irrelevant the traditional focus of the Federal Reserve Board on the nation's money supply. Total nonfinancial credit-market debt in the $23 trillion range, he argued, had effectively supplanted the $3 trillion money supply as the best guide to the actual economy.[19] However unlikely to persuade the Fed, Marks's analysis made a strong case that the U.S. economy was regrouping around credit, debt, and the side currents of financialization.

To carefully examine the pitfalls of U.S. debt—national, international, financial, corporate, and household—it is necessary to divide the overall bulk of the debt mountain into separate entities. But first, one more return to the decades before 1980 is in order. The debt mentality and problem did not just spring to life during the Reagan presidency. It gathered slowly, back in the 1960s and early 1970s, when debt creep was not yet seen as threatening. The national debt remained low as a share of GDP, while the usual small surplus in the current account meant that the U.S. international balance of trade in goods, services, and investments was

---

*In 1980 Americans collectively put aside a net 7.4 percent of national income. By 1990 that had fallen to 4.5 percent, and by 2005 to a record-low *negative* savings rate.

FIGURE 7

The Great American Debt Bubble (Act II)

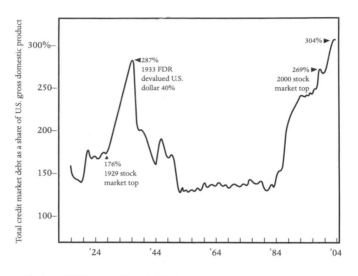

Source: Clapboard Hill Partners, *Barron's*, Feb. 21, 2005.

still favorable, even though imported automobiles, steel, and consumer electronics were capturing a growing share of the American market.

As for corporate debt, between 1960 and 1980 it soared, enlarged in the 1960s by "funny money"—the corporate debentures issued in a wave of conglomerate building and named for the possibility that they could become worthless if "the conglomerate house of cards had collapsed."[20] Corporations were still robust, despite paying 23 percent of all U.S. tax receipts in 1960. By 1990, after many new bond issues and favorable tax provisions, that share slipped to just 9 percent.

Household debt, while large and growing, represented the equivalent of only 50 percent of GDP in 1960 and 60 percent in 1980. This was well below the last binge levels at the time of the 1929 crash and its painful aftermath. Householders in the sixties and seventies were still somewhat constrained by memories of the Great Depression, which helped to keep the U.S. savings rate in the healthy 8 percent range.[21] Even so, economic chronicles count the sixties as a yeasty decade. Credit cards, launched in the 1950s, came of age during the "go-go" decade, although shenanigans in the rebounding mutual-fund industry are what furnished the nickname. Another clue was the attention that William McChesney Martin, that era's Federal Reserve Board chairman, got in 1965 for worrying about the sixties' resemblance to the twenties.[22] The Dow Jones Industrial Average touched 1000 for the first time in 1966, exciting stockbrokers, and the interaction of individual credit cards, television advertising, and ringing retail cash registers was as phenomenal as the effects of radio pitchmen and the introduction of installment buying in the 1920s. During the sixties alone, consumer debt increased by two-thirds. Mortgage debt, the largest individual ingredient of overall household debt, also ballooned, from $208 billion in 1960 to $474 billion in 1970 and $1,465 billion in 1980, as Americans filled in suburbia and carried on to exurbia.[23] State and local governments added their own new debt to the pile, notably for schools and roads.

The point of this brief backward glance is to underscore that the sixties, four decades removed from the twenties, laid a vital foundation by reattuning U.S. economic psychologies to consumerism, stock-market booms, and borrowing. In short, we must date the great twentieth-century U.S. debt-and-credit buildup back to that decade, even if the contours barely show on figure 7. It has now been eight decades since the last major rock slide.

Nevertheless, the eighties are when debt got out of hand, producing problems that hadn't even been thought of in the Coolidge-Hoover era. During the Reagan years, economists began to refer to "the twin deficits"— the federal budget deficit and the current-account deficit. No domestic red ink stained the twenties, because Washington ran successive budget surpluses from 1920 to 1930. The national debt had been paid down from $24 billion to $16 billion.[24] Internationally, the United States in the 1920s had a very favorable global payments balance, as befitted both the world's number-one creditor and a nation where exports far exceeded imports.

When Treasury Secretary Donald T. Regan observed in 1981 that "we're not going back to high-button shoes and celluloid collars. But the president does want to go back to many of the economic incentives that brought about the prosperity of the Coolidge period," fiscal prudence was the precedent he ignored.[25] During Andrew Mellon's long tenure as secretary of the treasury (1921–1932), Republican officials and economists pursued debt's reduction, not its expansion. Indeed, Mellon's weakness as the Depression unfolded was magnified by his impolitic statement in 1930 expressing utter lack of sympathy for debtors, farmers, or speculative investors, whose abuses could be liquidated to "purge the rottenness out of the system."

The Democratic presidential cycle that began in 1933 soon introduced willing use of deficitry and debtcraft, reflecting the spend-to-stimulate theories of John Maynard Keynes, whose view had become so widespread by 1970 that Richard Nixon acknowledged that "we're all Keynesians now."[26] In fact, the inflation of the 1970s was about to end Keynes's ideological reign. Yet many Republicans besides Nixon remained under partial influence. By the Reagan years, besides encompassing supply-side tax-cut theology and monetarist faith in currency expansion and shrinkage, the ranks of conservative Republicanism included tax-cut Keynesians (deficits are fine if you're giving money back to the folks who count), military Keynesians (the Pentagon houses government's most deserving function), pork-barrel Keynesians (more roads and projects, and then even more), and even bailout Keynesians (large or well-connected financial institutions have to be rescued). By the decade's end, as the philosophers of debt usefulness finished lining bookshelves with their paeans to junk bonds, leveraged buyouts, "deserving deficits," tax cuts no matter what, and the belief that current-account deficits signify only foreign hunger to invest in America, the debt fox was loose in the fiscal henhouse.

Compared to the straitlaced Republican fiscal policy of the 1920s, the 1980s were a Roman orgy. By 1992, with the federal budget deficit reapproaching 5 percent of GDP and the infamous savings-and-loan bailout making daily headlines, citizen outrage energized the most successful independent presidential candidacy in eighty years, mounted by peppery Texas billionaire H. Ross Perot. Preaching against the dangers of debt and deficits, Perot urged a string of reforms that pivoted on an anti-deficit constitutional amendment and a long-term trade strategy focused on debt and jobs.

The international economic supremacy of United States circa 1960 was becoming a memory. By the late 1980s and early 1990s Japan took over as the presumed threat. Smiling Tokyo billionaires were buying up trophy skyscrapers in Manhattan along with what appeared to be half of Hawaii. Historian Paul Kennedy's 1987 book *The Rise and Fall of the Great Powers* crystallized attention to the idea that the United States might be on the cusp of great-power decline. In 1988 Republican presidential hopeful Robert Dole had amended Ronald Reagan's 1984 claim that it was "morning again in America." Now, said Dole, it was "high noon"—time for the nation to face up to its global predicament, a point Perot and many others were to reiterate in 1992.

Deficit foes, for their part, challenged debt apologists through a series of influential books: *Beyond Our Means* (1987) by Alfred Malabre; *On Borrowed Time* (1988) by investment banker and former commerce secretary Peter G. Peterson; *Day of Reckoning* (1989) by Harvard economist Benjamin M. Friedman; and *The Indebted Society* (1996) by economists James Medoff and Andrew Harless.[27] Like Perot's, their indictments were unmistakable: debt jeopardized the U.S. future.

Yet the certainty about debt excesses was short-lived. Between 1998 and 2000 glum fiscal predictions appeared to wither on the vine as the technology-led stock-market boom swelled toward its ultimate bubblehood. For a while, its luminance convinced many Americans, particularly investors, that prosperity and solvency had returned. Cassandras were awed into silence. Moreover, the stock market developed enough momentum that surging federal capital-gains tax receipts washed away federal deficits. Unexpected federal budget surpluses replaced them in 1998, 1999, and 2000. Still buoyed by this, a heady George W. Bush, weeks after taking office in 2001, delivered State of the Union and budget messages proposing to both "pay down an unprecedented part of our national debt" and "double our Medicare budget over the next decade."[28]

The principal caution was international: the rapidly expanding U.S. current-account deficit, which combines the trade and investment flows. Briefly a small surplus in 1991 as allies from Saudi Arabia to Japan reimbursed Washington for its outlays in the Gulf War, this deficit resurged powerfully during the late 1990s. To be sure, the simultaneous stock-market boom facilitated soothing explanations: yes, Americans were loading up on goods made elsewhere, but foreigners were investing those dollars right back in soaring U.S. stocks. As for rising public consumption and its flip side, nonexistent personal savings, that duality also had excuses. Did people really need to save in banks when the values of their assets—stocks and real estate—were climbing like rockets? Wise or not, these were staple explanations.

By the end of 2001 the world had changed again. The one-two punch of a stock-market crash and a recession, followed by the trauma of September 11, cut short any economic reveries. Slowly, painfully, awareness refocused on the nation's unresolved debt problems. By the 2004 presidential election, circumstances were worse than those ten years earlier, aggravated by crises, financial developments, and White House missteps. Few people complained about outlays imposed by antiterrorist demands and the war in Afghanistan, or about the Federal Reserve Board's thirteen successive interest-rate reductions that drove borrowing costs to a forty-five-year low by the summer of 2003. More skepticism, however, attached to the deficit-swelling tax cuts that principally benefited the richest Americans, the ongoing hemorrhage of manufacturing jobs, the higher-than-expected cost in lives and dollars of the 2003 invasion and occupation of Iraq, the related disruptions and soaring prices in the oil markets, and the accelerating 2002–2004 decline in the value of the dollar. The economic clouds were thickening again.

Public and private debt levels bulked among them. As Federal Reserve Board chairman Alan Greenspan merged his massive interest-rate reductions with the Bush administration's tax cuts, the American people responded as Washington hoped. John and Jane Q. Public borrowed money cheaply and spent it liberally. All five U.S. debt colossi—national, international, financial, corporate, and household—kept setting records. At some points, even their momentum alone set records.

The underlying Washington strategy, which succeeded in stimulating the economy, was less to give ordinary Americans direct sums than to create a low-interest-rate boom in real estate, thereby raising the percentage of American home ownership, ballooning the prices of homes, and allowing householders to take out some of that increase through low-cost refinancing. This triple play created new wealth to take the place of that destroyed in the 2000–2002 stock-market crash and simultaneously raised consumer confidence.

But the benefits did not end there. The lowest interest rates in four decades—the Fed's overnight funds rate dropped to 2 percent in early 2002, hit 1 percent in 2003, and stayed in between through late 2004—also revitalized stocks by (1) giving business cheap capital, (2) allowing debt-burdened corporations to refinance, and (3) motivating individual investors to buy stocks instead of leaving cash in money-market accounts that paid negligible and even negative real interest. The Dow Jones

Industrial Average, which had sunk from a peak of 11,700 in 2000 to 7,197 in 2002, regained some three-quarters of that loss by late 2005, although the shattered Nasdaq recovered only one-quarter or so of its huge collapse.[29] As a result, $4 trillion of the $7 trillion shrinkage in stock valuation was regained, and rising home prices more than made up the difference. Figure 10 on page 332 shows both the wealth rebound and the stunning reversal in the importance of homes relative to stocks.

Nothing similar had ever been engineered before. Instead of a recovery orchestrated by Congress and the White House and aimed at the middle- and bottom-income segments, this one was directed by an appointed central banker, a man whose principal responsibility was to the banking system. His relief, targeted on financial assets and real estate, was principally achieved by monetary stimulus. This in itself confirmed the massive realignment of preferences and priorities within the American system.

Such was Greenspan's success. But if debt expansion per se was one large, gray cloud in the sky, the perception of a rebubbling of the economy was another. Nothing comparable had ever been tried. Critics such as Stephen Roach, Robert Shiller, and to an extent former Federal Reserve Board chairman Paul Volcker argued in varying degrees that the effect of Fed policy was to inflate a new real-estate and credit bubble on top of the older Nasdaq-centered froth. Roach, the chief economist at Morgan Stanley, described the Fed chairman as a "serial bubble blower."[30] By 2004 others spoke about an echo bubble or a double bubble or even referred to Greenspan as Chairman Bubbles. The expansion of debt was huge, indisputable, and a topic of spirited national conversation.

Likewise huge and indisputable but almost never discussed were the powerful political economics lurking behind the stimulus: the massive rate-cut-driven post-2000 bailout of the FIRE sector, with its ever-climbing share of GDP and proximity to power. No longer would Washington concentrate stimulus on wages or public-works employment. The Fed's policies, however shrewd, were not rooted in an abstraction of the national interest but in pursuit of its statutory mandate to protect the U.S. banking and payments system, now inseparable from the broadly defined financial-services sector.[31] To this end, the 2001–2003 rate cuts extended a more than two-decade pattern, relentless under Greenspan, of slapping large green liquidity Band-Aids on any financial wound that might get infected.

Large-scale peacetime government stimulus programs in the United

States have *always* been partly political—the New Deal's elevation of labor unions, public works, and activist government in the 1930s; the unleashing by the Reagan administration of corporate and financial animal spirits in the 1980s. However, as *The Economist* suggested, the Bush-Greenspan package, as history's biggest, dwarfed both. It also represents a bet—probably a gamble against human nature—on both the debt-management capacities of the Federal Reserve Board and the public-spiritedness of the financial-services industry.

The Emergence of the U.S. Debt and Credit-Industrial Complex

As the relative importance and profitability of U.S. manufacturing and finance exchanged positions, a larger national transformation took place, akin to the upheaval in the 1880s and 1890s as railroading and manufacturing jumped ahead of agriculture in value added to the U.S. economy.[32] In those days of agrarian despair, debt played a prominent role—it always seems to—in ruining overextended elements of the declining (farm) population while leveraging the ascent of the emerging (industrial) sector. Debt also has a well-known history of causing bubbles and periodic crises.

By Bush's second term, the debt problem that had agitated the late 1980s and early 1990s had reasserted itself. The 1997–2001 return of budget surpluses became a mirage; pessimists refocused their analyses on the long-term debt expansion arising out of the 1960s, 1970s, and 1980s. A graph for the 1965–2005 period of the critical debt measurements—public and private, domestic and international—would uncage a half-dozen climbing snakes, raising their heads for some sort of fiscal strike. The data are apples and oranges, but the problems are unmistakable.

The accelerating displacement of U.S. manufacturing by the financial-services sector, as we have seen, goes far back, greatly antedating both the late-1990s stock-market bubble and the terrorist strikes of September 11, 2001. Since those events, however, the evolution from physical production into debtcraft has accelerated alongside Washington's resort to massive stimulus of consumer borrowing and home refinancing. Debt and spending became fiscal patriotism, a way to strike back at al-Qaeda by supporting the U.S. economy in the automobile showrooms, mortgage offices, and shopping malls. Just before the 2004 election, columnist Daniel Gross caught the new spirit of this rate-cut Keynesianism: "The message since the Sept. 11 attacks has been . . . a strange and occasionally dissonant message of patriotism and consumption. As New Yorkers flocked to Ground Zero to volunteer, Mayor Rudolph Giuliani exhorted Gothamites to patronize TriBeCa restaurants. President Bush appeared in ads urging Americans to fly and stay in hotels. These days, it seems, they also serve who spend like there's no tomorrow."[33] Whereas during both world wars government posters beseeched Americans to save and buy U.S. bonds, now the media relayed a different "wartime" imperative: "Uncle Sam wants *you* to borrow." Taking advantage of zero-rate auto loans or re-financing your house was joining the nation's response to terror.

Never before have political leaders urged such large-scale indebtedness on American consumers to rally the economy. Debt has not previously been held out as a solution to a nation already overburdened by it—especially one vulnerable to restive global creditors. Moreover, it is difficult to believe that the rise of finance, the relative decline of manufacturing, and the polarization of incomes and wealth in the United States can be reversed if political control continues to pass to rentiers and credit vendors.

Think on the differences between the two sectors in income distribution. In the heyday of manufacturing, from the 1920s to the early 1970s, wave after wave of unionized blue-collar jobs lifted tens of millions of Americans into the middle class. Today, the American financial-services economy pushes in the opposite direction. Its narrowing employment base, some 8 million in 2004 out of a national workforce of 131 million, stood in sharp contrast to the much broader uplift of manufacturing in, say, 1960, when goods production employed 17 million Americans out of a workforce of 68 million.[34] This, too, is in keeping with the later stages of previous leading world economic powers: finance distributes its concentrated profits to a much smaller slice of the population.

Although any estimate must be subjective, some 30 to 40 percent of the manufacturing workers during the 1960s—unionized, high-wage men, for the most part—would have belonged to that era's emerging blue-collar middle class. At the top of the pyramid, some fifty to one hundred thousand or so senior manufacturing executives had compensation enough to put them in that era's top 1 percent income group. Yet in the manufacturing companies of that era, even chief executive officers made only twenty-five to forty times the pay of a median production worker. By contrast, as finance consolidated its hold in the nineties, corporate CEOs made three hundred to five hundred times the pay of a median employee. Glamorous financiers did better still. Compared with the relative egalitarianism of manufacturing in the Eisenhower and Kennedy years, the smaller workforce of the contemporary financial-services industry includes a much larger ratio of high earners—probably eight to ten times as many per thousand—whose $500,000-or-over incomes put them in the top 1 percent nationally. The shrinking blue-collar middle class is the glaring casualty of the new regime, but a considerable percentage (with more to come) of yesteryear's white-collar employees—secretaries, clerks, statisticians, and telephone operators—also face losing jobs to computers or high-school graduates in Hyderabad or Malaysia.

Since the late 1970s the loss of manufacturing jobs in the United States has pulled down inflation-adjusted wages for nonsupervisory employees. At the same time, huge income and assets gains in the top 1 to 2 percent, where investors, financial-services professionals, and wealth holders cluster, have enabled these percentiles to pull up overall national growth and income figures. The effect of this is to disguise the shrinkage elsewhere. By credible calculations, the top 1 percent of Americans in 2000 had as much disposable (after-tax) income as the bottom one hundred million or 35 percent of the population.[35] Thus, talk about the "average American income" is innately misleading.

Many economists explain these circumstances in impersonal terms, invoking technology, productivity, and education. These, however, miss another vital dynamic: the realignment of national interest-group influence and the escalating political clout of the financial-services industry. By the 1990s, policy favoritism had become epidemic.

In *The Indebted Society*, economists James Medoff and Andrew Harless advanced a central argument claiming that as debt burgeoned in the United States in the 1980s, it also realigned political power: "It is inevitable that lenders become more important in a society where debt becomes more important. Therefore, it seems likely that lenders also become more powerful. When lenders become more powerful, they have more influence over policy; and the policies chosen naturally reflect that influence."[36] Citing the importance of banks, investment firms, mutual funds, and other elements of the financial-services sector, Medoff and Harless noted the rise in the share of national income represented by net interest from 1 percent in 1950 to 5 percent in the early 1970s and 10 percent in the 1980s.[37] By the early 2000s, however, debt colored so many transactions that its proceeds entailed a much wider range of rewards than straight-forward interest. The term "borrower-industrial complex," cited by *The New York Times* and coined in a paper by economists Noriel Roubini and Brad Setser, caught the magnitude of the U.S. sector, led by credit-card operators, that had grown up around borrowers and their needs.[38] Use of the term "debt-and-credit industrial complex" would be more descriptive.

Candor about the escalating political influence of lenders, investors, and the financial-services industry has sometimes been colorful. In 1993 James Carville, an adviser to President Clinton, remarked that if he could be reincarnated, he'd want to come back as the bond market because it was so powerful. Referring to his 1993 economic proposals, Clinton himself said, "You mean to tell me that the success of the program and my re-election depends on the Federal Reserve and a bunch of f . . . . . . bond-traders?"[39]

In 1998 the financial-services industry successfully mobilized to repeal the Glass-Steagall Act, the New Deal statute mandating the separation of commercial banking, investment banking, and insurance. According to the Center for Responsive Politics, the FIRE sector laid out more than $200 million for lobbying in 1998 and contributed more than $150 million in the 1997–1998 election cycle.[40] Indignation from the left and elsewhere tended to be drowned in cheers for the soaring stock market, but its bubble popping relegitimated criticism. In 2000 the exposés in the *Buying of the President* and the *Buying of Congress* series published by Charles Lewis and the Washington-based Center for Public Integrity invariably dwelt on finance, its clout and political access. Between 1990 and 2002 the FIRE sector repeatedly topped the list of contributors to national elections, giving more than $1.3 billion.[41] In fact, the 2000–2001 fall of high tech only clarified the sectoral triumph of finance.

Some of the sector's political enthusiasm was specific to the Bush family. In mid-2004, the Center for Public Integrity tabulated the leading lifetime patrons of George W. Bush: the big four were Morgan Stanley, Merrill Lynch, PricewaterhouseCoopers, and MBNA, the credit-card giant.[42] The family's background also blended these same origins and commitment. No presidential clan has been so involved in banking, investments, and money management over so much time.[43]

As the younger Bush's second term began, the pervasiveness of debt and credit in the U.S. economy drew increasing attention. Beyond the familiar center-left economic critique—the argument that creditors and lenders by nature dislike rapid growth and inflation, preferring lesser economic momentum (2.5–3 percent) and the deflationary influence of cheap imports and a third-world labor pool—broader concern attached to the perception of a credit bubble. If housing prices weren't the second bubble in the Greenspan sequence, debt was. "If there's a bubble, it's in this four-letter word: debt," Merrill Lynch chief North American economist David Rosenberg had observed earlier. "The U.S. economy is just awash in it."[44]

Other worriers ventured kindred descriptions: the credit bubble, the mortgage finance bubble, the hedge-fund bubble, and the systemic liquidity (money-supply) bubble. The underlying premises were similar. Debt and credit had gotten out of control, even as the rest of the economy sometimes seemed to flirt with deflation.

Data from the 2000 census documenting the ascent of financial services became available in 2001 but received little initial public attention in a nation shell-shocked by the events of September 11. The ominous linkage between the escalation of private and public U.S. debt and the expansion of the financial-services industry was generally ignored, despite its imminent relevance when debt and home refinancing became such a conspicuous Washington priority. Investment strategists could be outspoken with important clients, but few officeholders held a similar 2004 dialogue with voters. In the words of Ray Dalio of Bridgewater Associates, a large Connecticut money-management firm, "The money that's made from manufacturing stuff is a pittance in comparison to the amount of money made from shuffling money around. Forty-four percent of all corporate profits in the U.S. come from the financial sector compared with only 10% from the manufacturing sector."[45] I have seen no rebuttals.

The numbers were hardly shocking. Public finance is one of the world economy's oldest profit centers. Research by *The Wall Street Journal* for a millennial retrospect on great wealth holders revealed public finance—the opportunity to handle the taxes, borrowings, and debts of kings, popes, and conquered provinces—as a major source of great fortunes since late medieval times.[46] Notables included Jacques Coeur, financial adviser to fifteenth-century French kings, and the Peruzzi, Medici, and Fugger families, whose relations to power centered on popes.

Three of the great British and French fortunes of the early nineteenth century were amassed by loan makers to governments: Nathan and James Rothschild and Gabriel Julien Ouvrard, the French wartime speculator and paymaster for Napoleon. Even in the early American Republic, four men counted among the richest—Robert Morris, William Bingham, Stephen Girard, and John Jacob Astor—owed significant portions of their wealth to investment or speculation in state and federal bonds and securities of the Bank of the United States.[47] Accounts of late-nineteenth-century public finance and wealth echo with names such as Jay Cooke, J. P. Morgan, and George F. Baker of New York's First National Bank.

Today, despite the prominence of moneymen such as Warren Buffett and George Soros, the importance of the financial-services industry rests less on glamorous individuals and more on a perverse interplay of magnitude and jeopardy. The magnitude lies in how finance has penetrated every nook and cranny of the U.S. economy, as well as the digitized world of cyberspace. From corner ATM machines and an average of eight credit cards per household to a $15 trillion stock market, $40 trillion of total credit-market debt, and a global total of derivative positions estimated at $270 trillion, the reach of finance is awesome—and as beyond our ken as awed New Yorkers found the first electric dynamos in the 1880s.[48]

If history teaches us anything, it's that this so-called cutting-edge finance is an accident waiting to happen, despite claims by the so-called new-macro economists that derivatives are tame and benign and that national debt and deficits are manageable within a new global savings pool in which national boundaries no longer matter so much.[49] Even Alan Greenspan occasionally owned to uncertainty about where speculators and new credit instruments—hedge funds and derivatives in particular—might be taking the country. Throughout 2004 and 2005 investment strategists and economists speculated that Greenspan was nervous about these markets. Some even interpreted his May 2005 speech citing the growing risk to banks and investors of a derivatives-driven liquidity crisis as a thinly veiled message to sell.[50] Their practical fear—that a rout in the bond market could follow any panicky hedge-fund selling of collateral debt obligations (CDOs)—mirrored uneasiness on the edge of the credit bubble.

The evidence of the last four centuries is that financial innovation and intensity regularly breed debt-and-credit crises, burst bubbles, and the like. In his still-unsurpassed 1978 study, *Manias, Panics, and Crashes,* Charles Kindleberger listed two dozen between 1720 and 1974–1975.[51] Their parenthood was principally Dutch, British, and (later) American, because these nationalities dominated global finance, central banking, markets, and trade during those years. The first modern financial mania collapsed in 1720 (the South Seas bubble) and the most recent, the high-tech (Nasdaq) bubble, splattered between 2000 and 2002. If human nature has changed, the gene modification must have occurred almost overnight.

The economists who called Greenspan a serial bubbler or condemned him for throwing money-supply or debt expansion at every crisis had documentation. Tabulations of M3, the broadest major money-supply measurement, showed a mushrooming from $4 trillion to $7 trillion between the early 1900s and the millennium as Greenspan lubricated crises involving Mexican debt, Russian debt, Asian currencies, the collapse of Long-Term Capital Management, and Y2K fears.[52] The Fed chairman's legitimate rebuttal rested on his responsibility for the safety of the banking system, although he discharged it well beyond any clear mandate in protecting nonbank linchpins such as Long-Term Capital Management, the large, wayward hedge fund on behalf of which Greenspan helped arrange a Wall Street bailout in 1998.

Indeed, the quarter century before 2005 could be described as a triumph of financial-sector protection over marketplace comeuppance. Figure 8 lists the principal U.S. governmental interventions, resuscitations, and rescue missions—high-level influence was a given and huge dollops of money commonplace—to preserve financial-sector interests and institutions. In the early 1980s, as these bailouts were getting under way, debate raged in Washington over a national industrial policy or strategy. That objective, originating with high-technology companies, was for Washington to support U.S. firms against the mercantilist alliances of business and government prevalent in Europe, Latin America, and Asia. Otherwise, said U.S. executives, American manufacturers would lose more global markets. Conservative officeholders and theorists generally disagreed, insisting that Washington "should not pick winners."[53]

However, by the end of the century it became clear that the federal government had done exactly that, picking finance to be the ascendant sec-

FIGURE 8

Bailouts, Debt, and the Socialization of Credit Risk, 1980–2005

Year	Rescue	Government Methodology
1982–1992	Mexico, Argentina, Brazil debt crisis	Federal Reserve and Treasury relief package to avoid domino effect on U.S. banks.
1984	Continental Illinois Bank aid	$4 billion Fed, Treasury, and FDIC rescue package.
Late 1980s	Discount window bailouts	Fed provides loans to 350 weak banks that later failed, giving big depositors time to exit.
1987	Post-stock-market dive rescue	Massive liquidity provided by Fed, and rumors of Fed clandestine involvement in futures market.
1989–1992	S&L bailout	U.S. spends $250 billion to bail out hundreds of S&Ls mismanaged into insolvency.
1990–1992	Citibank and Bank of New England bailouts	$4 billion to help BNE, then government assistance in arranging a Saudi infusion for Citibank.
1994–1995	Mexican peso rescue	Treasury helps support the peso to backstop U.S. investors in high-yield Mexican debt.
1997	Asian currency bailout	U.S. government pushes IMF for rescue of embattled East Asian currencies to save American and other foreign lenders.
1998	Long-Term Capital Management bailout	Fed chairman Greenspan helps arrange bailout for shaky hedge fund with high-powered domestic and international connections.
1999	Y2K fears	Liquidity pumped out by Fed to ease Y2K concern helps fuel final Nasdaq bubbling.
2001–2005	Post-stock-market crash rate cuts	Fed cuts U.S. interest rates to 46-year lows to reflate U.S. financial and real-estate assets and protect the U.S. economy's newly dominant FIRE sector.

Source: Adapted from Chart 2.15 in Kevin Phillips, *Wealth and Democracy* (New York: Broadway Books, 2002), p. 105.

tor in the U.S. economy and figuratively shrugging as American manufacturing lost its markets, profits, and prime political access. The electorate, of course, never got to vote on a decision that never had to be made formally. The financial sector, in fact, was *already* the statutorily designated constituency of Washington's second-most powerful officeholder—the chairman of the Federal Reserve Board—whose mandate was to supervise and regulate banks, implement monetary policy, and maintain a strong official payments system.[54] Here the reader may want to turn back to figure 6, on page 267, with its portrait of how U.S. manufacturing slid and finance took control, staking the American future on a sector with no record of sustaining earlier global economic hegemonies. The Federal Reserve Board was the principal architect.

So backstopped, the ascendant financial sector enjoyed the best of two seemingly contradictory worlds. On one hand, the Federal Reserve Board and sometimes the Treasury Department were available to rescue banks, bondholders, critical currencies, and even hedge funds too big to fail. Yet at the same time the financial-services industry enjoyed the cumulating benefit of three decades of deregulation: minimal regulatory constraint.

This triumph of neo–laissez-faire, as we will see, was almost as important as the government bailouts. Deregulation of financial services had been under way since 1980, but by the late 1990s the industry was like a long-distance runner coming down onto the flats for the last mile. The finish line—the promise of nearly unfettered financial capitalism, and devil take the hindmost—was so close the panting chief executives could see it.

Debtor Society, Credit-Card Nation

In jeopardizing the commonweal—through teenagers bearing credit cards, financiers leading politicians on golden leashes, and the Republic drowning in debt—the new economy mocks the dicta and beliefs of the nation's founding fathers. We can only wonder which one would have been most appalled: George Washington, who in the early 1770s decried London creditors for their treatment of Virginians; Benjamin Franklin, who deplored debt; John Adams, who publicly loathed banks; or Thomas Jefferson, who feared the rise of a financial elite. Lincoln, who put labor ahead of capital, would have been equally displeased, and likewise the two Roosevelts, Theodore and Franklin.[55] Even the lessons of Greece and Rome were relevant, as the men deliberating in 1787 had known from their readings.

For leading world economic powers of more recent vintage, the ins and outs and ups and downs of debt have been high-stakes rites of passage. If world history can be examined through the experience and saga of sugar, coal, spices, codfish, or technology, as bookshelves testify, debt also provides an important lens. One such volume, *A Free Nation Deep in Debt: The Financial Roots of Democracy,* recently came from a British investment banker, James Macdonald.[56] After explaining the role of debt, principally over the last five hundred years, Macdonald concluded that the rise of a massive, impersonal, and electronic global marketplace for public and private debt had all but dissolved the old nexus between citizen-creditors and democratic government. The emergence within the United States of the world's first large-scale debt and credit complex, analysis of which Macdonald did not pursue, may tell an even sadder tale.

A detailed chronicle of U.S. debt travails, looking back from 2015 or 2020, may rank the early 2000s as crisis years surpassing the 1890s, 1931–1933, and the early 1980s. During 2003 household debt jumped 11 percent, and 28 percent of Americans ended the year by giving debt priority in their New Year's resolutions, according to a poll by the Cambridge Consumer Index.[57] Amelia Warren Tyagi, coauthor of *The Two-Income Trap: Why Middle-Class Mothers and Fathers Are Going Broke,* told reporters that nearly one-third of bankruptcy filers owed an entire year's salary on their credit cards.[58]

During 2004 one unlucky American filed for bankruptcy every fifteen seconds. Antoinette Millard of Manhattan, after running up bills of nearly $1 million in local luxury emporiums, sued American Express for improperly soliciting her to sign up for a big spender's credit card.[59] By year's end consumer debt represented a record 85.7 percent of GDP. Overall, the U.S. economy had added $2.7 trillion in debt in twelve months.[60] Two thousand five, in turn, saw the household debt-service ratio reach 13.4 percent of after-tax income, the highest level since the Fed began publishing that data in 1980.[61] In California interest-only loans accounted for 60 percent of new mortgages, up from 47 percent in 2004.[62]

Multiple causes were at work. Human nature provided the greed and gullibility at which three decades of determined federal regulatory dismantling had unleashed credit vendors. U.S. financial overseers, in turn, were disinclined to establish social criteria or community welfare yardsticks for economic policies or activities. Finance also indulged one of its periodic compulsions to combine avarice, legal nonchalance, and clever innovation in the new speculative instruments—another sequence of the high-wire acts and bubble-blowing kits so recurrent in the four-century history of financial manias, panics, and crashes.

How the U.S. federal government became willing to dismiss memories of the 1920s and start deregulating banking and finance in the 1970s and 1980s makes a logical entry point for risk assessment. The stripping away of old safeguards in the name at the marketplace was relentless. Consider these post-1970 policy milestones, some taken from the *Financial Services Handbook,* but others added from explanations of relevant court rulings and Federal Reserve Board decisions.

In 1971 Washington stopped letting foreign central banks exchange their dollars for gold, thereby creating a buildup of excess U.S. currency in Europe—the advent of Eurodollars. This supercharged the foreign-exchange markets. In 1974 the U.S. government convinced Saudi Arabia and OPEC to price oil in dollars, which to some extent put the U.S. dollar on an oil standard. Many so-called petro-dollars received in oil payments were invested through U.S. banks, recycling some of the benefits of higher oil prices.

In 1978 the U.S. Supreme Court decided in the *Marquette* case to deregulate credit-card interest rates—practically speaking, a carte blanche that enabled credit-card companies to set up in states (South Dakota, Delaware, et al.) willing to allow full freedom.[63] Two years later, President Carter signed the Deposit Institutions Deregulation Act, voiding the longstanding 5 percent limitation on the interest rate that banks and savings institutions could pay, likewise a precondition for future innovations. In 1984 the Bank Holding Company Act was relaxed to allow banks to hold entire companies as if they were a portfolio of investments, even if they didn't perform banking-related functions.[64]

Permissiveness only broadened in the 1990s. In 1996 the U.S. Supreme Court held in the *Barnett Bank* case that banks could sell insurance. A second ruling that year, in *Smiley v. Citibank,* allowed credit-card issuers to charge *any* fees—penalties, for the most part—permitted by the states in which they were based. Within a few years, fees would begin to multiply like rabbits. In 1997 banks were allowed to buy securities firms.[65] In 1999, after the Federal Reserve Board had already approved a merger between Citigroup and Travelers, a major insurance company, the policy of allowing such mergers belatedly became official with the enactment of the Financial Services Modernization Act. That same far-reaching statute also repealed the Bank Holding Company Act of 1957, establishing a new category of financial holding companies (FHCs). These could not only hold banks, securities firms, and insurance companies under one umbrella but were also permitted to include nonfinancial enterprises. The 1995–2000 period had already seen a stunning crescendo of bank mergers—11,100. Within a year after passage of the financial-services mega-deregulation, five hundred new FHCs were created.[66]

This sequence, a powerful facilitator of the 1997–2000 stock-market bubble, simultaneously gave the financial-services industry essential wherewithal to consolidate its gains in share of GDP and soon to displace the toppled technology sector as the leader in U.S. stock-market capitalization. For all that financiers lost huge sums of paper wealth in 2001 and 2002, the underlying realignment of the U.S. economy remained in place.

Portions of the 1990s deregulation, it should be noted, rested on sound enough logic. Chairman Greenspan and others believed that the United States, handicapped by an old state-by-state banking structure rooted in Jeffersonian suspicions, required instead a phalanx of U.S. superbanks able to leapfrog state lines and abandon the 1930s-ordered separation of banking, investment, and insurance in order to compete with giant financial conglomerates in the Japanese, British, French, Swiss, and German mold. By 2003 three of the world's top ten banks were indeed American, up from none in 1988.[67] The downside, unfortunately, was institutional hubris.

Three U.S. banks became superbanks: Citigroup, the world's biggest; and the Bank of America and JPMorgan Chase, ranked further down. Compared to their predecessors of the 1980s, these institutions were powerhouses, goliaths with units that ran the gamut from insurance and merchant banking to consumer credit. However, as these giants flexed their new muscles, the public interest was often squeezed—witness the record of Citigroup. In late 1990 Citigroup was close to insolvency because of bad real-estate and foreign loans. However, Citigroup's size made it essential to any global strategy for U.S. banking, and Federal Reserve officials helped to arrange a cash infusion and rescue by Saudi Prince Awaleed bin Talal.[68]

By 2004 the firm's new global primacy was matched by its lead in ethical transgressions and large government fines. "Name any scandal of the last decade—Enron, Worldcom, Parmalat, biased [stock] research—and Citigroup's name will crop up," concluded *The Times* of London. Conspicuous abuses outside the United States included a 2004 effort to rig the European bond market and a wayward private-client operation in Tokyo that was shut down the same year by the Japanese government.[69] Within the United States, the bank's most notable chastisements included $215 million to settle Federal Trade Commission charges of applying predatory lending techniques to poor and unsophisticated borrowers, along with a $2 billion fine for allegedly colluding with Enron in defrauding investors. As part of Citigroup's agreement to pay the $2 billion, however, the company was allowed to deny the wrongdoing alleged.[70] Despite their size, such fines resembled hypothetically giving John D. Rockefeller a mere $50 million fine back in 1905, say, without making him admit the misbehavior of Standard Oil. No behavior would change. Just as in oil's emerging years, so much money was moving around within the swelling financial sector—Citigroup's revenues in 2004 topped $86 billion—that the practical effect of seemingly huge fines was hard to measure.

Much of the new financial galaxy was barely regulated. For a year Citigroup was able to flaunt a merger with Travelers that violated the Glass-Steagall Act, which was still on the lawbooks. Enron, in turn, gutted potentially inhibiting regulation of its own futures trading through the good offices of Texas senator Phil Gramm and his wife, Wendy Gramm, who chaired the Commodity Futures Regulatory Commission until she retired and joined the Enron board of directors.[71] Greenspan, as chairman of the Federal Reserve Board, declined to take action against an apparent speculative bubble in the stock market, while central banks elsewhere in the world—the European Central Bank, the Bank of England, the Bank for International Settlements—considered that pricking such bubbles might be in order. As we have seen, in 2002–2003 the office of the comptroller of the currency, within the Treasury Department, used its "regulatory" authority over bank credit cards to block activist regulators at the state level. Cole Porter's 1934 hit "Anything Goes" could have returned to Broadway with new lyrics.

One disenchanted investment banker summarized the jurisdictional anarchy that followed the 1999 passage of the Financial Services Modernization Act:

Financial holding companies got a regulatory green light to own any kind of financial service company as well as investments in companies that had little or nothing to do with finance. They became catchall structures to mask risky investments in nonbank corporations. Another festering problem created by the Financial Services Modernization Act was so-called functional regulation. The act claimed that each component of these new conglomerate institutions would be regulated by a different governmental regulatory body. This meant that different federal and state entities had oversight for different components of the same business, yet nobody had full oversight for the entire institution's activities as a whole. . . . So, functional regulation could more appropriately be called "dysfunctional regulation."[72]

Some of what we think of as the bubble of 1997–2000 was a side effect of massive, permissive deregulation—not just of finance but of energy and telecommunications, both in 1996. These were two other industries where egregious misbehavers, Enron and WorldCom, became poster children of speculative havoc. During the boom, the energy and telecom sectors each issued roughly one trillion dollars' worth of new debt, manna for the financial-services industry.[73]

Despite the enormous stakes, federal deregulatory and financial statutes provided scarcely more of a framework for imposing social values and behavioral requirements on newly ascendant financial services than had existed for railroads in the regulatory vacuum of the late nineteenth century. Those, of course, were the years when railroad became a verb as well as a noun—as in to "railroad" a bill through a supine legislature.

Parallels to the deficit in social consciousness on the part of the FIRE sector abound. The United States took decades in the late nineteenth century to regulate working conditions for children: current-day critics saw as much need to deal with the conditions that enticed young Americans into taking on crippling debt. Sociologist Robert Manning later detailed how banking deregulation during the late 1990s facilitated an "enormously successful mass marketing campaign" that "dramatically altered American attitudes toward consumer credit and debt," not least on the part of teenagers.[74] "The key is here," he had said, "as the marketing of consumption goes younger and younger and younger, we're talking about people who have never had jobs and haven't had to establish a budget."[75] Similarly Boston economist Juliet Schor argued that advertising had drawn children into rampant and gullible materialism.[76] Noting how consumer spending accounted for more than two-thirds of the $11 trillion national economy, *The New York Times* summarized that "the machinery of American marketing, media and finance all encourage the consumption habit. Many consumers are unable to resist the overpowering mantra: spend, spend, spend."[77]

True, "overconsumption" is not ideally addressed in a political arena, but considerations beyond finance pull it there today. For example, experts estimated that fraud—such as acceptance by lending institutions of inflated property valuations—was present in at least 20 percent of loans that wound up in foreclosure. Margot Saunders, an attorney at Washington's National Consumer Law Center, added a telling point: "Credit is not just a benefit; it is also a dangerous instrument. Everything from cars to toasters that have some danger are regulated, but loans which can cause such devastation when provided in the wrong situation are not regulated."[78] The need for a broader regulatory assessment of financial legislation seems to leap out.

Nor can market forces be the sole criteria in justifying how the debt-and-credit explosion made elderly Americans reaching retirement during the early 2000s less likely to own their homes than before. Those over sixty-five, said *The New York Times,* not only have "the fastest-growing home debt, but also the fastest-growing share of bankruptcy filings and the biggest growth in demand for credit-counseling. . . . More and more of the elderly are in outright financial distress. One in seven households headed by someone 65 or older was considered heavily indebted in 2001—devoting at least 40% of their incomes to debt payments, according to the Federal Reserve's Survey of Consumer Finances."[79] Such practices seem unsafe on the "micro" level as well as the "macro."

Worsening the burden on the elderly was the trend reported in a February 2005 study for the medical policy journal *Health Affairs.* Between 1981 and 2001 medical-related bankruptcies increased by 2,200 percent, a spike that far exceeded the 360 percent growth in overall personal bank-ruptcies during the same time period. Medical-related debt had become the second-leading cause of personal bankruptcy, partly because of the widening lack of health insurance (with the number of uninsured rising to forty-five million). One of the study's authors, Harvard Law School professor Elizabeth Warren, observed that "the people we found to be profoundly affected are not some distant underclass. They're the very heart of the middle class. These are educated Americans with decent jobs, homes and families. But one stumble, and they end up in complete fi-nancial collapse, wiped out by medical bills."[80]

Values beyond those of the market might also have reversed Alan Greenspan's decision not to prick the turn-of-the-century stock bubble. His case for not doing so, laid out in 2002 and again in 2004, withered alongside contrary theory and weighty evidence from the Bank for International Settlements (BIS), the International Monetary Fund, the European Central Bank, and elsewhere. A study prepared for the BIS, analyzing thirty-four countries since 1960, concluded, in the words of *The Economist*, that "a simultaneous surge in both credit and asset prices gives a pretty reliable warning of financial problems ahead. The case for a rise in interest rates is therefore stronger when asset-price rises go hand-in-hand with rapid growth in credit—as in America in the late 1990s."[81]

As for the serial liquidity that replaced the stock bubble with a housing bubble, the IMF in 2003 conducted a detailed study of previous property slumps in the United States and thirteen other industrialized countries. The conclusion was that a real-estate bust less than half as large as a de-cline in stock prices had typically proved twice as dangerous to national economies, with effects lasting twice as long.[82] Should a fall in real-estate prices in the 2000s bring the tumbling economic dominoes avoided ear-lier, the Federal Reserve Board's decisions might be reexamined under a cruel lens: can bubble popping be left to the whim of a central bank blinded by fealty to finance? Can unsafe credit practices be allowed when unsafe industrial practices have been regulated or prohibited?

We shall see. If the financial-services industry has risen to new heights of influence and economic dominance, its predilections and practices seem to march to a familiar drummer.

Greed and the 1995–2005 Credit Bubble

Philosophically, the several waves of Washington's conservative-led liberation of financial services contradicted the sounder sort of conservatism—the ideology of a John Adams, a George Washington, or a Theodore Roosevelt—cognizant of the effects of greed and the need to constrain it. Deregulatory thinking, predicated on an exaggeration of Adam Smith's vaunted "invisible hand," simply presupposed the legitimacy of whatever so-called market forces might produce. Preening after the enactment of the 1999 legislation, Phil Gramm, the chairman of the Senate Banking Committee, proclaimed that instead of regulation, "we believe freedom is the answer."[83] Freedom for the financial sector, that is.

What simultaneously triumphed, unfortunately, was ignorance of history and a classic onset of greed. Risk eloped with avarice in heady expectation, even while the memory of the Nasdaq crash and Enron was still fresh. These liaisons justified fear that the credit or serial-liquidity bubble was an extension and enlargement of the first crisis, not merely an aftershock.

Credit-card issuers turned buccaneer, helping to lure Americans into record debt, after gaining final approval in the late 1990s to charge customers virtually whatever interest rates and fees they wanted—and with flimsy excuses. By 2005, as we will see, nearly 40 percent of the typical issuer's profits came from penalty fees. Duncan MacDonald, a lawyer for Citibank in the 1996 Supreme Court case deregulating credit-card fees, told *The New York Times* in 2004, "I didn't imagine that some day we might have ended up creating a Frankenstein."[84] Hedge funds and exotic derivative instruments, including CDOs that pooled everything from snowmobile loans to plastic-surgery payment streams, picked up where Enron croupiers had left off. Financial-sector debt *doubled* during the five years following the Nasdaq crash. By 2005 it totaled three times as much as the Nasdaq equity vaporized earlier.

Housing may be part of the larger casino. As real-estate values soared with the help of Federal Reserve Board rate cuts, new varieties of mortgages, as we will see, turned homes into ATM machines and loan terms into crapshoots. Hundreds of different agreements facilitated a wide range of housing market, economic, and interest-rate gambles. By 2005 homes, not stocks, were the principal base of U.S. household net worth.

In contrast to what unfolded after 1929, the controversies over financial practices actually grew after 2000 as the Nasdaq crash led only into new dimensions of debt, themselves hinting at further global jeopardy. But we are getting ahead of ourselves. The United States is hardly the first nation to lose itself in financial ambitions and self-congratulation. The precedents of the earlier leading world economic powers, alas, make the fallibility and danger points all too clear.

9

Debt

History's Unlearned Lesson

The only thing new in the world is the history we don't know.
—Harry S Truman

Historically, the financialization of society has always been a symbol that a nation's economic position has entered a phase of deterioration.
—William Wolman and Anne Colamosca, *The Judas Economy*, 1997

The lesson of history is that we don't learn the lessons of history.
—Thomas G. Donlan, *Barron's*, 2005

BECAUSE THE PAST REPEATS ONLY IN GENERAL RESEMBLANCE, THERE IS always something different, something new. This truth, together with the usual effects of the passage of time, makes it easy for later generations to dismiss any awkward precedents—and so it has been with the demobilization of manufacturing and embrace of debt in the contemporary United States.

Like other leading world economic powers, we tell ourselves we are special, unique, *sui generis,* and God's chosen nation, the new people of the covenant. Economic as well as political and religious smugness threads through each historical sequence. A seventeenth-century Spaniard enthused: "Let London manufacture those fine fabrics, . . . Holland her chambrays; Florence her cloth; the Indies their beaver and vicuna; Milan her broaches; India and Flanders their linens . . . so long as our capital can enjoy them. The only thing it proves is that all nations train journeymen for Madrid and that Madrid is the queen of parliaments, for all the world serves her, and she serves nobody."[1]

A similar Dutch conceit was sculpted into the decorative exterior of the great Amsterdam town hall, begun in the glory year of 1648, which showed that city receiving the tribute of four continents—Europe, Africa, Asia, and North America—while a Dutch Atlas supported the globe on his back.[2] In Britain, economist W. S. Jevons caught the similar self-assurance of the Victorian era: "The plains of North America and Russia are our cornfields: Chicago and Odessa are our granaries; Canada and the Baltic are our timber forests, Australia contains our sheep farms, and in Argentina and on the western prairies of North America are our herds of oxen; Peru sends her silver, and the gold of South Africa and Australia flows to London; the Hindus and Chinese grow tea for us, and our coffee, sugar and spice plantations are all in the Indies, Spain and France are our vineyards, and the Mediterranean our fruit garden."[3]

Not anymore, of course. Few contemplate Madrid, the Dutch Atlas has put down his lonely burden, and the sun has set on the British Empire. The recent echoes of yesteryear's smugness come from the fanfares of American empire so popular before the occupation of Iraq fomented such disillusion. And still, conductors of the orchestra of American hubris wave star-spangled batons and the chorus resounds: Washington rules, the world manufactures for the United States, and our current-account deficit reflects nothing more than global anxiety to invest in U.S. prosperity. Who knows, the Treasury may even be planning a statue of an American consumer supporting the world on his back.

However, if pride goeth before a fall, cocksureness about the manageability of U.S. public and private indebtedness may as well, given threats that range from debt crises to currency humiliations. Crippling indebtedness is like the ghost of leading world economic powers past, a familiar Shakespearean villain come to stalk the current hegemon.

Finance: The Endgame of Champions

Nations do not easily become the leading world purveyor of financial services. Hapsburg Spain rode a flood of bullion from the New World, spreading it around Europe and employing the expertise of moneymen from Augsburg, Antwerp, Genoa, and Venice. The Dutch turned Amsterdam into Europe's top entrepôt, offered the continent's lowest-cost capital, and launched a maritime supremacy that stretched from Japan and the East Indies to New Amsterdam and the Cape of Good Hope. Britain constructed the world's greatest colonial empire and took over maritime and financial supremacy from the Dutch. The United States built the world's number-one industrial power, provided the oil and money for victory in two world wars, and assumed financial leadership from Britain.

None of these hegemons started with well-developed international finance. They began with simpler vocations. Castile, the heart of Spain, was a culture of high-plateau wool growers and skilled soldiers who had spent centuries reconquering the Iberian Peninsula from Muslim emirs before conquistadores found gold and silver in Central and South America. The Dutch, as we have seen, had a unique talent for vocations having to do with ships, seas, and winds. The English pioneered in coal development and superseded the Dutch as masters of the seas. But after several generations of success in soldiering, seafaring, or manufacturing, these peoples, in their respective heydays, were drawn farther in the direction of globalism, financial services, and capital management.

In the case of Spain, the reorientation came in mere decades, driven by the gold and silver mined in huge quantities in the Americas and shipped as bullion back to Seville in great treasure fleets. The Spanish Crown deployed that massive purchasing power to underwrite ventures from the Catholic Counter Reformation and war in the Low Countries to the expensive (and lazy) importation of manufactured goods. The Castilians who ruled Spain were not entrepreneurs, but by 1519 a multiple royal inheritance joined Spain to the Hapsburg empire. In addition to the new American colonies, this combined monarchy sprawled across the Low Countries, much of Italy, Portugal, and part of Germany.

These happened to be the European mercantile and financial centers of the sixteenth century. The extraordinary coming together occurred when Charles of Burgundy, the grandson of Ferdinand and Isabella of Spain on one side and Maximilian of Austria on the other, inherited the Spanish throne, Burgundy (the Low Countries), and Austria, and then became Holy Roman Emperor in his Hapsburg capacity. Without the commercial Flemings, Dutch, Lombards, and Genoese, a Spain captained by militarily and religiously driven Castilians might not have raised its economic flag so high. However, through its new Hapsburg reach, Castile enlisted much of Europe's financial acumen (even though revolt against Hapsburg rule broke out among the Dutch in 1568).

Arrayed together, Spain's wealth and Flemish, Italian, and German mercantile talents made Spain a financial power until its war-related ruination in the 1640s. In several unusual ways, to which we will return, Hapsburg Spain developed aspects of a financial-services empire. Hitherto, that specialty had been confined to small city-states, most notably Venice and Genoa. From the mid-sixteenth century to early in the seventeenth, however, many Genoese, Germans, and Flemings relocated to Madrid, Seville, Cadiz, and other Spanish centers. What Spain never enjoyed or passed through was a serious manufacturing era. As the gold and silver inflows mounted in the 1550s and 1560s, Spain became a financial feeding trough, its ports, commerce, and mercantile facilities largely controlled by outsiders.

Excluding the unusual case of Spain, the leading economic powers have followed an evolutionary progression: first, agriculture, fishing, and the like, next commerce and industry, and finally finance. Several historians have elaborated this point. Brooks Adams contended that "as societies consolidate, they pass through a profound intellectual change. Energy ceases to vent through the imagination and takes the form of capital." Will and Ariel Durant explained that "history repeats, but only in outline and in the large. We may reasonably expect that in the future, as in the past, that new civilizations will begin with pasture and agriculture, expand into commerce and industry, and luxuriate in finance."[4]

In 1908, as we have seen, Winston Churchill, then president of the British Board of Trade, vented a similar historical interpretation in finding "the seed of imperial ruin and national decay" in "the unnatural gap between the rich and the poor" and "the swift increase of vulgar jobless luxury." This bespoke finance, then emerging powerfully in the United Kingdom.[5] And the French scholar Fernand Braudel observed that

> the long perspectives of history suggest, perhaps fallaciously, that economic life is subject to slow-moving rhythms. The splendid cities of medieval Italy, whose decline took gradual shape in the 16th century, often began by building on the profits from road or sea transport.

It was thus with Asti, with Venice, with Genoa. This was followed by mercantile activity, then by industrial development. Finally, the crowning touch, the growth of banking. Inverse proof, the decline affected, successively, and sometimes at very great intervals—and not without occasional brief revivals—transport, then commerce, then industry, allowing banking activities to survive long after the others. In the 18th century, Venice and Genoa were still centers of finance.[6]

A leading twentieth-century historian of Spain, Sir John Elliott, related that nation's decline to its reliance on gold, silver, and debt—its passive acceptance of finance. He also ruminated on how many Spaniards—by 1600 becoming aware of their country's apparent *declinación*—repeated the analogies of Polybius, the Roman historian, who likened the life spans of great nations to the growth, maturity, and decay of living organisms.[7] In a 1997 book indicting the emerging U.S. version of what he called "the Judas Economy," William Wolman, chief economist for *BusinessWeek,* noted the reiteration of this familiar menace: "the best historians . . . have noticed that in each major phase of the development of capitalism, the leading country of the capitalist world goes through a period of financialization, wherein the most important economic dynamic is the creation and trading of abstract financial instruments rather than the production of genuine goods and services."[8]

This is a behavioral pattern—true enough, at least to date—that Americans must ponder. Spain, hardly a nation modern Anglo-Saxons pay much attention to, may have a unique relevance: the warnings it offers as the Western world's first major Judas Economy, where finance triumphed and work decayed. Spain became something that economists, particularly, have not grasped.

While the Netherlands, Britain, and the United States have all followed the familiar capitalist evolution in elevating finance, the perverse Spanish example is important. Before sixteenth-century treasure fleets crossed the Atlantic, Spain had the small outlines of wool, textile, and iron and steel industries, as well as a minor bourgeoisie. But the large-scale arrival of bullion, year after year, was inflationary and sent the prices of local products climbing to levels that made them noncompetitive and simultaneously diminished Spaniards' desire to work for anything but easy gains.

Historians have ascribed these changes to the fostering of a bonanza mentality and to the emergence of Seville, the chief treasure port, as an El Dorado symbol and magnet for fortune seekers.[9]

More broadly, the general verdict of commentators has been that gold and silver rained on Spain without ever greening its real economy. The would-be seventeenth-century reformer González de Cellorigo explained that "money was not true wealth" and that Spain's future was being "dissipated on thin air—on papers, contracts, *censos* [loans] and letters of exchange, on cash, and silver and gold—instead of being expended on things that yield profits and attract riches from outside to augment the riches within."[10] Foreign observers said much the same thing. One historian concluded that "for two centuries, Spain squandered its wealth and manpower."[11]

Perhaps, but for a limited comparison with the latter-day United States this description begs the issue. Nothing even resembling gross-domestic-product or gross-national-product data is available for sixteenth- and seventeenth-century Spain, but if it were what might it show? After gold and silver began flooding Spain, agriculture and what industry there was withered. Ambitious persons decamped for the Madrid of organized religion, the Hapsburg court, and the treasure port of Seville. Through 1620 or so these three were the flourishing economic sectors.[12] As such, they must have produced a significant GDP. Booming Seville, with a population of 150,000, became Europe's third city after Paris and Naples; and in 1585 the Spanish merchant fleet by one count "rivaled the Dutch, doubled the German [Hanseatic] and trebled the English and French."[13] Madrid, two-thirds the size of Seville, thronged with bureaucrats, court parasites, and luxury purveyors. We shall hear about the foreign financial-services vendors there momentarily.

No small part of Madrid's royal and church wealth came from bullion: the Crown took one-fifth of the gold and silver, and other fees, duties, and thinly disguised extortions were legion. The church and religious houses like the Jesuits, largely untaxed, drew great returns from Spanish America. By the eighteenth century the Jesuits, with their lands and mines, were reckoned to be the biggest slaveholders in South America.[14] The large foreign-dominated mercantile and financial communities in Madrid and Seville gorged on legitimate trade, bullion smuggling, tax collecting (on behalf of the government), silver brokerage, insurance arrangements, bills of exchange, and investments in various forms of debt instruments. The Castilian parliament, furious at the property rights and preferences accorded foreign financiers, protested in 1548 that "a consequence of Your Majesty's loans in Germany and Italy is that a great number of foreigners have come here. They are not satisfied just with their profits from banking, nor with obtaining property, bishoprics and estates, but are buying up all the wool, silk, leather and other goods." Of the twenty-nine million ducats Charles V borrowed from bankers, 21.9 million came from Genoese and Germans.[15] Historians and economists are only beginning to piece together the volumes and profits involved.[16]

Many of the nobility or lesser hidalgo class, along with churchmen and the various religious orders, were on the rentier side, deriving much of their income from offices purchased or awarded, investments in the colonies, and debt instruments called *juros*. The latter were cherished linchpins of "a highly elaborate credit system—a system which no doubt received much of its impetus from the exigencies of the crown's finances. Anyone with money to spare—a noble, a merchant or a wealthy peasant— or institutions, like convents, could lend it to private persons, or municipal corporations, or else to the crown, at a guaranteed five, seven or ten percent."[17] Such opportunities, indirectly enabled by bullion, shrank the pool of capital available for bolder ventures. Like debt in the U.S. GDP of the early 2000s, *juros* and other forms of indebtedness likely added up to a disconcerting share of the Spanish GDP circa 1600.

In addition to these components, the role of Spain in importing and diffusing New World gold and silver was a powerful global force during the sixteenth and early seventeenth centuries. Between 1540 and 1660 a total of 16,900 tons of silver and 181 tons of gold came to Europe, the largest proportional increase in bullion ever, and enough to expand the money stock of Europe by about 50 percent by 1660.[18] This was the all-important influx by which European wealth (and power) vaulted ahead of the hitherto larger treasuries of Mughal India, Ottoman Turkey, and Ming China.

Spanish bullion spread across Europe and around the globe. By one French analysis, "it was not just the King of Spain who was interested in the precious metals, but all the merchants of Sevilla, and all the merchants of Antwerp, Augsburg, Genoa and Rouen, who hastened to garner the profits on what they had exported. Once the returning *flota* hove into view . . . couriers carried the good or bad news to the four corners of the world."[19] War also sped the circulation of silver, as Spain used it to fund military campaigns in Morocco, Italy, and Holland.[20] Nor was the effect limited to Europe. The Manila galleons, based in the (Spanish) Philippines, carried so much commerce and coin—each year half the sum of the Atlantic traffic—that Spanish silver became the principal currency of Southeast Asia.[21]

Spain thus became the figurative lode mined by the embryonic western European financial-services industry. "The real figures for the trade, if we take into account all its sectors, are impossible to quantify," said historian Henry Kamen. "This vast commercial enterprise had the outward form of an empire dominated by Spain. Viewed from the inside, however, it was a structure in which all the essential arteries were controlled by non-Spaniards."[22] Like the Castilian parliament nearly eighty years earlier, the native merchants of Seville protested in 1627: "our people are without sustenance and income, the foreigners are rich; and Spain, instead of being a mother to her sons has ended up as a foster mother, enriching outsiders and neglecting her own."[23]

Manifestly, this draining, superimposed financial-services economy was not a framework for long-term Spanish economic success. González de Cellorigo, the economist-cum-reformer, was prescient in identifying the underlying problem. Money, he wrote, was not necessarily wealth unless it was "expended on things that yield profits and attract riches from outside to augment the riches from within." Instead of productive investment, the flow of bullion had created a false sense of wealth and diverted Spaniards from work to dreams.[24] At the same time, he erred in labeling the foreign moneymen as mere parasites. In fact, they were uniquely able to do what the Castilian ruling class wanted; employ European networks to finance Castile's noneconomic priorities of crossbow and crucifix.

For seventeenth-century Dutch and eighteenth- and nineteenth-century Britons, by contrast, the late-stage influence of finance evolved from earlier commercial and industrial strength. As we have seen, activities solidly rooted in the real economy—for the Dutch, fisheries, whaling, shipbuilding, and textile production; for the British, coal, maritime success, textiles, railroads, and iron and steel—prospered amid business climates of technological innovation, capital formation, and a timely energy source. Production of goods for export thrived. After two or three generations the innovation weakened, and the industries lost some competitiveness. Each nation's worldwide connections and buildup of capital and financial services encouraged a rising emphasis on stock and bond markets, insurance, brokerage, globe-girdling finance, and the emergence of large rentier communities.

As the imperial apogees approached, the potential return from investing money domestically came to seem inadequate, and both nations' creditor and financial classes began to move more and more funds into overseas investments. For the eighteenth-century Dutch these were principally British stocks and government debt, and for the British of 1900–1914 one could mention Indian tea plantations, American railroads, and Argentine ranches and banks. As industry lost its edge foreign scientists and students often left for home. Some native-born scientists, engineers, and skilled craftsmen decided to emigrate (from Holland to England, Germany, and Sweden; from Britain to the dominions and the United States). Wars became ever more of a budgetary and economic strain. Debt and currency crises grew increasingly frequent.

However, if the United States seems to be wandering down an altogether familiar pathway, that is not strictly the case. In the quarter century since 1980 manufacturing in the United States has diminished and been displaced by finance far beyond what happened in early-twentieth-century Britain. We will return to the comparative statistics, but Alan Greenspan's own comments have relevance. In the early eighties, as a private economist, he talked about reducing the federal budget deficit to help make U.S. manufacturing competitive again.[25] By July 2003, as chairman of the Federal Reserve Board, he voiced a different analysis: "Is it important for an economy to have manufacturing? There is a big dispute on this issue. What is important is that economies create value, and whether value is created by taking raw materials and fabricating them into something consumers want, or value is created by various services which consumers want, presumably should not make any difference so far as standards of living are concerned."[26]

This, indeed, is the dispute. Part is theoretical: the so-called post-industrial scenario versus the argument that "hard industries" still remain imperative. But another significant element, to which we now turn, is the influence that can entrench around a large rentier class or, as in America now, around a "debt and creditor" complex.

The Precariousness of Rentier Cultures

The word "rentier"—meaning a person living off unearned income—comes from the French, as do so many other words connected with money and plunder: financier, profiteer, buccaneer. Over the last four centuries, however, it was first Spain, then Holland and Great Britain, and now the United States that created the most notable rentier cultures. Each ultimately became vulnerable as a result.

Spain needs little further discussion, save for how its mounds of indebtedness bred an unproductive economic culture. When the initial large amounts of gold and silver arrived between 1540 and 1560, the financial system of Castile was late medieval, not commercially adept in the manner of Renaissance Italy's mercantile and banking centers. However, the flood of bullion enabled the Crown to borrow hitherto-unimaginable sums for grandiose purposes, often military campaigns. By 1574, with the Crown having gone through a kind of bankruptcy in 1557, King Philip II was already paying interest to his bankers in an amount that exceeded his revenues. Debt instruments, most of them *juros* in at least a dozen varieties, had been official money-raising tools since the days of Ferdinand and Isabella. The royal treasury not only sold *juros* but required subjects to accept them in payment when the king sequestered private shipments of bullion, seized businesses or estates, ordered renegotiation of short-term loans (a practice concomitant with the royal bankrupcties), and pressured nobles, merchants, or monasteries into making loans. With interest usually in the 5 to 7 percent range, many foreign bankers and financiers also subscribed.

The volume of *juros* swelled rapidly. In the words of one economic historian, "never before had western Europe enjoyed the buoyant sense of access to such unparalleled financial resources promising liquidity for both private and public enterprise. In 1598, perhaps as much as 4.6 million *ducados* annually were being paid to juro-holders from a [royal] budget of 9.7 million. In the 17th century, Philip IV managed to expand the public debt to twelve times Castile's annual revenues. . . . At the century's end, these instruments—now the foundations of Spain's long-term debt—allowed Spain's *clases privilegiadas* to live off interest income."[27] The upshot, said a second historian, was "the growth of a powerful rentier class in Castile, investing its money not in trade or in-

dustry" but in bonds, the redemption of which most holders strongly opposed.[28] In 1617 the Council of Finance acknowledged seeing no chance
for an economic revival in Castile so long as *censos* and *juros* paid better
interest than that to be had from investments in agriculture, industry, and
trade.[29] A few decades later the debt economy itself came unglued.

The Dutch, obviously, were a different people. Yet they got to much
the same place, albeit by a different route. To raise the money for their
revolution against Spain and Catholicism, they set up a funded debt and
backed it with heavy levels of taxation. Not only did this patriotic commitment bring in the necessary funds, but it soon made Dutch bonds
among the most creditworthy in Europe. Financing available at 5 percent
interest also established early-seventeenth-century Amsterdam as the
West's principal trade entrepôt and stock market, making many Dutch
merchants and bankers rich. In contrast to bullion-drenched but fiscally
fumbling Castile, the Netherlands was ruled by the same somber Calvinists
and capitalists who both underwrote the bonds and bought many of
them. According to investment historian James Macdonald, some sixty-
five thousand Dutch "citizen-creditors" held bonds in a nation that had
only one hundred thousand urban households: "Because the officers of
the state themselves held large portions of their fortunes in government
debt, every public creditor could be sure that his investment was safe."[30]

By the middle of the seventeenth century, however, the urban and
provincial leadership groups were no longer active merchants but
rentiers "deriving their income from houses, lands and money at interest."[31] Generations later, when Dutch industry was notably declining,
mid-eighteenth-century critics worried, as had Spanish reformers, about
a nation divided between rentiers and beggars.[32] Historian Simon
Schama has described the "aristocratization" of the Dutch Republic,
which some regarded as a betrayal of the nation's patrimony.[33] By another account, the typical mid-eighteenth-century family of the governing or regent class had 57 percent of its assets in Dutch bonds and more
than 25 percent in shares, obligations, and foreign funds.[34] A Dutch economic writer, Isaac Pinto, worried that such bonds, shares, and foreign
funds "were the linchpin of civic wealth and status, the principal pillar of
the social system, a situation quite unlike that existing in other countries."[35]

As Dutch society moved toward the credit crises, panics, and collapses
of the last three decades of the eighteenth century, critics grew more

pointed. "Seventy years ago," one foreign observer recorded in 1771, "the wealthiest businessman [in Amsterdam] did not have gardens or country houses comparable to those their brokers own today. The worst thing is not the building and immense expense of maintaining these fairy-tale palaces . . . it is that the distraction and negligence occasioned by this luxury often causes prejudice to business and trade."[36] "A further symptom of the collapse," observed historian Jonathan Israel, "was the astounding increase and transfer of Dutch capital abroad. Amsterdam banking houses with foreign connections plied a roaring business throughout the eighteenth century in exporting the capital the United Provinces had accumulated during the seventeenth."[37]

Besides owning something like 15 to 25 percent of Britain's public debt and a slightly larger ratio of stock in the Bank of England and the (British) East India Company, Dutch financiers of the 1770s found another rewarding venue: pushing money on foreign rulers, from Catherine the Great to Frederick of Prussia. Bankers who saw too little return in revitalizing the Zaandam industrial district or Friesland fisheries were happy to underwrite Russian capture of lands along the Black Sea from Turkey.[38] As British historian Charles Boxer has observed, "whether Dutch capital was invested at home or abroad, it was lent to bankers and brokers of commercial bills, rather than in developing home industries or fostering Dutch shipping."[39]

In the 1860s and 1870s British skeptics wondered if their nation might be doing its own imitation of the Dutch. However, nearer 1914, as the analogy really gained revelance, it was rarely raised. The number and influence of rentiers kept growing. According to one chronicler, "by 1871 Britain contained 170,000 'persons of rank and property' without visible occupation. . . . Stocks and shares, including shares in family firms formed into 'private companies' for this purpose, were a convenient way of providing for widows, daughters and other relatives."[40] Although not to the extent of Holland, Britain, too, was a nation of citizen-creditors, with many in politics or the government owning shares in the consolidated funds.[41]

The big British rentier growth was still to come. With each decade the percentage of investment going overseas grew like a springtime tulip bed. What had been just over £200 million in 1850 became £700 million in 1875, £1 billion in 1900, £3 billion in 1907, and £4 billion in 1914. By

1914 overseas investments were bringing the British investing classes a net annual return of £200 million—a sum that was barely taxed and exceeded the annual budget of His Majesty's government.[42] Owning 43 percent of the global total of foreign investments, Britons believed themselves to be almost invulnerable economically.

Reform-minded political officeholders such as Joseph Chamberlain, the Conservative party's leading economic nationalist, were dubious about this sense of safety well before 1914, and some academics assessing British decline make a similar complaint. "At the very moment when creativity and capital were needed for industrial renewal at home," said historian Paul Thompson, "resources were being siphoned away."[43] Clearly, though, the market dictate was clear: foreign investments earned considerably more than the returns available domestically.[44] Overall, one researcher of British capital migration concluded, preoccupation with dividends nurtured "the growth of a rentier governing class whose interests lay outside the community in which they lived and exerted influence."[45]

British historian Paul Kennedy, the dean of great-power-decline theorists, has emphasized the interplay of finance and the demands of war in charting the fates of Spain, the Dutch Republic, and imperial Britain—finance not as a late stage of national evolution but as a sinew (and sometimes an Achilles' heel) of a great power's military capacity. Kennedy was moved to note, however, that "this is not to say . . . that the financial element *always* determined the fate of nations."[46] We will revisit this relationship in chapter 10.

Because intermittent high debt ratios were so central to the evolution of each of the leading world economic powers, each became comfortable—too comfortable—with debt as a long-standing experience, practice, and tactic. Particular overconfidence was instilled by memories of how often previous debt problems had been surmounted, even at extreme levels (100 to 200 percent) of GDP or GNP. A few examples will make the point. By the time of its real peril in the 1630s—and despite growing cynicism—the Spanish kingdom had survived five previous royal bankruptcies (1557, 1575, 1595, 1607, and 1627), interest rates were still surprisingly low, and the prior ebbs of silver shipments from Mexico and Peru had been followed by renewed flows.[47] The embattled Dutch nation, in turn, had been surrounded by enemies and water at birth and was used to sticking its finger in financial dikes, as well as in the sea-restraining versions. The fact that its national debt rose to painful heights after the wars of 1688 to 1713 did not elicit the concern it should have.[48]

In the London of 1900–1914, complacency about Britain's rising debt in the aftermath of the Boer War reflected epochal industrial triumph after previous surges of war-related indebtedness. Men including David Hume and Adam Smith had doubted the nation's ability to survive the debt burden left by the several wars with France. In 1752 Hume had forecast national bankruptcy by the end of the century unless the trend reversed.[49] However, although the Napoleonic wars carried British debt to a new height—nearly 300 percent of GDP, as measured in the 1820s— even that was surmounted, despite severe pressures during the depressionary decade after Waterloo.[50] By the 1850s the historian Thomas Macauley could scoff at "the same cry of anguish and despair" that had always proved wrong.[51] Britain quickly shrank the Napoleonic-war debt with the profits from its manufacturing hegemony during the 1840s and 1850s, as factories and exports justified the description of Britain as the "workshop of the world." Then the hubris began to set in.

Understandable as this cockiness might be, history teaches a crucial distinction: nations could marshal the necessary debt-defying high-wire walks and comebacks during their youth and early middle age, when their industries, exports, capitalizations, and animal spirits were vital and expansive, but they became less resilient in later years. During these periods, as their societies polarized and their arteries clogged with rentier and debt buildups, wars and financial crises stopped being manageable. Of course, clarity about this develops only in retrospect. However, even though war-related debt seems to have been part of each fatal endgame, the past leading world economic powers seem to have made another error en route. They did not pay enough attention to establishing or maintaining a vital manufacturing sector, thereby keeping a better international balance and a broader internal income distribution than financialization allowed.

The Importance of Hard Industries

From seventeenth-century Spain to twentieth-century Britain, the dynamics of eventual decline supported the arguments of those who had contended that finance could not replace manufacturing and that na-

tional economies needed the broader base. The bluntest case for hard industries was made by Britain's former colonial secretary, Joseph
Chamberlain, in 1904. Whereas England was once the greatest manufacturing country, he said, "its people are now more and more employed in
finance, in distribution, in domestic service," but over the long term
Britain could not survive as merely a "hoarder of invested securities" if it
was not also "the creator of new wealth." Then he asked his audience of
bankers: "Granted that you are the clearing house of the world," but "are
you entirely beyond anxiety as to the permanence of your great position? . . . Banking is not the creator of our prosperity but the creation of
it. It is not the cause of our wealth, but it is the consequence of our
wealth; and if the industrial energy and development which has been going on for so many years in this country were to be hindered or relaxed,
then finance and all that finance means, will follow trade to the countries
which are more successful than ourselves."[52] But while this was one of
the most accurate predictions in British commercial history, it did not
carry the day.

Part of what made these contentions unpersuasive to elites was the
perception that finance and its services represented a higher stage of evolution, what late-twentieth-century observers would laud as postindustrialism. As Paul Kennedy has explained, complex finances made Britain
more rather than less vulnerable by the turn of the twentieth century. Yet
policy makers then were attracted to the idea that, should other nations
industrialize, Britain would become the financial- and commercial-
service center to the world. The United Kingdom was different, as one
observer put it, because it was the first frog-spawned egg to grow legs,
the first tadpole to change into a frog, the first frog to hop out of the
pond.[53]

Harvard economic historian David Landes saw the first steps toward
postindustrialism as having been taken even earlier:

> By the late 1700s, most wealthy Dutch were big landowners, high
> state officials or rentiers. Gone were the prosperous enterprisers of
> the "golden age": employers were now confined to the middle or
> lower ranks. In the process, the United Provinces abdicated as world
> leader in trade and manufacture and went into a postindustrial mode.
> Italy had gone that way before. In Venice, for example, the wool craft

had sunk under the burden of taxes, key industries had migrated to cheaper lands, and businessmen had reinvested their fortunes in agriculture on the mainland. . . . Both Venice and Florence were already taking on the role of tourist magnets, living on the wealth of erstwhile competitors. In the aggregate, Holland was still wealthy, as Adam Smith's observations show, but estimates of income or product per head in 1750–1870 have it going nowhere. Other, more active nations were passing it by.[54]

Postindustrialism, then, may be more a quest for genteel retirement than a real economics-based future for a major power. Weary global economic powers seem uniquely vulnerable. Those who insist that the manufacturing imperative still applies to the present-day United States invoke three powerful examples: Germany, Switzerland, and Japan. All three nations have wages or overall production costs higher than those in the United States. All have reasonably successful financial sectors and postindustrial accomplishments (tourism, ecological awareness, and renewable-energy emphases—wind in Germany, solar power in Japan). However, they balance these with highly developed manufacturing industries. For Germany, machinery, vehicles, chemicals, and metal products are the great exports; for Switzerland, chemicals, metal products, machinery, and mechanical-engineering products (especially clocks and watches); and for Japan, vehicles, electronics, and computers.[55] Each nation's products command global respect for quality.

Indeed, German, Japanese, and Swiss export prowess puts the once-mighty United States to shame. In 2003 and 2004 the U.S. trade deficit in manufactured goods rose from $470 billion to $552 billion. The three better-balanced economies, by contrast, enjoyed huge surpluses in trade in manufactured goods and large ones in their overall current accounts. A set of statistics will demonstrate the point. Estimates for 2004 provided by the CIA in mid-2005 put Germany first in the world with $893 billion in exports (mostly manufactured goods)—this from a national population of 82 million. The United States placed second with exports of $795 billion, not exactly a triumph because (1) the United States had a population of 296 million and (2) these exports were dwarfed by $1.3 trillion worth of imports. The Japanese, chalking up the world's third-highest export total, $538 billion, did so with a national population of 127 million. Pocket-sized

Switzerland was even more of a per capita powerhouse: with a national population of only 7.5 million, it exported $131 billion worth of goods in 2004.[56] Keep in mind the entire equation: the Germans, Japanese, and Swiss do this with workforce wages and benefits and industrial-production costs as high as or higher than those in the United States.

Needless to say, all three countries are net creditor nations, enjoy strong current-accounts surpluses, and have citizens who achieve relatively high savings rates. During the quarter century after 1980, while the U.S. economy was undergoing financialization, the Organization for Economic Cooperation and Development (OECD) credited all three with stronger growth rates than the United States.[57] One would not guess that from American media coverage; "Old Europe," in particular, is supposedly verging on economic palsy.

Even Britain, as it happens, has avoided the reckless deindustrialization allowed in the United States. Although British manufacturing exports lack the comparative heft they registered in 1870 or 1900, economic historians underscore that in 1990 merchandise exports represented 21 percent of British GDP, whereas in the United States they amounted to only 8 percent.[58] Between 2000 and 2003, the share of U.S. GDP represented by manufactured exports dropped from 7 percent to 6 percent, and it is chilling to contemplate what the ratios might be in 2010 or 2020.[59]

Chapter 10 will focus more on China and East Asia, but for the moment let us simply say that overall Chinese manufacturing and export levels may well vie with those of the United States by the 2020s. Moreover, China is already responsible for the bulk of the rapidly growing U.S. deficit ($37 billion in 2004) in what Washington calls ATP—advanced technology products. Here we are talking about major categories such as biotechnology, weapons, opto-electronics, and nuclear technology, not mere circuit boards or routine components.[60]

Clyde Prestowitz, the longtime president of the Washington-based Economic Strategy Institute, all but tolled the bell for U.S. manufacturing only a few years into the new century. The supposed 2003–2004 comeback of the U.S. technology sector after the Nasdaq stock collapse fell short across a range that included semiconductor production, laptops, and high-definition television. Serious renewal in the midwestern Rust Belt, meanwhile, was belied by the early 2000s disasters in the steel and automobile industries.[61] In *Three Billion New Capitalists: The Great Shift of*

Wealth and Power to the East, Prestowitz profiled a trio of critical weaknesses in America's "dying tech ecosystem": (1) research and development; (2) present and future workforce education, and (3) the particular peril posed to high-technology leadership by the nation's increasing inability to implement, test, or support that expertise in an actual manufacturing milieu.[62]

This seems to be a pervasive concern among both academic experts and captains of industry. The actual making of advanced technologies in the United States had slipped far enough that in 2003, Thomas S. Hartwick, former scientist at TRW and chairman of the Department of Defense's Advisory Group on Electronic Devices, told Congress that "the structure of the U.S. High Tech industry is coming unglued with innovation and design, losing their tie to prototype fabrication and manufacturing." These losses leave inventions on "the cutting floor because they cannot be manufactured."[63] The Department of Defense was particularly nervous because the advanced semiconductor production needed for a new generation of weapons was migrating to Asia.[64] Randall Isaac, former vice president for strategic alliances at IBM Technology, said, "You can't do effective R&D if you don't have the manufacturing to insure that the R&D is actually relevant. If the United States loses its manufacturing lead, it will lose everything else with it."[65] Governments elsewhere in the world try to maintain a wise balance, but not Washington.

Even the military side of the economy gives rise to what humorists like to call déjà vu all over again. Those familiar with British historian Corelli Barnett's searing indictment of British unpreparedness for World War I—his catalog of lackadaisical approaches and naïveté in everything from chemicals, coal tars, and munitions to ball bearings, and of Whitehall's lack of attention to how many essential processes, metals, and machine tools were in German or other foreign hands—must cringe at the latter-day U.S. parallels.[66] Four indicators compiled by Prestowitz make the point: the U.S. need to use Russian, Chinese, and European rockets to launch its space satellites; Boeing's decision to outsource production of the wings on its 787 Dreamliner; the lack of U.S. firms that have the capacity to manufacture the advanced systems for military "night vision capacity" (French licensees have sold equipment to China); and the U.S. dependence on China for a large number of strategic metals, including tungsten, yttrium, magnesium, antimony, and indium.[67]

Such evidence may carry more weight than laments about lost manufacturing and industry. Too many Americans wrongly view these sectors
through a rusty rearview mirror, calling to mind the 175-year-old redbrick
monuments to textile production still visible in New England, the derelict
steel mills of Indiana and Pennsylvania, or the sections of Cleveland's
Cuyahoga River that used to catch fire because of the flammable debris
that accumulated in it. But the industrial age is still with us. China has
many tens of millions of automobiles to produce in order to justify those
extraordinary Shanghai highways, and India has yet to even construct the
roads. The financial media in Delhi and Mumbai underscore the need
(and prospects) for local steel production by reminding readers that
the Chinese economy is already nearly ten times as steel-intensive as
India's.[68] Postindustrialism may be imminent in six or eight square miles
of information technology–driven Bangalore, but even modern manufacturing is rare across most of the nation, where the population will
soon exceed China's.

Part of the problem in recognizing the true industrial shape of the
world today, of course, lies in postindustrial theory and the proverbial dead
economists to whom many Washington conservatives somehow allowed
their thought processes to become enslaved. We now turn to them.

The Invisible Eighteenth-Century Hand in American Twenty-First-Century Strategy

Adam Smith, the worthy eighteenth-century Scottish economist who inclined to the American side in the Revolutionary War and sympathized
with colonial complaints about British mercantilism, commanded a very
enthusiastic press in the United States through the last quarter of the
twentieth century. Ties bearing his embroidered profile were said to have
sold far better in Washington than in, say, London or Edinburgh.

For the twenty-first century, however, some diminution of worship may
be expected. Smith's vaunted "invisible hand"—the inerrant guidance of
the market—has become too fumble-fingered for a growing percentage
of doubters, especially advocates of strategic thinking and the need to
consider political, economic, and cultural externalities ignored by more
than three decades of marketplace orthodoxy. As a side benefit of their

great-power analyses, historians such as David Landes, Paul Kennedy, and Jonathan Israel have held forth at some length describing how Smith's market theory and blinders caused him to misjudge or ignore many political, military, competitive, or strategic factors that influenced the rise or decline of the Dutch and British global economies.[69] Luckily, attention is also growing to the inadequacy of pure market theory in explaining developments in the United States.

Billionaire investor Warren Buffett, a critic of the proliferation of financial services and speculations in the United States, also poked fun at Smith and his hallowed marketplace. Instead of finding the "invisible hand" in stratagems such as derivatives, he likened such instruments to "an invisible foot kicking society in the shins."[70] We will return to Buffett's critique in chapter 10.

Trade specialist Prestowitz, preoccupied with strategic thinking, criticizes American economists for ignoring real-world "adjustment costs" like closed factories, blighted neighborhoods, lost skills, and uprooted communities. They cling to this myopia, he contends, "partly because they prefer the simpler world of Adam Smith and David Ricardo, with its magic unseen hand and climate-controlled comparative advantage– based trade."[71] "In *The Wealth of Nations*," adds Prestowitz, "Smith argued that the objective of economic activity is consumption," but the development models of Asian economies "all involve the suppression of consumption, along with a heavy emphasis on saving, investment and production. In Singapore, for example, the government mandates large contributions to a pension fund. In Japan, consumer credit is limited even today. Asian savings rates, at 30% to over 50% of GDP, are higher than Western rates have ever been except in wartime, which is perhaps not surprising given that industrial development is seen in Asia as a key element of national security and avoidance of Western dominance."[72] Worst of all, he concludes, the Bush administration "has no policy or strategy" and little understanding of many of the factors that should be involved in one.[73] Similarly, Jared Diamond, author of *Collapse: How Some Societies Succeed or Choose to Fail*, noted in a 2003 lecture that officials of the George W. Bush administration had acknowledged concentrating on situations headed for crises within ninety days.[74] No framework this short-term in orientation is compatible with strategic thinking.

In the case of the Bush administration, perhaps the magic of the marketplace leaves no room for the clutter of awkward cultural and political externalities. Faith may also be an explanation. In the triangle of evangelical belief, state, and marketplace, laissez-faire has two wellsprings, not one. But there have been no heavenly interventions on behalf of past leading international debtors. The United States is on its own.

10

Serial Bubbles and Foreign Debt Holders

American Embarrassment and Asian Opportunity

Decades of relentless urgings to borrow more and spend more, from the on-slaught of junk mail credit card pitches to the devotion of whole magazines to goods rather than words, have turned Americans into voracious consuming ma-chines. In 1981, Americans saved a net 8.5 percent of national income, accord-ing to the Bureau of Economic Analysis, and as recently as 1998, the figure was 6.5 percent; by 2003, the net savings rate had fallen to just 1.2 percent.

—Daniel Gross, *The New York Times,* 2004

Perhaps the crucial difference between then (Britain in 1914) and now is that Britain was a net exporter of capital, while the United States today is the op-posite. For the United States has used its dominance of the international bond market not to export *capital—which in net terms it did until around 1972—but to import it.*

—Niall Ferguson, *Cash Nexus,* 2000

PERSISTENT NEWSPAPER HEADLINES ABOUT DEBT ARE INNATELY WORRISOME. Their frequent appearances during the 1920s, 1930s, 1980s, and 1990s proved to be unhappy auguries. The tensions of the first decade of the twenty-first century, partly new, lay in the combination of American do-mestic credit excess and vulnerable international status. The world's biggest debtor had also became its largest ongoing borrower, a risky pairing.

The U.S. consumer, taking on record levels of debt and debt service and working record hours (sometimes holding two jobs), was hailed in 2003 and 2004 as the wheelhorse of the world economy, the global buyer of last resort. This dubious privilege was an unexpected outcome of the post–September 11 mobilization. "The world economy is leveraged to the U.S. consumer," reported CNN, "and the U.S. economy is leveraged to the hilt. . . . U.S. consumer spending accounts for around 70% of U.S. gross domestic product. . . . Indeed, consumer credit and mortgage debt are both a higher percentage of disposable income now than they've ever been before."[1] For households watching their disposable income shrink, their new international "locomotive" status was small consolation.

Because imported goods constituted a high percentage of those consumed by Americans, the several measurements of the U.S. trade deficits kept setting new highs. Export firms and central banks in China, Japan, Taiwan, and Korea accumulated so many dollars in payment that U.S. stock markets trembled at rumors that this or that Asian central bank might be selling greenbacks for other currencies. Economists in Tokyo and Beijing, all too aware of their nations' huge stakes, kept as close a watch as did dollar overseers in Washington. Like debt headlines, currency weakness is rarely a good sign. Britain, as a fading hegemon, had been troubled by sterling pressures and crises during the 1920s, 1930s, and 1940s, when the pound was yielding its global role to the dollar. Now the same shoe was pinching the American foot.

As U.S. wage income fell, American households pushed their debt and consumption levels to new heights. The U.S. current-account deficit, our thermometer of global imbalance, kept rising as a share of GDP: 5.0 percent in 2003, 5.7 percent in 2004, and an estimated 6.5 percent in 2005.[2] Asian central bankers, however, thought it generally wise to hold the dollars earned from selling popular products in the United States and reinvest many of them in American treasury debt, thereby loaning those funds back to the United States government. The Chinese and Japanese could sell so much in America partly because the United States made fewer and fewer of the manufactured goods that its citizens wanted or needed; neither export-focused nation wanted Washington to impose tariffs or quotas on their products.

Ordinary Americans took in the large, bold-faced debt headlines—the ones about extravagant credit-card fees, bubbling housing prices and mortgage loans, and the pivotal role being assumed by China—but absorbed relatively little of the technical explanation behind them. Press reporting on the debt didn't make it any easier: John and Jane Q. Public could not keep up with shifting domestic and international debt measurements, arcane definitions, and coded reports. Even experts winced at fathoming the latest wrinkles in credit derivatives, exotic mortgage instruments, and Beijing monetary policy. Besides, to grasp what the new debt levels threatened, worriers first had to find out how much indebtedness there actually was and what it represented. This involved considerable subjectivity. Moreover, any serious tabulation required going beyond just the "sovereign" or national debt that had monopolized discussion of Dutch vulnerability in 1715 or British peril in 1919. The fiscal jeopardy of the twenty-first-century United States was more complex.

On the occasion of George W. Bush's second inaugural, the national debt was $7.8 trillion, if we include both the debt held by the public ($4.6 trillion) and the debt held by government agencies ($3.2 trillion), principally the Social Security and Medicare trust funds. To those who counted nothing else, that total represented just 70 percent or so of the projected 2005 GDP. The threshold of real danger, experts agreed, came when government debt climbed into the range of 100 to 150 percent of GDP.[3] Britain's national debt had reached 200 percent of GDP during the eighteenth century and roughly 300 percent around 1820, neither of which encumbrances kept the United Kingdom from achieving its historical zenith and economic golden age between 1850 and 1870. Under certain circumstances, then, even levels over 200 percent could be managed successfully, especially in a manufacturing boom.

However, economists and journalists venturing a calculus for the U.S. debt usually weigh several additions. Given our federal system, combined state and local debt in the neighborhood of $1.7 trillion seems to warrant inclusion. A second plausible addition is the $3.7 trillion needed to make up a shortfall in the Social Security trust fund (to cover its expected obligations over the next seventy-five years). Including these raised the 2005 national debt to $13.5 trillion, a total representing 115 percent of GDP and approaching the danger zone.

The other possible add-on involved the expected obligations of Medicare funding over the next seventy-five years. These *The New York Times* described as follows: "Because nearly every one expects health care costs to keep rising faster than economic growth, the trustees of the Medicare fund warn that the nation faces an enormous shortfall. They report that the country would have to pay in $9 trillion today to make the trust fund big enough to cover its future obligations, and set aside an additional $21 trillion to cover supplementary obligations—for example, the prescription drug benefit—that lie outside the scope of the trust fund."[4] Against the backdrop of the national debts of Spain, the Dutch Republic, and Britain in their later days as great powers, including this $30 trillion seems excessive. Eighteenth- and nineteenth-century calculations never extended so far ahead. Even the seventy-five-year cost of Social Security is a reach, but the Medicare obligation is too remote and susceptible to a major policy shift toward national health insurance and drug price controls.

What also seems untenable is to isolate *public* debt from *private* debt. Too many critical interrelationships have developed over the last century, especially in the United States. No historical private-debt comparisons are plausible, even with the Britain of 1913. There, only 10 percent of the population owned homes (limiting real-estate borrowing), debtors' prisons had functioned well into the nineteenth century, and a fair part of private debt was extended within families. The total assets of British building societies (the housing lenders) in 1913 were just £65 million ($325 million). This equaled less than 2 percent of the £4 billion in overseas investments principally held by the rentier class.[5] This £4 billion was *four times* the size of the British national debt. These assets were Britannia's financial shield.

In the nineteenth-century United States, by contrast, much of the private lending and debt involved homes, lands, and crops in a society of a moving frontier, in which many adult white males voted and owned some acreage. Cheap credit and easy money became a democratic (and Democratic) war cry from Andrew Jackson to William Jennings Bryan, both famous as bank bashers outraged over the machinations of the moneyed classes. The millions of farmers, Bryan told the 1896 Democratic National Convention, were businessmen, too. Indeed, by 1914 the total of farm-mortgage debt alone was $4.5 billion.[6] Lending to the masses has long had its greatest commercial emphasis in the United States.

This is a vital backdrop to the current importance of U.S. private debt.

Taken together, household, corporate, and financial-sector debt represents roughly three-quarters of so-called total credit-market debt ($40 trillion) in the United States.[7] If there is a credit bubble, much of its vulnerable volume must be private.

In the United States of 2005, moreover, "private" debt had been swollen through the actions of the quasi-public Federal Reserve Board, encouraged by a president who was urging citizens to borrow and spend and further abetted by Vice President Cheney's broad assurance that "Reagan proved deficits don't matter." American private debt's foremost characteristic, however, is its sheer mass. No national vulnerability quotient can exclude it. As noted in chapter 8, the vastness of private credit-market debt in 2003 already dwarfed the official money-supply profiles, enough to suggest a case for credit as a new Federal Reserve yardstick. Financial markets watchers also made some interesting seat-of-the-pants observations. On top of other recognitions of parallels between debt and the financial-services industry, a CNN/*Money* analysis suggested that "the chart of the current account gap as a percentage of GDP, incidentally, looks almost exactly like a chart of consumer credit as a percentage of income."[8] Borrowing to consume—not inadequate savings—was at the heart of current-account deterioration.

"Private" financial borrowing manifestly cannot be borrowing in the "full faith and credit" sense, involving the backing of the U.S. government. Still, the lesson of the last quarter of a century is that private excesses, from savings and loans to hedge funds, have been bailed out by federal agencies and appointees, for public policy reasons. The "private" risk of high finance has been socialized, according to James Grant and other debt observers, even if the profits have not.[9]

Chairman Greenspan, as already noted, took policy responsibility in 2002 and again in 2004 for declining to prevent the buildup of credit or asset bubbles. Better, he said, to deal later with their subsequent ramifications by providing liquidity. Other central banks—the European Central Bank, the Bank of England, the Reserve Bank of Australia, the Bank for International Settlements—have contended that the greater harm may come from lack of prevention. For political calculations, can the Federal Reserve Board be presumed to have put the government behind its subsequent liquidity waves?

Theory this may be, but it is not remote. The management of private debt in the United States has a closer relationship than elsewhere to politics and government, and in the wake of the events of September 11, it became a thinly disguised instrument of public policy, stimulating consumer demand. This implies government obligations.

This brings us to mortgage debt, much of which is held by banks and other institutions in the financial services cohort. Given the Federal Reserve's central role in allowing mortgage debt to mushroom from $4.4 billion in 2000 to $7.5 trillion in 2004, maintenance of the upward revaluation of homes may be the next frontier of risk socialization.[10] Direct and repackaged consumer debt also bulks large—and in some very speculative forms—in the asset portfolios of the contemporary economy.

The entirety of the U.S. credit bubble, then—public and private alike—must be considered in judging the dangers of debt and the applicability of historic precedents. Unfortunately, the useful precedents are few, the hazards many.

The Indentured American Household?

Concern about Americans becoming "indentured servants" or "sharecroppers" laboring on behalf of whip-holding creditors—credit-card companies in the United States, dollar-holding central bankers in Asia—became a marginal political issue in 2005, struggling for attention but not getting much. The analogy did not strike a popular chord.

Indentured servitude had been allowed in the thirteen colonies of 1775 under British law, and it was not forbidden after the Revolution by the new American republic. The practice had been reinforced by imprisonment, reindenturing, and other penalties. Nevertheless, by 1800 it had largely withered. In the spirit of the Declaration of Independence, indenturing became unacceptable—at least for whites.

Two hundred years later, personal-bankruptcy filings under chapters 7 and 13 of the Federal Bankruptcy Code during the first Bush administration totaled close to five million, a record for a single White House term. Household pressures were becoming acute. In 2005 Congress passed and the president signed new federal bankruptcy legislation promoted by a worried credit-card industry. It required would-be bankrupts with incomes above a certain level to accept a new status under chapter 13. Instead of having their debts discharged, they would keep paying determined credit-card charges, medical bills, and other obligations.[11]

Proponents made the valid point that many filers shouldn't be allowed to use the permissive chapter 7 procedures to simply walk away from their debts. Opponents countered that the new procedures were extreme and could lend themselves to harsh implementation.[12] Some of the angriest foes, including House Democratic Leader Nancy Pelosi and Massachusetts senator Edward Kennedy, likened the future status of bankrupts to "modern-day indentured servants."[13] Few in the media took the interpretive bait.

The analogy is premature until we see how bankruptcy procedures under the 2005 act play out over a number of years. However, as figure 9 shows, the debilitation of wage earners is clear enough. Over the last four decades, as manufacturing employment has tumbled and finance has gained, wages have declined sharply as a share of personal income. Borrowing and spending as a percentage of wages, in turn, have both soared. For not quite half of the population, what some Democrats would picture as "involuntary servitude" can be summed up thus: the number of good jobs shrinks, wages decline, consumer appetites remain constant or intensify, credit cards are pitched endlessly and misleadingly, the credulous sign up, and cards are issued. Rates and charges eventually change, pain begins, and on go the plastic shackles. Because of the unusual harness yoking the American consumer to the world economy, a vague public sense of being used—dry political tinder of the first order—could develop. We have seen that the 1990s credit-card takeoff had several stages. It began, said Robert Manning, author of *Credit Card Nation,* in 1997, when credit-card issuers targeted young people and pursued them relentlessly.[14]

Consumer historian Peter Stearns described the national mind-set before September 11: "For many people, particularly in the United States, the commitment to consumerism introduced a new precariousness to material life. By 2001, despite unprecedentedly high incomes, over half of all Americans had almost no savings and a third lived paycheck to paycheck, often in considerable consumer debt. In some cases this situation reflected continued real poverty, but in others it followed from a sense that so many goods and trips had become absolutely essential."[15] That upward thrust of consumption after 1999 is clearly visible in figure 9.

A new stage came after September 11, when spending-as-patriotism combined with economic apprehension and the lowest interest rates in

FIGURE 9

The American Consumer: Slumping Wages and Accelerating Consumption

Rising U.S. Consumption as a Percentage of Gross Domestic Product, 1950–2005[a]

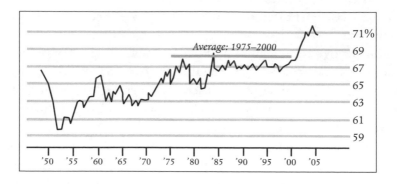

The Decline of Wage Income While Consumer Spending (and Borrowing) Soars[b]

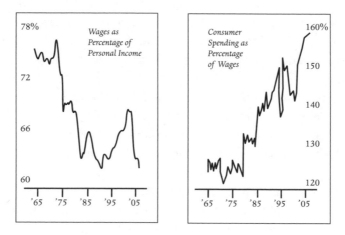

[a] Source: Stephen Roach; *Barron's*, Dec. 6, 2004. Data from China National Bureau of Statistics; Bureau of Economic Analysis; Morgan Stanley Research.

[b] Source: Stephanie Pomboy; MacroMavens, *Barron's;* April 25, 2005.

forty years to promote home refinancing and debt consolidation. Both usually provided spendable cash or mortgage-payment savings, and stimulated a weak economy. The downside was that between the presidential elections of 2000 and 2004, household debt grew by 39 percent.[16] Real disposable income, however, showed very little growth. In 2005 macroeconomist Stephanie Pomboy explained that over the three previous years consumers had leaned more heavily on new borrowing ($675 billion of non-mortgage debt) than on paychecks (up only $530 billion) to make possible the overall $1.3 trillion increase in their spending.[17]

The period after September 11 also saw a stepped-up Washington bias in favor of the credit-card industry, especially on the part of the Bush administration. For credit-card firms, the ability to borrow at 1 to 2 percent facilitated their ability to offer new cardholders sweet enrollment deals and often the chance to consolidate their debt in one place at seemingly great savings. However, once the new enrollee was hooked, the card companies were free to raise rates on just about any pretext— often from 6 or 11 percent into the 20 to 30 percent range—and to take advantage of the deregulation of fees authorized by the 1996 *Smiley* decision. Little or no attempt was made by the White House to rein in the card issuers with an appeal to "wartime" patriotism (unlike that made to consumers to spend "patriotically") and shared sacrifice. On the contrary, profiteering flourished. To call the fees lucrative is an understatement. Between 2000 and 2004 lateness and over-the-borrowing-limit penalties ballooned, and overall credit-card profits soared. According to CBS News, the portion of credit card–issuer profits represented by fees jumped from 28 percent in 2000 to 33 percent in 2002, 35 percent in 2003, and an estimated 39 percent in 2004.[18] The "hidden" costs of credit to consumers rode an up escalator even as the actual borrowing costs of the corporate issuers declined.

By late 2004 the main wave of card use for debt consolidation and consumption had crested but only after reshaping the U.S. credit landscape. Between 1990 and 2003 the number of people holding credit cards jumped by 75 percent—from 82 million to 144 million—but the amount actually charged exploded by 350 percent, up from $338 billion to $1.5 trillion.[19] By 2004 public attention was recentering on real estate, the prime lever of the Federal Reserve strategy for rebuilding the assets base of middle-, upper-middle-, and upper-bracket Americans.

Between 2000 and 2004, as we have seen, mortgage debt in the United States rose from $4.4 trillion to $7.5 trillion. Surging home values shared the limelight with bargain refinancing. The caveat was that although mortgage debt in the United States increased 66 percent between 2000 and 2004, Americans heeding the government's call to refinance at low rates usually spent the proceeds on consumer goods, not savings or home improvements. Thus, although the value of household real estate climbed 40 percent between the end of 2000 and the middle of 2004, owners collectively wound up having lower percentages of equity in their own homes.[20]

Adding to the uncertain prospects for stability, an increasing percentage of homeowners chose to take out interest-only loans or adjustable-rate mortgage variations, contracts that essentially bet on several more years of fast-rising prices. In states such as California, where interest-only loans represented some 60 percent of all those taken out in 2005, one-third of home buyers admitted to making an investment rather than selecting a long-term residence; even in the United States as a whole, 23 percent of home sales were to "investors."[21] Alan Greenspan, who had promoted the refinancing mentality, expressed concern in late spring 2005 about "the dramatic increase in the prevalence of interest-only loans, as well as the introduction of other relatively exotic forms of adjustable-rate mortgages." Indeed, these came in literally hundreds of packages and flavors. He added that "the apparent froth in housing markets may have spilled over into mortgage markets," a reference to loose lending practices.[22]

The Federal Reserve chairman's apprehensions prompted reassurances from mortgage bankers that the secondary market in mortgages assured wide dispersal of risk. But those concerned by the bubble were not convinced, and *The Washington Post* noted another worry: many of the frothiest housing markets were in San Francisco, Los Angeles, Boston, New York City, and Washington, cities that were also major financial centers.[23] One kind of speculation was helping to breed another.

Total household debt, which includes both consumer debt and mortgage debt, jumped from $6.5 trillion in 2000 to $10.2 trillion in 2004. This leap reflected the government's emphasis on stimulating private debt, and the sum exceeded most national-debt calculations. Precious few economists spoke of the actual national debt as anything resembling a bubble. The possible home-price bubble, by contrast, preoccupied cock-tail conversation from Long Island to San Diego. Although the stock-market crash between 2000 and 2002 had been contained, international historical research, as we have seen, suggested that a housing debacle in-volving even half the 2000–2002 wealth decline in stocks could produce a *greater* fallout in the overall economy. Forty percent of the new jobs cre-ated in the private sector between 2001 and 2005 were housing related.

In ordinary times, the idea of bankrupt Americans becoming "inden-tured" to credit-card operators could be taken as overwrought political propaganda. However, the fallout from a 10 to 20 percent national housing-price slump could make the analogy somewhat more credible. Bankruptcies or shattered credit might well put millions of cardholders in thrall to dozens of issuers and mortgage lenders. And if household America slowed its consumption, thereby ceasing to play locomotive to the world, the do-mestic and global effects could be incendiary.

Finance: The "Invisible Foot"?

More even than the future of Britain in 1914, the economic trajectory of the United States was in the hands of the financial sector. Chapter 9 de-veloped some of the historical reasons for concern, despite the talk of a new economic paradigm. Finance by itself has never been enough to sus-tain a leading world economic power.

Multibillionaire investor Warren Buffett, known for his dismissal of fi-nance as a den of vanity and profiteering, occasionally extended his mock-ery to Adam Smith's famous "invisible hand" and its supposed role in guiding markets to optimal outcomes, as we have seen. To Buffett, finance was no such boon. He first said as much in his 1983 annual message to Berkshire Hathaway shareholders: "Hyperactive equity markets subvert rational capital allocation and act as pie-shrinkers. Adam Smith felt that all non-collusive acts in a free market were guided by an invisible hand that led an economy to maximum progress; our view is that casino-type markets and hair-trigger investment management act as an invisible foot that trips up and slows down a forward-moving economy."[24]

Since then, although the Nebraskan's own fortune swelled to become the nation's second biggest, his comments on the financial sector remained disdainful. Derivatives were "financial weapons of mass destruction," and credit-default swaps were "a time bomb."[25] On top of this, he said that huge trade deficits threatened to turn the United States into a "share-cropper society," a mockery of White House talk about an "ownership society." In a 2005 letter to his shareholders discussing the company's prior-year results, Buffett grumbled that "in effect, the rest of the world enjoys an ever-growing royalty on the American output. Here, we are like a family that consistently overspends its income. As time passes, the family finds that it is working more and more for the finance company and less for itself."[26] For Buffett, the invisible foot was kicking even harder.

Whether Smith or Buffett had the better analogy may depend on the outcome of a second new private-debt expansion—undertaken by the financial sector—that exceeded even the credit-card and mortgage escalation of household indebtedness. Between 1995 and 2004 financial-sector domestic debt soared from $4.33 trillion to $11.79 trillion.[27] In 1980, financial-sector debt had been a mere $700 billion. This gargantuan increase explained much more than just the fin-de-siècle stock boom and bust. A rare convergence was at work, with a newly deregulated and ambitious financial sector taking advantage of the deregulation in 1996 of two other industries, merchant energy and telecommunications. The three-sector collusion created some $4 trillion in new bond and loan debt in the second half of the 1990s, the issuance of which peaked between 1998 and 2000 alongside the stock-market indexes.[28] Together with a seemingly endless parade of financial mergers and buccaneering hedge funds, and the deployment of a new array of speculative and derivative instruments and strategies, the result was what amounted to a grand financial-sector takeover of the economy.

In the fall of 1996 *Foreign Policy* published an article by John C. Edmunds, an academic economist, grandly entitled "Securities: The New Wealth Machine." Under the banner of securitization—the bundling of related or eclectic loans into asset-backed securities (ABSs)—the author hypothesized a new age in which a nation could increase its wealth by enlarging (through innovative structuring) the market valuation of its production assets.[29] Producing more goods and services wasn't actually necessary. While the jury is still out on the new age, ABSs were clearly an idea whose profitability had come. And they had a lot of company.

The torrent of new debt-related instruments and borrowing was central in lifting the relative weight of financial services from some 15 percent of GDP in 1980 to 20 percent in 2000, thereby staking out a clear predominance for the sector in stock-market capitalization after the Nasdaq debacle. The most important new instruments, far more complex structurally than the asset-backed securities of the early 1990s, were the categories of credit-default swaps (CDSs) and collateralized debt obligations (CDOs)—both sold by banks over the counter rather than traded through exchanges. The first allowed investors to insure the credit risk of their bond and loan holdings; the second represented purchasable pools of corporate credit, divided into three or more layers to reflect varying degrees of risk.

Despite the complexity of CDOs, which required extensive documentation by their bank issuers, credit derivatives became so popular that their global market expanded from embryonic status in 1997 to greater than $1 trillion in 2001, well over $3 trillion in 2003, and a projected $8 trillion in 2006.[30] Pricing these instruments is subjective, and they are illiquid to boot, making the potential cost of any debacle that requires their panic sale chilling. Similarly, while the combined derivatives markets grew to a nominal value of $270 trillion in 2004, no one knew what they would really be worth in a panic.

This immensity of early-twenty-first-century finance dwarfs the comparative expansion of railroad mileage, debt, and power in the 1850s and 1860s. Still, there is an unfortunate parallel to railroading's domination of federal, state, and local politics, as well as to its ability to long fend off most attempts at regulation. Financial services enjoyed a kindred position in the 1980s and 1990s. As innovation, computerization, and broad deregulation opened up grand vistas, politicians whose eyes saw contributor dollar signs at the very mention of names such as Citigroup, Merrill Lynch, and Goldman Sachs kept day-to-day regulators saluting respectfully.

The Federal Reserve, long the principal shepherd of the banking sector, became financial services' most important advocate. The board's anxiousness to see American financial-services giants emerge to challenge Japanese and European behemoths such as Mitsubishi, Credit Suisse, and Deutsche Bank expressed itself in thinly disguised collaboration. Potential stock-market constraints like higher margin requirements were left unused; putative financial collapses were transformed into expensive rescues; assets losing air were reinflated; and bubbles were rarely and be-

FIGURE 10
Stocks, Homes, and the Wealth Roller Coaster, 1998–2004

Wealth Rises Again in 2003–2004
After the 2000–2002 Stock Collapse[a]

Year-over-year percentage change in household net worth

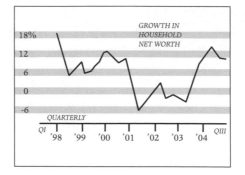

The Replacement of Stocks by Housing as the Pillar of U.S. Wealth Creation[b]

Value of U.S. stocks and homes, as percentage of GDP

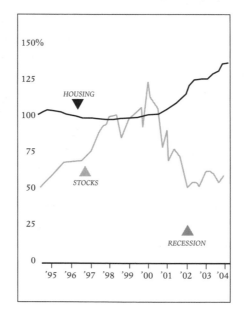

[a] Source: Federal Reserve; Global Insight, Inc.

[b] Source: Federal Reserve; Commerce Department via Economy.com.

latedly noticed (and never, ever pricked). Even the railroads had not done so well.

From 2001 to 2004—and especially after September 11—the Federal Reserve managed an economic architectural triumph on the scale of the Great Pyramids at Luxor. The financial and real-estate base of American wealth was rebuilt, shifting primacy from stocks back to home values. Figure 10 shows the magnitude and timing. In many ways, the rescue was extraordinary. The downside, obviously, lies in the debt used to bring it about. Perhaps we can now take a better inventory.

The national debt, having been expanded to pay for stimulus, must make the list; so, too, consumer borrowing and mortgage debt. The expansion of corporate debt, part of it refinancing at the lowest rates in nearly half a century, helped to rebuild stock-market capitalization. As for the incredible expansion of financial-sector debt, some of it doubtless strengthened Adam Smith's invisible hand, and a considerable amount propelled Warren Buffett's invisible foot. The point is that easy private credit became public policy—and to a unique degree.

However, with so much new debt created, the stimulus per dollar showed a significant decline. Although economists used different yardsticks and ratios, the message was essentially the same. From 1988 to 2000 the ratio of nonfinancial debt to GDP had stayed at 1.8 to 1, but then from 2001 to 2003 the ratio widened: $4.2 trillion more in debt turned out to add only $1.3 trillion in new GDP.[31] In 2005 another economist acknowledged "diminishing marginal returns on credit, in that it takes more and more debt now to fuel each marginal dollar of consumption. It now takes 11 cents of new debt to generate each additional dollar of consumption. That's up from just three cents in 1992."[32]

The burdens on consumers, meanwhile, became heavier. In the first quarter of 2005 households paid out 10.35 percent of their income to service mortgages, the highest since 1991. At 13.4 percent, the overall (consumer and mortgage) household debt-service ratio—debt payments to disposable income—was at an all-time high. The broader ratio of household outlays for all financial obligations—adding rent, auto lease payments, homeowner's insurance, and property taxes—was 18.4 percent, just under the 2001–2003 peak.[33] With respect to automobile loans, some 40 percent of those buying new cars with the zero financing of

334   BORROWED PROSPERITY

2003–2004 were trading in vehicles on which they owed more than the auto was then worth.

The other emerging predicament was global: the massive current-account deficit, which reflected a United States living beyond its means, and the uncertain duration of the unusual willingness of Asian central banks to fund it by buying and holding U.S. debt.

And Now, Over to Asia . . .

To Abraham Lincoln, war was too important to be left to generals, and other presidents have had more or less the same concern about the state of the economy: it is too important to be left to economists. For example, accurate and dramatic discussion of the ballooning U.S. current-account deficit—the broadest measurement of how much more Americans buy or pay out overseas than they sell or bring back—has been impeded by sterile economic parlance. Academic experts have tended to link current-account deficits to federal budget deficits or to an inadequacy of national savings, explanations that have failed to motivate citizens and noneconomist decision makers, especially elected ones.

A more engaging explanation might go something like this. Yes, Americans have saved too little because they consume too much. Still, there are several reasons for having consumed a steadily higher amount relative to wages. On one hand, wages aren't the same share of national income that they used to be, and over this same period Americans—young people especially—have been increasingly fixated on consumption. As for why so much of the consumption has involved imports—in 2004 the United States imported goods worth 54 percent more than those it exported—two practical explanations stand out. First, the United States competitively makes fewer and fewer manufactured goods; second, data confirm that the fifty states produce less than half of the oil consumed here. Unelaborated jargon about "savings" fuddles much of the serious politics involved: the increasing U.S. dependence on manufactured and petroleum imports from East Asia and the Middle East.

Asians and continental Europeans, who tend to take a more nationalistic view of trade, cannot understand how Americans can sit around with so little concern over their red ink–stained current-accounts ledgers. The British are also amazed. Niall Ferguson, a Harvard historian well versed in economics, makes the perfectly valid point that although Britain circa 1910 saw her manufactured exports weaken, they remained substantial—and so did fiscal conservatism in Downing Street.[34] Thus, whereas Britain in her prime remained a lopsided creditor nation, the United States since the late 1980s has used its global sway to pursue a *borrowing* mode.

Alas, the United States is the first leading economic power to take this path since Spain. A quarter century of public and private American affinity for debt—the term "overconsumption" loses the fiscal half of the message—has helped erect the largest national current-account deficit the world has ever seen. Both political parties have abetted this, but the Republicans more so.

In a 2004 speech to a meeting of international economists, former U.S. treasury secretary Lawrence Summers candidly described the fiscal elephant in the American parlor: "The U.S. current account deficit is currently running well in excess of $600 billion at an annual rate, in the range of 5.5% of GDP. It represents well over 1% of global GDP and absorbs close to two-thirds of the cumulative current account surpluses of all the world's surplus countries. All of these figures are without precedent. The United States has never run such large current account deficits and no single nation's deficit has ever bulked nearly as large relative to the global economy."[35] Figure 11 on page 362 displays the close 1990–2004 relationship between rise in U.S. consumption as a share of GDP and the surge in the nation's current-account deficit. During this same period, though, two other measurements failed to maintain their long-assumed causal connections. For example, as the federal budget deficit metamorphosed into a surplus for 1998 to 2000, the current-account deficit kept getting worse. That should not have happened. The decline of the U.S. dollar from 2002 to 2004 likewise failed as an antidote; the current-account deficit widened further during that time period.

The disarray in the nation's current accounts did not preoccupy George W. Bush when he became president, and the events of September 11 soon provided a compelling distraction. By 2004, however, the gravity of the deteriorating U.S. international balances could hardly be avoided. The world's number-one debtor had also become its biggest borrower, in itself unprecedented, and dollar holders from Zurich to Beijing asked themselves what was likely to happen.

The question was particularly important for the central banks of China,

Japan, Taiwan, and South Korea. In the wake of the 2000–2001 stock-market crash, private investors outside the United States had lost much of their interest in holding dollars, which added to the greenback's slow decline. However, beginning in a major way in 2002, Asian central banks stepped into the breach, buying U.S. Treasury debt on a grand scale, which worked to limit the dollar's erosion. The Congressional Budget Office (CBO) later calculated the purchase of U.S. assets by foreign governments at $113 billion in 2002, $280 billion in 2003, and $399 billion in 2004.[36] "Almost all" of the purchases, said the CBO, came from Asia.

In June 2004 the *Financial Times* reported a milestone: "demand for U.S. government bonds at foreign central banks has for the first time lifted overseas holdings to more than half the paper [Treasury debt] in circulation."[37] As of that March, 50.6 percent of liquid Treasury bonds were in foreign hands, up from about 20 percent in 1995. The Atlanta Federal Reserve Bank in 2005 summed up that "since 2001, Asian central banks' U.S. dollar reserves have increased by $1.2 trillion, roughly two-thirds of the cumulative U.S. current account deficit over that period."[38] Two well-known international economists, Nouriel Roubini and Brad Setser, have argued that "the role of central banks in financing the U.S. budget deficit is much larger than some studies consider, since actual central bank purchases exceed recorded central bank purchases. Since 2000, all of the net new supply of Treasuries has been purchased by nonresidents, and about 80 to 90% of the new supply by foreign central banks."[39]

Politically the implications were grave but enigmatic. The chugging of the U.S. economic locomotive, powered by the indebted American consumer, was really being financed by the central banks of the same countries selling John and Jane Smith their shoes, slacks, televisions, laptops, and Toyotas. The question was why, and answers were many. Officials of the Bush administration credited the ability of market forces to provide access to a globalized savings pool. However, cynics scoffed that because Asian central banks were losing money through purchasing short-term Treasuries with negative real returns, their obvious motivation was to keep lucrative export markets open. Peter Morici, a University of Maryland professor who earlier served as director of the Office of Economics of the U.S. International Trade Commission, went further, saying that China "abuses global markets to obtain an objective": dominance.[40]

The importance of the American export market was real enough. Whereas U.S. manufacturing had been able to stage some recovery in the late 1980s with the help of a declining dollar, the underlying circumstances of 2004–2005 were much less yielding. More and more industries had been hollowed out by import penetration and by U.S. manufacturers' inability to compete with low-cost Asian production. By one calculation foreign goods made up 38 percent of all durable-goods purchases, including 54.5 percent of automobiles, 56 percent of computers and office equipment, 57 percent of semiconductors, 57 percent of all communications equipment, 71 percent of consumer electronics, 78 percent of apparel, and 99 percent of all footwear.[41]

Nor was this likely to change much. New investments in industries that manufactured tradable goods were ebbing in the United States because returns were better elsewhere. In 2004 U.S. investors and corporations got almost twice the return on their foreign direct investments, especially in Asia, that foreigners got on direct investments in the United States.[42] The Dutch and British precedents were certainly relevant here.

Imported petroleum, meanwhile, was riding a twin escalator. Its share of U.S. consumption was rising almost as fast as its cost per barrel. Economist Setser, noting that outlays for oil imports had been some $100 billion in 2002, $130 billion in 2003, and $180 billion in 2004, predicted a 2005 oil-import bill in the $232 billion range.[43]

Structural calcifications like these did not augur well for the U.S. current-account deficit, which led serious economists back to the essential conundrum: what would happen to the dollar—and also to the willingness of Asian central banks to maintain and expand their dollar reserves to accommodate a further expansion of the U.S. current-account deficit?

Certain problems were already obvious. If interest rates in the United States rose to, say, 4 to 5 percent on two- to five-year Treasury notes, the federal government would face a considerably higher burden in servicing its huge debt, mostly short term. Meanwhile, as Summers and others had noted, foreign central-bank collaboration was not assured. "I would suggest," the former treasury secretary had observed in 2004, "that if one is seeking to draw lessons from the last 15 years of monetary experience, here is one that is very powerful: fixed exchange rates with heavy intervention have enormous capacity to create an illusory sense of stability that could be shattered very quickly. That is the lesson of Britain in 1992, of Mexico in 1994, of emerging Asia in 1997, of Russia in 1998, and of Brazil in 1998."[44]

We can mark this down as a fourth danger zone of indebtedness. The national debt is the first, provided the reasonable additions that peg it in the $10 trillion to $15 trillion range. Household debt, deliberately ballooned by Washington policy makers, is the second. Financial-sector indebtedness— the half-speculative nervous system that conjoins risky mortgages, shaky hedge funds, illiquid credit derivatives, and superbank overreach—is a third. The current-account deficit belongs on the list, not least because of the unprecedented dimensions laid out by Summers and others.

Not surprisingly, the previous leading world economic powers offer no precedent for the interplay of so many debt dimensions. I cannot help but think that the United States, like Spain in its day, has become something of a Judas Economy for the average American, with Wall Street in the profitable bullion-handling role of early-seventeenth-century Seville, the Asian central banks as uncertain Genoan financiers, and George W. Bush as the dull and prayerful Hapsburg dynast.

The caution about the United States using its global power to borrow, not to loan in the British manner, needs a bit more elaboration. Actually, the Kissinger deal with the Saudis and OPEC to recycle petro-dollars in the 1970s and 1980s (discussed in chapter 3) and the recent tacit arrangement with the East Asian central banks share a common design: recycling by foreigners of U.S. payments for imports through channels that work to uphold the value of the U.S. currency. The possibility that both strings could soon run out as disillusionment with the United States sets in will be discussed in the concluding chapter.

Not that any world currency winds down overnight. The Dutch guilder had a long process of being superseded by the British pound sterling, and some Britons understood by 1916 and 1917—never mind 1919— that the future might belong to the dollar. One historian has noted that the British Treasury warned the War Cabinet that by the end of 1916 "the American executive and the American public will be in a [financial] position to dictate to this country."[45] Several decades and two war-related global realignments later, that financial dependence was a fact.

But before trying to add up the historical analogies, one more context requires pursuit: the likelihood of the United States being drawn into a war—terror based, resource based, or as some extension of the existing combats in Iraq and Afghanistan—akin to the expensive confrontations that helped to scuttle Spanish, Dutch, and British hegemony.

War: The Military and Economic Unmaking of Global Hegemons

If the God of Tim LaHaye and the *Left Behind* series turns out to be otherwise preoccupied—as he seems to have been during the later wartime embroilments of Spain, Holland, and Britain—then, lacking heavenly intervention, any major military confrontation in the Middle East or anywhere else could easily have results similar to those of the past. U.S. global supremacy could drain away more in five to twenty years than most Americans would have thought possible.

In the months after September 11, 2001, Washington could have shaped a multilateral response able to maintain much of the worldwide goodwill volunteered to the United States in the wake of the shocking attacks. Instead the administration's response was fundamentalist, unilateralist, and Manichaean, trumpeting a confrontation—briefly even termed a "crusade"—pitting good against evil. The invasion and occupation of Iraq, another poorly planned agenda, provided an environment that enabled overseas terrorism and radicalism to renew itself around a more acceptable anti-American cause. If terrorism remains center stage in a Middle Eastern war of attrition, that battle could last long enough—flaring into guerrilla wars and even civil wars—to wear the United States down militarily and economically. Osama bin Laden has hinted at exactly these hopes.

Other outbreaks could be more conventional. The beginning deployment of the U.S. military as an oil-defense force, bunched around oil-production centers—the Middle East, the Caucasus, and west Africa—and also along pipeline routes and oil-transportation sea-lanes, crystallizes the possibility of periodic resource wars. For the United States, these would involve oil, but among other nations water resources represent a second focus of contention. The Pentagon, as already noted, has prepared scenarios in which climate changes provoke resource wars.

The annals of the leading world economic powers, however, show a clear pattern of major wars playing a central role in the upending of one hegemon and the emerging of another. Small conflicts can provide hints, but the great confrontations—the Thirty Years War, the wars of 1688–1713, the Seven Years War, the French Revolution and Napoleonic wars, World War I, and World War II—have been decisive catalysts. While the two twentieth-century world wars carry their global magnitude in their names, the others were forerunners.

The Thirty Years War was a religious and political clash in Europe, but it had colonial and economic overtones elsewhere. Paul Kennedy notes that "Dutch military expeditions struck at Brazil, Angola and Ceylon, turning the conflict into what some historians describe as the first global war."[46] After peace came in 1648, the Dutch were the major beneficiaries, Spain the unhorsed leading power.

The conflict of 1688–1713—precise historians divide it into two separate wars—marked Britain's emergence and relative Dutch weakening in trade if not in global loan making. Like the Thirty Years War, the conflicts of 1688–1713 reached around the world, and British gains at the peace table included Gibraltar, Minorca, Nova Scotia, and Newfoundland. The Seven Years War and the Anglo-Dutch theater of the 1780–1784 global war that grew out of the American Revolution finished off Dutch pretensions and confirmed British predominance, a stature elevated by the Napoleonic wars and confirmed at Waterloo.

The twentieth-century wars, obviously, marked the two-stage undoing of British imperial and financial hegemony and the emergence of the United States in that role. But if war and its financial underpinnings are hallmarks of hegemonic rise and fall, a good case can be made for the simultaneous overlay of other forces, such as religion, natural resources, and culture (including so-called decadence). One common feature of Spanish, Dutch, and British commentaries during their respective heydays was attention to how the rhythms of the life cycles of nations resemble those of living organisms: youth, maturity, old age, and passing. During the later part of these national spans, more weakens than simply the fiscal and economic underpinnings of empire.

Probably that is why the great wars have been grim reapers of international hegemonies, as well as of so many individual lives. In addition to the various reformations and counterreformations, maritime regimes, resource supremacies, and cultural rhythms, watershed changes in the intensity and cost of the major wars have also been decisive, as Paul Kennedy makes clear. The most important were far enough apart in time and in technological and economic demands that the cost of military success in the seventeenth century, for example, brought down a Spain that had been able to push Islam out of the Iberian Peninsula in the fifteenth century and usually control Italy in the transitional sixteenth.

For Spain, suppressing the revolt in the economically and militarily determined and sophisticated Netherlands was a particularly crippling eighty-year burden. "The war in the Netherlands," said one Spanish councillor, "has been the total ruin of this monarchy."[47] The added effects of the 1618–1648 war were fatal. In Kennedy's words, depleted resources, bankruptcies, and smaller treasure fleets became a persistent drain:

> By scraping together fresh loans, imposing new taxes, and utilizing any windfall from the Americas, a major military effort . . . could be supported; but the grinding costs of war always eroded these short-term gains, and within a few more years, the financial position was worse than ever. By the 1640s, in the aftermath of the Catalan and Portuguese revolts, and with the American treasure flow much reduced, a long, slow decline was inevitable. What other fate was due to a nation which, although providing formidable fighters, was directed by governments that consistently spent more than two or three times more than ordinary revenues provided?[48]

For the Dutch, military and financial depletion attended the late-seventeenth- and eighteenth-century wars with France. Their exposed southern flank facing France required what for the republic was a huge army—119,000 at its peak between 1702 and 1713—and a costly chain of barrier forts. These outlays forced the Dutch to neglect their maritime and naval needs, and each of the French wars added more debt and also cost trade and foreign markets. Historian Jonathan Israel observes that "in terms of men and resources, the Republic mounted the largest and most sustained military and logistical effort in its history. . . . Yet, despite the raising of expenditure and troop levels, it was clear the Republic was failing to keep pace with the growth of the armies, and power, of France, Britain, Prussia and Austria."[49]

After peace came in 1713, military expenditure was reduced sharply, but the country's public debt remained at an unprecedentedly high level [more than 200 percent of GDP] while the provincial governments showed no inclination to increase taxation so as to be able to reduce the funded debt. While the war of 1672–78 had left Holland with a public debt of 38 million guilders, by 1713 this had risen to a staggering 128 millions, a burden which had a paralyzing effect on the Republic's diplomacy and military establishment. This was part of the burden for having fought the War of the Spanish Succession principally on credit, avoiding large increases in taxation. Furthermore, the army cuts, and continuing high levels of debt provoked new inter-provincial tensions.[50]

The Netherlands remained neutral during the 1756–1763 war pitting Britain and her allies against France and her allies, but Britain—quashing Dutch hopes—blocked neutrals from carrying cargoes into and out of France. Then the 1780–1784 fighting between Britain and the Netherlands completed the process, having "terminal consequences for the Dutch 'Old Regime.' . . . It simultaneously bankrupted the treasury and provided the 'creditors' of the government—in the Netherlands, not only the regents of Holland but countless humbler stockholders below them—with a much more aggressively insurrectionary language with which to verbalize their grievances."[51] The ability of the Dutch elite to be lenders to the royal and princely houses of Europe while much of the country decayed was all but over.

The British did take some of these lessons to heart, and when war broke out in 1914 their national debt was relatively small—certainly compared to its ratios in the eighteenth century and after 1815—and Britian's status as global creditor was impeccable. What no one expected, despite surprise at the expense of the Boer War, was the imminent new face of war in the twentieth century: technological intensity, all-out mobilization, and corresponding financial burdens. For the British people, four years of it produced massive disillusionment. For British financiers and Treasury officials, the watershed was grim but hardly fatal. While in debt to the United States, Britain was otherwise still a global creditor, albeit to a much depleted extent.

The Second World War completed the pauperizing process. Britain was stressed by the military budget demands of 1937–1939 rearmament, then bled further by the early stages of the war when the nation stood alone against Germany, paying by liquidating what was left of British overseas assets. Although a few historians quibble, the broad consensus was summed up in 2004 by *The Economist:* "After two costly world wars and economic mismanagement, [Britain] became a net debtor and the dollar usurped sterling's role. Dislodging an incumbent currency can take years. Sterling maintained a central international role for at least half a century after America's GDP overtook Britain's at the end of the 19th century. But it did eventually lose that status."[52] Ferguson, the British historian, further distilled the lesson for the United States. It was a lot better, he said, to decline over five centuries than to telescope decline into a short period as Britain had done.[53]

The relevance to the United States today is unmistakable. In the 1980s the national psychology ranged from "morning again in America" to late-decade fear of Japan's rising sun. In 1991 concern over the U.S. budget deficit was such that Washington dunned its allies in the Gulf War to pay for the U.S. troops and their support, eliciting comments about latter-day Hessians. Then in 2004 and 2005 the initial ferocity of the national response to September 11—in both Oval Office speeches and the invasion of bin Laden–sheltering Afghanistan—gave way to military disarray in Iraq and fiscal disrepair at home. Indeed, the various fiscal deficits were joined by a serious political-leadership deficit.

By 2005 public opinion had turned against the earlier White House decision to invade and occupy Iraq, while support for withdrawal mounted. Ironically, shrinking budgets in London had haunted the earlier British occupation of Iraq in 1921–1922. The U.S. load in that country, however, was incomparably larger, as well as more provocative to global opinion. It also, even CIA officials admitted, stimulated terrorist recruitment around the Islamic world. There is something about Iraq—most cynics would nominate oil, but the influence of the Bible is also relevant—that clouds the competence of Anglo-American invaders and occupiers.

If one relies on Spanish, Dutch, and British precedents, the international realignment that might cripple the United States and elevate Asia could be expected to come from a new bout of expensive global warfare. However, given that history doesn't repeat itself exactly, perhaps economically focused terrorism or a series of regional resource wars could satisfy the

Fates, even if a substantial portion of the Republican constituency does appear to be hoping for Armageddon and Christ's return.

Social Security and Medicare

No debate has so focused on America's potential future indebtedness as that involving Social Security and Medicare, including the enormous projected costs of prescription drugs. To ensure the future of Social Security through 2080 or thereabouts, it is broadly agreed that something like $3.7 trillion must be injected into the system.[54] Optimists, however, cite the Social Security Administration's own analysis that it will be able to pay all the promised benefits through 2042 and three-quarters of them thereafter.[55] Medicare and the prescription-drug program, in turn, are estimated to require another $30 trillion to be adequately funded for another seventy-five years.

The idea of advanced funding for a seventy-five-year projection seems odd. The Pentagon has not guesstimated the burden of World War III or 2.63 regional wars over the next half century, and the Energy Department has not weighed in on how to deal with annual oil-import "deficits" likely to hit $500 billion per year by 2015. The Treasury has not projected the cost of a debt-and-credit implosion if one of those bubbles pops. One major skeptic of the crisis over Social Security, Merton Bernstein, staff director of the 1983 Social Security Commission, dismisses long-term projections as unreliable: "Is there an economist or financial adviser who's going to tell you what's going to happen between right now and the end of [the year]? So why do we know that in 2042, the [Social Security] trust fund will have been used up?"[56]

Part of the reason that Social Security has been such a priority for policy makers involves the near-term desire of elements of the financial-services industry to privatize it, in whole or (more likely) in part. George W. Bush, who as governor of Texas had privatization targets that originally even included the University of Texas, spent political capital in 2005 on an unsuccessful proposal to partially replace Social Security with private accounts.[57] By some calculations, because the Treasury would have had to borrow some $2 trillion to implement the plan, and the system's long-term viability would not have been addressed, privatization stands out as the fundamental objective.

The Social Security system, which presently enjoys an annual surplus of $150 billion per year, had already been enlisted in one finance-related recalculation. For many years the system's surplus has been counted to reduce the actual federal budget *deficit* by that same amount. Thus, while the 2004 federal budget deficit was officially published as $412 billion, the true deficit was $567 billion, with the Social Security surplus being used as an offset.[58]

It is not quite fair to say that the effect of this bookkeeping has been to encourage higher deficits, but the blurring involved is definitely bond-market friendly. If all of a sudden the U.S. budget deficit was admitted to be $150 billion higher, one can imagine the tenor of the meetings that would be convened by central banks in Tokyo, Beijing, Seoul, and Taipei.

After all is said and done, of course, the private-sector forces that have interests in Social Security privatization or its use in deficit camouflage also make a telling point: the resources needed to support the outlays presently projected could start falling short between 2018 and 2042. Liberals say that the problem could be avoided by ending the upper-bracket-focused tax cuts enacted since 2001. Because these are projected to cost $11 trillion over seventy-five years, their elimination would more than pay for the $4 trillion Social Security needs over that period.[59] If one can be computed, presumably the other can, but the inevitable political battle is not likely to produce that kind of simple choice.

The ruckus over Medicare and the cost of prescription-drug benefits is another story. With all the oil and debt problems on the horizon, the assumption that Medicare is going to unfold as planned over seventy-five years seems like a thought from cloud-cuckoo-land. Perhaps one-third of the Republican electorate is paying little attention because of religious preoccupations, while the leaders of American corporations in embattled legacy industries such as airlines and automobile and parts manufacturers are starting to favor a national health system as an enabler of their own survival. Depending on the severity of economic pressures, the 2010s could be the decade of decision. In the short run, though, Social Security and Medicare may continue as the issues that catalyze national discussions of deficits and debt.

Somewhat longer-term, the emerging debt and oil dangers could produce trouble in such a relatively proximate time frame—from just ahead through 2020 or 2025—that *they* are likely to control the parameters of the pension, old-age, and medical-coverage questions rather than vice versa. Planning for 2080 pales alongside the perils of failing to plan for the treacherous decade ahead.

Absent a shift in Washington policy, former Federal Reserve chairman Paul Volcker was only the most prominent of many Americans to express worry recently about the vulnerability of the U.S. economy. David Walker, the comptroller general of the United States, remarked that "the greatest threat to our future is our fiscal irresponsibility," calling 2004 possibly the most fiscally reckless year in the history of the Republic.[60]

The other two dangers—oil dependency and radical religion—only made things worse. In August 2005, on the day that George W. Bush signed the much-touted energy bill that had finally passed Congress, global oil markets saluted its presumed unimportance by kicking the price of oil over sixty-three dollars per barrel, a record. Moreover, four years of ineptness in dealing with the oil crisis was hardly the only weakness the Bush administration brought to global affairs. From Tokyo to Toronto, even old allies worried about the resiliency of a United States that could muddle so many critical national judgments while indulging a religious constituency hostile to science and significantly dedicated to extreme interpretations of the Book of Revelation. Unfortunately, the three perils fed on one another—and they also drew on a shared political base.

11

The Erring Republican Majority

There are disturbing trends: huge imbalances, disequilibria, risks—call them what you will. Altogether the circumstances seem to be as dangerous and intractable as any I can remember. . . . I don't know whether change will come with a bang or a whimper, whether sooner or later. But as things stand right now, it is more likely than not it will be financial crises rather than policy foresight that will force the change.

—Paul Volcker, former Federal Reserve chairman, *The Washington Post*, 2005

We're not only outsourcing manufacturing to China and services to India, but we've managed to outsource our financing to Asia.

—Stephen Roach, chief economist, Morgan Stanley, 2004

As far as I know, there is not a single contingency plan in place or currently being written by any of the think tanks of the world that sets out a model illustrating how the world can continue to function smoothly once it is clear that Saudi Arabian oil has peaked. In a nutshell, it is this total lack of any "alternative scenario thinking" that makes this unavoidable event so alarming.

—Matthew Simmons, *Twilight in the Desert*, 2005

If religious extremism is only one large set of bodies in this fringe constellation [of Republican interest groups], it is a powerful one. That is why federal agencies reject scientific reports on ecological, stem cell, contraceptive, and abortion issues. They sponsor not only faith-based social relief, but faith-based war, faith-based science, faith-based education, and faith-based medicine.

—Garry Wills, *The New York Review of Books*, 2005

NO EXPLANATION OF THE THEME OF THIS BOOK—U.S. OIL VULNERABILITY, excessive indebtedness, and indulgence of radical religion—can ignore the encouragement of the Republican party and its electoral coalition, especially since 2000. Policy excesses and blind constituency commitments have a long history of developing around a stagnant but entrenched politics that has overstayed its national usefulness. This, alas, is an established pattern in the United States, with its long cycles of party domination in Washington.

It does not really matter which of the three is primary at any given moment. Some crisis may suddenly resolve the question, or appear to—a war, a popping financial bubble, a religious event, another major terrorist attack, five-dollar gasoline. History, however, tends to interrelate events, and threats that necessarily have been discussed separately in this book show further signs of integration—oil and the debt-and-credit crunch; true-believing religion and the substitution of faith for science and national strategy.

The Republican electoral coalition, near and dear to me four decades ago, when I began writing *The Emerging Republican Majority*, has become more and more like the exhausted, erring majorities of earlier failures: the militant, southernized Democrats of the 1850s; the stock-market-dazzled and Elmer Gantry–ish GOP of the 1920s; and the imperial liberals of the 1960s, with their Great Society social engineering, quagmire in Vietnam, and New Economy skills expected to tame the business cycle. Now the Republicans are again the miscreants.

In some ways the Emerging Republican Majority is becoming the Emerging Republican Theocracy, although that might still be kept from fuller fruition. More broadly, suffice it to say that the nation's most troublesome circumstances owe much to the fealty of an erring Republican majority to its most important constituencies. The inadequacy of the Democrats—every four years they seem to resemble the Not Ready for Prime Time Players who made *Saturday Night Live* a byword three decades ago—complicates things but hardly excuses what the Republican party has become: a vehicle of special interests that have become entrenched in crippling commitments and biases. What we must now look at is the interplay of these constituencies and favoritisms with wrongheaded decision making.

After Iraq: Oil, Debt, and the Dollar

The interrelationship of oil and the U.S. dollar, while increasingly strained, does hark back many years. If the Allies floated to World War I victory on a sea of American oil, as one European statesman observed, the dollar shared in that new buoyancy, becoming a potential replacement for sterling as the world's leading currency. World War II, another oil-facilitated victory, led to American hegemony, making the dollar the world's reserve currency.

When a new global oil regime emerged from the Middle East upheaval between 1973 and 1981, Washington took pains to assure that black gold still worked to maintain the supremacy of the dollar. Through the good offices of Saudi Arabia, OPEC agreed to price oil in dollars, which meant that a Belgian or Peruvian had to obtain greenbacks to purchase it. Also to the point, the oil-producing nations, especially the Persian Gulf states under U.S. influence, usually deposited much of the oil payment they received—the appropriately named petro-dollars—in U.S. banks. Not a few wound up being invested in U.S. Treasury debt. In consequence, the migration of oil-production leadership away from North America, so vivid by the 1980s and 1990s, did not dethrone the dollar, which still enjoyed a critical link to petroleum.

In the meantime the United States began spending money like a drunken sailor, also indulging its inheritance of the sort of finance that has nursed the lion's share of global manias, panics, and crashes. By the 1990s, as we have seen, financial services, led by the growth of debt, became the ascendant sector in the U.S. economy. Thereafter, finance fattened during the early 2000s—this notwithstanding the 2000–2002 collapse of the stock-market bubble—on a feast of low-interest enablement, credit-card varietals, exotic mortgages, derivatives, hedge-fund strategies, and structured debt instruments that would have left 1920s scheme *meister* Charles Ponzi in awe.

By mid-decade, however, the reports of ever-higher American debt had been augmented by estimates of ever-lower U.S. oil production. The latter fed the former. Experts pondered whether, as 2010 approached, the cost of U.S. oil and petroleum product imports—potentially six to eight billion barrels a year at $50 to $70 per barrel or worse—could approach

$400 billion per year.[1] Such an outflow could well uncouple the U.S. dollar from its last oil prop. Petroleum producers would no longer want to be paid in dollars, conceivably preferring euros, a new Asian currency, or a basket of currencies. As economists mulled over the predictions by Paul Volcker and others, many such scenarios were posed.

The failure of the U.S. invasion of Iraq with respect to oil supplies became one of the great underreported stories of the decade. Far from achieving the covert aims discussed in chapter 3—flooding the world with cheap Iraqi production, breaking the back of OPEC, installing ExxonMobil in the rich Majnoon fields, and living happily ever after on twenty-dollar to thirty-dollar oil for America's SUVs and McMansions—the outcome was disastrous.[2] Iraqi oil production shrank in the face of sabotage and relentless insurgent attacks on the major pipelines. OPEC survived, and oil prices soared. The havoc wreaked by hurricane Katrina on the Gulf of Mexico oil facilities in 2005 heightened the U.S. predicament, but the critical failure came in Washington's flawed calculations in the Middle East.

The dollar, already declining before the invasion, sank further in 2003–2004 as a number of OPEC nations moved to reduce their dollar holdings, while investing in their own rising stock markets and real estate. Whereas in 2002 the United States had paid $100 billion for its imported oil needs, that rose to over $230 billion in 2005, with expectations of considerably worse to come. No U.S. military commitment, perhaps not even in Vietnam, so utterly failed in its unspoken objectives. Financial dominoes shook or toppled, from the price of oil on the New York Mercantile Exchange to OPEC's ebbing commitment to the dollar.

Should the dollar's decline persist, the world's reasonable perception, or so many economists argued, would be that the United States was attempting to depreciate and inflate its way out of its huge debts. Foreign central banks—in Asia, first and foremost, but also elsewhere—would be unwilling to buy or hold large quantities of U.S. Treasury debt in their reserves. Such disillusionment would further depress the greenback, making the cost of oil, by that point no longer priced in dollars, continue to rise for Americans.

Of course, a sharp downturn in the U.S. economy—hypotheses included a sudden surge in interest rates, a stock-market slide, a speculative debacle, a house-price implosion, a recession, or some unnerving combination—would curb U.S. demand for manufactured imports and oil, reducing those pressures. That kind of slump, however, would pose other dangers: a spreading assets deflation, trade protectionism, different reasons for foreign banks to unload their dollars, and so forth. The Internet chatroom conversations of global economists, cloaked in anonymity, tended toward pessimism.[3]

In this economic world turned upside down, others hinted at the problem the United States might face in paying higher interest on mounting national debt. Amid 2002–2004 interest rates low enough to be negative after adjustment for inflation, the Treasury had refinanced so as to make most of its debt under five years in duration and cheap to carry. As a result, whereas Washington in 1997 had paid $356 billion worth of interest on $5.4 trillion worth of debt, by 2003, with rates at rock bottom, $318 billion sufficed to cover the interest on $6.8 trillion.[4] However, should short-term rates linger in the 4.5 to 5.5 percent range, almost double those of 2003, the interest payable on $8 trillion to $9 trillion of debt could rise to $400 billion to $500 billion, a major strain on the year-to-year U.S. budget.

The Republicans in control of Congress and the White House, meanwhile, conducted both fiscal and energy policy in a state of denial—denial, at least, of any potential crisis. The Bush administration energy legislation enacted in 2005 left the global energy markets sufficiently unimpressed that oil prices made new highs. Skeptics observed that the most important sections of the bill were those deleted at various stages, meaningful provisions requiring the government to find ways of reducing U.S. oil demand, automakers to improve fuel efficiency, and utilities to generate 10 percent of electricity from renewable energy sources.[5] Powerful constituencies found such strictures unacceptable, although the federal government had raised the standards of energy efficiency for refrigerators, for example, six times since the 1970s with enough success that comparable new units use only one-fourth as much electricity. Any remotely similar gain in automobile and truck efficiency would go a long way to ease oil-import demands.

Conservatives in the White House and Congress also continued to insist on making the 2001–2003 tax cuts permanent, despite unimpressive cost-benefit analyses. Over seventy-five years, as noted earlier, these changes were projected to cost $11 trillion, dwarfing the $4 trillion price tag of fully funding Social Security benefits. Furthermore, the tax reductions were skewed toward the upper-income brackets in ways that lessened their stimulative effects. The lowered rates on capital gains and dividends, for example, were calculated to produce only 9 cents of stimulus for every dollar of forgone revenue, and the reduction of overall rates only 59 cents on a dollar.[6] By contrast, the small amount of federal aid to state governments in the Bush package was rated at a more effective $1.24 of stimulus for every dollar.

If U.S. excesses of debt and energy consumption remained on giddy and converging trajectories, the reactions overseas were wary. Among the oil producers, as we saw in chapter 3, Iran, Indonesia, Malaysia, Venezuela, and others had moved earlier to reduce their use of dollars or to take other measures against U.S. financial domination of the oil markets. In 2005 Russia, Singapore, and Malaysia all announced small but significant shifts in their central-bank reserves from dollars to euros.[7]

Even rumors or careless comments about possible currency diversification in the East Asian nations, which had made huge purchases of U.S. Treasury bills and notes—at least $399 billion in 2004, if not as much in 2005—produced moments of panic in the U.S. financial markets. One such episode in South Korea was described as follows: "As the Korean comment ping-ponged around the world, all hell broke loose, with currency traders selling dollars for fear that the central banks of Japan and China, which hold immense dollar reserves . . . might follow suit. That would be the United States' worst economic nightmare."[8]

Economists in the United States worked up models and estimated the impact of various Chinese central-bank actions, ranging from significant sales of the dollar to simply halving China's purchases of U.S. Treasury debt. The U.S. economy could be hurt by interest rates on bonds that were between four tenths of 1 percentage point and 2 full percentage points higher than they otherwise would have been.[9]

As in so many critical arenas, the U.S. government had no clear strategy, save for allowing the dollar to weaken in 2003–2004 while professing to uphold its strength. In both oil consumption and currency management, the clock of American vulnerability was ticking.

Religion and the Republican Coalition

As commentators on oil and debt pondered leaden gray skies, the 30 to 40 percent of the Republican coalition that read the *Left Behind* series or believed in the rapture were looking toward the heavens more hopefully. Fundamentalist preachers, Sunday gospel hours, and end-times Web sites monitored the countdown, analogizing events to biblical predictions and speculating about advancing time horizons.

In 2005 42 percent of Americans described themselves to survey takers as born-again, only slightly below the readings of 2001 and 2002.[10] George W. Bush reassured the faithful that summer and autumn by endorsing the teaching of "intelligent design"—implicit godly design, to be sure—alongside evolution in U.S. schools, and by choosing nominees who were conservatives on the abortion issue to fill two U.S. Supreme Court vacancies. Because the retiring Sandra Day O'Connor had been a swing vote in earlier high-court rulings, her replacement was expected to be decisive. The president also reassured the faithful by renewing his promise to veto any legislation to liberalize stem-cell research, its lopsided public support notwithstanding.[11]

One peril to Republicans lay in growing voter skepticism about the influence on national policy wielded by the religious right and the wisdom of mixing religion and politics. In 2002 and 2003 the average American had favored more religiosity in public officials rather than less, results that encouraged Bush in his open religiosity and biblical phraseology. However, the polls had begun to change in 2004, and soured further in 2005, with twice as many respondents saying the Christian right had too much influence in Washington as said it had too little.[12]

The 2004 presidential election campaign had raised questions about Bush's religious intensity, including a perception that he saw himself speaking for God. Then the Schiavo dispute provoked particular national disillusionment and belief that the president and Congress were pandering to the religious right. Voters were also displeased by White House attempts to build friendly churches into a political machine, opposing that kind of involvement by more than two to one in public opinion polls.[13]

With George W. Bush and Vice President Dick Cheney both retiring in 2008, jockeying by would-be presidential candidates began quickly within the Republican party. Among those getting early attention were Senate Republican leader Bill Frist of Tennessee, Senator John McCain of Arizona, and former New York City mayor Rudolph Giuliani. Florida governor Jeb Bush, in turn, was watched carefully for any sign of a Bush family effort to prolong its White House dynasty.

Because the religious right had so much power within the party, few observers thought that McCain could prevail at a national party convention, even if he had done well in the primaries. The Arizona senator's age—he would be seventy-two in 2008—and his uncertain health were also drawbacks. Giuliani, although far to the right on law-and-order issues, had offended evangelical and fundamentalist sensitivities on gay rights and abortion rights, which he had upheld during his mayoralty years. Senate leader Frist, with his high-profile party role and 100 percent rating from the Christian Coalition, sometimes sought to appear moderate, raising particular hackles on the right in 2005 by endorsing congressional legislation to expand stem-cell research.

If Jeb Bush wanted to take up the Christian conservative mantle, he had some chance of success, although several pundits also discussed the possibility of a McCain-Bush arrangement. With McCain's advanced age in 2008, they speculated, Jeb Bush could take the vice presidency and then run for president in his own right in 2012.[14]

What also began to weigh on Republican strategists was the likelihood of a serious intramural contest, including the new complex of moral issues that tied into voters' religious beliefs, denominational affiliations, and churchgoing intensities. Religious themes had been secondary but significant in three previous intra-GOP presidential contests: John Anderson's bid for the 1980 Republican nomination, followed by his springtime party bolt to run that year as an independent; next, the 1992 infighting as culture warrior Patrick Buchanan opposed George H. W. Bush for the party nomination, and longtime GOP activist H. Ross Perot wound up running as an independent; and then in 2000, John McCain's short-lived but bitter challenge to George W. Bush's nomination drive.

Each contest focused incremental attention on the Republican party's political geography of culture and religion. Congressman John Anderson, a liberal Republican from a Yankee and Scandinavian section of northern Illinois, led off by crystallizing northern moderate-GOP suspicion of

Ronald Reagan's Sun Belt cultural conservatism and ties to the fast-rising Moral Majority of Virginia fundamentalist preacher Jerry Falwell.

In 1992 Ross Perot's principal emphasis was on the failure of George H. W. Bush's economic policies. However, the maverick Texas computer-services billionaire had relatively little appeal in the South, taking his best vote in secular northern and western areas characterized by low church affiliation, high technology, or a youthful libertarian-minded (but non-university) population.

In 2000 McCain reiterated the same broad geography: strength against the younger Bush in the secular North and West, glaring weakness in the Baptist and Pentecostal South. By now there was a familiar pattern. The identification of both Bushes with southern regionalism and the courtship of emotional Protestantism—visible with the elder Bush in 1992, for his son in 2000 and 2004—provoked a persisting counterforce among northern and western elements of the old Republican coalition.

Barring some extraordinary fluke or arrangement, these groups, marshaling only 10 to 20 percent of Republican self-identifiers, had little chance of winning a GOP presidential nomination. Where they could have effect, though, was in third-party leverage or playing a swing role in a close general election, a capability that deserves some detail.

The swing component was missing in 1980. John Anderson's ultimate 7 percent of the total vote—through most of the autumn he had drawn 10 to 15 percent in national surveys—made no real difference to the outcome. His Yankee-centered independent and moderate-Republican vote would probably have split slightly in favor of Carter over Reagan, but the latter won on Election Day by a decisive nine percentage points. In retrospect, however, we can note that a fair number of the Anderson Republicans in the Northeast, in the upper Midwest, and along the Pacific coast were moving out of the GOP as it southernized, and in 1984 a solid majority of Anderson voters backed Democrat Walter Mondale against Reagan.[15]

The cultural dimensions of the Perot vote in 1992 have been thoroughly developed by Albert J. Menendez, a statistician with a fascination with religious politics. His 1996 book *The Perot Voters and the Future of American Politics* probed beyond the usual emphasis on the Texas billionaire's quirky economics, giving useful attention to the campaign's less noticed religious undercurrents. Perot, Menendez concluded, had cat-

alyzed a large Election Day turnout and major opposition to George
H. W. Bush among low- and middle-income white Protestant Republicans of the secular and less church-attending variety across the
rural, small-town, and suburban North. Distaste for the elder Bush's attention to the religious right, on parade that summer, aggravated dissatisfaction with his administration's economic record. In dozens of
counties where Bush had gotten 63 percent or even 67 percent of the
vote in 1988, his 1992 backing shrank to 46, 41, or even 39 percent. In the
fourteen counties across the country where Perot actually led both Bush
and Clinton on Election Day, Bush's aggregate vote plummeted by
twenty-seven percentage points.[16] That was leverage.

Overall, Menendez noted, in capturing just under 20 percent of the
national vote, Perot took 22 percent of nonfrequent churchgoers and
won 24.2 percent in the twelve states with the largest ratios of religiously
nonaffiliated individuals.[17] Some 29 percent of liberal Republicans supported Perot and 21 percent of moderate Republicans, 24 percent of
nonevangelical Protestants, and 28 percent of conservative independents.[18]
According to Menendez, "Mainline Protestants, a mainstay of the Republican party since 1856, were far less likely to support Bush than any
previous Republican president. These voters, economic moderates but
social-issue liberals, may have reacted against the extremism perceived at
the Republican convention in August and the party's embrace of
Religious Right platform positions." Instead of their usual 60 percent,
mainline Protestants "gave Bush just 38% nationwide. Clinton won
slightly over 38% and Perot won 24%. 'Yankee' Protestants all over New
England deserted their party in droves as Clinton carried Cape Cod,
Nantucket, Wellesley, and scores of similar communities."[19]

Not surprisingly, Perot's support in New England, the upper Midwest,
and the Pacific Northwest showed substantial correlation with Anderson's
twelve years earlier. But the larger point, in contemplating the 2008 election,
is the reappearance of the same broad division in John McCain's 2000 primary campaign against the younger George Bush, and then in the emphatic
sectionalism of the narrowly decided 2000 and 2004 presidential elections.

McCain, in 2000, got trapped—and without sufficient funds to fully
engage the front-runner—in a barely hidden battle of religious politics
that made the debates of 1980 and 1992 look like kindergarten stuff.
Campaigning day after day in the early New Hampshire primary, McCain

had won handily in what for the GOP had traditionally been a bellwether contest. This stunned Bush advisers, who turned to crush McCain in the upcoming South Carolina and Virginia primaries, fundamentalist and evangelical venues where they could call up support from such stalwarts as Bob Jones III of Bob Jones University, Pat Robertson, and Jerry Falwell. McCain lost—he never had any real chance below the Mason-Dixon Line—but not before obliging a worried Bush to hold a symbolic rally with the far-right Bob Jones in Greenville, South Carolina.[20] McCain then went on to attack Robertson and Falwell as "agents of intolerance," even describing Bush as "a Pat Robertson Republican."

The Arizona senator was defeated in South Carolina, and then again in Virginia, after venting anger that verged on recklessness.[21] Although the nomination contest was all but over, McCain went on to win primaries in Michigan—partly by running ads that tied Bush to the anti-Catholic comments of Bob Jones—as well as in Arizona, Vermont, Massachusetts, Rhode Island, and Connecticut. Not only did these embarrassments hurt Bush for the general election, but McCain's own lingering resentment was so well known that in 2001 Democrats wooed him to switch parties, a course some of his own advisers recommended. Even in 2004, the Bush campaign was not quite sure McCain would resist blandishments to become the Democrat John Kerry's running mate, but he did.

Preliminary jockeying for the 2008 election recalled some of these memories and tensions—further stimulated in the 2005 milieu of deepening national disillusionment with the Bush administration, public worry about White House attempts to pack the federal courts, and intra-party disgruntlement with the religious right. McCain, however, was hardly the only potential contender facing national Republican religious litmus tests. Former mayor Giuliani and even Tennessean Frist likewise faced true-believer skepticism.

Despite the huge numbers of born-again and frequent church-attending voters, theological correctness stands to be a Republican Achilles' heel. Its influence periodically forces the Republican party to lean too far to the right. The issue clusters involving sex, life and death, the First Amendment, and church-state relations—to say nothing of the larger biblical worldviews out of which they grow—still face their greatest philosophic and courtroom battles in the years ahead. Unfortunately, comparable challenges confront the economics of U.S. international hegemony.

The Greenback at Bay

In guiding the weakening dollar through its global gauntlet, top U.S. economic officials found themselves facing a new set of foreign economic
policy arbiters. The United States had been a net global creditor until the
late 1980s, ill preparing Washington policy makers for the post-2001 surveillance of a hard-eyed Asian power elite: the central banks of creditor
nations rapidly accumulating large sums of U.S. Treasury debt.

As debt-prone Americans ratcheted up their international borrowing
in the late 1990s, media attention first ran to short stories, not headlines.
In 1997 net U.S. international indebtedness rose to $360 billion, and in
1999, to a trillion dollars. The year of the attack on the World Trade
Center saw U.S. net international indebtedness reach $2.3 trillion.[22]
Thereafter, as we have seen, the total swelled in 2003 to $2.7 trillion, and
ballooned to $3.3 trillion in 2004, with a 2005 figure in the $4 trillion
range.[23] Gradually the issue of which nations held American debt, for
what purposes, and with what risk of potential ambuscades, began to
make the front pages, especially in the financial press.

Some of the large holders were major U.S. allies—Britain, Canada,
and Germany—whose central banks had long kept dollars in reasonable
proportions as part of their reserves. The second holders, more problematic, were the major and middling oil-pumping nations collecting a
flood of greenbacks from the escalating price of petroleum. These included the OPEC members, as well as Mexico and Russia. According to a
survey by the Bank for International Settlements, between 2001 and 2004
OPEC nations dropped the share of their reserves held in dollars from 75
percent to 61.5 percent.[24] Major OPEC producers such as Iran and
Venezuela held fewer dollars because their hostility to the United States
had become overt, but even moderates in OPEC ranks saw the growing
wisdom of putting reserves into a wider array of currencies.[25]

The collapse of U.S. oil strategy in the botched invasion and occupation of Iraq was a further aggravant. OPEC had been an indirect target of
Washington's ambition to open the oil spigots in a subjugated Iraq and
drive down oil prices. When the U.S. blueprint miscarried, OPEC appeared to have taken full advantage. For starters, the former oil-price
band of twenty-two to twenty-eight dollars per barrel was quietly
dropped. Some analysts also concluded that OPEC decision makers had

begun to calculate informally in euros—logical enough, considering that the European Union was the Middle East producers' biggest customer. Doing so would have allowed the oil price to mirror the sharp rise in the EU currency, albeit the invoices were still in dollars. In December 2004 the survey released by the Bank for International Settlements noted the speculation that OPEC central-bank reductions in dollar holdings prefaced a larger policy move.[26]

As we saw in chapter 3, some OPEC member nations—not just Iran, Iraq (under Saddam), and Venezuela, but also Malaysia and Indonesia— were pushing discussions to stop pricing oil in dollars and switch to euros or a basket of currencies. By 2004–2005, other proposals seriously discussed included setting up a global oil exchange in Iran to rival London and New York; establishing a Middle East regional currency (the gold dinar); and rallying around an Acu (Asian currency unit) anchored by the Japanese yen.[27] The United States enjoyed some respite in 2005 as the dollar gained strength from Federal Reserve Board interest rate hikes.

Washington also directed attention toward the Asian nations whose central banks were rapidly accumulating dollars and U.S. Treasury debt: Japan, China, Taiwan, and South Korea. In contrast to the greenbacks OPEC received in payment for oil imports, these stalwart exporters collected them for automobiles, television sets, laptops, advanced technology, and, in China's case, in part for filling half of the shelves at Wal-Mart. By late 2004 Asian central bankers had become nervous enough about the U.S. current-account deficit—would it break the dollar or oblige Washington to curb imports?—to head off any imminent crisis by buying $200 billion worth of Treasury debt in the fourth quarter alone.[28] Figure 11 shows the mounting foreign ownership of U.S. assets.

In contrast to the gambits of OPEC malcontents, there was no East Asian plot to break the dollar. On the contrary, Japan, South Korea, and Taiwan were longtime U.S. allies well accustomed to sheltering under the U.S. military umbrella. However, their motivations were more complex than presumed by conservative economists, given to happy theories about the United States' fortunate ability to access a new transnational savings pool. As adherents of commercial realpolitik have argued, the Asian nations tend to follow national strategies of economic self-aggrandizement.[29] In these systems, the visible hand of government often manages a stronger international grasp than the so-called invisible hand.

One can only imagine the private conversations—the blunt economic language—in the conference rooms of Asian financiers and exporters, each group as confident of its contingent's coming hour as executives in Manhattan and Chicago circa 1919 were of America's: "Why don't the Americans take care of their industry and invest in it? Why do they dither over primitive and antiscientific religion? Why are their children so far behind our own students? Why can't they cut back on their foolish and unaffordable overconsumption of oil? How far can we—should we—support them?"

Satisfactory rebuttals are elusive. The implosion of American manufacturing, while hardly planned, has manifestly been tolerated in the U.S. capital. Since the mid-1990s, as China has reemerged in the world economy, its massive, minimal-wage labor force has sat on any chance of a broad U.S. manufacturing reemergence. Investment in such domestic plant, not illogically, has little more appeal for Americans than kindred home-front opportunities did for the Britons of 1900–1914 or for eighteenth-century Dutch financiers. Their nods, too, had gone to more lucrative foreign investments or transactions—shares in Canadian banks or Argentine railroads, loans to Catherine the Great.

Investment data underscore the parallel. In 2004, for example, the total of U.S. direct foreign investment (ownership of plants and equipment, not local securities) was $3 trillion, roughly the size of foreign direct investment in the United States. The comparative returns, however, were a matter of night and day. Americans earned almost twice as much from their holdings, especially those in Asia, as foreigners did from their U.S. holdings.[30] For many American companies, sinking more money into U.S. plant, equipment, and payroll made little sense.

Here the evidence is stark. Capital outlays by U.S. corporations, low or negative during 2001 and 2002, grew sharply between mid-2003 and mid-2004, as shown by official gross private-investment figures. Thereafter, they softened again, despite the usual rule that high profits at a cyclical economic crest bring high capital spending. As summarized by *New York Times* columnist Anna Bernasek, "instead of investing, corporate America has been accumulating cash—big piles of it. According to the most recent figures from the Federal Reserve Board, nonfinancial corporations increased their liquid assets by 20 percent to a record $1.3 trillion, from the start of 2003 to June, 2004. Think about all that money for a minute. It's about 10 percent of the total economy, and much of it is virtually stuffed into a mattress."[31]

Part of that comforting corporate mattress was overseas, in convenient tax havens such as the Bahamas, Ireland, and Singapore. Profits earned abroad and left there sidestepped the 35 percent tax usually payable on funds repatriated to the United States. At the end of 2004, estimates put the stash as high as $750 billion. To tempt the prodigal sums to return, federal tax legislation enacted that autumn gave multinational corporations a chance to be taxed at only 5.25 percent on profits earned before 2003 and held in foreign subsidiaries, provided the money was brought back to the U.S. before the end of 2005 and used for purposes that stimulated job creation and the economy.[32]

The eventual definition of the allowable purposes ensured that much of the repatriation—the U.S. Treasury hoped for $300 billion—would produce enlarged dividends, debt retirement, pension-fund shoring up, and acquisitions that involved relatively little job creation.[33] However, the stock market also benefited, and watchers identified a further boon: short-term support for the embattled dollar in currency markets as U.S. foreign assets came home.[34] What received little attention, even in the financial press, was the watershed occasion of another erstwhile world economic power turned global debtor beginning to repatriate overseas assets in the manner of Britain between, say, 1915 and 1948.

Closer attention was doubtless paid in Tokyo, Beijing, and Seoul, where the near-term prop under the dollar was welcomed. Little U.S. progress, however, would have been perceived on the vital energy front, where consumption and price pressure continued to grow. So, too, for the continued shortfall in the education of young Americans and the deterioration of the U.S. lead in training engineers and scientists. Such difficulties would not be easily overcome.

Economist Stephen Roach at New York–based Morgan Stanley was caustic, observing that the United States had begun to outsource its financing as well as its manufacturing. Investment strategist Raymond T. Dalio stated matter-of-factly that "our need for foreign capital is going to continue to grow at the same time China's desire to buy our bonds will diminish. We are substantially dependent on foreign lending."[35] Such

FIGURE 11

The Hocking of America: Massive U.S. International Debt as the Price of Domestic Overconsumption

Domestic Overconsumption and the Hemorrhage of the U.S. Trade Balance[a]

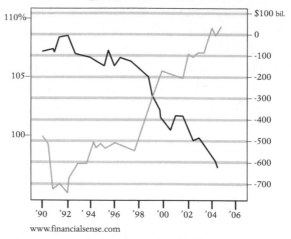

www.financialsense.com

Note: The rising line represents the relationship of U.S. real private consumption to global real GDP. The declining line represents the ballooning annual U.S. trade deficit in billions of U.S. dollars.

The Rise in Net U.S. Assets Held by Foreigners, 1982–2004[b]
(Percentage of U.S. gross domestic product)

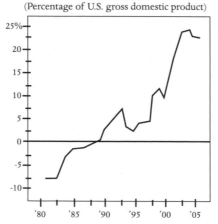

Note: Net U.S. assets held by foreigners are the difference between foreign-owned U.S. assets and U.S.-owned foreign assets. Both are measured using a market-value method.

[a] Source: BCA Research, Int'l BCA, Feb. 2005.
[b] Source: "Recent Shifts in Financing the U.S. Current Account Deficit," Congressional Budget Office, July 12, 2005, p. 2, based on data from the Department of Commerce, Bureau of Economic Analysis.

comments raised a further analogy to Britain, in the 1920s, when concern about foreign debt and the need to enlist the help of foreign central bankers—usually in the United States—had augured the worse financial straits to come.

Each year, more U.S. economists seemed to break away, or at least to edge away, from the quarter-century suasion of economic conservatives who had become content simply to hold Adam Smith's invisible hand and proclaim the omniscience of market forces. But the established wisdom remained particularly unyielding in the councils of Republican Washington, where—as Paul Volcker observed in explaining his fears—policy was not a good bet to change.[36]

Clyde Prestowitz, the onetime senior counselor in Ronald Reagan's Commerce Department who thereafter went on to found and head Washington's Economic Strategy Institute for two decades, summed up:

> America needs to recognize that many of the assumptions guiding its economic policy are at odds with the realities of today's global economy. Its performance in a broad range of areas—including saving, education, energy and water conservation, critical infrastructure and workforce upskilling—is far below the standard of many other nations. America needs to understand that its refusal to have a broad competitiveness policy is, in fact, a policy. And it gives leading U.S. CEOs no choice but to play into the strategies of other countries. This policy, according to its proponents, leaves decisions to the unseen hand of the market. Actually, however, it leaves them to the highly visible hands of lobbyists and foreign policymakers. It is a policy that ultimately leads to impoverishment.[37]

What kind of politics—or crisis—could overcome the combination of Bush administration strategic neglect, Washington interest-group entrenchment, and parochial Republican constituency pressures no one quite knew.

Cultural and Political Fundamentalism: The Theology of U.S. Domestic and Foreign Policy

In summing up the Republican "theology" of tax cutting as an item of faith, not logic, former Republican commerce secretary Peter Peterson identified a pervasive weakness.[38] Much of what the Republican party stood for had become based on faith, not reason—and this across a spectrum that ranged from domestic economics, science, and constitutional jurisprudence to souring relationships with Europe and the United Nations, and preemptive war-making in the holy lands of the Middle East.

As we have seen, the strong religious imprint on foreign policy came from the broad ranks of fundamentalist, evangelical, and Pentecostal Protestants, many of whom believed in Armageddon and represented, along with a smaller, like-minded Catholic minority, something like 25 to 30 percent of the U.S. population and 50 to 60 percent of the George W. Bush electoral coalition. As figure 12 shows, a commitment to making U.S. foreign policy implement a biblical worldview jumps out in the evangelical response to a mid-2004 survey taken by the Pew Research Center, portions of which queried the interaction between religion and foreign policy.

As overall public support for the invasion of Iraq declined, evangelicals became the mainstay of minority backing for the occupation and for the larger doctrine of preemptive invasions. Most of them, in all likelihood, were guided by what House Majority Leader Tom DeLay termed in his own case a "biblical worldview." While the Pew Center survey did not include an "Armageddon" question in its poll, one taken for Newsweek in 1999 (see figure 1 on page 102) had found 45 percent of U.S. Christians expecting Armageddon, including 71 percent of evangelicals but only 28 percent of mainline Protestants and 18 percent of Catholics.[39] About the same percentages believed that the antichrist was already on the earth, adding to the sense of immediacy.

Support for Israel is another part of this biblical worldview. In mid-2003, after the U.S. invasion of Iraq, another survey taken for the Pew Center found 63 percent of white evangelical Protestants calling the state of Israel a fulfillment of the biblical prophecy of the second coming of Jesus, whereas only 21 percent of mainline Protestants did so.[40]

We can fairly assume a large constituency overlap among (1) putting a top priority on following religious principles in foreign policy; (2) adhering to a Bible-centered worldview; and (3) favoring U.S. military intervention in the Middle East to promote the fulfillment of end-times prophecy and the second coming of Christ. To be sure, few media poll-takers chose to cut too close to the bone of U.S. Christian belief by dis-

FIGURE 12

What Should Guide Foreign Policy?

Percent who considered "following religious principles" a top priority for foreign policy

White evangelical Protestants	55%
White mainline Protestants	27
White Catholics	26
Seculars	13

Source: The Pew Research Center, "Foreign Policy Attitudes Now Driven by 9/11 and Iraq," August 18, 2004 (polling, July 8–18, 2004).

playing the religiosity in the cross-tabulations. Politically, however, one is hard put to think of an interrelationship with greater relevance: religion has been the principal denominator of the aggressiveness of the GOP rank and file in the Middle East.

Because of the makeup of the Bush electorate, religion, probably more than anything else, shaped the biblical "good-versus-evil" wrap thrown around September 11, as well as the related, deliberate merging of the terrorist crisis with a targeting of Saddam Hussein's "New Babylon" regime in Iraq. Furthermore, throughout much of 2002 and 2003, the administration's commingling of theology and antiterrorism shaped a climate in which George W. Bush enjoyed job approval in the 65 to 70 percent range. This strength, in turn, allowed him to prevail in Congress on different issues, principally economic, where he might otherwise have been stymied.

By 2005 Bush's broad job approval had dissipated, but the biblical and evangelical influence over American foreign policy remained in place. It was visible not only in the Middle East but in the extraordinary, conjoined global posture of the United States on a half-dozen other fronts. One was the so-called Mexico City policy of denying U.S. financial assistance (through funding by the Agency for International Development or the State Department) to any international organizations extending support to abortion, even if the activity objected to had non-U.S. funding. Another posture involved insistence on "abstinence-only" alternatives for dealing with sexually originated circumstances such as AIDS, abortion, or sexually transmitted diseases. A third circumstance, with international ramifications, was the withholding of official approval within the United States for a number of medications and drugs: the so-called morning-after pill (EC—emergency contraception); vaccines against the HPV virus that leads to cervical cancer; Intrinsa, a women's hormone; and genetic anti-viral AIDS drugs.[41] Yet another involved the backhanding of international women's programs and conferences, such as those under United Nations auspices, lest they give any recognition to abortion as a human right.

Different, but also biblically connected, was unwillingness to take part in international climate-change convocations or the implementation of treaties that recognized global warming—supposedly incompatible with the Book of Genesis—as a human-caused atmospheric problem. Then came the White House commitment to blocking serious stem-cell re-search in the United States. This arrayed the United States alongside the more religious nations in Europe (Ireland, Italy, and Poland) but set back the prospects for joint U.S. programs with leading biotechnology re-search centers such as Britain, Korea, Switzerland, and Singapore.[42]

Officials in international organizations in Europe and in Asia reacted with outrage to the U.S. AIDS-related policies. One 2004 analysis by *The Observer* in Britain quoted Poul Nielson, member of the European Union Commission in charge of development and humanitarian aid, indicting the United States for "preaching one line only and denying people's rights by trying to push them into abstinence. It will weaken the battle against AIDS, and the unfortunate reality is that it will directly endanger the lives of millions of women." Dr. Peter Piot, executive director of UNAIDS, the agency responsible for relief efforts, was equally straightforward: "We are not in the business of morality. Condom promotion should be part of education about sexuality for young people." Europeans have stepped in, *The Observer* elaborated, to fill what Nielson called the "decency gap" by funding both the UN Population Fund and the International Planned Parenthood Federation after the United States had withdrawn its support. Britain, too, decided to contribute an additional £80 million over four years.[43]

At a 2002 Asian conference in Bangkok, the abstinence policy offered by the United States was rejected by a ringing 32–1 vote, and at the United Nations Special Session on Children the same year, the United States found itself aligned with Iran, Iraq, Libya, Sudan, and the Vatican in failing to gain support for abstinence-only.[44] British commentators noted the irony of United States overlap with Islamic militants on women's rights issues.[45]

Because polls show Americans heavily in favor of high school sex education courses that promote abstinence and explain contraception, rather than just one aspect, the abstinence-only campaign is risky foreign policy and domestic politics, resting on narrow theology. Garry Wills explains that an influential fringe of the Christian right believes that "whenever human semen enters any ovum God pops a soul in along with it—though almost 50 percent of the resulting 'people' perish instantly by failing to achieve nidation [implantation in the uterus]."[46]

The Government Accountability Office, the investigative unit of Congress, released a report in early 2005 criticizing the Bush administration for its stance on the global use of AIDS drugs. The administration's obstruction, it said, was at odds with the strategies of international health groups and contrary to the views of the nations needing assistance. The GAO specifically criticized the administration for withholding FDA approval of generic antiretroviral AIDS drugs, which had been accepted by the World Health Organization and other international agencies.[47]

Never before has the U.S. government been so aggressive internationally on these themes, and it is not surprising that European commentators and diplomats are stunned. They see people from the American Medical Association replaced in U.S. delegations by activists, for example, from the conservative evangelical Family Research Council or Concerned Women for America, the organization founded two decades ago by Tim LaHaye's wife, Beverly. Such groups are not objective; they represent a theocratically minded Christian right.

Over the last quarter century, negative portrayals of women's rights activists—the element stereotyped for bra-burning and creating material such as *The Vagina Monologues*—have been a boon for the Christian right. The radical image of parts of the women's movement has been a foil to be played off of. However, implicit within the anger of the feminist left is a core analysis that, when well distilled, could threaten conservative Republican credibility with centrist women.

This is the perception that some religious conservatives have a somewhat Taliban-like philosophy—or perhaps simply an Old Testament one—of returning women to their traditional place in a world of male supremacy. What at first glance seems to be an unrelated patchwork of incidents adds up to a theological quilt. Brazil, for example, was cut off from U.S. AIDS assistance because its government did not explicitly condemn prostitution.[48] Ironically, a U.S. conservatism that once stood for domestic and global realpolitik has come to promote the panacea of abstinence—a kind of cultural idealism about as sociologically plausible in the third world (or Manhattan) as liberal plans in the 1960s for suburban school busing in the U.S. metropolitan areas. In the early 2000s, the right seems to have taken the lead in promoting unworkable social-planning abstractions.

This possibility has been lying in wait for decades. In 1982 I suggested in *Post-Conservative America*, which described a radical conservatism displacing the old genteel variety, that "any Sun Belt hegemony over our politics has a unique potential—not present in the Jackson-to-Bryan frontier or the Adams-to-Taft eastern establishment—to accommodate a drift toward apple-pie authoritarianism. . . . The morality of the majority would be upheld and enforced, though with politically convenient lapses; the 'Star Spangled Banner' would wave with greater frequency and over many more parades; increased surveillance would crack down on urban outbreaks and extreme political dissidents."[49] We are seeing it now: church, family, and flag, and more than a few hints of something more.

Liberals discern a lip-smacking element in conservative neopuritanism, especially in the religious right's submission of lists of AIDS scientists and programs to be denied federal funding, as well as in the disclosure by scientists at both the National Institutes of Health and Centers for Disease Control and Prevention that research proposals with the terms "homosexual," "prostitute," or "drug-user" in their title—monitored by zealous congressional staffers—were routinely rejected for funding.[50] Kay Cole James, the former dean at Pat Robertson's Regent University who was named to head George W. Bush's federal Office of Personnel Management, had likened gays to alcoholics, adulterers, and drug addicts in her 1995 book *Transforming America: From the Inside Out.*[51] Only Jesus Christ can bring about the societal change needed to stop AIDS, preacher Franklin Graham told a 2002 Washington conference on the evangelical response to the crisis.[52]

Even harsher theology abounds on the far right, especially in the fringe Christian Reconstruction movement, which endorses biblical punishments. Walter Olson, a gay conservative, penned an analysis of the "Recons," noting their penetration of the home schooling movement and some elements of antigovernment libertarianism, but going on to chuckle about how their positions—such as favoring stoning for adulterers—enabled others on the right to feel moderate. What with one Christian Reconstructionist faction "proposing the actual judicial murder of gays, fewer blink at the position of a Gary Bauer or Janet Folger, who support laws exposing them to mere imprisonment."[53]

Some of the humor is inadvertent, born of salacious gusto. Liberal columnist Katha Pollitt quoted Virginia state legislator Robert Marshall arguing that the "day-after" pill would "turn young women into chemical Love Canals for frat house playboys."[54] Jokes about the Spanish Inquisition come easily enough to mind, or some latter-day Nathaniel Hawthorne profiling a Christian Coalition visit to Salem.

But disappointment is equally in order, because the conservative case against the prurient society, which had genuine merit, has now become a caricature—its fervor more posture than plausible solution. Zealots have helped to enact so-called covenant marriage (disavowing divorce except for adultery, abandonment, imprisonment, and suchlike), as an option in three states—Louisiana, Arizona, and Arkansas. However, to the glee of liberals, only 2 percent of those getting married locally so opt.[55] Nor do the values of evangelical Protestantism uniformly prevail in Utah, where minor degrees of Mormon harem-keeping persist. Polygamous marriages are estimated to be in the tens of thousands, and child-bride laws have been enacted to curb that pernicious aspect.[56] But from the GOP perspective, Mormons are swell: in 2004 Utah gave George W. Bush his largest statewide percentage.

Feminists decry another hypocrisy. While the Christian right and the U.S. Food and Drug Administration blocked sex-linked medications for women—a vaccine to prevent HPV, the virus responsible for most cervical cancers, and Intrinsa, a testosterone patch intended to raise libido in women whose ovaries have been removed—male use of Viagra was encouraged. For five years, until the discovery of the practice in 2005, New York State handed out free Viagra (under Medicaid) to sex criminals because state authorities thought that federal rules so required.[57]

Beyond any doubt, early in the Bush years the abstinence cause also became a vehicle for channeling large amounts of money to a wide variety of organizations that were faith-based and connected to the religious right—pregnancy-crisis centers, abstinence programs, anticondom organizations, and passion-for-prayer clubs—totaling perhaps $1 billion through 2004, with another $170 million budgeted for the 2005 fiscal year.[58] Activists in social work, feminist organizations, gay-rights groups, and population research were generously funded by friends in past Democratic administrations, so such patronage was hardly new. What can be said, though, is that the motivation on the Republican side was less ideological than religious, a distinction that raises First Amendment issues.

From Afghanistan to Arkansas, researchers of religious and political fundamentalism have found that the subordination of women is often a significant secondary objective. In *Fundamentalism and Gender,* religion scholar John Stratton Hawley amplifies "the critical role of gender in the larger complex," through fundamentalists' commitment to "femininity" in a motherhood-and-domesticity model and a desire to recapture a traditionalist past.[59] In *Strong Religion: The Rise of Fundamentalisms Around the World,* the authors similarly pointed out that in 1999 "the Southern Baptist Convention voted to re-enforce traditional gender roles."[60] But let us confine ourselves to the politics. Talk about the religion gap supplanting the gender gap in U.S. voting patterns ignores a larger interrelation: how conservative religious politics now includes its own collection of gender gaps and inequalities, a potentially explosive aspect.

To policy makers elsewhere in the world, Washington's espousals of these priorities in the American South is one thing; pushing them globally is something else. These gender and sex-related postures have gone hand in hand with opposing the Kyoto Protocol, embracing a concept of unilateral preemptive war, declining to accept the jurisdiction of the International Criminal Court, and appointing as the U.S. ambassador to the United Nations a man such as John Bolton, whose previous attacks on the world body—some admittedly justified—bore a more polished resemblance to the name-calling in the *Left Behind* series.

Realistically, these events and circumstances hardly encourage foreign central bankers, diplomats, or political leaders to buy and hold U.S. Treasury bonds, support American energy profligacy, join U.S. ventures in the Middle East, or believe that young people unskilled in mathematics, addled by credit cards, and weaned on so-called intelligent design instead of evolution will somehow retool American science for another generation of world industrial leadership. Dismissing global opinion is easy in Idaho or suburban Houston, but in the world beyond the GOP core constituencies, such attitudes keep exacting a price.

The all-important domestic political side of the same complex of issues can be thought of as a quadrangle bounded by stem-cell research; by the many dimensions of abortion and women's rights; by life-support situations as in that of Terri Schiavo; and by the question of gays, their status, and what makes a marriage. Abstinence, a critical thread of conservative neopuritanism, touches two sides of the quadrangle. All of these controversies have become staples of the religification of the U.S. party structure, the national arousal over judicial selection, and the ongoing tension between faith and science. However, the notion that these are issues Americans would do better to keep out of politics, although appealing in the abstract, ignores any democratic definition of governance and its responsibility to public opinion. All sides happily rush to milk any advantage from popular sentiment.

The right faces lopsided public disagreement with its more obvious theocratic tendencies—the attempt during the 2004 campaign to make churches into Republican adjuncts, televangelists' disdainful comments on the separation of church and state, and open efforts to supplant public schools with home schooling or religious instruction. All of these pursuits are opposed by clear national majorities. As we will see, these positions, however popular with fundamentalists and evangelicals, enjoy relatively little support beyond these belief groups.[61]

Liberals, for their part, face popular constraints on issues such as school prayer, the posting of the Ten Commandments in public buildings, schools' teaching intelligent design (along with evolution), and the display of Christmas manger scenes in towns such as Bethlehem, Connecticut. Because only 20 to 30 percent of Americans object to these, opponents who wave the banner of secular purity seem strident and anti-religious in San Diego and South Dakota, not to mention Greenville, South Carolina.[62]

The pivotal battles of religious politics are taking place around the quadrangle. Here Republicans are more divided than Democrats, although between 2000 and 2004 the GOP usually offset that weakness with sharper strategic skills. In fact, with the partial exception of the important political distinction between gay marriage and gay unions, the center of gravity of the four critical positions seems to be where mainline Protestantism and Catholicism meet mildly secular centrism.

The weight of national opinion on abortion widely supports women's rights, with caveats regarding the stage of the pregnancy and the conditions of the abortion, coupled with a strong popular preference for requiring parental notice where teenagers are involved. Gay marriage draws 40 to 45 percent support in public opinion surveys—at least until the issue heats up and becomes emotional, as in the 2004 ballot initiatives in a dozen states. The parallel claimed between homosexual and heterosexual marriage, being disbelieved by swing voters, is an effective conservative target. By contrast, popular majorities seem ready to support gay unions and legal rights without the marriage label.

Stem-cell research broadened its support in 2004 and 2005, with one Pew Center poll capturing the critical nuances as follows: 57 percent thought it more important to conduct research for new medical cures than to avoid destroying the potential life of embryos, 30 percent disagreed. As for the Schiavo case, majorities of 65 to 75 percent were angry with Congress and the White House for trying to interfere. However, without that circumstance, the divisions would have been closer, inasmuch as opinion only narrowly supports (51 percent to 40 percent) giving terminally ill patients the means to end their own lives.[63]

What makes these issues so pivotal, obviously, is that they touch most families. They pluck at the theology of virtually every religious denomination and belief system. Equally to the point, the beliefs involved put public policy makers in every young woman's medical consultations and in every aged parent's last hospital room or hospice. The greater the scientific advances in biomedicine and drug therapy, the greater the potential response of officeholders anxious to ingratiate themselves with the demands of the Traditional Values Coalition, the Southern Baptist Convention, the Christian Coalition, and Concerned Women for America. These prospects dwarf the old "culture wars" of the 1980s, with their shallow confrontations over the famous Willie Horton advertisement designed to inflame racial feelings, and the proposed constitutional amendment to prohibit flag-burning.

Zealots burden both sides. Theocrats promoting church-state collusion will hurt their conservative friends. So, too, for inquisitors out to terrorize the National Institutes of Health with lists of sexually unacceptable research projects. Gay bashers in Georgia may hurt conservatism, but gay marriage demonstrators in the streets of San Francisco do no favor to liberals. Indeed, demonizing the other side's extremists has often been a particularly successful tactic.

From 2000 through 2004, as noted, the Republicans were generally shrewder. To begin with, they held the votes of economic conservatives who were secular but little influenced by the cultural and religious debate. Right after the 2004 election, the commentator E. J. Dionne pointed out that Bush got the votes of 38 percent of those who believed abortion should be legal in most cases, and 22 percent of those who favored gay marriage.[64] Similarly, after constructing a profile of "gray-area" voters on the abortion issue, *Newsweek* found that Democrats narrowly lost these voters in 2002 and 2004, even though more of them leaned pro-choice, in considerable part because liberal rhetoric attuned to the solidly pro-choice voter did not work for those more philosophically conflicted.[65]

The judicial vacancies of 2005 sharpened voter awareness of both the influence of the religious right in Washington and the stakes of the new nominations and the eventual Supreme Court battles. Some politicians and pundits saw the Democrats benefiting as the threat posed by realigned courts to abortion rights under *Roe v. Wade* became more tangible. Conservatives had enjoyed kindred benefits in the late 1960s and early 1970s as the federal courts were seen by many swing voters to align themselves with permissive criminology—defendants' rights supposedly being put above victims' rights—and unpopular proposals for educational and residential racial balance. This new agenda displaced the woeful 1964 dialogue in which conservatives had been electorally mauled for opposing basic civil rights in such areas as public accommodations and voting.

The 2004 election, by confirming the conservative stranglehold on power in Washington, made medical and reproductive privacy seem less safe. Mid-2005 polls by the Garin-Hart-Yang Research Group for Emily's List, a women's political organization, found one-third of the women who had voted for Bush in 2004 planning to back Democrats for Congress in 2006. Besides dissatisfaction over the economy and Iraq, switchers cited the Schiavo case and privacy considerations. In one question, 58 percent of Republican women believed government should not impose any moral or religious view on the country.[66]

The threat perceived from conservative-dominated courts gained as Bush's 2005–2008 nominations took the spotlight. In the early summer of 2005, 65 percent of Americans told Gallup that they favored appointment of a justice who would uphold *Roe v. Wade,* a majority that included 47 percent of Republicans.[67] The same summer, a Pew Center survey asking voters whether *Roe v. Wade* should be overturned found 65 percent saying no, while just 29 percent said yes, although a second question spotlighted the range within the *Roe*-upholding 65 percent. Among the entire sample, 35 percent said abortion should be generally available, but 23 percent chose "more limited"; 31 percent said illegal except in cases of rape, incest, or saving the mother's life; and 9 percent said abortion should never be available.[68] Some of the pro–*Roe v. Wade* majority is soft. Even so, loss of *Roe v. Wade* protection to new judicial appointees approved by the religious right became an increasingly tangible apprehension.

Some polls even showed red states turning a little more purple, while purple states took on bluer tones. The idea of theocrats marshaling government intervention, as in the Schiavo case, struck a negative chord. Many Europeans found the confrontation hard to fathom, perceiving that in some way the United States was still locked in the religious militance and radical sectarianism that had riven sixteenth-century and seventeenth-century Europe, but then had faded into the Enlightenment of the eighteenth century. Indeed, colonial America did take in many immigrants born in or descended from those radical streams—Puritans; English, Dutch, and German Anabaptists; Mennonites; Amish; Moravians; Quakers; French Huguenots; Scottish and Scotch-Irish covenanters. Thereafter, as chapter 4 discussed, the American population kept the radical and sectarian pot ever bubbling. The United States also took in large numbers of Methodist, Baptist, and other nonconformist immigrants from nineteenth-century England, including numerous radicals— English converts won to polygamous Mormonism and Plymouth Brethren followers of John Nelson Darby, the nineteenth-century trailblazer for the *Left Behind* series.

No longer, as in the 1970s and early 1980s, could the rightward movement in the early 2000s be characterized as simply one of people of faith countermobilizing against the disdain for religion shown by elements of secular liberalism. New forces were being interwoven. These included the institutional rise of the religious right, the intensifying biblical focus on the Middle East, and the deepening of insistence on church-government collaboration within the GOP electorate. By the 2000s the moral counterrevolution had manifestly fallen short in some areas—control of pornography, the sexual revolution, and the erosion of families (divorce rates were actually highest in born-again states). Even so, the ascent of the Christian right, George W. Bush's emergence as its leader, and the surprising religification of the Republican party shifted the relative danger away from secular excesses to the influence of the new mass power base and its motivations.

We have seen the unfortunate precedents. Militant Catholicism helped undo the Roman and Spanish empires; the Calvinist fundamentalism of the Dutch Reformed Church helped to block any eighteenth-century Dutch renewal; and the interplay of imperialism and evangelicalism led pre-1914 Britain into a bloodbath and global decline. The possibility that something similar could propel the United States into war in the Middle East—and that once again, God would decline to rescue his chosen people—is the precedent that needs to be kept in mind.

In the meantime, though, there are plenty of people in the financial community who have their own considerable worries about a different kind of Armageddon.

Financialization: A Volckerian Götterdämmerung?

By 2005, as U.S. wise men of great financial wealth or the exalted status of former Federal Reserve Board chairmen—the Warren Buffetts, Paul Volckers, et al.—watched the global markets in Wagnerian contemplation, waiting for the clichéd fat lady to sing, no one could deny the dramatic circumstances of potential economic crisis. Even Alan Greenspan had commented on "exotic forms of adjustable-rate mortgages" and the uncertain dangers posed by hedge funds.[69]

For the U.S. financial system to avoid a crisis would take a miracle, some thought, because policies by the Bush White House, the GOP Congress, and a sympathetic Federal Reserve Board had brought about excesses ranging from huge tax cuts and deficit finance to deregulation and growth of a massive credit bubble. In this context, a half-dozen circumstances and practices—the fodder, perhaps, for some future book in the style of *Manias, Panics, and Crashes*—stood out for speculative conflagrational potential.

Several of the new derivative instruments were front and center. Collateralized debt obligations (CDOs) became popular in the late 1990s, conjoining the unprecedented total of consumer borrowing—papers of indebtedness incurred for purchases that ranged from cars and boats to face-lifts—with the financial sector's own innovative packaging talents. In a descriptive nutshell, CDOs in the multiple millions of dollars are pasted together by banks and investment firms from almost any kind of debt that lenders are willing to sell. These confections are then sliced up—"tranched" is Wall Street's preferred word—and sold off by risk levels, according to mathematical models of how they will behave in the aggregate. The high-priced guesswork, not surprisingly, commands rich fees. One investment firm, for example, set aside a $100 million litigation fund in 2005 to deal with a federal securities regulatory challenge into how it determined a fair value and priced a CDO package. By then, CDOs represented a huge, multitrillion-dollar market. However, because they were complicated and sold only institution to institution, skeptics worried about dangerous illiquidity in a panic.

The second major variety of credit derivatives, so-called credit-default swaps (CDSs), elicited this distillation from one investment banker: "Credit default swaps offered a way to 'short' corporate bonds, or bet on them to decline in value, without paying high borrowing costs for money to actually purchase and then sell them. Moreover, they provided a way to buy and sell the perceived credit risk of a corporation without actually exchanging the underlying corporate bonds."[70] These, too, grew from peanuts in the mid-1990s to multiple trillions in less than a decade.

Regulation of what had become a $5 trillion over-the-counter credit-derivatives market by 2005 was negligible in the United States. In Britain, though, a more vigilant Financial Services Authority warned that the volume of these arrangements had caused banks to fall behind in documenting and confirming the complex terms involved.[71] Unfortunately, the lesson of financial history—that debacles often involve the untested cutting edge of innovation, such as Enron in 2001, and so-called portfolio insurance back in 1987—is that credit derivatives could play a role if push came to shove. Warren Buffett, as we have seen, called them "a time bomb."

Which brings us to hedge funds, the coteries of clever people who make money by playing angles too chancy for regulated institutions. Hedge funds are not regulated. But between 1990 and 2005, they multiplied from only a few hundred to about 8,500 in the United States alone, many rushing boldly onto the credit-derivatives playing field.[72] In mid-2005 the Fitch credit-ratings company issued a special report: "Hedge Funds: An Emerging Force in the Global Credit Markets." Estimating that 30 percent of the $8.4 trillion credit-derivatives market was controlled by the funds, Fitch saw potential for "a far-reaching liquidity squeeze and price dislocation across multiple credit markets due to hedge funds' presence."[73]

The interaction between the hedge funds and the banks they borrow from could also be electric. Because they borrow so much money to pursue their strategies, the hedge funds have been among the best customers of the big banks. The banks have indulged them, just as several indulged Enron to the point of being almost co-conspirators.[74]

The housing and mortgage markets, especially after 2001, had blended into the larger financialization of America in multiple and unnerving ways. Simply put, for many people, homes had become vehicles of household financing—"my home is my castle" giving way to "my home is my ATM machine." As such, and with the collusion of the Federal Reserve Board, homes became financial assets in everything but statistical classification. Beyond that, they became tools of speculative finance in that persons mortgaging or refinancing had to choose from a dizzying array of options, many of which held out, in credit-card fashion, unusual attractiveness in the first months or years. In June 2005 Chairman Greenspan deplored some of the most egregious, allowing that "the dramatic increase in the prevalence of interest-only loans, as well as the introduction of other relatively exotic forms of adjustable-rate mortgages, are developments of particular concern."[75]

In fact, reported *The Washington Post,* there were some two hundred different kinds of mortgage products on the market, differentiated by interest-rate schedules, down-payment requirements, payback terms, fees, and potential penalties. Douglas Duncan, the chief economist of the Mortgage Bankers Association, told the newspaper that the "exotic" loan referred to by Greenspan was probably the "option adjustable rate mortgage," which permits borrowers to decide themselves how much to pay, how long the loan term should be, and when they can convert from a fixed rate to a variable rate or back again.[76]

Even credit cards were tied into the speculative side of finances. For several years issuers had been merchandising credit cards tied to home-equity lines of credit.[77] This took place at the same time as home purchases and mortgages themselves were taking on speculative characteristics.

Worriers over the possibility that the United States had exchanged a stock-market bubble for an even larger credit bubble even had their own Web sites where the latest developments and nuances could be monitored with professional aplomb or trepidation.[78] History, to be sure, backed the case for trepidation.

While these examples peel back only the first layers of the speculative onion, as opposed to showing a full cross section, they do capture its rank flavor. Between 2000 and the market bottom in 2002, when U.S. stocks lost $7 trillion of their $15.5 trillion value, home values held up and then spurted ahead. To critics, the rescue was essentially a rebubbling. Should a credit and financial collapse follow that second stage in the manner that Volcker and others feared, stock and home prices would presumably sink together, making that second downturn the more destructive of the two. In which case, imploding consumer debt and the harsh provisions of the new federal bankruptcy code could interact to yoke middle-class debtors in the quasi-indentured status Democrats predicted.

To those Americans who say that it can't happen here, the answer is that something almost as harsh did overtake Britain in the 1940s and the Dutch Republic in the 1770s and 1780s. A generation earlier, few would have believed such comedowns possible. Such a painful upheaval overtakes a leading world economic power only when it is losing or has lost that global laurel. Whether that time is at hand for the United States or still decades away, no one can say. On the other hand, in light of the trends in manufacturing and the credit markets alike, there is little doubt left about the next dominant continent, Asia, and the next leading world economic power—China, possibly in the 2030s, barring some extraordinary disruption. This prospect, coupled with China's emergent role as a leading U.S. creditor, is part of what has to warn Americans, just as the surging economic growth of both the United States and Germany became a warning to Britain in the 1890s.

Globally, the prospect has two faces. The first, of course, is the threat to the United States and the well-being of its people. The final act of a Volckerian opera, in which the fat lady of misfortune finally does sing, could be tragic not just for many in the United States, but conceivably for world stability. At the same time, there is a fascination—not least in the

United States—with the implications of a new economic supremacy in Asia. Every year brings more attention to the rising skyline of Shanghai and China's extraordinary industrial growth, to the emergence of India as the communications back office of the English-speaking world, to the emergence of South Korea as the world's most advanced broadband telecommunications society, to the location of the world's tallest buildings in Kuala Lumpur, Malaysia, to the world's first "seven-star" hotel in Dubai, to the urban model of Singapore, to the money being made in Middle Eastern stock markets, and to the growing belief in the West as well as the East that global leadership will pass to Asia by 2040 or even 2030. The belief held in some Asian circles—that the balance of power and wealth is shifting back to Asia for the first time since unbeatable Western warships passed through the Strait of Malacca in the fifteenth century—could well turn out to be true. Not a few Asian Americans, educated or even born in the United States, are returning to grasp a future in Taiwan, Korea, India, and China.

In the Middle East, the oil price surge that grew in 2003–2005 after the Bush administration failed in its Iraq-centered oil policy has elevated what was already a major new wave of regional economic development. Industrialization is growing, bolstered by oil and natural gas availability. Finance is becoming more locally oriented—Middle Eastern stock markets were among the world's best performing in 2004–2005—and less tributary to the United States and Britian. Cities and resorts are becoming sophisticated enough that tourism and duty-free shopping are booming from Bahrain to Abu Dhabi. The next decades should be extraordinary.

The economic realignment favoring southwest and central Asia that flows from recent and projected oil and natural gas prices already resembles that occurring in East Asia because of the migration of manufacturing, not least from North America. If, as some believe, some 30 to 35 percent of world energy will come from natural gas by the 2020s, the principal beneficiaries will be major gas producers—Qatar, Iran, Turkmenistan, and Russia hold more than half of the known reserves, but Venezuela and North Africa are also important. The energy outflow of American dollars, in short, can only burgeon under an oil and gas regime. Besides the currency flowing to East Asia and the Middle East, two other buildups deserve note: Russia's international reserves ballooned from $18 billion at the end of 1997 to $124 billion as 2004 closed, principally because of oil and gas, while India's jumped from $24 billion to $126 billion in the same period.[79] Computer software and office-job outsourcing played major roles for India and probably will continue to do so. Even in biotechnology, India is surging, with local publications crowing about how secular Hinduism is compatible with science while evangelical constituencies cripple U.S. stem-cell research.[80] With all of these transfers occuring or anticipated, by the 2010s it is hard to see what forces—except possibly military forces—could keep the no-longer-almighty dollar enthroned as the world's reserve currency.

By the 2020s, if not earlier, China is expected to become the principal economic rival of the United States. The dynamics of this rise have been pursued by others and—save for U.S. politics and the dearth of capable national leadership—are beyond the scope of this book. Still, a few amplifications are in order. To begin with the challenge, economic and growth comparisons between China and the United States are complicated by the former's massively undervalued currency and huge purchasing-power disparities, but two major financial firms, Goldman Sachs and HSBC (Hong Kong and Shanghai Banking Corporation), have ventured predictions. In late 2003, Goldman anticipated that China would pass Japan in GDP by 2015 and would overtake the United States by 2040; in 2005, HSBC calculated that bank assets in China would overtake those of the United States by 2034. None of this is far-fetched. Based on 2003 data, one analyst pointed out that China consumed half of the world's cement and one-third of its steel, and is now the world's biggest market for mobile phones and the second biggest for personal computers.[81]

The above estimates may be conservative. At Washington's Economic Strategy Institute, Clyde Prestowitz, citing the Goldman Sachs analysis and a kindred set of evaluations by the International Monetary Fund, suggested that if analysts eschew converting Chinese yuan and U.S. dollars based on exchange rates and instead calculate "in terms of China's domestic purchasing power . . . its GDP could be effectively as large as America's by 2025."[82] This could bring a serious U.S.–China contest by the 2010s.

To be sure, many things can go wrong with such forecasts—wars, energy shortages, stock-market crashes, and economic depressions. On the other hand, if some British expert had contended in 1850 that by 1895, the United States would lead the world in manufacturing, he would have been correct—and despite the dislocations of the Civil War, several stock-market panics, and the depression of 1873. The supporting argument to make for China's ascent rests on several basic strengths, from its saving rate and technological history down to its current rapid rise in scientific capacity. "Impressive" is too weak an adjective.

As of 2005, China had a savings rate in the 43 percent range, while the savings rate in the United States had turned negative—savings were being drawn down. On top of which, in 2003, China passed the United States as the top global recipient of foreign direct investment.[83] Another important factor is China's long-standing talent for technology. As one U.S. business publication set forth, "History shows that inventiveness is firmly planted in China's DNA: gunpowder, rocketry, wheel-barrows, cast iron, compasses, paddle-wheel boats, block-printing, stirrups, paper-making and mechanical clocks—all came from China, often centuries before they appeared in the West."[84]

Within a generation or so, China may well resume its pioneering. A 2005 study by Harvard economist Richard Freeman, director of the Labor Studies Program at the National Bureau of Economic Research, documents how U.S. technology is threatened by a dramatic realignment of scientific specialists and research facilities away from the United States to Europe and especially Asia. In 2001, he says, the European Union gave 40 percent more doctorates in science and engineering than the United States did, and China's gains are even steeper: "China is expected to surpass the United States in numbers of engineering doctorates by 2010. At the college level, statistics show a waning interest among U.S. students in science-related careers; in 2001, only 17 percent of all bachelor degrees in the United States were in natural science and engineering, compared to a world average of 27 percent and a Chinese average of 52 percent." Equally to the point, Freeman worries that a combination of advanced science and low-cost labor, which he calls "human-resource leapfrogging" will weaken the U.S. global trade position, forcing difficult adjustments in the U.S. economy and labor force.[85]

In the meantime, the difficulties facing the United States in oil supply, burgeoning debt, loss of dollar hegemony, and the ultimately unbearable burden of Medicare and Social Security suggest their own harsh timetable. In part I of this book I suggested that a number of countdowns—by oil geologists, the big oil firms themselves, currency watchers, ecologists, and counters of public and private debt, as well as the end-times religious element—had already become powerful, if rarely acknowledged, pressures in the making of U.S. domestic and foreign policy.

These various trends and countdowns include too many different circumstances to lend themselves to an actual chart, so perhaps an imagined one is best. First, put in one column the earlier estimates as to when China might or might not start to catch up with and even pass the United States in gross domestic product. Next to that sequence put a middle-range forecast for several decades—the 2010s, probably—when global oil production outside OPEC might peak. In the next imaginary column, visualize two related trend lines—the cost of oil per barrel and the annual expense of the growing amount of oil and gas the United States will have to import. The adjacent column should list the prospects over the next fifteen years for the U.S. current account deficit—and one column beyond that, the reader can mentally jot down the unfolding prospects for the U.S. dollar during the same stressful and high-powered time frame.

Beyond these, of course, it will also matter what happens to Social Security, Medicare, the federal budget deficit, and the various tabulations of U.S. public, private, and total credit-market debt. The 2010s could easily be a very troubled decade, and the 2020s after them. Many cautionary time frames are converging just at a time when the political leadership of the United States—much like that of past leading economic world powers in their later days—is not in the most competent hands.

Secularism, Sclerotic Politics, and Disillusionment

But let us briefly return to religion. If there is one current description that characterizes Spain, Holland, and Britain in the early twenty-first century, we can safely exclude "religious." The fervor that professed chosen nationhood or marched to an evangelical drumbeat is long gone. Less than one-fifth of the people in these nations still attend weekly religious services. Spain recently legalized gay marriage; today's Church of England casts a small shadow compared with its historic cathedrals; and the Netherlands still supposedly has a Dutch Reformed "Bible Belt" near Amersfoort, twenty miles southeast of Amsterdam, but a tourist would be hard-pressed to find it.

Few historians have paid much attention to the loss of faith, but one explanation may be safely ventured. Organized religion did not profit from the great disillusionment when the various chosen peoples turned out not to be. For Britain, the lesson followed a century in which British Christianity had moved in many of the directions that we have later seen in the United States—evangelical religion, global missionary intensity, end-times anticipation, and sense of biblical prophecy beginning to come together in the Middle East. Indeed, recent studies of British religion during the 1875–1914 period have also identified major growths of orientalism, spiritualism, and even Victorian-era speaking in tongues, akin to recent U.S. trends, save that the British version of other-directed speech was occultism and a fascination with mediums who would have remote experiences reported from the "other side" and putting seekers in touch with departed relatives and friends.[86]

But when the Armageddon of 1914–1918 brought forty million deaths instead of Christ's return, the embarrassment was not limited to flag-bedecked Anglican churches or nonconformist chapels that had joined in the parade. Religion in general seemed to have failed, and British church attendance shrank—and then shrank again. It is not hard to imagine something similar happening in the United States by 2030 or 2040 as two or three decades of cynicism claim religious as well as economic and political victims. Evangelicalism under George W. Bush probably expanded to levels of adherence and belief that it will be unable to sustain much further into the twenty-first century. However, that will certainly not happen overnight, because the end-times imagery of the early twenty-first century—from tsunamis and terrible hurricanes and the AIDS crisis to the rise of Iraq, followed by China, the trauma of oil, and even financial panic—lends itself too well to religious end-times explanation to dissipate in the face of anything much less than a World War I equivalent.

In the meantime much of the rest of the world—even Europe and to a smaller extent Britain, Canada, and Australia—has come to talk about the United States' becoming undependable and even an altogether different culture from itself. The widespread biblical and *Left Behind* sort of religiosity is often cited as the explanation, although few foreign observers comprehend its contours or depth. In the first wave of world disillusionment with the United States in late 2002 and 2003 as the invasion of Iraq loomed, international polling by the Pew Center and others found many respondents singling out George W. Bush for blame, not Americans as a whole.[87]

The first international polls taken as the United States was preparing to invade Iraq surprised Americans with findings that most foreigners were hostile to the invasion, but focused much of their negativism on George W. Bush. By 2004 and 2005, however, the result became hostile in a deeper way. The Pew Global Attitudes Study for 2004, based on some sixty-five hundred interviews in eight countries in addition to the United States, found that respondents in every nation but the United States said the war in Iraq had hurt, not helped, the war on terrorism. Only in Britain did a majority of those queried believe the U.S. war on terror was sincerely directed against international terrorism; others thought it was insincere and principally aimed at controlling Middle Eastern oil. People from four participating countries belonging to NATO—allies like Britain, Germany, Turkey, and France—favored Western Europe's taking a more independent approach to diplomatic and security affairs and reducing its association with the United States.[88]

In 2005, the Pew Global Attitudes probe found new dimensions of dissatisfaction. Startling majorities said their views of the United States had become less favorable because of the reelection of George W. Bush (77 percent in Germany, 75 percent in Canada, 74 percent in France, 62 percent in Britain). In France, the Netherlands, Britain, and Germany, majorities or pluralities said the United States was too religious, and most participants favored the emergence of some nation or multinational union as a military counter to the United States. When respondents were asked to indicate favorable or unfavorable attitudes toward five specific nations—the United States, Germany, France, Japan, and China—the British, French, Germans, Spanish, Dutch, and Russians gave their lowest marks to the United States. Only Canadians did not, but their criticism flared up in other ways, because Canadians gave Americans the highest negatives for being violent and greedy.[89] Not only have the last several years witnessed the most global defeat for the U.S. public diplomacy and the nation's reputation since the interplay of defeat in Vietnam and the Watergate scandal in the 1970s, but the direct tie to the Bush administration is unmistakable.

Indeed, the divisions within the U.S. electorate make it difficult to suggest that Bush is unique. Whereas Americans who declined to vote for Bush generally agreed that U.S. policy has made enemies and disaffected much of the world, the bulk of Bush's huge evangelical, fundamentalist, and Pentecostal constituency did not think so. Its members believe that the United States remains both strong and respected. The problem, to an extent, is that within the United States they have their own communications system and culture built around belief, both religious and scriptural. Many of the evangelical, fundamentalist, and Pentecostal churches, especially the megachurches, become the principal source of both belief and information in their congregations' lives. Broadcast, publishing, and direct-mail empires have grown up around these fellowships and communities, creating umbrellas against the effects of secular communications. The viewpoints of so-called sophisticates have little access to the minds of the faithful.

Thus, for example, majorities of Americans continue to believe in Noah's Ark and the Book of Genesis version of creation even though a recent report by genome researchers found that chimpanzees and humans share a very similar genetic blueprint—a 96 percent overlap, which scientists call overwhelming evidence of Darwin's theory of evolution.[90] Similarly, even though the major oil companies have started to concede that a peak of world oil production may be close, true believers continue to believe that God will provide. If holders of these religious views were not a very large, albeit minority, bloc of the population, George W. Bush would not have been reelected. Their ranks may be close to their peak, but that prediction cannot be offered as fact.

Difficult politics thus lies ahead. Unfortunately, the history of past leading world economic powers is that they have not been able to throw up the sort of leadership needed to reverse the tides involved. In consequence, the nations in the process of being dethroned as the world's economic leader have faced a difficult period of twenty to forty years, at very least, in making the transition from yesterday's hegemony to a lesser but eventually comfortable role in a differently shaped world.

In the United States, elements of economic sclerosis seem to go hand in hand with the political variety. In mid-2005, for the first time since measurement began, household incomes failed to increase for five straight years. Median pretax income, said the Census Bureau, was at its lowest point, adjusted to inflation, since 1997.[91] Meanwhile, buoyed by federal policy, those enjoying the top 1 percent of U.S. incomes continued to increase their share of the national pie. When Federal Reserve chairman Greenspan acknowledged that 7 percent of personal disposable income in 2004 had come from households borrowing against home values—up from 3 percent in 2000 and 1 percent in 1994—he followed an earlier and equally telling admission: that asset values had become a prime focus of Washington decision making. "Our forecasts," said Greenspan, "are becoming increasingly driven by asset price changes."[92] Edwardian England and mid-eighteenth-century Holland shared some of those preoccupations.

American energy policy had its own ennui and interest-group commitments. Ineptitude in Iraq worsened matters, but the government took no serious measures to curb public fuel consumption—or, for that matter, to curb attitudes that offended oil- and gas-supplying nations, from Canada and Venezuela to the Muslim Middle East. In 2004, *The New York Times* pointed out, the U.S. Energy Information Administration issued forecasts that by 2020 Saudi Arabia would produce 18.2 million barrels of oil a day. No reliable information was involved; the agency "simply assumed that Saudi Arabia would be able to produce whatever the United States needed it to produce."[93]

This complacency had its own precedents. As coal-rich Britian went to war in 1914, it became clear that for a century her politicians had neglected the strategic raw materials, from bauxite and nonferrous metals to oil, that would eventually become vital. Four years after the First World War ended, *The History of the [British] Minister of Munitions* candidly described the severity of the negligence.[94] The early-twenty-first century United States, in turn, seems as neglectful of the Chinese challenge as early-twentieth-century Britain was of the German one. As we have seen, in 2005 polls, the populations of many supposed U.S. allies rated China more favorably than they did the United States, and scarcely a week goes by without reports of the Chinese cutting new oil and gas deals with Canada, Latin America, and the Middle East. On top of this, the Chinese have the sort of pioneering record in energy that the Germans circa 1900 had in science, chemistry, and engineering. Not long ago, one Chinese Web site posted impressive petroleum-related references from the eleventh-century Mengxi Bitan volumes.[95]

The lesson of the past is that timely reforms do not emerge, and deep, unanswerable national issues generate weak and compromising politicians or zealous bumblers. Second-raters certainly dominated in Spain and Holland.[96] So, too, in Britain. Indeed, the collapse of the World War I coalition government under Lloyd George was followed—in the nearly two decades prior to Winston Churchill's wartime accession in 1940—by a quartet of second-rate prime ministers and ineffective coalitions. The four prime ministers in question—Bonar Law, Ramsey MacDonald, Stanley Baldwin, and Neville Chamberlain—are remembered as historical pygmies in the towering company of the Walpoles, Pitts, Gladstones, and Disraelis who governed during Britain's eighteenth- and nineteenth-century ascent. Depending on how history looks back from the 2010s and 2020s, the two Bush presidents could be associated with U.S. decline in a way that the hard-to-remember leaders of ebbing Spain, Holland, and Britain avoided.

The U.S. difficulty in facing these problems has been matched by a similar failure of leadership, incapacity of the parties, and aristocratization or sclerosis of institutions. One troubling aspect is the phenomenon I discussed in 2004 in *American Dynasty*. This is the emergence within the U.S. system of a great-family politics, most vivid on the Republican side in the mediocre father-son inheritance of the Bush dynasty, but also debilitating for the Democratic party. The 2000 Democratic nominee, Vice President Albert Gore, was the son of a U.S. senator and ill positioned to challenge the politics of privileged descent. Bush's challenger in 2004, Massachusetts senator John Kerry, operated under a similar handicap. He was sponsored by another political dynasty, the Kennedys, was married to the rich widow of a Republican U.S. senator, was a member (like George W. Bush) of the elite Skull and Bones society at Yale, and he even possessed another revealing link: he had served as lieutenant governor of Massachusetts under Governor Michael Dukakis, the 1988 Democratic presidential nominee who was defeated by the elder George Bush. Never before had two men who had served simultaneously as governor and lieutenant governor of a state both run for president many years apart, and both been defeated by two different presidents of the other party (to say nothing of two who were father and son).

Inbred and sclerotic vie as appropriate descriptions of the two parties' selection processes. Such continuity of power elites suggests little capacity for challenging the status quo. And of course, the front-running Democrat for the 2008 presidential nomination is Hillary Clinton, from America's third major dynasty.

For those of us who grew up thinking that the United States was different, the prospect that it probably is not different is a chastening one.

AFTERWORD: THE CHANGING REPUBLICAN PRESIDENTIAL COALITION

The two major-party presidential coalitions in the United States are a bit like mutating organisms. They change constantly in a minor way, and occasionally in a major way.

Over the last half century, both coalitions have been undergoing considerable and interrelated upheavals. My own focus has been on the GOP, which had a significant—and ultimately inauspicious—transformation as it took over the South. In *The Emerging Republican Majority,* published in 1969, I argued that the collapse of the old Civil War framework would create a conservative and Republican presidential majority.

This took place in two stages. First, Richard Nixon, with 61 percent of the national vote in 1972, and Ronald Reagan, with 59 percent in 1984, put together the new coalition including the South, while still keeping most of the old support in the North, albeit slipping in places like Vermont, Cape Cod, Princeton, and the fashionable neighborhoods of Manhattan and San Francisco. That slippage on the margins was to be expected. The chart on the facing page shows how much northern support continued in the 1972 and 1984 races.

This ended under the two Bushes. By 1992, after President George H. W. Bush had redefined his politics toward the South and the religious right, he carried none of these nine states. In 2000 and 2004, George W. Bush carried only one—Ohio—and by much smaller margins than Eisenhower, Nixon, or Reagan. The 1992 election, as this book's narrative makes clear, had potential watershed significance. Without Bill Clinton's personal moral shortcomings, the Democrats would have consolidated during the 1990s, won the 2000 election, and been in power to enjoy the rally-round effect after September 11, 2001. Instead, the increasingly

Share of the Total Vote for President Won By

State	Eisenhower, 1956	Nixon, 1972	Reagan, 1984
Massachusetts	59%	45%	51%
New York	61	59	54
New Jersey	65	62	60
Pennsylvania	57	59	53
Ohio	61	60	59
Michigan	56	56	59
Wisconsin	62	61	54
Oregon	55	53	56
California	55	55	58

religion-oriented and southernized Republicans won the White House in 2000 by a Supreme Court decision, enjoyed the rally-round benefits of September 11, and still managed only a narrow victory in 2004.

Bluntly putting it, I believe that a careful electoral analysis shows that what can be called the Bush coalition is too narrow to govern successfully and was empowered to win only by a succession of odd circumstances in both 2000 and 2004. Indeed, by 2006, George W. Bush had followed in his father's unique presidential footsteps—in 1991–1992, the forty-first president had become the first White House incumbent to see his job approval plummet by more than fifty points, and between 2002 and 2005, his son followed suit. Both times, failed policies in Iraq were factors. Over-ambition combined with ineptness and more than a little deceit.

By 2003 and 2004, the professed religiosity of the Republican electorate and congressional leadership, coupled with George W. Bush's periodic asides that God spoke through him, was becoming ever more defining of the GOP coalition and what it stood for. Prior to 2003, many of the new votes that the Republicans gained from religion took place in an essentially supportive crisis climate. The horrors of September 11 had fed a sense of end times among the faithful while seeming to legitimize the younger Bush's biblical language and righteous nationalism. During this period, the theocratic implications, the depressing relation of Bush policies to aspects of the *Left Behind* series, and the pandering associated with the 2005 Schiavo episode were still little perceived.

By 2005, the concern about the influence of the religious right visible in 2004 had taken hold, both in the polls and in national discussion. Thus, although no one can be sure what issues will dominate the next several presidential elections, it is useful to look at the Republican presidential coalition from a standpoint of religion, denominational biases, interest-group power, theological correctness, and the consequent national vulnerabilities these entail.

As map 4 on page 199 shows, the red-state-versus-blue-state dimension of the 2000 and 2004 elections can plausibly be viewed in religious terms. For the Republicans, the old mainline denominations are no longer the pillars. Map 4 emphasizes three new regional underpinnings—the Southern Baptist Convention, the Mormons (Latter-Day Saints), and the Lutheran denominations that capture upper Midwest Protestantism. The fourth element, too dispersed to map well although most numerous in the South, Middle West, and West, includes (1) the Pentecostals (notably the Assemblies of God) and (2) the so-called primitive and holiness denominations. The latter include the Churches of Christ, the Christian Churches, the Church of God, and the Church of the Nazarene.

This Republican presidential coalition is weakest, in turn, in states with relatively large Catholic populations, sizable Jewish constituencies, high percentages of nonbelievers, and smaller Protestant populations with large mainline ratios (Episcopalian, Presbyterian [USA], Congregationalist [UCC], and Methodist). States meeting these cultural criteria concentrate in the Northeast, the Great Lakes, and the Pacific coast.

The battleground or "new border" states can also be located by a religious calculus. In the Northeast, Pennsylvania has the closest equivalent of an in-state Bible Belt and is not out of reach for the religious Republican coalition. Next-door Ohio is the ultimate swing state, with the Cleveland area—two hundred years ago the "Western Reserve" of Connecticut—trending against the GOP coalition in 2004. Meanwhile, the Republicans gained among white born-again Protestants in southern Ohio and among rural and small-town Catholic and Lutheran Germans in the state's west. As noted in chapter 6, the Southern Baptist Convention is mounting an expensive religious mobilization and conversion campaign in metropolitan Cleveland. This should benefit the GOP, as do the flows into southern and central Ohio from Kentucky, Tennessee, and West Virginia.

In 2004, West Virginia, Kentucky, Tennessee, and Missouri, the border states of 1861–1865 Civil War politics, lost that marginality because of their high ratios of Southern Baptists, Pentecostals, and holiness-denomination and other sectarian Protestants. Culturally, of course, John Kerry was a weak Democratic nominee. Still, if religion stays central and outweighs the economy, these states would probably again be more Republican than the nation as a whole.

In both 2000 and 2004, Florida was the tightest state in the South for the GOP, being another cultural crossroads. However, religion doesn't seem to have been a particular net plus or minus.

Moving elsewhere, a slight caveat is necessary in describing Lutheranism as the religious linchpin in a bloc of states including Wisconsin, Minnesota, Iowa, Nebraska, and the Dakotas. Some distinctions must be made among the several Lutheran denominations. The Evangelical Lutheran Church in America is centrist and more Scandinavian (especially Swedish and Norwegian) than German. By contrast, the more conservative and pro-Bush Missouri Synod and Wisconsin Synod Lutherans are predominantly German.

While there are no recent studies to cite, my sense is that German ethnicity may have a closer correlation than Lutheranism per se with upper middle western support for religiously infused conservatism in the 2000 and 2004 elections. Catholic German rural counties in the region, back in the late nineteenth century largely Democratic, began trending Republican in response to two world wars, consolidating that sentiment during the Reagan years. They are religious, traditional, and nationalistic, with an America First slant and a distaste for foreign aid and entanglement. In 2004, Bush did very well in these areas, as he did among Catholics and Lutherans but perhaps even more among the various German-sprung sects—Old Order Amish, Hutterites, Moravians, Mennonites, and the like—that are often found interspersed in counties with high German Catholic or Lutheran populations.

Behaviorally, if Wisconsin, Minnesota, Iowa, Nebraska, and the Dakotas represent the region with the nation's highest ratios of Lutherans—and they do—they also represent the region with by far and away the nation's highest ratios of Germans. For those interested, a county-by-county map of the intensity of German-American population appears on p. 535 of my 1999 book *The Cousins' Wars*. In the first three of these states, all close in 2004, my guess is that Bush easily carried the Germans (Catholic, Lutheran, and sectarian) and probably lost the heavily Lutheran but more liberal Norwegians. However, if the U.S. involvement in Iraq continues to be embarrassing to Republicans through 2008, they could pay a major price among upper midwestern Germans, who tend to turn against such overseas imbroglios if they drag out. Ross Perot, among other things a critic of U.S. Middle Eastern policy, won a huge 1992 protest vote in the upper Midwest.

As for the West, part of it is drawn to a conservative religious coalition, and part of it is not. The Pacific coastal areas of Washington, Oregon, and California are among the most secular portions of the United States, especially from Seattle and Portland south to San Francisco Bay and Silicon Valley. The Catholic, Jewish, and mainline Protestant ratios are also too high to support a conservative evangelical and fundamentalist religious coalition. However, the eastern interior sections of these states are more conservative and more like the Rocky Mountain states. On balance, though, Bush lost all three states in 2000 and 2004.

The mountain states—Arizona, New Mexico, Colorado, Utah, Nevada, Idaho, and Montana—all supported Bush in 2004 (and all but New Mexico did in 2000). Nevertheless, it is an oversimplification to say they all support a conservative religious coalition. Those most committed in that direction—Utah, Idaho, and Wyoming—all rank among the nation's most conservative states. Utah and Idaho do so because of their heavy Mormon ratios, and Wyoming because its oil and ranching combine with a conservative Protestantism.

Two of the mountain states stand to be marginal. Nevada's rapid growth and substantial Catholic, Jewish, and California émigré populations tilt its culture toward California. However, it also has substantial conservative (Mormon and Southern Baptist) religious populations. Like Ohio and Florida, Nevada is a demographic crossroads. New Mexico is marginal, partly because an atypical concentration of Hispanic Catholics offsets the Southern Baptist coloration of eastern New Mexico's "Little Texas."

Montana is another crossroads, between the plains and the mountains, but leans conservative nationally. Arizona and Colorado, by contrast, are increasingly sophisticated states with progressive urban centers as well as Mormon, Southern Baptist, and other evangelical populations.

In both 2000 and 2004, Arizona and Colorado briefly looked like swing states before coming down on the Bush side of the electoral ledger.

Revealingly, as the fifty states sort out on a cultural and religious basis, the Republican coalition is starting to look like the reverse of the one that existed for generations after the Civil War. Not only does it rest on the Greater South instead of on Greater New England, but within key states like Ohio and Florida, Republican party internal strength in presidential elections has reversed from the old Yankee geography of the 1940s and 1950s—higher support in northern Ohio and in Yankee-settled south Florida. The new pattern involves greater Republican strength in southern and western Ohio and in "cracker" northern Florida.

In short, the GOP support base in the North is slowly moving toward the constituencies most comfortable with an essentially southern-leaning and religious Republican politics. However, this is an innately narrowed constituency, kept from any unnecessary broadening that might dilute its ideological and theological commitments. By pursuing these views, the new religious coalition draws attention to its narrowness and controversial theological mainsprings, which must then increase the controversy and electoral backlash—unless, of course, another war or set of terrorist attacks can somehow restore the good-versus-evil moral and religious climate that existed in 2002.

But this begs a second important question: whether the GOP coalition is fatally flawed from a national-interest standpoint. I think so, but not because of the basic cultural conservatism that did so well in the Nixon and Reagan landslides of 1972 and 1984. Both those coalitions had a flavoring of populist conservatism, but nothing resembling the current mix.

Never before has a U.S. political coalition been so dominated by an array of outsider religious denominations caught up in biblical morality, distrust of science, and a global imperative of political and religious evangelicalism. These groups may represent only a quarter to a third of the U.S. population, but they are mobilized, as the turnout in 2004 showed.

They also have important allies. As we have seen, the financial sector—and a large majority of the richest Americans—understandably finds the alliance convenient. Many of the fundamentalist, evangelical, and Pentecostal faithful are too caught up in religion, theology, and personal salvation to pay much attention to economics, and they are easily rallied for self-help, free enterprise, and disbelief in government. With much of the GOP's low- and middle-income electorate listening to conservative preachers, the corporate and financial agenda not only prevails but often runs riot.

For the oil and gas industries, however, the alliance is a two-edged sword. True, the religious right and oil have developed a working compatibility in states like Louisiana, Texas, Oklahoma, and Colorado, and the religious-right leadership generally disdains environmentalists and alternative-energy backers. Still, much of the real world as seen by cosmopolitan energy geologists and executives cannot be publicly described in Republican national politics. The Book of Genesis and the *Left Behind* series both get in the way. We cannot be running out of oil; God makes the climate; and White House explanations about what the United States is doing in Iraq or elsewhere in the Middle East have to square with the fight between good and evil as the end times draw nigh. Much like intervention in Iraq, national energy strategy takes weak shape in a vacuum of candor.

To be sure—as so many believers are sure—this time the prophecies could truly be on the verge of fulfillment. History, however, suggests that if the hour was not at hand for Rome, Spain, the Dutch Republic, or Britain circa 1914, despite their convictions of God's favor and heaven's special attention, then God may also spurn his Republican faithful in and out of Washington. And should religious excess and overambition become part of an epitaph for the twenty-first-century United States, as it did for some of the others, the current GOP national coalition will share in the ignominy.

This is not a cheery thought. In one way or another, I have been studying and writing about the emerging Republican presidential coalition for half a century now. I particularly regret this latest evolution under the two Bush presidents, and my last three major books—*Wealth and Democracy* (2002), *American Dynasty* (2004), and *American Theocracy* (2006)—could be said to represent a trilogy of indictments, something I never imagined when I started writing *The Emerging Republican Majority* back in 1966.

ACKNOWLEDGMENTS

Like all books, this one has had helpers and facilitators. I would like to thank my wife, Martha, for her help in obtaining federal economic data; my agents, Bill Leigh and Wes Neff; my editor at Viking, Wendy Wolf; and senior production editor Bruce Giffords, who surmounts production obstacles.

For religious data, I must cite the research and compilations of the Glenmary Research Center and John Green of the University of Akron. On the economic side, my thanks go to *Barron's* and several investment firms, most notably Goldman Sachs Global Investment Research, for its 1974–2004 data on the growth of the U.S. financial sector.

NOTES

Preface

1. Leading world economic powers have seen homosexuality become an issue in their later years. For the Dutch and the British, the scandals of the later years are mentioned in general histories. However, controversies in Spain are little discussed. See Daniel Eisenberg, "Research Topics in Hispanic Gay and Lesbian Studies," *Lesbian and Gay Studies Newsletter*, users.ipfw.edu/jehle/deisenbe.
2. William Safire, *The New Language of Politics* (New York: Collier Books, 1972), p. 273.
3. *Time*, February 14, 2005.
4. Bill Moyers, speech to the Center for Health and Global Environment at Harvard Medical School, December 4, 2004.

Chapter 1: Fuel and National Power

1. "Oil," www.answers.com/topic/oil.
2. Clifford Ashley, *The Yankee Whaler* (Boston: Houghton Mifflin, 1938), p. 9.
3. "17th Century Dutch and Flemish Art," www.theotherside.uk.
4. Jonathan Israel, *Dutch Primacy in World Trade, 1585–1740* (Oxford, U.K.: Clarendon, 1989), p. 357.
5. "The History of Whaling and the International Whaling Commission," World Wildlife Federation, www.panda.org.
6. Federal Writers' Project, *Massachusetts* (Cambridge, Mass.: The Riverside Press, 1937), p. 561.
7. Ibid., p. 286.
8. Ashley, *Yankee Whaler*, p. 41.
9. Brian Black, *Petrolia* (Baltimore: The Johns Hopkins University Press, 2000), p. 14.
10. Ibid., p. 17.
11. Sarah Searight, *The British in the Middle East* (New York: Atheneum, 1970), p. 126.
12. Simon Schama, *The Embarrassment of Riches* (Berkeley: University of California Press, 1988), p. 75.
13. Ibid., p. 35.
14. "The Evolution of the Dutch Windmill," Radio Netherlands, www2.rnw.nl/rnw/en/features/dutchhorizons.
15. Israel, *Dutch Primacy*, p. 357.
16. "Dutch Windmill."
17. Ibid.
18. John Nef, *The Rise of the British Coal Industry* (London: Routledge, 1932).
19. Sir John Clapham, *A Concise Economic History of Britain* (Cambridge, U.K.: Cambridge University Press, 1957), p. 231.

20. Barbara Freese, *Coal* (New York: Penguin, 2004), p. 69.
21. John Stevenson, *British Society: 1914–1945* (London: Penguin, 1984), p. 22.
22. Correlli Barnett, *The Collapse of British Power* (London: Sutton Publishing, 1997), p. 88.
23. Ibid., p. 87.
24. Adrian Vaughn, *Railwaymen, Politics, and Money* (London: John Murray, 1997), p. 170.
25. Aaron Friedberg, *The Weary Titan* (Princeton, N.J.: Princeton University Press, 1988), p. 87.
26. Michael Sisson and Philip French, eds., *The Age of Austerity* (London: Penguin, 1964), p. 258.
27. Freese, *Coal*, p. 137.
28. H. C. Allen, *Great Britain and the United States* (New York: St. Martin's Press, 1955), p. 218.
29. "Extreme Oil: The History," Public Broadcasting System, September 2004, www.pbs.org/wnet/extremeoil/history/pre-history.html.
30. Ida Tarbell, *The History of the Standard Oil Company*, vol. 1 (New York: McClure, Phillips, 1904).
31. Anthony Sampson, *The Seven Sisters* (New York: Bantam, 1976), p. 25.
32. John Nichols, *Dick* (New York: The New Press, 2004), p. 17.
33. Sampson, *Seven Sisters*, pp. 22–23.
34. Matthew Yeomans, *Oil* (New York, The New Press, 2004), p. 41.
35. Ibid., pp. 26–37.
36. Charles W. Schmidt, "Possibilities in the Pipeline," *Environmental Health Perspectives*, January 2002.
37. In the 1940s, Hubbert turned his studies of the life cycle of oil fields into a mathmatical model predicting that U.S. oil production would peak sometime between 1965 and 1970. His thesis was presented at a national conference of petroleum geologists in 1956, few of whom believed it.
38. The Association for the Study of Peak Oil and Gas, based in Uppsala, Sweden, maintains a Web site with few if any equals in monitoring global developments and analyses of the peaks or prospective peaks in global oil and gas production, as well as those of individual nations. Its Web site is www.peakoil.net.
39. During 2004 and 2005, expert opinion swung widely, but the trend in 2005 has been toward skepticism of Russian output potential. In *Twilight in the Desert* (pp. 304–7), Matthew Simmons likens the uncertain future of Samotlor, the principal Siberian oil field, to what he believes are the overstated prospects of Ghawar, Saudi Arabia's supergiant.
40. Matthew R. Simmons, "The World's Giant Oilfields," M. King Hubbert Center for Petroleum Studies, Colorado School of Mines, January 2002.
41. Andrew Callus, "BP Says Will Miss Output Target in 2002," Reuters, September 4, 2002.
42. William Engdahl, *A Century of War* (Ann Arbor, Mich.: Pluto Press, 2004), p. 262.
43. "Big Oil Warns of Coming Energy Crunch," *Financial Times*, August 4, 2005.
44. Ibid.
45. "The Oil Uproar That Isn't," *The New York Times*, July 12, 2005.
46. Adam Porter, "Bank Says Saudi's Top Field in Decline," *Al Jazeera*, April 12, 2005; Josef Auer, "Energy Prospects After the Petroleum Age," *Deutsche Bank Research*, December 4, 2004.
47. "Oil's Well," *Barron's*, April 4, 2005.
48. Paul Roberts, "Over a Barrel," *Mother Jones*, November–December 2004.
49. Richard Heinberg, *The Party's Over* (Gabriola, B.C., Canada: New Society, 2003), pp. 103–4.
50. Paul Roberts, *The End of Oil* (New York: Houghton Mifflin, 2004), p. 55.
51. Heinberg, *Party's Over*, p. 115.
52. Peter Schwartz and Doug Randall, "An Abrupt Climate Change Scenario," U.S. Department of Defense, October 2003.
53. Heinberg, *Party's Over*, p. 126.
54. Roberts, *End of Oil*, p. 181.
55. Ibid., p. 182.
56. "Annual Rankings," *Petroleum Intelligence Weekly*, December 13, 2004.

57. Michael Renner, "Washington's War on Iraq," *Foreign Policy in Focus*, January 2003, p. 4.

58. "Black Gold: Controlling Global Oil from Iraq to Saudi Arabia to China to Venezuela and Beyond," *Democracy Now*, transcript for June 3, 2004.

59. "Oil Giants Look Ahead," *The Wall Street Journal*, April 17, 1995.

60. James A. Paul, "The Iraq Oil Bonanza: Estimating Future Profits," Global Policy Forum, January 28, 2004.

61. Roberts, *End of Oil*, p. 172.

62. "Growing Its Own Future," *Houston Chronicle*, June 3, 2004.

63. Ibid.

64. Heinberg, *Party's Over*, p. 61.

65. "Ford Says '05 Earnings Will Fall," *The New York Times*, January 26, 2005.

66. "Car Talks," *The NewsHour with Jim Lehrer*, September 19, 2003.

67. www.fdic.gov/bank/analytical/fyi/2004/011304fyi.html.

68. "Ford Sees Lower Profits in '05," Associated Press, January 25, 2005.

69. "Finance: Tail Wags the Dog," *Ward's Auto World*, December 1986.

70. Bradford C. Snell, "American Ground Transportation: A Proposal for Restructuring the Automobile, Truck, Bus and Rail Industries," presented to the Subcommittee on Antitrust and Monopoly of the United States Committee on the Judiciary, February 26, 1974, Washington, D.C., U.S. Government Printing Office, 1974.

71. Ibid.

72. "Automatic Fuel Economy Program," U.S. Department of Transportation, November 2004, chart II-3.

73. See "Detroit's Nine Lives" in *The Economist* of September 2, 2004, for a lengthy discussion of the near-death experiences of the big automakers.

74. "Car Companies and Climate Change: Measuring the Carbon Intensity of Sales and Profits," World Resources Institute, 2003, adapted from chapter 3 of Duncan Austin and Amanda Sauer, *Changing Drivers: The Impact of Climate Change on Competition and Value Creation in the Automotive Industry* (Washington: World Resources Institute, 2003).

Chapter 2: The Politics of American Oil Dependence

1. Robert Engler, *The Politics of Oil* (Chicago: University of Chicago Press, 1961), p. 403.

2. Roberts, *End of Oil*, p. 15.

3. Yeomans, *Oil*, p. 36.

4. "The Rockefellers," *American Experience*, PBS Home Programs, www.pbs.org/wgbh/amex/Rockefellers.

5. For the rise of oil-related Texan political clout in Washington, see Robert Bryce, *Cronies: Oil, the Bushes and the Rise of Texas* (New York: Public Affairs, 2004).

6. Thomas Ferguson, *Golden Rule* (Chicago: University of Chicago Press, 1995).

7. "Connally Hot Oil Act of 1935," Handbook of Texas Online, http://www.tsha.utexas.edu/handbook/online/articles/print/cc/mlc.3html.

8. Different two-tier systems have been in effect between the 1930s and the 1970s, the most recent following the Emergency Petroleum Allocation Act of 1973. This law provided that oil from known domestic reserves had to be sold at a lower price than that permitted for oil imports or newly discovered U.S. oil. It was ended in the early 1980s.

9. Engler, *Politics of Oil*, p. 402

10. Robert Caro, *Lyndon Johnson: The Path to Power* (New York: Knopf, 1982).

11. Samuel Lubell, *The Revolt of the Moderates* (New York: Harper Bros., 1956), p. 186.

12. The information on per capita income in Texas comes from 1940–1970 census data and other samplings for 1919 and 1933. Even by 1970, per capita income in Texas had not caught up with the overall national figure, but it was much closer.

13. Michael Klare, *Blood and Oil* (New York: Henry Holt, 2004), p. 37.
14. Roberts, *End of Oil*, p. 41.
15. Ferguson, *Golden Rule*, pp. 83–84.
16. Carlo D'Este, *Eisenhower* (New York: Henry Holt, 2002), pp. 140–45.
17. Bob Shallit, *California: Triumph of the Entrepreneurial Spirit* (Northridge, Calif.: Windsor Publishers, 1989), pp. 119–21; Kevin Starr, *Material Dreams* (New York: Oxford University Press, 1990), pp. 85–89.
18. Starr, *Material Dreams*, p. 87.
19. Roger Morris, *Richard Milhous Nixon* (New York: Henry Holt, 1990), pp. 65–67.
20. Ibid., p. 207.
21. Discussions of Nixon's energy policies can be found in books about his administration but rarely in much depth. They were driven more by politics than energy expertise or ideology.
22. See, for example, Allan J. Matusow, *Nixon's Economy* (Lawrence: University of Kansas Press, 1998), p. 245.
23. Robert Dreyfuss, "The Thirty-Year Itch," *Mother Jones*, March–April 2003.
24. Hoover's years as a very successful mining engineer—he retired before World War I with a $5 million fortune—often saw him evaluating oil properties and proposals. He would have known more about the oil business than any U.S. president before the two Texans, Lyndon Johnson and George H. W. Bush.
25. Roberts, *End of Oil*, p. 295.
26. "Oiling the Political Engine," *Financial Times*, August 2, 2002.
27. Antoine Lerougetel, "Elf Verdict Reveals State Corruption," Global Policy Forum, November 25, 2004.
28. "Escaping the Curse of Oil? The Case of Gabon," International Monetary Fund, 2002.
29. "H. Ross Perot," www.infoplease.com/CRG/peopleA0838476.html.
30. David Ignatius, "Political Oil Slick," *The Washington Post*, July 30, 2002.
31. Kevin Phillips, *American Dynasty: Aristocracy, Fortune, and the Politics of Deceit in the House of Bush* (New York: Viking, 2004).
32. Paul H. Giddens, *Pennsylvania Petroleum, 1750–1872* (Harrisburg: Pennsylvania Historical and Museum Commission, 1947), pp. 378–79.
33. "Confederate Raid on Burning Spring," www.civilwar.com.
34. James Paul, "Oil Companies in Iraq: A Century of Rivalry and War," Global Policy Forum, November 2003, p. 3.
35. Sampson, *Seven Sisters*, p. 31.
36. Ibid., p. 72.
37. Ibid., p. 73.
38. See, for example, Sampson, Engdahl, Pelletière (see n. 43, below), and Daniel Yergin, *The Prize* (New York: Simon & Schuster, 1991).
39. Two examples are Frank Hanigher, *The Secret War* (New York: John Day, 1934), and Anton Mohr, *The Oil War* (New York: Harcourt Brace, 1926).
40. R. A. Dwyer, "British War Debts," quoted in Engdahl, *A Century of War*, p. 51.
41. Edward Edgar, quoted in ibid., p. 64.
42. Ibid., p. 60.
43. Stephen Pelletière, *Iraq and the International Oil System* (Washington, D.C.: Maisonneuve Press, 2004), pp. 39–40.
44. Benjamin Strong, the head of the New York Federal Reserve Bank, worked closely with the Bank of England and supported sterling at critical junctures in 1924 and 1927.
45. Engler, *Politics of Oil*, p. 192.
46. Greg Easterbrook, "How Oilmen in the White House See the World," *The New Republic*, June 4, 2001.
47. Sampson, *Seven Sisters*, p. 80.

48. The sequence of arrangements between Socal and Texaco are spelled out in ibid., pp. 104–12, and Pelletière, *Iraq and the International Oil System*, pp. 64–66. They are a measure of how far British dominance in Arabia and the Persian Gulf came undone during the 1930s.
49. Sampson, *Seven Sisters*, p. 74.
50. "The Landscape of Spinning Sombreros and Electrified Teepees," *Society of Commercial Archaeology Journal*, Spring 2004.
51. "Norman No. 1," Skyways.lib.ks.us/history/norman1.html.
52. Washington's purchase of 250 acres including an oil spring in what is now West Virginia is described as making him "the first petroleum industry speculator" in the United States by the Oil and Gas Museum of Parkersburg, West Virginia. See http://little mountain.com/oilandgasmuseum.
53. "The Evolution of the Dutch Windmill."
54. Roberts, *End of Oil*, p. 218.
55. Ibid., pp. 153 and 218.
56. "Changes in Energy Intensity in the Manufacturing Sector, 1985–91," www.eia.doe.gov.
57. Stephen Koff, "Crude Awakening," *Cleveland Plain Dealer*, October 2, 2005.
58. James L. Williams, "Oil Price History and Analysis," www.wtrg.com/prices.htm.
59. Yeomans, *Oil*, p. 182.
60. Roberts, *End of Oil*, p. 220.
61. "Drivers of Large SUVs Support Bush, Kerry Finds Votes Among Drivers of Small Imports," www.aiada.org/article.asp?id_25827.
62. Ibid.
63. "Bush Series: Nascar Emerges as a Power Source for the GOP," *Norfolk Virginian-Pilot*, October 31, 2004.
64. "So Long, Soccer Moms," Battleground 2002 Poll, June 26, 2002, www.evote.com.
65. C. Kenneth Oraki, "The Emerging Influence of the 'Micropolis,'" www.joelkotkin.com/Commentary.
66. "GOP Won State Along I-4," *Palm Beach Post*, November 10, 2004; "Rural Vote Gave State to Bush," *St. Petersburg Times*, November 14, 2004.
67. "For Political Trends, Think Micropolitan," *USA Today*, November 23, 2004.
68. Robert Lang, "Micropolitics: The 2004 Vote in Small-Town America," Metropolitan Institute Census Note 04:03, November 2004.
69. While micropolitan areas have some overlap with the nation's fastest-growing counties, it is important to differentiate between them. Micropolitan areas are by definition small, while the hundred fastest-growing counties include many large suburban jurisdictions.
70. Ronald Brownstein and Richard Rainey, "Bush Dominated in Outer Suburbs," *Los Angeles Times*, December 1, 2004.
71. "For Political Trends."
72. Roberts, *End of Oil*, p. 154.
73. John Kiewicz, "2003 Mercury Marauder VT," *Motor Trend*, September 2003.
74. "A Supersizing Influence," *Road & Track*, September 1, 2003.
75. Celinda Lake's postelection survey, which makes more sense out of the male-female divisions than most other samplings, was done for the International Women's Studies Institute. Good analyses by the media include Al Swanson, "Security Moms Decided the Election," UPI, *Washington Times*, November 12, 2004, and "Unmarried Women," *San Jose Mercury-News*, November 16, 2004.
76. "Rural Vote Gave State to Bush," *Palm Beach Post*.
77. "Interview with Former Interior Secretary James Watt," *Western Perspective*, 2004.
78. The difficulty, in the United States of the early 2000s, is that "fringe" views can be held by 20 to 30 million people, which is more than a fringe—demographically, at least.
79. Russ Bellant, *The Coors Connection* (Somerville, Mass.: Politics Research Association, 1990).

80. Brewing magnate Coors had ties to both Watt and Hodel. Much more information is available, but in a nutshell, he bankrolled the Mountain States Legal Foundation, of which Watt was the first president. He also played a role in launching the Council for National Policy and was serving on its board when Hodel later became its president.
81. Cited in Bill Berkowitz, "God Hates Environmentalists," *Working for Change,* June 22, 2001; see also Geisler at http://www.normgeisler.com.
82. For details, see the Interfaith Council for Environmental Stewardship's Web site, www.stewards.net.
83. The National Religious Partnership for the Environment, established in 1993, serves as the centrist-to-liberal environmental vehicle of four groups: the National Council of Churches of Christ, the U.S. Conference of Catholic Bishops, the Evangelical Environmental Network, and the Coalition on the Environment and Jewish Life. It advocates "environmental sustainability and justice." See http://www.nrpe.org.
84. Martin Marty, "Rossing's Rapture," *Sightings,* July 5, 2005, the Martin Marty Center, the Institute for the Advanced Study of Religion at the University of Chicago, http://martycenter.uchicago.edu/sightings/archive_2005/0705.shtml.
85. The predictions cluster in places like Matthew 24:7 and Revelation 8:8–11. Raptureready.com, a popular end-times Web site, includes oil-supply and price data as one of its end-times yardsticks.

Chapter 3: Trumpets of Democracy, Drums of Gasoline

1. White House press conference, February 6, 2003 (Bush/Fleischer); *CBS News,* November 14, 2002 (Rumsfeld); *The Times* (London), January 15, 2003 (Blair).
2. Engdahl, *A Century of War,* pp. 24–25.
3. James A. Paul, "Oil Companies in Iraq: A Century of Rivalry and War," Global Policy Forum, November 2003, p. 7.
4. Ibid., p. 17.
5. Pelletière, *Iraq and the International Oil System,* p. 71.
6. Hannu Batatu, *The Old Social Classes and the Revolutionary Movements of Iraq* (Princeton, N.J.: Princeton University Press, 1978), p. 468.
7. Glubb Pasha, *Britain and the Arabs* (London: Hodder and Stoughton, 1959), pp. 238–47.
8. British novels and accounts covering this period include John Harris, *The Thirty Days War;* Somerset de Chair, *The Golden Carpet;* and part of a semi-autobiography by John Masters, *The Road Past Mandalay,* which is half history, half adventure.
9. Pelletière, *Iraq and the International Oil System,* pp. 32–40; Paul, "Oil Companies in Iraq"; Engdahl, *A Century of War.*
10. Tanya Hsu, "U.S. Plans for Occupation of Saudi Arabia," Institute for Research on Middle Eastern Policy, Inc., July 12, 2004, www.twf.org.
11. Miles Ignotus (nom de plume), "Seizing Arab Oil," *Harper's Magazine,* February 1975.
12. Dreyfuss, "The Thirty-Year Itch," p. 41.
13. Sampson, *Seven Sisters,* pp. 7–8.
14. Richard Sale, "Saddam Key in Early CIA Plot," United Press International, April 10, 2003.
15. Alan Friedman, *The Spider's Web* (New York: Bantam, 1993).
16. It is a measure of how closely U.S. and British activities in Iraq have overlapped since the 1980s that even the investigations, judicial inquiries, and special prosecutors looking into illegalities—first Iraq-gate (illegal arms to Iraq) in the 1980s and then deceitful practices in 2002–2003—display transatlantic parallels. While the two Bush presidents have been pursued by congressional committees, Justice Department investigators, and special prosecutors, the governments of Margaret Thatcher and Tony Blair have been subjected to official judicial inquiries and reports—by Lord Justice Scott in 1994 and Lord Justice Hutton in

2003–2004, the latter in the matter of whether Blair misled the nation on Iraq's supposed weapons of mass destruction. Little has come of them.

17. Pelletière, *Iraq and the International Oil System,* p. 240.

18. In his book *A History of Bombing* (New York: The New Press, 2001), Swedish journalist Sven Lindqvist explains that in the years after World War I, the European colonial powers—Britian, France, and Italy, in particular—had huge fleets of no-longer-needed military aircraft, and hundreds were used to employ bombing as a relatively cheap way of policing recalcitrant territories in North Africa, the Middle East, and India. Most of the targeted populations were Muslims. Winston Churchill, as Britain's colonial secretary, played a prominent 1921–1923 role in using bombing to police Iraq. See Christopher Catherwood, *Churchill's Folly* (New York: Carroll and Graf, 2004).

19. Engdahl, *A Century of War,* p. 270.

20. Oliver Kuhn, "Odyssey of Oil," www.cseg.ca/recorder/pdf/2000/2000/_Dec/01_Dec2000.pdf.

21. Engdahl, *A Century of War,* p. 41.

22. Sampson, *Seven Sisters,* pp. 7–8.

23. Pelletière, *Iraq and the International Oil System,* pp. 132–33.

24. "Oil Giants Look Ahead," *The Wall Street Journal,* April 17, 1995.

25. "World Energy Outlook, 2001," International Energy Agency, cited in *The Observer,* October 6, 2002.

26. Klare, *Blood and Oil,* pp. 70–72.

27. Linda McQuaig, "Iraq's Oil," *Znet,* September 27, 2004.

28. Leonardo Maugeri, "The Virgin Oil Fields of Iraq," *Newsweek,* July 5, 2004.

29. McQuaig, "Iraq's Oil."

30. Oliver Warner, *The Sea and the Sword* (New York: William Morrow, 1965), p. 41.

31. Charles H. Hill, *The Danish Sound Dues and Command of the Baltic* (Durham, N.C.: Duke University Press, 1926), p. 165.

32. Niall Ferguson, *Empire* (New York: Basic Books, 2003), p. 368.

33. "The Word from the CIA: It's the Oil, Stupid," *The Melbourne Age,* September 23, 2002.

34. The Reagan and Bush administrations covertly provided arms to Iraq during the 1980s, and some reports suggest that the White House was trying to stay on good terms with Saddam Hussein right up until he invaded Kuwait in August 1990. Saddam badly needed funds after Iraq's drawn-out (1980–1988) war with Iran, and he and his advisers met several times with U.S. State Department representatives to complain about how Kuwait was digging slant wells into the Rumaila oil fields on Iraq's side of the border and producing far above Kuwait's own OPEC quota in order to push down oil prices and block Iraqi economic recovery. A few analysts have interpreted these unusual conversations—in which Saddam was told the United States had no obligation to protect Kuwait—as giving Saddam a "green light" to invade. These various relationships and events are described on pages 302–8 of *American Dynasty.*

35. Klare, *Blood and Oil,* p. 50.

36. Mark Fineman, "The Oil Factor in Somalia," *Los Angeles Times,* January 18, 1993.

37. Zbigniew Brzezinski, *The Grand Chessboard* (New York: Basic Books, 1998).

38. F. William Engdahl, "Iraq and the Problem of Peak Oil," *Current Concerns,* January 2005, p. 4; www.currentconcerns.ch.

39. "The War for Pipelineistan," *Asia Times,* January 6, 2002.

40. "Go-Ahead for Balkan Oil Pipeline," *BBC News,* December 28, 2004.

41. Paul, "Oil Companies in Iraq," p. 12.

42. "The War for Pipelineistan."

43. In the wake of September 11, Osama bin Laden several times cited the presence of U.S. troops on the sacred soil of Saudi Arabia—Islam's preeminent holy places are there—as a reason for his surprise attack. Few in the media referred to these claims, but one reason to

invade Iraq in 2003 was to establish it as an alternative principal Middle Eastern base so that U.S. troops could be withdrawn from Saudi Arabia (as they soon were in August 2003).

44. "Cheney, Energy and Iraq Invasion," *San Francisco Chronicle*, March 21, 2004.
45. Klare, *Blood and Oil*, p. 14.
46. Michael Klare, "Transforming the American Military into a Global Oil-Protection Service," *Foreign Policy in Focus*, October 2004.
47. Daniel Smith, "U.S. Military on the Scent of Oil," *Foreign Policy in Focus*, November 20, 2004, pp. 2, 5, and 8.
48. See David Eisenhower, "Global Manifest Destiny," *Peoples Week World Newspaper On-line*, January 22, 2005.
49. Klare, "Transforming the American Military," p. 3.
50. Ibid., pp. 2–3.
51. Greg Jaffe, "In a Massive Shift, U.S. Plans to Reduce Troops in Germany," *The Wall Street Journal*, June 10, 2003.
52. "U.S. Military Commander to Visit African Oil Producers," Irin News Service, August 23, 2004; Klare, "Transforming the American Military," p. 5.
53. "U.S. Military Commander."
54. "Who Knew?" *Asia Times*, August 13, 2001.
55. Klare, *Blood and Oil*, p. 7.
56. Report of the Energy Task Force of the Center for Strategic and International Studies, vol. 3, cited in Klare, *Blood and Oil*, p. 22.
57. "Escaping the Curse of Oil? The Case of Gabon," International Monetary Fund, 2002.
58. Very few discussions appeared in the U.S. press, to a degree that the California-based journalism group Project Censored later selected this topic—"U.S. Dollar Versus the Euro: Another Reason for the Invasion of Iraq"—for one of its 2003 citations. See www.projectcensored.org/publications/2004/19.html.
59. Peter Schwartz and Doug Randall, "An Abrupt Climate Change Scenario and Its Implications for United States National Security," Department of Defense, October 2003.
60. "Prophetic Ten," Raptureready.com.
61. Text of speech of Dick Cheney at the London Institute of Petroleum, 1999, www.peakoil.net/Publications/Cheney_peakoil_fed.pdf.
62. Colin Campbell and Jean Laherrère, "The End of Cheap Oil," *Scientific American*, March 1998.
63. Heinberg, *The Party's Over*, p. 127.
64. Roberts, *End of Oil*, p. 172.
65. Michael Renner, "Fueling Conflict," *Foreign Policy in Focus*, January 2004, p. 26.
66. Roberts, *End of Oil*, p. 111.
67. Paul, "Oil Companies in Iraq," p. 7; Roberts, *End of Oil*, p. 82.
68. Michael Meacher, "Plan Now for a World Without Oil," *Financial Times*, January 4, 2004.
69. Ibid.
70. Paul, "Oil Companies in Iraq," p. 10.
71. Ibid., p. 18.
72. "Black Gold: Controlling Global Oil from Iraq to Saudi Arabia to China to Venezuela and Beyond," *Democracy Now*, January 3, 2004, transcript.
73. Dreyfuss, "The Thirty-Year Itch."
74. Ibid.
75. "Black Gold."
76. Howard Fineman, "In Round 2, It's the Dollar vs. Euro," *Newsweek*, April 23, 2003.
77. "Russia to Price Oil in Euros in Snub to U.S.," *Daily Telegraph*, October 10, 2003.
78. Chavez was motivated, at least in part, by his belief that the U.S. government was plotting his assassination, or at least coups to overthrow him. Iran, in turn, was the target of off-and-on U.S. sanctions.

79. "Indonesia May Dump Dollar," Bloomberg.com, April 17, 2003.

80. Coilin Nunan, "Petro-Dollar or Petro-Euro," *Feasta Review,* June 2003, pp. 126–28.

81. Ibid.

82. Although Bill Clinton backed the Kyoto Protocol, Democrats in the U.S. Senate joined Republicans in 1997 in supporting a resolution in opposition to any Kyoto-like treaty. It passed by a margin of 95–0. By the time George W. Bush became president in 2001, belief that the Kyoto agreement was flawed was clearly bipartisan.

83. Glenn Scherer, "The Godly Must Be Crazy," *Grist Magazine,* October 27, 2004. Senator Inhofe has not denied this quote, which doesn't get him in trouble in Oklahoma as it would in, say, Manhattan.

84. *Air America,* http://shows.airamericaradio.com.

85. "The Bible and the Apocalypse," Time/CNN Poll, *Time,* July 1, 2002.

Chapter 4: Radicalized Religion: As American as Apple Pie

1. Charles Kimball, *When Religion Becomes Evil: Five Warning Signs* (San Francisco: HarperSanFrancisco, 2002), p. 7.

2. Scholar George Marsden used this phrase in 1980, but the focus intensified during that decade and even more in the 1990s, as disarray in the Middle East and the rise of the religious right in the United States promoted attention to U.S. religious radicalism and fundamentalism as part of a worrisome global pattern.

3. Harvey Cox book-jacket quote for Barbara Rossing, *The Rapture Exposed* (Boulder, Colo.: Westview Press, 2004).

4. Even the centrist religious frequently analogize the suburban megachurches to shopping malls, in terms of both satisfying every need and offering so many different options.

5. Peter Halvorson and William P. Newman, *The Atlas of Religious Change in America, 1952–1990* (Atlanta: Glenmary Research Center, 1994), pp. 2–4.

6. Walter McDougall, *Promised Land, Crusader State* (New York: Houghton Mifflin, 1997), p. 99. The quotation from the Book of Matthew (28:19) is "Go ye therefore and teach all nations. . . ."

7. Mark Noll, *The Old Religion in a New World* (Grand Rapids, Mich.: Eerdmans, 2002), p. 162.

8. Diana Eck, quoted in Kimball, *When Religion Becomes Evil,* p. 8.

9. Noll, *Old Religion,* p. 185.

10. Ibid., pp. 196–97.

11. Ibid., p. 197.

12. With respect to Pentecostals in the United States, data is notably imprecise. The estimates of religious adherency found on www.adherents.com show Pentecostal adherency rising from 3.2 million in 1990 to 6.2 million in 2004, but individual estimates range from 4 million persons affiliated to 11 million. It is relevant, too, that Pentecostals may well constitute the largest element within the 6 million U.S. Hispanics estimated to be Protestants. As of the early twenty-first century, Pentecostal faith appears to be the fastest-growing element of global Christianity, with an estimated 400 million global believers.

13. Noll, *Old Religion,* pp. 263–66.

14. Polls seem to have found the highest percentages of Americans claiming to have been born again in 2001–2003 in the wake of September 11. By 2005, the number was down to 42 percent.

15. Mark Noll, ed., *Religion and American Politics* (New York: Oxford University Press, 1990), p. 271.

16. Noll, *Old Religion,* pp. 268–71.

17. Ibid., p. 195.

18. Rodney Stark and Roger Finke, *The Churching of America, 1776–1990* (New Brunswick, N. J.: Rutgers University Press, 1993), p. 237.

19. Noll, *Old Religion,* pp. 283–86.

20. Ibid., pp. 176–78.
21. Stark and Finke, *Churching,* p. 275.
22. "Young Europeans," *The New York Times,* April 23, 2004.
23. Stark and Finke, *Churching,* p. 85.
24. Whitney A. Cross, *The Burned-Over District* (New York: Harper Torchbooks, 1965), p. 3.
25. Stark and Finke, *Churching,* pp. 58–59.
26. Ibid., p. 113.
27. Christine Heyrman, *Southern Cross* (New York: Knopf, 1997), pp. 265–66.
28. Ibid., p. 27.
29. Starke and Finke, *Churching,* p. 58.
30. Ibid., p. 95.
31. Noll, *Old Religion,* pp. 66–67; Edwin Gaustad and Philip L. Barlow, *New Historical Atlas of Religion in America* (New York: Oxford University Press, 2001), pp. 178–87, figures 2.109 and 2.110.
32. Noll, *Old Religion,* p. 101.
33. William Sweet, *The Story of Religion in America* (Grand Rapids, Mich.: Baker Book House, 1979), pp. 274–77; Randall Miller, Harry Stout, and Charles L. Wilson, eds., *Religion and the American Civil War* (New York: Oxford University Press, 1998), p. 102; Gaustad and Barlow, *New Historical Atlas,* p. 232.
34. Gaustad and Barlow, *New Historical Atlas,* p. 258.
35. R. Laurence Moore, *Religious Outsiders and the Making of Americans* (New York: Oxford University Press, 1986), pp. 136–39.
36. Edwin Gaustad and Leigh Schmidt, *The Religious History of America* (San Francisco: Harper-San Francisco, 2002), p. 282; Gaustad and Barlow, *New Historical Atlas,* p. 196.
37. Stark and Finke, *Churching,* p. 165.
38. Moore, *Religious Outsiders,* pp. 4–5.
39. Stark and Finke, *Churching,* pp. 145–47.
40. Moore, *Religious Outsiders,* p. 14.
41. Stark and Finke, *Churching,* p. 55.
42. Ibid., p. 146.
43. Joel Carpenter, *Revive Us Again: The Reawakening of American Fundamentalism* (New York: Oxford University Press, 1997), pp. 8, 13.
44. Ibid., p. xii.
45. Moore, *Religious Outsiders,* p. 142.
46. Stark and Finke, *Churching,* p. 208.
47. Noll, *Old Religion,* p. 160.
48. Ibid., pp. 176, 158–59.
49. Carpenter, *Revive Us Again,* p. 131.
50. Ibid., p. 7.
51. Ibid., p. 231.
52. Stark and Finke, *Churching,* p. 16.
53. Carpenter, *Revive Us Again,* p. 6.
54. Ibid.
55. Ibid., p. 7.
56. Ibid., p. 236.
57. Ernest R. Sandeen, *The Roots of Fundamentalism* (Chicago: University of Chicago Press, 1970); George Marsden, *Fundamentalism and American Culture* (New York: Oxford University Press, 1980).
58. Philip Goff and Paul Harvey, eds., *Themes in Religion and American Culture* (Chapel Hill: University of North Carolina Press, 2004), p. 58.
59. Gaustad and Barlow, *New Historical Atlas,* p. 282.

60. Moore, *Religious Outsiders,* pp. 141–43.

61. Starke and Finke, *Churching,* p. 248.

62. Noll, *Old Religion,* p. 176.

63. Ibid., p. 177.

64. Ibid., p. 178.

65. Stark and Finke, *Churching,* second edition, 2005; Noll, *Old Religion,* pp. 183–84; Carpenter, *Revive Us Again,* p. 237.

66. Donald E. Miller, *Reinventing American Protestantism: Christianity in the New Millennium* (Berkeley: University of California Press, 1997).

67. The Toronto Airport Vineyard Church was expelled for allowing so called holy laughter to degenerate into animal noises—squeals, barks, clucks, and the like. A good account can be found in the "Vineyard Churches" profile on the New Religious Movements home page of the University of Virginia Web site; see www.religiousmovements-lib-virginia.edu/ nrms/vineyard.html. Defenders of holy laughter argued that this was unusual, and that no other Vineyard churches had been so disciplined.

68. Mark Shibley, *Resurgent Evangelicalism in the United States* (Columbia: University of South Carolina Press, 1996).

69. Noll, *Old Religion,* p. 179.

70. Stark and Finke, *Churching,* p. 260.

71. Ibid., pp. 259–60.

72. Ibid., p. 273.

73. Ibid.

74. Dean Hamer, *The God Gene: How Faith Is Hardwired into Our Genes* (New York: Doubleday, 2004).

75. Noll, ed., *Religion and American Politics,* p. 355.

76. Kevin Phillips, *The Cousins' Wars: Religion, Politics, and the Triumph of Anglo-America* (New York: Basic Books, 1999).

77. Miller, Stout, and Wilson, *Religion and the American Civil War,* pp. 4–5.

78. A number of political scientists—Richard Jensen, Paul Kleppner, Ronald Formisano, and others—have looked at the denominational aspects of that era's political cleavages. A broad overview can be found in Daniel Walker Howe, *The Political Culture of the American Whigs* (Chicago: University of Chicago Press, 1979), pp. 150–67.

79. Miller, Stout, and Wilson, *Religion and the American Civil War,* p. 409.

80. Oran P. Smith, *The Rise of Baptist Republicanism* (New York: New York University Press, 1997), p. 4.

81. Susan Page, "Churchgoing Closely Tied to Voting Patterns," *USA Today,* June 2, 2004.

82. Conrad Cherry, ed., *God's New Israel: Religious Interpretations of American Destiny* (Chapel Hill: University of North Carolina Press, 1998), p. 26.

83. Schama, *Embarrassment of Riches,* p. 94.

84. Anthony Smith, *Chosen Peoples: Sacred Sources of National Identity* (New York: Oxford University Press, 2002), pp. 45–46.

85. Ibid., pp. 77–78.

86. Donald H. Akenson, *God's Peoples* (Ithaca, N.Y.: Cornell University Press, 1992).

87. Anthony Smith, *Chosen Peoples,* p. 78.

88. Akenson, *God's Peoples,* p. 4.

89. Ibid., pp. 359, 363, 365, 366.

90. Anthony Smith, *Chosen Peoples,* pp. 138–41.

91. Cherry, *God's New Israel,* p. 11.

92. Ibid., p. 19.

93. Hubertis Cummings, *Scots Breed and Susquehanna* (Pittsburgh: University of Pittsburgh Press, 1964), pp. 298–99.

94. D. W. Meinig, *The Shaping of America*, vol. 3 (New Haven: Yale University Press, 1998), p. 104.
95. David Goldfield, *Still Fighting the Civil War* (Baton Rouge: Louisiana State University Press, 2002), p. 22.
96. W. J. Cash, *The Mind of the South* (New York: Knopf, 1941), p. viii.

Chapter 5: Defeat and Resurrection: The Southernization of America

1. Among Newt Gingrich's Civil War novels, cowritten with William R. Fortschen, the one that rescripts that pivotal battle into a Confederate victory is *Gettysburg* (New York: Thomas Dunne Books, 2003).
2. William R. Taylor, *Cavalier and Yankee* (New York: Anchor Books, 1961), p. xvi.
3. Phillips, *Cousins' Wars*, pp. 32, 57–59.
4. Joseph L. Davis, *Sectionalism in American Politics, 1774–1787* (Madison: University of Wisconsin Press, 1977), p. 10.
5. Ibid., p. 12.
6. David C. Hendrickson, *Peace Pact* (Lawrence: University of Kansas Press, 2003), pp. 9, 205.
7. Phillips, *Cousins' Wars*, p. 318.
8. Grady McWhiney, *Cracker Culture* (Tuscaloosa: University of Alabama Press, 1988), pp. xiii–xiv, xxi–xxii, 3–8, 16–20.
9. Ibid., p. 18.
10. John Shelton Reed, *One South: An Ethnic Approach to Regional Culture* (Baton Rouge: Louisiana State University Press, 1982), p. 3.
11. Phillips, *Cousins' Wars*, pp. 353–54.
12. Ibid.
13. Ibid., pp. 327–54; Hendrickson, *Peace Pact*, pp. 225–29.
14. Phillips, *Cousins' Wars*, p. 347.
15. Miller, Stout, and Wilson, *Religion and the American Civil War*, pp. 374–75.
16. Goldfield, *Still Fighting*, p. 6.
17. Goff and Harvey, *Themes in Religion*, p. 54.
18. Books dealing with the South's battle to define a renewed nationalism after the Civil War and to shape the national interpretation of those events made memory itself a battlefield. This has become a major book subject in recent years, and beyond those I cite in the text, the subject is also addressed by two other recent volumes: William Blair, *Cities of the Dead: Contesting the Memory of the Civil War in the South, 1865–1914* (Chapel Hill: University of North Carolina Press, 2004); and W. Fitzhuge Brundage, ed., *Where the Memories Grow: History, Memory and Southern Identity* (Chapel Hill: University of North Carolina Press, 2000).
19. Maurice Isserman and Michael Kazin, *America Divided: The Civil War of the 1960s* (New York: Oxford University Press, 2004), p. 2.
20. William Doyle, *An American Insurrection: The Battle of Oxford, Mississippi, 1962* (New York: Archer Books, 2003).
21. Isserman and Kazin, *America Divided*, p. 3.
22. Kirkpatrick Sale, *Power Shift* (New York: Random House, 1975); Carl Oglesby, *The Yankee and Cowboy War* (New York: Berkley Medallion Books, 1977).
23. John Egerton, *The Americanization of Dixie: The Southernization of America* (New York: Harper & Row, 1974), p. 195.
24. Paige Williams, "Sneak Peeks," review of *Dixie Rising*, by Peter Applebome, *Salon.com*, November 11, 1996.
25. Richard Holbrooke, "Our Second Civil War," *The Washington Post*, August 28, 2004.
26. William Schneider, "Politics Remain Stalemated," *Los Angeles Times*, March 31, 2002.
27. Michael Barone, *U.S. News & World Report*, November 17, 2003.

28. Isserman and Kazan, *America Divided*, p. 302.

29. Richard E. Beringer, Herman Hattaway, Archer Jones, and William N. Still Jr., *Why the South Lost the Civil War* (Athens: University of Georgia Press, 1986), p. 440.

30. Alice Fahs and Joan Waugh, *The Memory of the Civil War in American Culture* (Chapel Hill: University of North Carolina Press, 2004), introduction.

31. Edward Sebesta and Euan Hague, "The U.S. Civil War as a Theological War: Confederate Christian Nationalism and the League of the South," *Canadian Review of American Studies* 32: 3, 2002.

32. See James McBride Dabbs, *Haunted by God* (Richmond, Va.: John Knox Press, 1972).

33. While I know of no precise analysis, the spate of volumes on the South's unusual history and compulsion largely parallels the rise of the religious right, the Southern Baptist Convention, and southern Republican influence in Washington during the 1990s and then under George W. Bush.

34. The biblical passages supporting slavery, or appearing to, have been analyzed in a number of places. Discussions on the Internet include "Christianity and History: Bible, Race and Slavery," http://atheism.about.com/es/christianityhist/, as well as "The Bible and Slavery," http://www.bible-researcher.com/slavery.html.

35. Mitchell Snay, *The Gospel of Disunion* (Chapel Hill: University of North Carolina Press, 1993). p. 11.

36. Miller, Stout, and Wilson, *Religion and the American Civil War*, p. 79.

37. Snay, *Gospel of Disunion*, pp. 190–91, 194–95.

38. Ibid., p. 196.

39. Ibid., p. 192.

40. Ibid., p. 204.

41. Miller, Stout, and Wilson, *Religion and the American Civil War*, p. 411.

42. Goldfield, *Still Fighting*, p. 52.

43. Ibid., p. 29.

44. Reid Mitchell, "Christian Soldiers?" in Miller, Stout, and Wilson, *Religion and the American Civil War*, pp. 297–308.

45. Charles Reagan Wilson, *Baptized in Blood: The Religion of the Lost Cause, 1868–1920* (Athens: University of Georgia Press, 1980).

46. Goldfield, *Still Fighting*, p. 4.

47. Miller, Stout, and Wilson, *Religion and the American Civil War*, p. 15.

48. Historians have paid more attention to the chronology and explanations of the three major U.S. denominations' splitting regionally and theologically as the Civil War approached than to the attempts, obstacles, and slow processes of national reunification after the war. By the late twentieth century, however, the Southern Baptist Convention was the sole holdout, likewise remaining the only prominent U.S. religious denomination to include "Southern" in its name.

49. Snay, *Gospel of Disunion*, p. vi.

50. Daniel Stowell, *Rebuilding Zion* (New York: Oxford University Press, 1998), p. 23.

51. Ibid., pp. 169, 180.

52. Ibid., p. 107.

53. Ibid., p. 113.

54. David W. Blight, *Race and Reunion* (Cambridge, Mass.: Harvard University Press, 2001), p. 22.

55. Goldfield, *Still Fighting*, pp. 51–52.

56. Stowell, *Rebuilding Zion*, p. 115.

57. While the famous movie was titled *The Birth of a Nation*, it was based on a book, *The Clansman*, whose author, Thomas Dixon Jr., was a friend of Woodrow Wilson from university days.

58. Goldfield, *Still Fighting*, p. 52.
59. The term "backward glance" is a widely used description of the South's preoccupation with history and regional self-explanation and self-justification.
60. Oran Smith, *Baptist Republicanism*, pp. 10–11.
61. Paul Harvey, *Redeeming the South* (Chapel Hill: University of North Carolina Press, 1997), p. 9.
62. Gaustad and Barlow, *New Historical Atlas*, p. 70.
63. Harvey, *Redeeming the South*, p. 6.
64. Winthrop Hudson, quoted in Oran Smith, *Baptist Republicanism*, p. 20.
65. Miller, Stout, and Wilson, *Religion and the American Civil War*, pp. 171–72.
66. Ibid., pp. 176–80.
67. Stowell, *Rebuilding Zion*, p. 113.
68. Ibid., p. 169.
69. Oran Smith, *Baptist Republicanism*, pp. 18–19.
70. Miller, Stout, and Wilson, *Religion and the American Civil War*, p. 178.
71. Ibid., p. 10.
72. Ibid., p. 179.
73. Ibid., p. 366.
74. Harvey, *Redeeming the South*, p. 30.
75. Smith, *Baptist Republicanism*, p. 32.
76. Ibid., pp. 20–21.
77. Gaustad and Barlow, *New Historical Atlas*, figures C4 and C6.
78. Harvey, *Redeeming the South*, p. 3.
79. Ibid., p. 87.
80. Oran Smith, *Baptist Republicanism*, p. 34.
81. Ibid., p. 38.
82. Ibid., p. 48.
83. Ibid., pp. 38–54.
84. Ibid., p. 38.
85. Ibid., p. 46.
86. Ibid., pp. 78–80.
87. Ibid.
88. Gaustad and Barlow, *New Historical Atlas*, figures C8 and C10.
89. "Will the Real Fundamentalists Please Stand Up," *Baptist Standard*, July 31, 2001.
90. Marty and Appleby put Southern Baptists into the fundamentalist category in their book *Fundamentalisms Observed* (Chicago: University of Chicago Press, 1994); while Kimball did so in *When Religion Becomes Evil.*
91. Jerry Falwell and Ed Dobson, *The Fundamentalist Phenomenon* (New York: Doubleday 1981).
92. Oran Smith, *Baptist Republicanism*, pp. 11–15.
93. Bruce Lawrence, *Defenders of God: The Fundamentalist Revolt Against the Modern Age* (San Francisco: Harper & Row, 1989).
94. Oran Smith, *Baptist Republicanism*, pp. 11–14.
95. Historians and observers touching on the notion of the Southern Baptist Convention as a "folk church" of the South include Paul Harvey, Oran P. Smith, and others with respect to its ruralism and regionalism, as well as others for its regional and patriotic commitment during the years before, during, and after the Civil War.
96. Oran P. Smith, who writes more as a political observer than academician, emphasizes the unique Southernness and larger dimensions of what he calls Bapticity across a broad range of cultural, regional, and evangelical traits. But similar emphases on the blurring of Southern Baptist religion and regional history, culture, and politics can be found on page after page of the analyses of Paul Harvey, Mitchell Snay, Samuel S. Hill, and Charles Reagan Wilson. It seems to me that while nuances can be debated, the basic analysis is all but irrefutable.

97. George Frederickson, *The Comparative Imagination* (Berkeley: University of California Press, 1997), p. 4.

98. Norman Yance, *Religion Southern Style* (Anderson, S.C.: National Association of Baptist Professors of Religion, 1980).

99. Oran Smith, *Baptist Republicanism*, p. 39.

100. The maps are from Raymond Gaskil, *Cultural Regions of the United States* (Seattle: University of Washington Press, 1975), p. 27, and John S. Reed, "The Heart of Dixie: An Essay in Folk Geography," *Social Forces* 54 (June 1976).

101. Earl Pomeroy, *The Pacific Slope* (New York: Knopf, 1965), p. 75.

102. Alvin Josephy, *The Civil War in the American West* (New York: Knopf, 1991), pp. 233–34; Dorothy O. Johansen, *Empire of the Columbia*, 2nd ed. (New York: Harper & Row, 1967), pp. 260–62.

103. Johansen, *Empire*, p. 262.

104. Josephy, *Civil War*, pp. 234–37; Meinig, *The Shaping of America*, p. 53.

105. Josephy, *Civil War*, p. 234.

106. Meinig, *The Shaping of America*, p. 125.

107. Ibid., p. 393.

108. Johansen, *Empire*, p. 266.

109. Ibid., p. 268.

110. Pomeroy, *Pacific Slope*, p. 78.

111. Ibid., p. 77.

112. Tom Sargent, "The Civil War in Montana," http://www.newpsych.org/virginia/cwmt.htm.

113. Josephy, *Civil War*, p. 19.

114. Ibid., pp. 293–94.

115. Federal Writers' Project, *Georgia Guide* (Athens: University of Georgia Press, 1946), pp. 383–84.

116. Ted Morgan, *Shovel of Stars* (New York: Simon & Schuster, 1995), pp. 352–53.

117. Thomas C. Donnelly, ed., *Rocky Mountain Politics* (Albuquerque: University of New Mexico Press, 1940), p. 204.

118. Josephy, *Civil War*, p. 264.

119. Pomeroy, *Pacific Slope*, p. 78.

120. Johansen, *Empire*, p. 347.

121. Pomeroy, *Pacific Slope*, p. 226.

122. Peter Applebome, *Dixie Rising* (New York: Times Books, 1996), p. 10.

123. Ohio Writers' Project, *Ohio Guide* (New York: Oxford University Press, 1962), p. 168.

124. Ibid., p. 281.

125. James W. Loewen, *Lies Across America: What Our Historic Sites Got Wrong* (New York: The New Press, 2001).

126. E. W. Hunke, *Southern Baptists in the Intermountain West* (Franklin, Tenn.: Providence House, 1998), p. 227.

127. Gaustad and Barlow, *New Historical Atlas*, p. 82.

128. Applebome, *Dixie Rising*, pp. 5–6.

129. Michael Emerson and Christian Smith, *Divided by Faith* (New York: Oxford University Press, 2000), pp. 93–113.

130. Ibid., p. 170.

131. "Southern Baptist Surprise," *Christianity Today*, September 2004.

132. Mark Shibley, "Southernization," *Encyclopedia of Religion and Society* (Walnut Creek, Calif.: Alta Mira Press, 1998).

133. Ibid.

Chapter 6: The United States in a Dixie Cup: The New Religious and Political Battlegrounds

1. Secretary of State Cass was old and not far from senility, but he resigned on December 11, 1860, over President James Buchanan's failure to reinforce beleaguered Fort Sumter. See, for example, Roy F. Nichols, *The Disruption of American Democracy* (New York: Collier Books, 1962), pp. 404–5.
2. Cash, *The Mind of the South.*
3. The many historians who apply the term "Second Reconstruction" to the civil-rights struggle following World War II don't all use the same time period. However, if you take the quarter century from 1948 to 1973—a time frame that overlaps with most of the marches, civil-rights statutory enactments, major judicial decisions, urban riots, and black political enfranchisement—it matches very closely with the chronology in which the South made its great journey from Democratic presidential support to Republican presidential support as shown in figure 2, p. 177.
4. Earl Black and Merle Black, *The Vital South: How Presidents Are Elected* (Cambridge, Mass.: Harvard University Press, 1992), p. 305.
5. Oran Smith, *Baptist Republicanism,* p. 159.
6. Two astute British observers of U.S. politics have touched on these events and possibilities—Robert Mason in *Richard Nixon and the Quest for a New Majority* (Chapel Hill: University of North Carolina Press, 2004), pp. 198–99; and Godfrey Hodgson, *The World Turned Right Side Up* (Boston: Houghton Mifflin, 1996), pp. 123–27.
7. Clinton's unmilitary image was a break in the usual post–World War II pattern of presidents who had served in uniform, if not always in harm's way.
8. Black and Black, *Vital South,* p. 197.
9. Ibid., p. 309.
10. "On His Watch," *St. Petersburg Times,* January 14, 2001.
11. Black and Black, *Vital South,* p. 309.
12. Paul Kleppner, *The Cross of Culture* (New York: The Free Press, 1970), and Michael Jensen, "The Historical Roots of Party Identification," paper delivered to annual meeting of the American Political Science Association, September 1969.
13. William Schneider, "Politics Remain Stalemated," *Los Angeles Times,* March 31, 2002.
14. Page, "Churchgoing Closely Tied to Voting Patterns."
15. Geoffrey Layman, *The Great Divide: Religious and Cultural Conflict in American Party Politics* (New York: Columbia University Press, 2001).
16. Louis Bolce and Gerald De Maio, "The Party of Unbelievers," *The Public Interest,* Fall 2002.
17. Oran Smith, *Baptist Republicanism,* p. 159.
18. Samuel Lubell, *The Future While It Happened* (New York: Norton, 1973), pp. 61–62.
19. Herman Kahn, *Single Magazine,* February 1974, p. 34.
20. Oran Smith, *Baptist Republicanism,* pp. 51, 159.
21. Glenn H. Hutter and John W. Storey, *The Religious Right* (Santa Barbara, Calif.: ABC-CLIO, 1995), pp. 110–37.
22. Oran Smith, *Baptist Republicanism,* p. 153
23. Ibid., pp. 51, 215.
24. William Schneider, *The Election of 1980* (Washington: American Enterprise Institute, 1981), p. 242.
25. Dan Carter, *From George Wallace to Newt Gingrich* (Baton Rouge: Louisiana State University Press, 1996), p. 59.
26. Oran Smith, *Baptist Republicanism,* p. 221.
27. Howard Fineman, "Bush and God," *Newsweek,* March 10, 2003, p. 25.

28. James L. Guth and John C. Green, eds., *The Bible and the Ballot Box* (Boulder, Colo.: Westview Press, 1991), p. 39.
29. Ibid., p. 113.
30. Ibid., p. 18.
31. Ibid., pp. 73–90.
32. Ibid., p. 19.
33. Ibid.
34. Ibid., p. 116.
35. Oran Smith, *Baptist Republicanism*, p. 225.
36. Ibid., p. 163.
37. Bolce and De Maio, "Party of Unbelievers," p. 3.
38. Oran Smith, *Baptist Republicanism*, pp. 174, 228.
39. Ibid., p. 194.
40. John Green and Mark Silk, "The New Religion Gap," Center for the Study of Religion in Public Life, Trinity College, Hartford, p. 2.
41. "Nation Divided at Outset of '04 Campaign," *Baptist Press*, January 2004, www.lifeway.com.
42. Page, "Churchgoing Closely Tied to Voting Patterns."
43. *USA Today* political writer Susan Page, in "Churchgoing Closely Tied to Voting Patterns," outlines the Clinton connection but does not dwell on how the Clinton scandals fed George W. Bush's dynastic, moral, and religious appeal, facilitating his coming to power.
44. "Race, Religion Gap Growing," *Nashville Tennessean*, March 10, 2004.
45. Page, "Churchgoing Closely Tied to Voting Patterns."
46. Green and Silk, "The New Religion Gap."
47. Ibid., citing John Green, "The Undetected Tide," *Religion in the News*, Spring 2003.
48. Pollster George Gallup and others have commented that roughly half of those who call themselves born again do not fit the strict definition of the term, based on follow-up questions about their personal experience and commitment to leading others to Christ. Thus, Gallup finds that although two-fifths of Americans call themselves born again, only one-fifth fit the strict definition.
49. Page, "Churchgoing Closely Tied to Voting Patterns."
50. "Nation Divided at Outset of '04 Campaign."
51. *PBS Perspectives*, November 5, 2004, pp. 1–2.
52. Ibid., p. 3.
53. "Bush Gets Major Support from Orthodox Jews," *Haaretz*, November 11, 2004.
54. The Muslim data comes in a number of versions, but at least one prominent Republican strategist, Washington-based Grover Norquist, analyzed the Florida Muslim vote—some fifty thousand, heavily for Bush—as having been the ironic pivot of the 2000 election. For Norquist's case, see his article in the June 2001 issue of the *American Spectator*. For a broader analysis, see Alexander Rose, "How Did Muslims Vote in 2000?" *Middle East Quarterly*, Summer 2001.
55. *PBS Perspectives*.
56. Kathleen Flake, *The Politics of Religious Identity* (Chapel Hill: University of North Carolina Press, 2004), pp. 45–48.
57. The figure of "almost 90" percent is taken from the postelection surveys by John Green and the University of Akron, which found Bush getting 88 percent in 2000 and 89 percent in 2004. It might not be quite that high. After looking at the county returns in Idaho and Utah, I would go for a number in the mid- to high 80s. Small counties in both states listed no local religious adherents but Mormons usually gave Bush 85 to 90 percent in 2004.
58. Gaustad and Barlow, *New Historical Atlas*, maps 23.106, 2.109, 2.110, 2.117, 2.121, 2.124, 2.126.

59. Halvorson and Newman, *Atlas of Religious Change in America, 1952–1990*, p. 62.
60. Gaustad and Barlow, *New Historical Atlas*, map 3.10.
61. As yet, there are no good studies of the Lutheran vote in 2004. The Missouri Synod Lutherans are mostly German and very conservative. So, too, for the Wisconsin Synod Lutherans. The Evangelical Lutheran Church in America has a German minority, but also a larger Scandinavian component. Scandinavian Lutherans in Minnesota, Wisconsin, and Iowa may have split roughly fifty-fifty, and presumably the more churchgoing were the more Republican.
62. Gaustad and Barlow, *New Historical Atlas*, map 4.17.
63. Studies make quite clear that seculars and nonbelievers are strongest in and around Boston, Manhattan, and the Pacific Coast between Seattle and San Francisco and Silicon Valley. Details can be found in the Howard University–sponsored social-capital community benchmark survey taken in 2000 and focused on community social values and beliefs; *The Directory of Religious Congregations and Memberships, 2000* includes, on p. 584, a county-by-county map of the percentages of residents stating no religious adherence.
64. No studies have as yet (2005) identified the religious denominations and sects showing the strongest pro-Bush trends between 2000 and 2004. However, white Protestant fundamentalists and evangelicals in West Virginia, Kentucky, and Tennessee would be near the top, as would the ultra-Orthodox Jews discussed in the *Haaretz* survey previously cited.
65. Religiously, West Virginia, Kentucky, Missouri, and Oklahoma are states with a heavy Baptist flavor—the latter three, in particular, have been strong post–World War II growth states for the SBC. As for the Mormon church, its Republicanism is more overt now, and Mormon numbers have surged in many western states. Bush's large gains over Goldwater in Utah, Idaho, and Wyoming would reflect that. Alaska and Hawaii, too, have substantial and growing numbers of Mormons. Alaska's unusual Protestant ratios all but ensure a conservative pattern: the top three denominations are the Southern Baptist Convention, the Mormons, and the Pentecostal Assemblies of God.
66. Kaplan, "With God on Their Side."
67. Martin Marty and R. Scott Appleby, eds., *Fundamentalisms Observed* (Chicago: University of Chicago Press, 1991), pp. 822–23.
68. Kimball, *When Religion Becomes Evil*, pp. 161–70.
69. Charles Kimball lecture, Baltimore, 2004, Institute for Christian and Jewish Studies, www.icjs.org/scholars/kimballlecture.
70. Bruce Lincoln, *Holy Terrors* (Chicago: University of Chicago Press), p. 20.
71. Ibid., pp. 30–31.
72. "How Bush Speaks in Religious Code," *Boston Globe*, September 12, 2004.
73. Ibid.
74. David S. Domke, *God Willing? Political Fundamentalism in the White House* (Ann Arbor, Mich.: Pluto Press, 2004), p. 2.
75. Ibid., pp. 3, 16; and David Domke, "God's Will According to the Bush Administration," Counterpunch.org, September 10, 2004.
76. David Domke, "Bush's Fundamentalism: The President as Prophet," *Seattle Times*, September 23, 2004.
77. David Domke, "Divine Dictates," *Baltimore Sun*, February 6, 2005.
78. "Bush and God," *Newsweek*.
79. Domke, *God Willing?*, p. 93.
80. "How Bush Speaks in Religious Code."
81. Domke, "Bush's Fundamentalism."
82. "Bush Quietly Meets with Amish Here," *Lancaster New Era*, July 16, 2004.
83. "Just How Devout Do Americans Want Their President to Be?" *Time*, June 21, 2004.
84. Page, "Churchgoing Closely Tied to Voting Patterns."

85. Building political strength through social programs and social-welfare spending has been a staple of Democratic politics, and save for the larger theocratic framework in which faith-based social programs cradle, the Republican imitation would be shrewd. The Democrats obviously politicized labor during the 1930s, and poverty and welfare during the 1960s, but the Republicans in doing so with church-based programs face unique constitutional constraints.

86. "Democrats Hope to Draw Swing Voters," *Christian Science Monitor,* October 26, 2004.

87. Ibid.

88. "The God Gap," *CWN/CBN News,* October 15, 2004.

89. "Across Europe," *Christian Science Monitor,* February 22, 2005.

90. One Georgia newspaper pursued a story in late October that GOP strategists sought to maximize turnout in Georgia, Texas, and South Carolina, although all three were safe for Bush, to guard against the chance that Bush might lose the popular vote again even while winning in the electoral college.

91. "Bush Campaign Seeks Help from the Congregations," *The New York Times,* June 3, 2004.

92. Ibid.

93. "Evangelicals Say They Led Charge," *The Washington Post,* November 8, 2004.

94. Ibid.

95. Derrick Jackson, "Bush's Vatican Strategy," *Boston Globe,* June 15, 2004.

96. "GOP Wants Catholic Parishes to Turn Over Membership Rolls," Associated Press, July 29, 2004.

97. Steven Waldman and John Green, "It Wasn't Just (or Even Mostly) the Religious Right," *Beliefnet,* November, 2004.

98. This is based on the author's research into nineteenth-century Ohio voting patterns for his biography *William McKinley* (New York: Henry Holt, 2003).

99. *Religious Congregations and Membership, 2000* (Nashville, Tenn.: Glenmary Research Center, 2002), pp. 351–70.

100. A discussion of Green's religious typologies can be found under "Religious Landscape" on the research page of the University of Akron Web site at www.uakron.edu/6/iss.

101. Waldman and Green, "It Wasn't Just."

102. Based on the author's own election research.

103. "Southern Baptists Focus on Cleveland," Cleveland *Plain Dealer,* January 10, 2005.

104. "Movement in Pews Tries to Jolt Ohio," *The New York Times,* March 27, 2005.

105. Goff and Harvey, *Themes in Religion,* pp. 357–58.

106. Oran Smith, *Baptist Republicanism,* pp. 33, 134, 168, 170, 171.

107. Ibid., p. 6.

108. Flake, *Politics of Religious Identity,* p. 5.

109. Goff and Harvey, *Themes in Religion,* p. 351.

110. Ibid., p. 62.

111. Ibid., p. 185.

112. *Religious Congregations and Membership, 2000,* p. 564.

113. "Jerry Falwell," Wikipedia at www.wikipedia.org/wiki/Jerry_Falwell.

114. Oran Smith, *Baptist Republicanism,* p. 103.

115. "Bob Jones Lets the Theocratic Agenda Slip Out," *Dispatches from the Culture Wars,* November 12, 2004, www.stcynic.com/blog/archives/2004/11.

116. Maureen Farrell, "On a Mission from God," Buzzflash.com/farrell/04/03.

117. Phillips, *American Dynasty,* pp. 234–35.

118. Frederick Clarkson, "Theocratic Dominionism Gains Influence," *The Public Eye Magazine,* vol. 8, part 3, March–June 1994, pp. 2–3, online at www.publiceye.org.

119. The furtiveness of the religious right does not simply exist in the minds of its detractors; it has existed for decades—and occasionally been acknowledged—in the minds of many of

its most capable strategists. Much has been written about the tactics of top Georgia Republican Ralph Reed during his years as the top political operative of Pat Robertson's Christian Coalition. A recent detailed exposition—"Stealth, Secrecy Are Reed's Calling Cards"—appeared in the October 23, 2005, *Atlanta Constitution*. For the rhetorical and organizational deceptions of the Christian Reconstructionist movement, see a series of articles by Frederick Clarkson in the March–June 1994 issue of *The Public Eye*.

120. Pew Center poll, June 2004.
121. "Church and State Poll: Most American Think Church Should Steer Clear of Politics," ABC News.com, June 4, 2004.
122. Ibid.
123. Page, "Churchgoing Closely Tied to Voting Patterns."
124. Speech of Rabbi David Saperstein, Center for American Progress, June 9, 2004, www.americanprogress.org.
125. Page, "Churchgoing Closely Tied to Voting Patterns."
126. Besides being praised on religious-right Web sites, these proposals are described, critically indeed, on the Web site of Theocracy Watch, www.theocracywatch.com.
127. Republican representative Shay's description of the GOP as a theocracy is quoted in *The New York Times* of March 23, 2005.

Chapter 7: Church, State, and National Decline

1. Bolce and De Maio, "Party of Unbelievers," p. 4.
2. Rossing, *The Rapture Exposed*.
3. James L. Guth and John C. Green, eds., *The Bible and the Ballot Box: Religion and Politics in the 1988 Election* (Boulder, Colo.: Westview Press, 1991).
4. Of the four empires, each was the leading commercial or financial power; Rome was the leading military power, as was Spain; the Dutch and British never had dominant armies, but they enjoyed naval supremacy to support their far-flung trade and commerce.
5. Henry Kamen, *Empire* (New York: HarperCollins, 2003), pp. xxiii–xxv.
6. Edward Gibbon, *The Decline and Fall of the Roman Empire*.
7. Michael Grant, *The Fall of the Roman Empire* (New York: Collier Books, 1990), p. 171.
8. J. H. Elliott, *Imperial Spain* (New York: Mentor Books, 1966), pp. 239–44.
9. Kamen, *Empire*, p. 375.
10. Elliott, *Imperial Spain*, pp. 308–23, 363–64.
11. Charles Kindleberger, *World Economic Primacy, 1500 to 1900* (New York: Oxford University Press, 1996), p. 74.
12. Elliott, *Imperial Spain*, p. 363.
13. Paul C. Allen, *Philip III* (New Haven, Conn.: Yale University Press, 2000), p. 244.
14. Jonathan Israel, *The Dutch Republic*, pp. 1019–37.
15. Simon Schama, *Patriots and Liberators* (New York: Vintage, 1992), p. 17; Israel, *The Dutch Republic*, pp. 1067–78.
16. In 1795, with revolutionary French military backing, the Dutch established the so-called Batavian Republic, which in 1796 disestablished the Dutch Reformed Church.
17. Corelli Barnett, *Collapse of British Power*, pp. 23–24.
18. Paul Thompson, *The Edwardians* (New York: Routledge, 1992), pp. 173–74.
19. Elmer Towns and Douglas Porter, *The Ten Greatest Revivals Ever* (Ann Arbor, Mich.: Servant Publications, 2000), pp. 3–4.
20. Charles Freeman, *The Closing of the Western Mind* (New York: Knopf, 2002).
21. Ibid., p. 322.
22. Elliott, *Imperial Spain*, p. 293.
23. Kamen, *Empire*, p. 505.

24. Ibid., p. 506.
25. David S. Landes, *The Wealth and Poverty of Nations* (New York: Norton, 1998), p. 181.
26. Israel, *The Dutch Republic,* p. 1043.
27. Ibid., pp. 1062–65.
28. Barnett, *Collapse of British Power,* p. 25.
29. Freeman, *Closing of the Western Mind,* p. 26.
30. Elliott, *Imperial Spain,* p. 306.
31. Charles Boxer, *The Dutch Seaborne Empire* (London: Penguin, 1988), p. 305.
32. Kevin P. Phillips, *Wealth and Democracy* (New York: Broadway, 2002), p. 171.
33. George Dangerfield, *The Strange Death of Liberal England, 1910–14* (New York: Capricorn Books, 1961), p. 259.
34. Karl Beckson, *London in the 1890s* (New York: Norton, 1992).
35. Arthur Sullivan, "Thanksgiving for Victory," 1902.
36. Cecil Eby, *The Road to Armageddon: The Martial Spirit in English Popular Literature, 1870–1914* (Durham, N.C.: Duke University Press, 1987), p. 5.
37. Russell's prophecy drew considerable attention in 1914.
38. Between the "Christian nation" platform adopted by the Texas Republican party in 2004 and the kindred action by the Arizona GOP in 1988, dozens of other related pronouncements have been made by state parties, mostly in the South and West. The Oklahoma GOP, for one, came out against the separation of church and state. Amazingly, no full compilation exists.
39. The details of the 2004 Texas GOP platform can be perused at www.theocracywatch.com.
40. Kaplan, *With God on Their Side,* p. 134.
41. Ibid., p. 34.
42. Ibid., p. 134.
43. Ibid., pp. 135–36.
44. Ibid., pp. 34–35.
45. Ibid., p. 39.
46. Hamil R. Harris, "Putting Worship into Their Workdays," *The Washington Post,* November 19, 2001.
47. Indeed, many of the GOP's House and Senate leaders earned 100 percent ratings.
48. Ron Suskind, *The Price of Loyalty* (New York: Simon & Schuster, 2004), p. 292.
49. www.raticol.org/ratville/CAH/DiIulio.html.
50. "Joe, I don't do nuance." George W. Bush to Senator Joseph Biden as quoted in *Time,* February 15, 2004.
51. "Bush Mixes Humor with Humility in Commencement Talk," *Yale Daily News,* May 22, 2001.
52. Ron Suskind, "Without a Doubt," *The New York Times Magazine,* October 17, 2004.
53. Kaplan, *With God on Their Side,* p. 4.
54. Shays was quoted in *The New York Times* of March 23, 2005; Chafee in Suskind, "Without a Doubt."
55. Such results came in various flavors, but one of the most revealing followed the Schiavo controversy, when an NBC/*Wall Street Journal* poll reported one-third of Republicans saying that Congress should prevent Bush and party leaders from "going too far in pushing their agenda." John Harwood, "Republicans Splinter on Bush Agenda," *The Wall Street Journal,* April 7, 2005.
56. The viewpoints and activities of the two groups can be studied online at www.acton.org and www.stewards.net.
57. Since 1998, Acton has received $100,000 from Exxon, according to Exxonsecrets.org.
58. Bill Berkowitz, "God Hates Environmentalists," *Working for Change,* June 22, 2001.
59. "Theologians Warn of 'False Gospel' in Environment," National Council of Churches

news release, February 14, 2005, available at www.nccusa.org/news/14.02.05godsearth. html.

60. "Stem Cell Wedge," *The Nation,* June 20, 2005, p. 8.

61. On the Brazilian-U.S. aid cutoff, see "Prostitution Puts U.S. and Brazil at Odds on AIDS Policy," *The New York Times,* July 24, 2005.

62. Some activists not only advocate the death penalty but support biblical death by stoning.

63. Indeed, March 2005 polling by CBS News found 82 percent opposing presidential and congressional intervention. See www.cbsnews.com/stories/2005/03/23politics.

64. Kaplan *With God on Their Side,* pp. 114–15.

65. Ibid., p. 147.

66. For discussion of the limited roles of women in the three faiths—the Assemblies of God, Roman Catholicism, and Orthodox Judaism—see "Women's Ordination: Priests, Pastors, Ministers, Rabbis" at www.religioustolerance.org/femclgy.htm; "The Role of Women in Ministry," General Council of the Assemblies of God, www.ag.org/top/beliefs; and "The Roles of Women in Judaism," Wikipedia, http://en.wikipedia.org/wiki/role_of_women_ in_judiasm.

67. R. Albert Mohler, "The Baby Gap: Parenthood and Politics," ChristianPost.com, January 14, 2005.

68. Akenson, *God's Peoples,* pp. 17–20.

69. There is no movement "platform," but the zealots take many such viewpoints.

70. The important question is whether the more respectable groups recognize the Christian Reconstructionist movement as an important ally from which some distance must be kept or whether the partial philosophical overlap is coincidental and unimportant.

71. Clarkson, "Theocratic Dominionism Gains Influence," parts 1 and 2.

72. John Sugg, "America the Theocracy," *Creative Loafing,* March 25, 2004.

73. According to *The American Prospect,* Titus took the lead in drafting the Constitution Restoration Act for congressional conservatives. See Sam Rosenfeld, "Disorder in the Court," *The American Prospect,* July 3, 2005.

74. For a broad overview of the political connections of the Christian Reconstructionist movement, with specific reference to Olasky, see "Operation Potomac," by Rob Boston of Americans United for the Separation of Church and State, dated October 2001, on its Web site at www.au.org.

75. "New Child Welfare Head in Florida Is Drawing Fire," *The New York Times,* August 16, 2002.

76. "Inside the Council for National Policy," ABC News, May 2, 2002.

77. Frank Rich, "A High-Tech Lynching in Prime Time," *The New York Times,* April 24, 2005.

78. "2 Evangelicals Want to Strip Court's Funds," *Los Angeles Times,* April 22, 2005.

79. Kaplan, *With God on Their Side,* p. 117.

80. Ibid., pp. 93, 126.

81. Letter to the editor on Russell E. Train, "When Politics Trumps Science," *The New York Times,* June 21, 2003.

82. "Scientific Integrity in Policymaking: An Investigation into the Bush Administration's Misuse of Science," February 2004. See the Web site of the Union of Concerned Scientists at www.ucsusa.org.

83. Maureen Dowd, "Tribulation Worketh Patience," *The New York Times,* October 9, 2002.

84. John Danforth, "In the Name of Politics," *The New York Times,* March 30, 2005.

85. Glenn Scherer, "George Bush's War on Nature," Salon.com.

86. Anti-evolution activity ballooned in the "red" states in 2005, according to pro-evolution chroniclers and activists. But the latter were cheered by a November 2005 victory for pro-evolution forces in a school board election in Dover, Pennsylvania. Dover was the first school district in the nation to order the introduction of "intelligent design" in a science class curriculum.

87. For more details, see Barbara Forrest and Paul Gross, *Creationism's Trojan Horse* (New York: Oxford University Press, 2004).
88. Clyde Prestowitz, *Three Billion New Capitalists* (New York: Basic Books, 2005), pp. 8, 135.
89. Kaplan, *With God on Their Side*, p. 271.
90. "M.I.T. Chief Urges Research Funds Boost," *Financial Times*, March 7, 2005.
91. Forrest and Gross, *Trojan Horse*, p. 186.
92. Goff and Harvey, *Themes in Religion*, p. 290.
93. Ibid.
94. "Cameras Rolling," *Christianity Today*, July 10, 2000.
95. Concord Coalition talking points for Peterson's book appearances for *Running on Empty*, 2004.
96. See, for example, Geoffrey Hindley, *The Crusades* (New York: Carroll and Graf, 2003), p. 259.
97. Peter Hopkirk, *Like Hidden Fire* (New York: Kodansha International, 1994), pp. 21–24.
98. Niall Ferguson, *The Pity of War* (New York: Basic Books, 1999), pp. 208–9.
99. See, for example, Thomas E. Woods, Jr., *The War for Righteousness* (New York: ISI Books, 2004).
100. Jerry Falwell was prominent among the religious-right leaders identifying the Soviet Union as the biblical enemy.
101. "Seeing Islam as 'Evil Faith,' Evangelicals Seek Converts," *The New York Times*, May 27, 2003.
102. Paul Boyer, "When U.S. Foreign Policy Meets Biblical Prophecy," *Alternet*, February 20, 2003, www.alternet.org/story/15221/.
103. Ibid.
104. Ibid.
105. Kaplan, *With God on Their Side*, p. 30.
106. Rossing, *Rapture*, pp. 173–74.
107. Ibid., p. 99.
108. Ibid., pp. 4, 42.
109. The three Catholic critiques of the rapture are Carl E. Olsen, *Will Catholics Be Left Behind?* (San Francisco: Ignatius Press, 2003); Paul Thigpen, *The Rapture Trap* (West Chester, Pa.: Ascension Press, 2001); and David Currie, *Rapture: The End-Times Error That Leaves the Bible Behind* (Manchester, N.H.: Sophia Institute Press, 2003).
110. Fyrkholm, quoted in Rossing, *Rapture*, p. 98.
111. "Bush and God," *Newsweek*, March 10, 2003.
112. Hugh McLeod, "Protestantism and British Identity," in Peter Van der Veer and Hartmut Lehmann, eds., *Nation and Religion* (Princeton, N.J.: Princeton University Press, 1999), pp. 58–59.
113. Arthur Marwick, *The Deluge* (New York: Macmillan, 1965), p. 297.
114. David Fromkin, *A Peace to End All Peace* (New York: Henry Holt, 1989), pp. 268–69.
115. Karen Armstrong, *Holy War* (New York: Anchor Books, 2004), p. 521.
116. Eby, *Armageddon*, p. 7.
117. Ibid., p. 206.
118. Hindley, *The Crusades*, p. 259.
119. Ibid., p. 258.
120. Fromkin, *Peace*, pp. 268–70, 276–301.
121. Armstrong, *Holy War*, p. 522.
122. Fromkin, *Peace*, pp. 263–75.
123. Ibid., pp. 281–83, 301.
124. Ibid., pp. 558–60.
125. Ibid., pp. 398–99.
126. Ibid., pp. 298–99.

127. Ben McIntyre, "Bush Fights the Good Fight with a Righteous Quotation," *The Times* (London), March 7, 2003.
128. Kaplan, *With God on Their Side*, p. 13.
129. Goff and Harvey, *Themes in Religion*, p. 58.
130. Kaplan, *With God on Their Side*, pp. 13–15; "Seeing Islam as 'Evil Faith.'"
131. "U.S. Christian Missions in the Middle East," *Los Angeles Times*, March 18, 2004.
132. "Evangelicals Building a Base in Iraq," *The Washington Post*, June 23, 2005.
133. Boyer, "Biblical Prophecy," p. 3.
134. Ibid.
135. For details on the cognitive dissonance involved, see "Bush Supporters Still Believe Iraq Had WMD or Major Program," Program on International Policy Attitudes, University of Maryland, October 21, 2004, www.pipa.org/OnlineReports.

Chapter 8: Soaring Debt, Uncertain Politics, and the Financialization of the United States

1. The manufacturing number is not one that senior government officials like to acknowledge; they prefer to talk about productivity or output.
2. *Financial Services Fact Book for 2005*, copublished by the Insurance Information Institute and the Financial Services Roundtable. It is available online at www.financialservicesfacts.org.
3. Ibid.
4. Stephen Leeb, "The Hot Financial Sector," *The Complete Investor*, August 2004, p. 1.
5. "America's False Profits," August 24, 2004, Economist.com.
6. Ibid.
7. Loan-sharking, however, now involves much higher rates.
8. Eamonn Fingleton, *In Praise of Hard Industries* (Boston: Houghton Mifflin, 1999).
9. Johnson's critics used the term "guns and butter" to argue that his attempt to have both was unrealistic.
10. Historical Tables, *Budget of the United States Government, Fiscal Year 2000* (Washington, D.C.: U.S. Government Printing Office, 1999), pp. 21–22.
11. Bush proposed that fast-food restaurants be reclassified in the manufacturing sector in the *Economic Report of the President 2004*. For a month or so it was the subject of considerable amusement.
12. Paul Kasriel, chief economist at Northern Trust Company, quoted in "Spending Our Way to Disaster," *CNN/Money*, October 3, 2003.
13. "A Phony Recovery," *The Economist*, February 26, 2004.
14. "America's False Profits."
15. "Best of All Possible Worlds?" *The New York Times*, January 21, 2005.
16. Paul Kasriel, "Householders Run Record $324 Billion Deficit," Northern Trust Company, October 24, 2004, www.northerntrust.com.
17. Ibid.
18. By the end of 2005, total credit-market debt as a percentage of GDP was probably 310 to 315 percent.
19. Robert Marks, "The Case for Credit," *Barron's*, August 9, 2004.
20. John Brooks, *The Go-Go Years* (New York: John Wiley, 1999), p. 160.
21. Table B-75, Mortgage Debt Outstanding, *Economic Report of the President, 2005*, p. 300.
22. Brooks, *Go-Go Years*, p. 99.
23. Table B-32, Gross Savings and Investment, 1959–2004, *Economic Report of the President, 2005*, p. 249.
24. John D. Hicks, *Republican Ascendancy* (New York: Harper & Row, 1960), p. 107.

25. Kevin P. Phillips, *Post-Conservative America* (New York: Random House, 1982), p. 9.
26. Supposedly, Nixon made the comment privately to newscaster Howard K. Smith in 1970, and Smith repeated on ABC News in January 1971.
27. Alfred Malabre, *Beyond Our Means* (New York: Random House, 1987); Peter G. Peterson, *On Borrowed Time* (New York: Simon & Schuster, 1988); Benjamin M. Friedman, *Day of Reckoning* (New York: Random House, 1989); James Medoff and Andrew Harless, *The Indebted Society* (Boston: Little, Brown, 1996).
28. This quotation is from Bush's address to Congress, February 27, 2001.
29. As of December 2005, the Dow-Jones Industrial Average, from its low, had regained some 80 percent of the ground lost between 2000 and 2002.
30. Stephen S. Roach, "Global Economic Forum," Morgan Stanley, January 9, 2004, www.morganstanley.com/GEFdata/digests/20040109=fri.html.
31. The basic mandate of the Federal Reserve Board, as set out in the Federal Reserve Act of 1913, was to furnish an elastic currency, to afford a means of rediscounting commercial paper, and to establish a more effective supervision of banks. These ends, along with maintaining the official payments system, are still central in the current responsibilities of the Federal Reserve, as set out in Title 12 of the *U.S. Code*, but in fact its national and global role has expanded enormously.
32. Phillips, *Wealth and Democracy*, p. 45.
33. "Asking Big Spenders to Be Big Savers, Too," *The New York Times*, October 17, 2004.
34. The workforce of the FIRE sector in 2000 was not quite 8 million, according to data from the Bureau of Labor Statistics published by the Labor Research Association (www.laborresearch.org); the 17 million employment in manufacturing in 1960 is taken from the *Statistical History of the United States*, citing the *Handbook of Labor Statistics*, 1972, p. 89. The overall workforce for both years—65 million in 1960 and 128 million in 2000—is from current census data.
35. Phillips, *Wealth and Democracy*, p. 103.
36. Medoff and Harless, *Indebted Society*, p. 65.
37. Ibid., p. 66.
38. *The New York Times* used the term in "Maybe It's Not All Your Fault," December 5, 2004.
39. Bill Clinton made this remark in spring 1993. Some media ran the quote with the expletive included, but more deleted it.
40. "Breaking Glass-Steagall," *The Nation*, November 15, 1999.
41. Nomi Prins, *Other People's Money* (New York: The New Press, 2004), p. 13.
42. "The Buying of the President, 2004," Center for Public Integrity, www.publicintegrity.org/bop2004/reportaspx.910-220.
43. See Phillips, *American Dynasty*, pp. 119–28.
44. Kasriel, "Spending Our Way to Disaster."
45. Ray Dalio, "The Money Shuffler's Vig," *Bridgewater Daily Observation*, September 22, 2004.
46. "Fifty of the Wealthiest People of the Past 1,000 Years," *The Wall Street Journal*, January 11, 1999.
47. Phillips, *Wealth and Democracy*, p. 216.
48. The total of U.S. credit market debt is generally taken as $40 trillion, but government data shows a rise from $25.3 trillion in 1999 to $38.1 trillion in the second quarter of 2004 (*Federal Reserve Statistical Release*, September 21, 2005). The estimate of $270 trillion in global derivative positions was frequently cited during 2005 by the press and on the Internet but was obviously less than precise.
49. A relaxed view of massive derivative positions and a comfortable belief in a new globalized savings pool mark the early-twenty-first century frontier of confidence among market economists, most of whom count both as forces for stability.

50. "Greenspan's Warning," *Barron's*, May 23, 2005.
51. Charles P. Kindleberger, *Manias, Panics, and Crashes* (New York: Basic Books, 1978), pp. 253–59.
52. By 2002, this broadest of monetary bases had *doubled* in a decade, from $4 trillion to $8 trillion.
53. The term is used, for example, in Prestowitz, *New Capitalists*, p. 210.
54. The authority and policy-making reach of the Federal Reserve Board has in itself been vital to the rise of the financial-services sector since the 1980s. Besides having responsibility for the U.S. monetary and payments system, the Fed regulates much of the banking system and has assumed the further role of bailing it out when necessary. Considering that the Class A and Class C directors of the twelve individual Federal Reserve banks are elected by member commercial banks in those districts, the financial-services sector has a unique and privileged status within the U.S. political economy.
55. Phillips, *Wealth and Democracy*, Chapter 7 (pp. 293–316, especially 298–303).
56. James Macdonald, *A Free Nation Deep in Debt: The Financial Roots of Democracy* (New York: Farrar, Straus and Giroux, 2003).
57. "U.S. Consumer Debt Reaches Record Levels," January 15, 2004, www.wsws.org/articles/2004/Jan2004/debt-j15.shtml.
58. Ibid.
59. "Maybe It's Not All Your Fault."
60. "Tipping Points," *Financial Sense Online*, May 20, 2005, www.financialsense.com/stormwatch/2005/0520/html.
61. "U.S. Household Debt Service Ratio Hits All-Time High," Dow-Jones Newswires, June 16, 2005.
62. "Tipping Points," p. 7.
63. The deregulation of interest rates between 1978 and 1980, while necessary as inflation soared during those years, wound up enabling a twenty-first-century framework—the credit-card industry, in particular—in which high interest rates and fees often bore no relationship to the (low) federal funds rate and discount rate set by the Fed.
64. Prins, *Other People's Money*, p. 129.
65. See the testimony of Arthur Levitt, chairman of the Securities and Exchange Commission, before the Committee on Banking and Financial Services of the U.S. House of Representatives, March 15, 1995.
66. Prins, *Other People's Money*, pp. 38–39.
67. "Top 1,000 World Banks," *The Banker*, July 2, 2004.
68. Bob Woodward, *Maestro* (New York: Simon & Schuster, 2000), pp. 72–73.
69. Why Is Citigroup the Bank That Everyone Loves to Hate?" *The Times* (London), May 25, 2005.
70. This is commonplace. Such settlements often allow a denial of the wrongdoing alleged despite the contradictory aspect of making such a large payment.
71. Phillips, *American Dynasty*, pp. 158, 165.
72. Prins, *Other People's Money*, p. 38.
73. Ibid.
74. "U.S. Economy Slows as Global Consumer Debt Rises," American Sociological Association press release, August 15, 2004.
75. "Debt Nation," *Jim Lehrer NewsHour Extra*, April 15, 2001.
76. "Maybe It's Not All Your Fault."
77. Ibid.
78. "Erase Debt Now (Lose Your House Later)," *The New York Times*, October 10, 2004.
79. "As Bills Mount, Debts on Homes Rise for Elderly," *The New York Times*, July 4, 2004.
80. "Your Money or Your Life," *The Nation*, February 21, 2005.
81. "To Burst or Not to Burst," *The Economist*, September 7, 2002.

82. "Hear a Pop? Watch Out," *The New York Times,* May 25, 2005.
83. Prins, *Other People's Money,* p. 131.
84. "Soaring Interest Compounds Credit Card Pain for Millions," *The New York Times,* November 21, 2004.

Chapter 9: Debt

 1. Kevin Phillips, "Hegemony, Hubris and Overreach," *The Iraq War Reader* (New York: Touchstone, 2003), p. 633.
 2. Ibid., p. 634.
 3. Ibid.
 4. Will and Ariel Durant, *The Lessons of History* (New York: Simon & Schuster, 1968), p. 88.
 5. Phillips, *Wealth and Democracy,* p. 171.
 6. Fernand Braudel, *On History* (Chicago: University of Chicago Press, 1980), p. 88.
 7. J. H. Elliott, *Spain and Its World, 1500–1700* (New Haven, Conn.: Yale University Press, 1989), p. 248.
 8. William Wolman and Anne Colamosca, *The Judas Economy: The Triumph of Capital and the Betrayal of Work* (New York: Addison-Wesley, 1997), p. 186.
 9. Stanley J. Stein and Barbara H. Stein, *Silver, Trade and War* (Baltimore: The Johns Hopkins University Press, 2000), p. 26; J. H. Elliott, *Imperial Spain, 1479–1716* (New York: Mentor Books, 1966), p. 184.
10. Elliott, *Imperial Spain,* p. 313.
11. Kamen, *Empire,* p. 493.
12. Elliott, *Imperial Spain,* p. 307.
13. Anthony J. Cascardia, *Ideologies of History in the Spanish Golden Age* (University Park: Pennsylvania State University Press, 1997), p. 174.
14. Kamen, *Empire,* p. 282.
15. Ibid., p. 89.
16. However much Spain wound up as an economic has-been by 1660, its role in the European and world economies of the sixteenth and early seventeenth century was huge. Spanish officials interlocked with the financial elites in other Hapsburg spheres of interest like Italy, Germany, and Flanders. Many of these moved to Spain and helped run the system by which New World gold was fed into Europe's money supply, commerce, and even war mobilization. This system would have to be a major component in any hypothetical calculus of a European, Hapsburg, or Spanish gross domestic or gross national product—even if most of the Spanish people got little or no benefit.
17. Elliott, *Spain and Its World,* p. 233.
18. Macdonald, *Deep in Debt,* p. 119.
19. Stein and Stein, *Silver,* p. 3.
20. Ibid., p. 21.
21. Kamen, *Empire,* pp. 292, 297.
22. Ibid., p. 297.
23. Ibid., p. 298.
24. Elliott, *Imperial Spain,* p. 313; Elliott, *Spain and Its World,* p. 25.
25. Ravi Batra, *Greenspan's Fraud* (New York: Palgrave Macmillan, 2005), pp. 195–96.
26. House hearings: Greenspan's testimony, "Semi-Annual Report on Monetary Policy," Federal News Service, July 15, 2003.
27. Stein and Stein, *Silver,* p. 376.
28. Elliott, *Imperial Spain,* p. 204.
29. Elliott, *Spain and Its World,* p. 233.
30. Macdonald, *Deep in Debt,* pp. 155 and 157.

31. Kevin P. Phillips, *Boiling Point* (New York: Random House, 1993), p. 206.
32. Ibid., p. 199.
33. Schama, *Embarrassment of Riches*, p. 286.
34. Israel, *Dutch Republic*, p. 1007.
35. Ibid.
36. Phillips, *Boiling Point*, p. 20.
37. Israel, *Dutch Republic*, p. 1003.
38. Fernand Braudel, *The Wheels of Commerce* (New York: Harper & Row, 1982), p. 535.
39. Boxer, *Dutch Seaborne Empire*, p. 329.
40. Phillips, *Boiling Point*, p. 207.
41. Macdonald, *Deep in Debt*, p. 353.
42. Phillips, *Boiling Point*, p. 207.
43. Thompson, *The Edwardians*, p. 154.
44. Niall Ferguson, *Cash Nexus* (New York: Basic Books, 2001), p. 279.
45. David Thomson, *England in the Nineteenth Century* (London: Penguin, 1953), p. 166.
46. Kennedy, *Rise and Fall*, p. 86.
47. The dates for the royal bankruptcies—in some ways processes better described as refinancings—can be found in most Spanish histories. As for the flow of silver from the New World, yearly data records levels between 1616 and 1625 not so far removed from those of the late-sixteenth-century glory years. Stein and Stein, *Silver*, p. 24. Then, just as Spanish success in the Thirty Years War tailed off, so did the bullion arrivals.
48. Historians agree that the Dutch taxed themselves at very high rates to pay for their eighty-year war to break free of Spain. Thus the fiscal burden imposed by the French wars between 1688 and 1713—public debt was estimated to have risen above 200 percent of GDP—could have been seen as a manageable extension of this earlier challenge. But it was not.
49. Macdonald, *Deep in Debt*, p. 238.
50. Ibid., p. 352.
51. Ibid., p. 350.
52. Friedberg, *Weary Titan*, pp. 75–76.
53. Kennedy, *Rise and Fall*, p. 158.
54. Landes, *Wealth and Poverty*, pp. 445–46.
55. CIA, *The World Factbook*, June 2005, www.cia.gov/cia/factbook/geos.
56. Ibid.; CIA export estimates for 2004 by country.
57. Author Eamonn Fingleton (*In Praise of Hard Industries*) cites the 1998 edition of *OECD in Figures* to make the case that U.S. per capita income trailed that of the export powerhouses, Germany, Switzerland, and Japan. He adds that the three nations, as well as some others in the OECD, beat the United States in income growth between 1980 and 1996 (pp. 7–8). The U.S. gains in recent years are regarded by many in Europe and Asia as fueled by unsustainable borrowing.
58. Ferguson, *Cash Nexus*, p. 294.
59. The decline from 2000 to 2003 in U.S. merchandise exports as a share of GDP is set out in recent data from the International Trade Administration, Table 3, *U.S. Trade in Goods, 1982–2004*, http://ita.doc.gov. By the 2010s, it is easy to imagine a further decline to just 4 to 5 percent.
60. The categories counted as advanced-technology products are listed in the Advanced Technology Product definitions published as part of the Census Bureau's foreign trade statistics. The Web citation is http://www.census.gov/foreign-trade/reference/glossary/a/atp.html.
61. Prestowitz, *New Capitalists*, pp. 126–28.
62. Ibid., pp. 130–34.
63. Ibid., p. 130.

64. "$600 Million over Ten Years," *Manufacturing & Technology News*, February 3, 2004.
65. Prestowitz, *New Capitalists*, p. 132.
66. Barnett, *Collapse of British Power*, pp. 81–90.
67. Prestowitz, *New Capitalists*, pp. 128, 130–31, 157–58.
68. Subir Roy, "India Gets Competitive in Steel," (Mumbai) *Business Standard*, February 23, 2005.
69. Landes, *Wealth and Poverty*, pp. 443–44; Kennedy, *Rise and Fall*, p. 152; Israel, *Dutch Primacy*, pp. 400–401.
70. Fingleton, *In Praise of Hard Industries*, p. 76.
71. Prestowitz, *New Capitalists*, p. 210.
72. Ibid., p. 177.
73. Ibid., p. 213.
74. Jared Diamond, "Why Do Some Societies Make Disastrous Decisions?" Lewis Thomas Prize lecture, March 2003, www.edge.org.

Chapter 10: Serial Bubbles and Foreign Debt Holders

1. "Spending Our Way to Disaster," CNN/*Money*, October 3, 2003.
2. "The U.S. as a Net Debtor: The Sustainability of the U.S. External Imbalances," November 2004, available at www.rgemonitor.com/Roubini-Setser-US-External-Imbalances.pdf.
3. Anna Bernasek, "The Outer Limits of National Debt," *The New York Times*, May 1, 2005.
4. Ibid.
5. E. Victor Morgan, *A History of Money* (New York: Penguin, 1965), p. 73.
6. Ben J. Wattenberg, ed., *The Statistical History of the United States* (New York: Basic Books, 1976), p. 491.
7. Not everyone follows the same calculus. Some private commentators use $40 trillion, but the last government figure was $38.1 trillion (see note 48, chapter 8). By the end of 2005, to be sure, the official data presumably neared $40 trillion.
8. "Spending Our Way to Disaster," p. 2.
9. Grant, the publisher of *Grant's Interest Rate Observer*, is widely credited with coining the term and concept of "the socialization of credit risk."
10. *Flow of Funds Report*, U.S. Treasury, June 19, 2005, www.bopnews.com.
11. See "New Bankruptcy Law Changes Debtor's Responsibilities," Internal Revenue Service, November 2005 (FS-2005-18), for a summary of the changes.
12. For the criticisms voiced by House Democratic Leader Nancy Pelosi, see "U.S. Congress Enacts Bankruptcy Bill to Force Debt Repayment," *Bloomberg News*, April 14, 2005. *New York Times* columnist Paul Krugman used the term "debt-peonage." See www.pkarchive.org/column/030805.html.
13. "U.S. Congress Enacts Bankruptcy Bill."
14. See, for example, Manning's June 12, 2003, testimony before the Subcommittee on Financial Institutions and Consumer Credit of the House Committee on Financial Services. He describes the crystallizing 1990's focus not only on young people, but on other gullible elements of the population.
15. Peter Stearns, *Consumerism in World History* (New York: Routledge, 2001), p. 128.
16. "Asking Big Spenders to Be Big Savers, Too," *The New York Times*, October 17, 2004.
17. Alan Abelson, "Thank You, Shortsellers," *Barron's*, April 25, 2005.
18. "Credit Extra," *The Early Show*, CBS News, April 24, 2004.
19. The data from American Consumer Credit Counseling is set out in "The Midas Touch to Debt Problems," February 9, 2005, http.www.dcbtconsolidationcare.com.
20. *Flow of Funds Brief*, U.S. Treasury, September 16, 2004.
21. Alan Abelson, "Yuan Upsmanship," *Barron's*, July 25, 2005.
22. "Greenspan Wary of Risky Mortgages," *The Washington Post*, June 10, 2005.

23. Ibid.
24. Warren Buffett, annual message to Berkshire Hathaway, Inc., shareholders for 1983, Omaha, March 1984, www.berkshirehathaway.com/letters/1983.html.
25. Prins, *Other People's Money*, pp. 108, 112.
26. Warren Buffett, annual message to Berkshire Hathaway shareholders for 2004.
27. The surge in financial sector domestic debt from $4.33 trillion in 1995 to $11.79 trillion in 2004 is detailed in figure 6.1, Credit Market Debt Outstanding, *Flow of Funds Accounts of the United States,* June 9, 2005, www.federalreserve.gov/releases/z1/current/annuals/a/1994-2005.pdf.
28. Prins, *Other People's Money*, p. 46.
29. John C. Edmunds, "Securities: The New Wealth Machine," *Foreign Policy,* Fall 1996.
30. "Move to Speed Up Derivatives Trading," *Financial Times,* March 3, 2005.
31. Daniel Gross, "The Next Shock: Not Oil, but Debt," *The New York Times,* September 5, 2004.
32. "Handling the Truth," *Barron's,* February 3, 2005.
33. www.federalreserve.gov/release/householddebt/default.htm.
34. Ferguson, *Cash Nexus,* p. 293.
35. Lawrence H. Summers, "The U.S. Current Account Deficit and the Global Economy," *The Per Jacobsson Lecture,* October 3, 2004, www.perjacobsson.org/2004/100304.pdf.
36. *Economic and Budget Issue Brief,* CBO, July 12, 2005, p. 3.
37. "Most Treasuries in Foreign Hands," *Financial Times,* June 14, 2004.
38. "The Evolution and Implications of the U.S. Current Account Deficit," *EconSouth,* First Quarter, 2005.
39. Nouriel Roubini and Brad Setser, "Will the Bretton Woods II Regime Unravel Soon? The Risk of a Hard Landing in 2005–2006," pp. 9–10, www.rgemonitor.com/blog/roubini/91190.
40. "The China Trade Gets to Bush," *Barron's,* April 18, 2005.
41 Jim Puplava, "Tipping Points," *Financial Sense Online,* May 20, 2005.
42. Brad Setser, "6.4% of GDP Current Account Deficit in Q1," *Brad Setser's Web Log,* June 17, 2005, www.roubiniglobal.com./setser/archives/2005/06.
43. Brad Setser, "Oil and the U.S. Current Account Deficit," *Brad Setser's Web Log,* October 13, 2004, ibid.
44. Summers, "U.S. Current Account Deficit," pp. 9–10.
45. Fromkin, *Peace,* p. 253.
46. Kennedy, *Rise and Fall,* p. 40.
47. Ibid., p. 50.
48. Ibid., p. 48.
49. Israel, *The Dutch Republic,* pp. 970–71.
50. Ibid., p. 986.
51. Schama, *Patriots and Liberators,* p. 61.
52. "The Disappearing Dollar," *The Economist,* December 2, 2004.
53. Bernasek, "The Outer Limits."
54. The estimate of $3.7 trillion being needed to make the Social Security trust fund able to meet current obligations through 2075 comes from the Social Security system's own trustees.
55. Daniel Altman, "Social Security's Future?" *The New York Times,* February 6, 2005.
56. "Social Security Budget Woes Mean Painful Choices Loom," *USA Today,* March 15, 2005.
57. Nothing came of Bush's hopes of privatizing institutions like the University of Texas, but such thinking helps to explain his later willingness to joust unsuccessfully with Social Security.
58. In 2005, congressional Democrats contended that since 2001, the Republicans had used $670 billion in Social Security surpluses to support other programs. See www.waysandmeans_democrats/socsec/new-plan-and-budget.pdf.

59. "Social Security Budget Woes."
60. Nicholas Kristof, "A Glide Path to Ruin," *The New York Times*, June 26, 2005.

Chapter 11: The Erring Republican Majority

1. As 2005 opened, an assumption of a $40 to $50 per barrel oil price yielded an estimate of a $232 billion import burden. Should the imports needed rise to 6 to 8 million in 2010 at a $50 to $70 per barrel price, then $400 billion a year for foreign oil would be plausible enough. Few experts were venturing such predictions, but in early autumn 2005, the oil futures markets were pricing light sweet crude for December 2010 at $60 a barrel.
2. The possibility that ExxonMobil might get the Majnoon field, Iraq's biggest, was noted by journalists during the run-up to the Iraq war. Exxon had been a major player in Iraq before the 1969 nationalizations. In 1998, Saddam Hussein had tentatively earmarked Majnoon for France's Total, and loyally Republican Exxon would have been the logical major U.S. developer had the U.S. invasion and occupation been the hoped-for success.
3. Besides the bearish investment advisers, the Web site of economists Nouriel Roubini and Brad Setser (www.rge.monitor.com) generally represents this kind of polished mix of academic proficiency and skepticism.
4. Gross, "The Next Shock: Not Oil, but Debt."
5. As of late 2005, follow-ups to the weakened midyear energy legislation were being pursued.
6. "Painting the Economy into a Corner," editorial, *The New York Times*, August 12, 2004.
7. Despite the firming dollar, 2005 saw some significant adjustments of central-bank dollar reserves. In August, Russia dropped the dollar share of its reserves from 70 percent to 65 percent. Immediately after China's midsummer yuan revaluation, Malaysia's central bank shifted from dollar-based reserves to a basket of currencies.
8. "Warning from the Markets," *International Herald-Tribune*, February 25, 2005.
9. Goldman Sachs economists estimated that Asian intervention reduced the yields on U.S. bonds by only 0.4 percent, but economists Roubini and Setser estimated a much larger reduction—keeping yields down by some 2 percent. See Nouriel Roubini and Brad Setser, "Will the Bretton Woods II Regime Unravel Soon? The Risk of a Hard Landing in 2005–2006."
10. "42% in Gallup Poll 'Born-Again,'" *Religious News Service*, June 8, 2005.
11. Bush's statement was made in a White House press conference, May 25, 2005. See text, White House Press Office, May 25, 2005, www.whitehouse.gov/news/release/2005/05/20050525-5.html.
12. Gallup polls in May 2005 found 43 percent of Americans saying the Christian conservative movement had too much power, while only 22 percent thought it had too little. Gallup/*USA Today*/CNN polling for April 29 to May 1, 2005, www.usatoday/com/news/polls/tables.
13. Some 69 percent thought it improper for parties to ask for church rosters for voter registration drives. Pew Forum poll, "GOP Religion-Friendly Party," August 27, 2004, http://pewforum.org/docs/index.
14. E. J. Dionne, "McCain May Be Bush's Ticket," *The Washington Post*, June 14, 2005.
15. Albert J. Menendez, *The Perot Voters and the Future of American Politics* (Amherst, N.Y.: Prometheus Books, 1996), p. 41.
16. Ibid., p. 57.
17. Ibid., pp. 176, 216.
18. Ibid., p. 32.
19. Ibid., pp. 179–80.
20. See text of February 28, 2000, speech in Virginia by John McCain, posted on www.everything2.com/index/pl?node_id=489542.

21. Richard Land, the top Southern Baptist Convention representative in Washington, called McCain's comments "a remarkable two-day spasm of anger and badly mistaken electoral calculus," www.beliefnet.com/story_1574_2.html.

22. This number represents the U.S. net international investment position (NIIP) for 2001. See Roubini and Setser, "The U.S. as Net Debtor: The Sustainability of the U.S. External Imbalance," revised draft, November 2004.

23. Ibid.

24. "OPEC Sharply Reduces Dollar Exposure," *Financial Times,* December 6, 2004.

25. Ibid. The *Financial Times* also speculated that OPEC might be preparing to shift its oil pricing out of dollars.

26. The BIS survey implied more reserve changes to come, which partly proved out, but was constrained during 2005 by the effects of higher U.S. interest rates and corporate overseas profits repatriation in supporting the dollar.

27. The Asian currency possibilities are discussed, for example, in Prestowitz, *New Capitalists,* pp. 238–39, 276–77.

28. Brad Setser, "6.4 Percent of GDP Current Account Deficit in Q1," June 17, 2005, http://www.roubiniglobal.com/setser/archives/2005/06/64_of_gdp_curre.html.

29. See Prestowitz, *New Capitalists,* for a chillingly effective analysis.

30. Setser, "6.4 Percent of GDP."

31. Anna Bernasek, "Long on Cash, Short of Ideas," *The New York Times,* December 5, 2004.

32. "The Cash Heads Home," *Business Week,* December 27, 2004.

33. The Treasury's hopes for a repatriation in the $300-billion range were widely put about and cited.

34. See "Money Washes Ashore, Not Jobs," *Chicago Tribune,* May 31, 2005. The article quoted Jack Ablin, chief investment officer at Harris Bank, seeing "a huge boost for the dollar near-term if $300 billion is repatriated." By way of comparision, he observed that only $600 billion a year was moved between central banks.

35. "Bipolar Disorder," *Barron's,* June 13, 2005.

36. Paul Volcker, "An Economy on Thin Ice," *The Washington Post,* April 10, 2005.

37. Prestowitz, *New Capitalists,* p. 256.

38. Promotion material for Peterson, *Running on Empty.*

39. "Prophecy: What the Bible Says About the End of the World," *Newsweek,* November 1, 1999.

40. "Religion and Politics: Contention and Consensus," *Pew Forum on Religion and Public Life,* July 24, 2003.

41. This is my mid-2005 list based on news stories and opinion columns. There may have been changes and additions.

42. Trade publications in some of these countries also commented on the advantages to be derived from diminished U.S. competition.

43. "Experts Attack Bush's Stance in AIDS Battle," *The Observer,* July 11, 2004.

44. For the Asian conference, see Kaplan, *With God on Their Side,* pp. 239–41; for the alignment with Islamic stalwarts and the Vatican, see "Exporting Ineffective Policy: The Globalization of American Abstinence-Only-Until-Marriage Programs," SIECUS Public Policy Fact Sheet, October 2003, and *With God on Their Side,* p. 243.

45. "It Will Take All Our Energy to Stand Still," *The Guardian,* March 8, 2005.

46. Garry Wills, "Fringe Government," *The New York Review of Books,* October 5, 2005.

47. In 2004, the General Accounting Office changed its name to the Government Accountability Office. For an explanation see the comments by Comptroller General David Walker on July 19, 2004, http://www.gao.gov/about/rollcall07192004.pdf.

48. "Brazil's Fight Against AIDS," *The New York Times,* July 31, 2005.

49. Phillips, *Post-Conservative America,* p. 239.

50. For the NIH episodes and harassment, see Kaplan, *With God on Their Side*, pp. 96–104. For the religious right's dealings with the Centers for Disease Control, see ibid., pp. 120–21, 190–93.

51. Ibid., p. 84.

52. Ibid., p. 189.

53. Walter Olson, "Invitation to a Stoning," *Reason*, November 1998.

54. Katha Pollitt, "Toothpaste, Cough Drops, Aspirin and Contraception," *The Nation*, March 15, 2004.

55. "Convenant Marriage Statistics," http://marriage.about.com/cs/covenantmarriage. According to this data, only one quarter of 1 percent opted for covenant marriage in Arizona, and even fewer in Arkansas.

56. A major 2003 story about polygamy and child brides in Morman Utah ("In Depth: The Dysorder," Las Vegas *Review-Journal*, November 2, 2003) quoted University of Utah law professor Ed Firmage saying that "within a hundred miles from where I stand now, you can find a hundred thousand polygamists in every direction."

57. Katha Pollitt, "Virginity or Death," *The Nation*, May 30, 2005, and "Stiffed," *The Nation*, June 13, 2005.

58. The $170 million was provided for in the 2005 federal budget. Calculations of 2001–2004 expenditures vary with the breadth of inclusion.

59. John Stratton Hawley, ed., *Fundamentalism and Gender* (New York: Oxford University Press, 1994), pp. 19–32.

60. Almond, Appleby, and Sivan, *Strong Religion*, p. 29.

61. Besides the public's 65 to 70 percent opposition to churches taking sides or endorsing candidates, a 2005 Zogby International poll found 59 percent of Americans calling it important or very important to maintain separation of church and state, while only 18 percent thought it was not important. On schools, voters favor vouchers, prayers, and sometimes aid to religious schools, but then cool if the activity is seen as jeopardizing the public school system.

62. Only 20 percent to 30 percent of Americans oppose teaching creationism or having the ten commandments on the walls of public buildings, but the level of support for creationism presupposes that evolution is also being taught.

63. Pew Research Center for the Public and the Press, July 2005 national poll released on August 3, 2005.

64. E. J. Dionne, column, *The Washington Post*, November 8, 2004.

65. "Roe's Army Reloads," *Newsweek*, August 8, 2005.

66. Garin-Hart Poll, "Women at the Center of Change," June 22, 2005.

67. CNN/Gallup Poll, late June 2005.

68. Pew Center Poll, July 2005

69. "Greenspan Wary of Risky Mortgages."

70. Prins, *Other People's Money*, p. 108.

71. "Move to Speed Up Derivatives Trading."

72. In June 2005, the *Wall Street Transcript* noted that the world's 8,500 hedge funds controlled at least $1 trillion in assets.

73. "Hedge Funds' Presence in Credit Markets Could Exacerbate Credit Problems—Fitch," Credit-derivatives.com, July 29, 2005, http://www.credit-derivatives.com.

74. Numerous banks in the United States and Canada were fined for their complicity with Enron.

75. "Fed Chief Warns of Housing Froth," *The Washington Post*, June 10, 2005.

76. Ibid.

77. By 2001, even the Federal Reserve Board felt constrained to discuss the perils of credit cards linked to available home-equity loans on its Web site, http://federalreserve.gov/pubs/equity/equity_english.htm.

78. The best credit bubble Web site, not surprisingly, is Doug Noland's *Credit Bubble Bulletin*, available through www.prudentbear.com.

79. Eduardo Porter, "Another Drink? China Is Paying," *The New York Times*, June 5, 2005.

80. Pankaj Mishra, "How India Reconciles Hindu Values and Biotech," *The New York Times*, August 21, 2005.

81. John Mauldin, "China: One Coin, Two Faces," January 23, 2005, 321.gold.com.

82. Prestowitz, *New Capitalists*, p. 74.

83. Ibid., p. 61.

84. "China," *Fortune*, October 4, 2004.

85. "Overseas Insourcing," *Harvard Magazine*, November–December, 2005, pp. 15–18.

86. The religious quirks of late Victorian and Edwardian Britain bear some resemblance to those visible in the United States over the last quarter century. Besides pervasive evangelicalism and the powerful 1904–1907 Welsh revival, Britain had large numbers of female mediums, spiritualists, and healers given to trances, voices, touching, and healing, with a cousinship to the Pentecostalism emerging in the twentieth-century United States. See, for example, Alex Owen, *The Darkened Room: Women, Power and Spiritualism in Late Victorian England* (Chicago: University of Chicago Press, 1989). Orientalism, in turn, was seeping in from India and the Far East, as was the occult. In the meantime, the established Church of England was losing some privileges, especially in Britain's Celtic peripheries.

87. Pew Center poll data.

88. "Poll Finds Hostility Hardening Towards U.S. Policies," *The New York Times*, March 17, 2004.

89. "U.S. Image Up Slightly but Still Negative," *Pew Global Attitudes Survey*, June 23, 2005.

90. "Humans, Chimps Almost a Match," *USA Today*, September 1, 2005.

91. "U.S. Poverty Rate Up Last Year," *The New York Times*, August 21, 2005.

92. "U.S. Consumer Spending Might Be on Borrowed Time," *Wall Street Journal Europe*, September 27, 2005; "Greenspan Warns Successor," *Financial Times*, August 27, 2005.

93. Peter Maass, "The Beginning of the End of Oil," *The New York Times Magazine*, August 21, 2005.

94. See Barnett, *The Collapse of British Power*, pp. 82–83.

95. "The History of Rock Oil," *Falun Dafa in Europe*, May 4, 2003, http:clearharmony.net/articles/200305/12105p.html.

96. Both Spain and the Netherlands support the thesis that leading world powers passing their peaks and mired in special-interest politics have trouble finding or elevating first-rate national leadership. The eighteenth-century Dutch did not produce any leader whose name leaps out of the history books. Likewise for seventeenth-century Spain, with the exception of the Count-Duke of Olivares, the reform-minded chief adviser to Philip IV for two decades. But Olivares did not succeed—and no one else matched him.

INDEX

431